# The Subject of Liberty

# The Subject of Liberty

TOWARD A FEMINIST
THEORY OF FREEDOM

*Nancy J. Hirschmann*

For Michael,

With Thanks for my year at
IAS, which made this book so
much better

Nancy

PRINCETON UNIVERSITY PRESS

PRINCETON AND OXFORD

Published by Princeton University Press, 41 William Street, Princeton, New Jersey 08540
In the United Kingdom: Princeton University Press, 3 Market Place, Woodstock,
Oxfordshire OX20 1SY

0-691-09624-4 cloth
0-691-09625-2 paper
British Library Cataloging-in-Publication Data is available

This book has been composed in Sabon
Printed on acid-free paper ∞

www.pupress.princeton.edu
Printed in the United States of America

1 3 5 7 9 10 8 6 4 2

For Chris, once again and forever

*And The Girls, of course*

# CONTENTS

# PREFACE

DOES A WOMAN who stays with her abusive husband freely choose to do so? Does the practice of veiling indicate that women in Muslim countries are oppressed? Does welfare provide women with economic independence, or does it make them dependent on state-funded handouts? These kinds of questions sit at the heart of this book, which examines the idea of freedom in modern Western political theory through women's lived experiences. I argue that a gendered perspective on freedom that puts the often invisible and excluded aspects of women's experience at its center can demonstrate the inadequacy of dominant theoretical conceptions of freedom and point the way to new and better ways to think about it. Freedom, I argue, is centrally about choice, a claim with which many mainstream freedom theories would agree. But choice is constituted by a complex relationship between "internal" factors of will and desire—impacting on the preferences and desires one has and how one makes choices—and factors "outside" the self that may inhibit or enhance one's ability to pursue one's preferences, including the kind and number of choices available, the obstacles to making the preferred choice, and the variable power that different people have to make choices. Many theorists of freedom recognize that desires and preferences are always limited by contexts that determine the parameters of choice: if chocolate and vanilla are the only flavors available, I am not free to choose strawberry, but that does not alter the fact that I would have preferred strawberry if it were available.

What is not addressed by most freedom theories, however, is the deeper, more important issue of how the choosing subject is herself constructed by such contexts: could the repeated absence of strawberry eventually change my tastes so that I lose my desire for it? This question, as I conceive it, involves more than the "adaptive preferences" problem of rational-choice theory, or even the possibility of "oppressive socialization" that some feminist theorists of autonomy critique, both of which I will discuss in chapter 1. Rather, it involves the more complex and subtle process of social construction. Choices and the selves that make them are constituted by context, discourse, and language; such contexts make meaning, self-hood, and choices possible. Yet feminists have clearly shown over the past several decades of critiquing patriarchy that some contexts are better than others at providing women with genuine alternatives from which they can choose. Though the notion of the choice-making agent who can form, express, and act on desires is central to most theoretical understandings of freedom, the ways in which this agent is constructed by social contexts so as to shape her desires and indeed make them possible is generally not addressed by political theory and philosophy. This is an important omission, however, for key to freedom is what or who the "self" is that makes these choices. I use the lived experiences of women to demonstrate how existing freedom theories fail to challenge the duality of the internal and external dimensions of freedom; and I argue that attending to women's experiences requires political theorists to rethink the relationship between these two dimensions. This theoretical approach reveals that the inner self—preferences, desires, self-conceptions—is constructed by and through outer forces and social structures, such as sexism. Who we are—the "choosing subject"—exists within and is formed by particular contexts, contexts which for the most part exhibit varying degrees and forms of gender hierarchy and oppression. By failing to recognize this, the ideal of the subject utilized by most freedom theory—and in turn, the concept of freedom itself—is simplistically overdrawn and deeply problematic.

Two days after I completed my revisions of this book, in the largest and most organized terrorist attack on the United States in its history, two U.S. commercial-carrier jet airplanes out of Boston were hijacked and flown directly into the twin towers of the World Trade Center in New York, which completely collapsed a short time after. A third hijacked jet was crashed into the Pentagon, and a fourth, apparently also headed for Washington, D.C., crashed in rural Pennsylvania, apparently after its passengers attacked the terrorists. The country was in shock; the president was declaring a "war on terrorism"; Afghanistan was being threatened with military attack for harboring Osama bin Laden and the al Quaeda network. By the time I was finished going over the copyedited manuscript several months later, the United States had launched a full-scale military operation in Afghanistan, the Taliban had been ousted from its ruling position in Afghanistan, and a coalition government was formed between the Northern Alliance and various ethnic factions and tribal groups. The new provisional cabinet includes two female members, and Interim Prime Minister Hamid Karzai has signed the Declaration of the Essential Rights of Afghan women.

Given the rapid pace with which events have unfolded over the past four months, who knows what further developments will have occurred by the time I receive my page proofs, let alone by the time the book is released? Will bin Laden and Mullah Mohammed Omar, the former leader of the Taliban government, still be targets of an international manhunt? Will the anthrax scare that gripped the nation in the autumn of

2001 be resolved or revived? Will any further terrorist attacks, which have been repeatedly rumored and explicitly threatened over the past several months, actually be launched? I leave it to my comparative-politics colleagues to keep up with the rapid pace of change and predict what will and will not happen in the Middle East in the coming years. My observations here, rather, focus on the issue of freedom as it pertains to the September 11 tragedy, because it seems to me to be a serious concern, both materially and discursively.

Freedom emerged as a thematic trope almost immediately after the events of September 11, when President George W. Bush characterized the attack as one on freedom: the United States, he declared, and other "freedom-loving" nations, had been victimized by "barbarians"—a term that invokes a long history of Western attitudes toward Islam as inferior and irrational—who "hated freedom." It is incontestable that the thousands of people who died in these attacks were, in part, casualties of the United States' open borders and respect for individual liberties, a respect that has made antiterrorist measures difficult to deploy. But one could also argue that many Middle Easterners have been casualties of the U.S. ideal of freedom too. The military campaign in Afghanistan was given the unfortunately ambiguous name "Enduring Freedom," as if the United States' version of freedom was something that Afghanis must endure. And from a Middle Eastern perspective, "endure" may have been an appropriate term, for in the interest of plentiful and cheap oil, the United States has long given its support to oppressive regimes. Our relations with Saudi Arabia, which is obviously antidemocratic and in which women cannot work outside of the home, or even drive, are only the most obvious example of how the United States tries to look the other way when it is in our economic interest. The U.S. tendency to form expedient alliances, heedless of long-term results, has resulted in significantly diminished freedoms for large numbers of people in the Middle East and elsewhere. Indeed, the Taliban itself came to power in part because of U.S. support for Afghan rebels, whom the Reagan administration ironically called "freedom fighters" during Afghanistan's occupation by the former Soviet Union. Since the Soviet Union instituted certain policies that arguably heightened women's freedom, however, such as mandatory education, it is relevant to ask what kind of freedom, not to mention whose, the rebels now known as the Northern Alliance actually supported. As I will discuss in chapter 6, the post-Soviet Afghan ruling authority, made up of these so-called freedom fighters, was allegedly responsible for many atrocities against women, including rape and kidnapping. But U.S. government leaders, and indeed many U.S. citizens, fail to see the ways in which we may have contributed to this loss of freedom; we have failed to recognize the relationship between freedom and responsibility, that the freedom to choose entails taking responsibility for our choices. It may be fair to say that our foreign policy does not really care about freedom for Middle Eastern people—"exotic others" who may not even be seen as fully human subjects entitled to liberty. For us, it seems, the "subject" of liberty is an American.

In the United States itself, freedom has been under serious attack, however, as racial profiling—now of Arabs and Arab Americans, rather than African Americans—seems to have gained a new legitimacy. Increased wiretapping authority granted to the FBI, permission for prison guards to listen to conversations between certain prisoners and their attorneys if terrorist connections are suspected, calls for military tribunals to replace criminal trials for any terrorists who may be caught, military control of information available to the press, including control of surveillance satellites—all such measures challenge fundamental freedoms that Americans have come to take for granted. The exchange of freedom for security may be worthwhile, depending on the freedom that is being sacrificed. But we are in fact no safer. The futility of increased security efforts at airports is only the most ludicrous example; though Congress voted to federalize aviation security, and there is talk of increasing funding to restore the "air marshal" program, so that armed federal officers would accompany many flights, such measures are still in the works. In the meantime, security agencies pay minimum wage to poorly trained employees who officiously confiscate fingernail clippers but let knives and box cutters slip through. Europe may be doing no better—security agents in Paris recently permitted boarding to a man with a brand new passport, a one-way ticket paid for in cash, and explosives in his shoes—but in the United States, the need to "do something" has resulted in a wide range of useless, wheel-spinning gestures that may heighten anxiety but not security. Signs saying "Passengers should not make security related jokes" flash at the check-in counter, and passengers making innocent remarks remotely relating to security concerns are detained for questioning. People who are described as acting "kind of strange" are detained. So much for John Stuart Mill's defense of "eccentricity" as vital to freedom. The absurdity of such policies is self-evident; the metal silverware that used to be served on board most airlines could hardly cut your overcooked meal, let alone be used as a weapon. But such absurdity should not obscure the very real and frightening power of surveillance given to these poorly trained individuals. For at the same time, one of President Bush's Secret Service detail was denied entrance to a flight to Texas because he was carrying a gun. He also happened to be an Arab American.

Those who think that taking their shoes off for x-ray scrutiny is merely an inconvenience (or perhaps even an amusing Laurel and Hardy routine) fail to see the continuum of official power being exercised over us. To take one example, most diabetics I know have severely curtailed, if not altogether eliminated, airline travel because of the threat that their insulin syringes will be confiscated. FAA and airline policy allows syringes on board aircraft; it requires only that the insulin be carried as well, to serve as proof of the need for syringes, without further documentation. And, in recognition of widely accepted medical research that x-rays decompose and compromise the potency of insulin, the FAA does not require insulin to be put through x-ray. Yet airport security guards, who have evidently not learned the policies they are supposed to enforce, insist on putting insulin through x-ray; they demand to see notes from doctors verifying the passenger's illness (which most diabetics I know now carry, like five-year-olds bringing permission to go on a field trip); and they try to confiscate syringes. Such surveillance is humiliating, as the intimate details of private life are splayed before a gawking, needle-phobic, public audience. It also produces its own form of terror, by threatening to take away control of medication that is essential to surviving this illness (particularly given the unpredictability of airline delays, it can prove disastrous for a diabetic to check her medication rather than carrying it on board). If anyone ever needed concrete proof that Foucault was onto something about the micropolitics of the surveillance society, this is it.

I am not sure which is more depressing: the pointlessness of these new rules, the frequent racism behind their implementation, or the enthusiastic support that Americans show for them, declaring that they feel "safer," even though such feelings are unjustified. This situation of intensified surveillance in which we now find ourselves makes it imperative that we think critically about the relationship between the "external" and "internal" aspects of freedom. We must be wary of enthusiastically embracing, out of fear, new restrictions on our choices and behavior. We must resist the desire to abandon basic legal rights and curtail freedom of expression and travel. For such restrictions will in turn affect the social construction of subjectivity and desire. As anti-Islamic sentiment manifests itself more and more overtly, as Americans express their desire for revenge, calling it "justice," as they unquestioningly support military action, as they view with approval governmental lockdowns and the closing of borders, as they voluntarily give up freedoms for the sake of security: new identities, subjectivities, and understandings of ourselves as Americans, as well as conceptions of what we want, what we desire in terms of freedom, will be produced and pushed in new directions. Understanding where these conceptions and desires come from, and what they mean, is vital to fully understanding and appreciating what we are giving up and why we are doing so. We must be aware and self-critical about how we conceptualize freedom, about how we define and use the term in our everyday dealings with other people, as well as about the choices we make, the options that are perceived, presented, and pursued. It is the purpose of this book to contribute to a deeper understanding of these processes, and it is offered in the hope of a world in which freedom does not have so high a price.

# ACKNOWLEDGMENTS

THIS BOOK began and ended in two residential fellowships. Its framework and founding questions first germinated at the Bunting Institute of Radcliffe College, with funding from the American Council of Learned Societies. Thanks to the Bunting and ACLS for a wonderful and productive year. Until its transformation into the Radcliffe Institute for Advanced Study (with the demise of Radcliffe as an independent women's college), the Bunting was one of the few, possibly the only, research institute in the United States exclusively for women. In residence that year were a number of scholars from a variety of disciplines, including medicine, law, psychology, and poetry, who were writing about or studying domestic violence, and it was in conversations with them that this book really took shape. The battered woman who chooses to remain with her abuser became my paradigm for the ways in which women's experiences challenge the dominant conceptions of freedom found in political theory, because it grew clear over the course of the year that the most common understandings of domestic violence were reductive and simplistic. Patricia Traxler and Hilary Astor were particularly instrumental in helping me grasp the complexity of choice within the parameters of intimate abuse. Other "sister-fellows," particularly Susan Eaton, Mary Hamer, Margot Kempers, Madeline Kunin, and Anna Deveare Smith, in addition to then-director Florence Ladd, provided many stimulating hours of conversation and brain-picking that helped shape my approach to the book and led me to see the linkages between domestic violence and other forms of oppressive experience in women's lives. Abby Zanger of Harvard University also was a valuable colleague and friend during my fellowship year.

The Institute for Advanced Study in Princeton was where I (almost) completed the book, funded in part by the National Endowment for the Humanities; thanks to both for their resources and support. This was quite a different experience from the Bunting, particularly since women were in a distinct minority, but the strong feminist presence of faculty member Joan Scott and other fellows, namely, Susan Brison and Elizabeth Weed, provided inspiration, critical insights (particularly into my social construction chapter), and psychological support. But of course one did not need to be surrounded by feminist women to enjoy the camaraderie and challenging intellectual stimulation of the institute. Exchanges of critical commentary with IAS faculty member Michael Walzer and fellows Kamran Ali, Nahum Chandler, Tom Flynn, Evelyn Huber, Jim Mittleman,

Michael Mosher, Gordon Schochet, John Stephens, and Dana Villa, were particularly helpful. Additional thanks go to Amy Gutmann and George Kateb for including me in the stimulating events offered by the Princeton Department of Politics and the University Center for Human Values.

Only two colleagues have read this manuscript in its entirety; Joan Tronto deserves special thanks for her detailed and thoughtful commentary. Deep gratitude also goes to Will Kymlicka for many very helpful insights and ideas (particularly the nudge I needed to act on the knowledge, which I had been resisting, that my original lengthy manuscript was really two separate books). Other colleagues read individual chapters, or earlier incarnations of chapters in the form of papers, and to them I am extremely grateful as well: Rebecca Allahyari, Liz Bussiere, Fred Dallmayr, Cyndi Daniels, Christine Di Stefano, Matt Evangelista, Dick Flathman, Nancy Fraser, Susan Hekman, Eva Kittay, Isaac Kramnick, Ulrike Liebert, Molly Shanley, Ian Shapiro, Marion Smiley, Tracy Strong, Karen Zivi, and a number of anonymous reviewers. Additionally, portions of the work were presented in talks in numerous places, in addition to the Bunting and the Institute for Advanced Study at Princeton, and I appreciate the feedback and ideas offered on those occasions as well. Particularly notable were the New York Society for Women and Philosophy; the Comparative Studies Public Intellectuals program in the Dorothy Schmidt College of Arts and Letters at Florida Atlantic University (special thanks to my dear friend Teresa Brennan for arranging a most memorable hurricane during my visit); the Walt Whitman Center at Rutgers University; the Odyssey Project at California State University at Long Beach; and the Gender and Politics Seminar at Harvard University. I am also indebted to Anne Norton and Deborah Harrold for particularly helpful discussions about Islamic political thought and women's veiling. Still other colleagues and friends have provided insight, guidance, suggestions, ideas, support, and delightful distractions during the course of writing this book, particularly Martha Fineman—who has also provided a great deal of intellectual stimulation through the feminist legal theory workshop conferences she runs at Cornell Law School—Susan Buck-Morss, Mary Katzenstein, Kirstie McClure, Julie Mostov, Jonas Pontusson, and Carol Smith. Thanks to my students at Cornell, graduate and undergraduate, for rewarding classroom experiences in which I sometimes tried out new ideas and arguments for my book, and in which I always gained new insights about the canonical texts and contemporary feminism. Thanks to Cornell University for research funds and various chunks of leave time that made it possible for me to continue working on this book. Thanks also to Ian Malcolm of Princeton University Press for his encouragement and assistance in getting the book into print, as well as to Sara Lerner for her help in production. A very special debt of gratitude goes to Vicky Wilson-Schwartz for her superb copyediting of the manuscript. Thanks to Shannon Mariotti for her help in constructing the index. If there is anyone I have forgotten to mention, I hope they will forgive me. I alone, of course, am responsible for the flaws and inadequacies that doubtless remain in the book.

My family also deserves mention for their support of me over the years, not only for my work but in the trials and tribulations of health problems. My mother deserves special mention for her saintly patience, constant checking up and concern, generosity of time and thoughtfulness, countless homemade microwave meals when I became (for a limited time, fortunately) too disabled to cook for myself, and general all-around good humor in the face of always impending disaster. Thanks also to my father for constantly reminding me of the absurdity of life, and that when you can't find something, it's always in the first place you looked, not the last. Thanks to my sister for her positive spirit and for providing a new brother; thanks to the old brother for stiffening my spine to withstand the hardships that the unfairness of life inevitably throws our way. Deepest gratitude goes to my husband, to whom I dedicate this book, for everything.

Finally, in the context of a book on freedom in which the theme of "internal" barriers plays an important role, it is also appropriate to thank the coterie of doctors who have kept me going over the past dozen years. Though I will never be free from the medical problems that sometimes make my life less than wonderful, my physicians have certainly helped me to understand and even gain some measure of control over the bizarre (truly statistically anomalous) panoply of things that can go wrong in a single body. I cannot name all of my physicians, but Seth Braunstein deserves foremost mention for putting up with me the longest, and for overseeing my most serious condition and the plethora of related problems to which it has given rise. Notable thanks also go to Mark Brown, Robert Guerra, Gary Lichtenstein, and Albert Maguire.

Last but definitely not least, I will gladly risk appearing totally ridiculous by thanking all of the cats who have graced my life over the past two decades, bringing grace, calm, entertainment, distraction, joy, and comfort. Be free! Be free! The meaning of life is cats.

Sections of this book have been previously published as the following articles: "Toward a Feminist Theory of Freedom," *Political Theory* 24, no. 1 (1996): 46–67, reprinted by permission of Sage Publications; "Eastern Veiling, Western Freedom?" *Review of Politics* 59, no. 3 (1997): 461–88, reprinted by permission of the *Review of Politics*; "Eastern Veiling, Western Feminism, and the Question of Free Agency," *Constellations: An International Journal of Critical and Democratic Theory* 5, no. 3 (1998), reprinted by permission of Blackwell Publishing; "A Question of Freedom, a Question of Rights? Women and Welfare," in *Women and Welfare: Theory and Practice in the United States and Europe*, ed. Nancy J. Hirschmann and Ulrike Liebert, © 2001 by Nancy J. Hirschmann, reprinted by permission of Rutgers University Press.

# The Subject of Liberty

## Chapter One

# INTRODUCTION

A TWENTY-THREE-YEAR OLD, unemployed single mother in West Virginia became pregnant as a result of date rape. Due to recent cuts in federal funding, "Meg" had trouble locating an abortion clinic but finally found one four hours away in Charleston. She was told that she was 17 weeks pregnant, and that the clinic performed abortions only up to 16 weeks, so she was referred to a clinic in Cincinnati which would perform an abortion up to 19 1/2 weeks for a cost of $850. When she went there 1 1/2 weeks later, however, she was told that she was actually 21 weeks pregnant and referred to a clinic in Dayton that would perform the abortion for $1,675. She refinanced her car, sold her VCR, borrowed money, and went to Dayton. There she learned that she was a high-risk patient because of an earlier cesarean delivery and would therefore have to go to Wichita, where the procedure would cost $2,500. "I just didn't think I could manage that," she says. "Now that I know I have to have it, I'm trying to get used to the idea. . . . I'm not thinking about adoption, because I've never understood people having a baby just to give it away. So I've been thinking a lot about trying to love this baby the way I love my daughter."[1] Can we say that this woman has freely chosen her role as mother?

Susan is beaten by her husband and is admitted to a hospital. This is the second time she has been severely beaten this year. An advocate from the local battered women's shelter visits her and gives her information about the resources they have, as well as information about pressing charges and prosecuting her husband for assault. Susan is angry at her husband, and very frightened of him, but she is reluctant to press charges with the police because she doesn't want to put her children through such an ordeal. Her husband, meanwhile, sends her a dozen bouquets of lovely flowers and comes to the hospital with lavish gifts and profuse apologies, declaring his love and promising never to hit her again. The battered-women's advocate tells her that she should not believe him, that he will do it again, but Susan decides to return to him. She says that he has apologized and that she forgives him; that he is basically a good person and has promised to change; that he loves her and is a good father; that she loves him; that it was partly her fault anyway. Is she free if she returns to her husband?

In the novel *Mrs. Bridge*, the title character is a woman who seems to subordinate herself completely to her husband. She defers to him, is extremely self-deprecating, rarely ventures a political opinion, and has so effectively effaced herself that at the end of the novel, she risks freezing to death while trapped in her car because she won't yell for help; the implication is that she doesn't want to disturb anyone and simply waits passively, until her husband gets home to rescue her. She doesn't appear to be holding these views out of fear or coercion. Her husband is somewhat overbearing but not violent; he doesn't overtly seek to control her, he clearly loves her, and demonstrates his consideration and respect for her in various ways. Is Mrs. Bridge free or not?[2]

When Greta got married, her husband and she agreed that she would quit her job as a secretary so that they could raise a family. Greta's mother always worked when she was a child, and Greta has always believed it is better for children to have a full-time mother. She had three kids over the course of the next seven years. Shortly after the birth of the third child, her husband left her. It turns out he was having an affair, but he told Greta that he felt smothered by the routine of their domestic life and all the kids. Although she eventually was able to file for divorce, she was never able to collect child support or win any other financial settlement from her husband, and so she was forced to find a job. But her former secretarial skills were sorely out of date, so the only jobs she could obtain were barely above minimum wage. After paying for child care and transportation, she has less money than she would receive on welfare. Greta grew up in a family that always scorned those on public assistance, however; and her mother, who is horrified by the prospect of her daughter's becoming "one of those welfare mothers," argues that Greta brought this on herself by quitting her job when she got married. She will, after all, receive a raise every six months if she continues to work. Greta knows that economic security is years away at this rate, and she feels trapped by her situation. Is she trapped, or is her mother right that freedom requires taking responsibility for one's choices?

Charlene, a lesbian, is an attorney with an extremely conservative Wall Street firm that has never had a woman partner. Charlene wants very badly to become a partner. Accordingly, she is not open about her sexuality. Her lover, Sally, believes this is a mistake, not only tactically, but from the perspective of personal cost as well. Though Charlene declares that their relationship is more important to her than anything, she has become so fearful about colleagues finding out about it that she and Sally have virtually stopped going out of the house together; and the stress is affecting not only Charlene's health but the relationship as well. Sally is beginning to contemplate "outing" Charlene. She believes that this would liberate Charlene from her fears, her anxiety, her extra stress, and save the relationship. Is she right?[3]

These scenarios are not particularly special or unusual; they are common examples of the everyday dilemmas many women (and some men) face. And precisely because of their familiarity, many of us probably have immediate, perhaps even gut-level, reactions to them. For instance, most people would probably say—at least initially—that the pregnant woman is unfree[4] and that Sally is wrong. The other stories might give us more pause. It is difficult, for instance, to imagine that a victim of domestic violence really knows what she is doing when she "chooses" to return to her abuser; Greta could not know that her husband would abandon her; and Mrs. Bridge might seem rather hopelessly repressed to many but quite normal to others. I want to suggest, however, that there is really no simple answer to the question of freedom in any of these cases.

This complexity is partly due to the amazing ambiguity of the term "freedom" in its popular usage, not to mention the vast disagreements among political philosophers over the meaning of the term, as well as over individual instances of "freedom" and "unfreedom." But it is also partly due to the fact that the dominant discourse of freedom in philosophy and political theory—which founds as well as reflects popular, everyday conceptions—is inadequate to fully encompass this complexity. Moreover, it is a central contention of this book that feminism—which many might assume would maintain that the women in all four stories are unfree—highlights both this complexity and this inadequacy.

## A Masculinist Theory of Freedom?

Implicit in these introductory questions is the more fundamental issue of what the term freedom means. This is a central bone of contention among liberty theorists;[5] but most, if not all, conceptions of liberty have at their heart the ability of the self to make choices and act on them. The contested terrain, therefore, generally covers differences about what constitutes the process and activity of choosing and what constitutes the product, or an "actual" choice. Theorists disagree also on what constitutes a "restraint on" or "barrier to" choice, what prevents certain options from being made available, or what prevents me from taking a particular choice that is normally available. Many of these questions—and indeed, much freedom theory—are arguably "semantic" rather than normative; that is, concerned with distinguishing freedom from other terms, such as equality, justice, and obligation, or with the features that constitute a "restraint" (as opposed to an "inability"). Subsidiary to and implicit in these debates, however, though often not addressed, is the more normative and political question of what or who the "self" is that makes these choices; in other words, what constitutes the "choosing subject" of liberty.

While definitions and conceptions of freedom can be quite varied, ranging from neo-Hobbesian descriptivist accounts of behavior to the most value-laden prescriptive accounts of actions,[6] most formulations still divide along the lines offered by Isaiah Berlin in his famous 1958 essay "Two Concepts of Liberty," of "negative" and "positive" liberty.[7] According to Berlin, negative liberty consists in an absence of external constraints. The individual is free to the extent that she is not restrained by external forces, primarily viewed as law, physical force, and other overt coercion. So, for instance, if I wanted to leave the house but my husband broke my leg to prevent me, he would be restricting my freedom. "By being free in this sense I mean not being interfered with by others. The wider the area of non-interference, the wider my freedom."[8] Berlin's general notion that restraints come from outside the self, they are alien to the self, or "other," is an important basic feature of negative liberty; specifically, other humans' direct (or, in some cases, indirect) participation "in frustrating my wishes" is the relevant criterion in determining restraint.[9]

And these "wishes," or desires, preferences, interests, and needs which I must be able to pursue unimpeded if I am to be free, are seen as coming from me and from me alone. Desires in negative liberty do not necessarily need to be "brute," that is, immediate, physical, and compelling, as some theorists have maintained.[10] Although brute desire is an important concept in negative liberty, desire can just as easily be seen as long term, well thought out, and rational. The point for negative liberty, however, is that whether the desires are long term or immediate, "brute" or "rational," what matters is that they are desires that the agent has formulated by herself. That is, a desire may be formed in reaction to external stimuli—I may want to leave the house because I can no longer stand listening to the televised football game my husband is watching in the next room—but this desire is *mine*, say the negative libertarians, and I am responsible for acting on or resisting it.

Similarly, the desire in question must be *conscious*: I must know that I have it. Certainly, desires may be responses to unconscious feelings—perhaps my aversion to televised football stems from repressed childhood memories of fear of my father, who would yell angrily at the television as his team lost yet again—but the relevant point for negative freedom is *that* I want it, and that I *know* I want it, not *why* I want it. Thus, negative liberty draws clear-cut lines between inner and outer, subject and object, self and other. This kind of freedom, as Taylor puts it, is "toughminded," because of the strict notions of individual responsibility and accountability that it finds conceptually necessary to "choice."[11] It is also "toughminded," however, in the way it starkly differentiates between freedom and various other political concepts, such as equality and justice. As Berlin says, "Everything is what it is: liberty is liberty, not equality or fairness or justice or culture, or human happiness or a quiet conscience."[12] Thus, negative liberty defines itself in opposition to concepts such as obligation and authority; these things, while perhaps necessary to human society, or even to individuals' pursuit of their desires and possibly even to greater freedom in the future, are nonetheless limitations on freedom. As John Rawls argued, while equality, or wealth, or other factors may affect the "worth" of an individual's liberty by enhancing or inhibiting her ability to pursue opportunities, these factors are distinct and separate from the liberty itself, which is measured by the absence of external restraints, such as laws.[13] The central question for negative liberty, according to Berlin, is "What is the area within which the subject—a person or group of persons—is or should be left to do or be what he is able to do or be, without interference by other persons?"[14] For this reason, Taylor calls negative liberty an "opportunity concept": the significant factor in determining whether I am free is that no other person or thing is actually preventing me from doing what I want, nothing or no one is barring me from taking advantage of opportunities that I could otherwise pursue but for this restraint.[15] Berlin similarly says that "Freedom is the opportunity to act, not action itself."[16] What is important is that I be allowed to make choices, rather than that I make a particular choice. Freedom is "constituted by the absence of obstacles to the exercise of choice."[17]

Thus, Berlin holds that freedom is determined by "the number of doors open to me"; the more doors that are open, regardless of whether I go through any of them, or even *want* to go through any of them, the freer I am. Berlin does concede that "the extent to which [doors] are open," as well as the relative importance of these various doors and paths, are relevant to freedom; but given the necessarily subjective dimensions of such evaluations, "the number of doors" is ultimately determinative. Freedom is thus in an important sense quantitative on the negative-liberty model, even quantifiably measurable.[18] More importantly, freedom operates from an "objective" rather than subjective notion of choice. Recognizing the "adaptive preference" phenomenon—that when faced with a limited range of options, I can increase my freedom by simply accommodating my desires to availability—Berlin insists that freedom requires "a range of objectively open possibilities, whether these are desired or not."[19] Freedom "consists in the absence of obstacles not merely to my actual, but to my potential choices . . . it is the actual doors that are open that determine the extent of someone's freedom, and not his own preferences."[20] The presence of options themselves, objectively defined, is key to freedom; I may not want many, or even any, of the alternatives available, but I am nevertheless freer than if there was only one option. If choice is paramount in the definition of freedom, then the more choices I have, the freer I am.

Defining freedom in the objective terms of available options rather than the subjective expression of desire is supported by many contemporary theorists, such as Stanley Benn, W. L. Weinstein, Joel Feinberg and Christine Swanton,[21] because it allows us to circumvent the fact that subjective desire is almost always contingent on social circumstances. For instance, one could not claim that an African slave was free simply because she said she did not want to leave the plantation, because this desire could be seen as the final effects of colonization. But at the same time, this "available options" conception is somewhat counterintuitive: if there are only two options, one of which is the one I want, I would seem to be less free than if what I want is not available at all amidst dozens of other options. Accordingly, other negative-liberty theorists, such as Richard Flathman, Robert Nozick, and William Parent, reject this account and insist on the relevance of the more traditional, Hobbesian notion of being able to make the choice I want.[22] But even for the latter theorists, such ability presupposes coherence between subjective desire and objective circumstance—I cannot have what I want if it is unavailable—so they favor the availability of more rather than fewer options.

Such arguments may appear to be little more than semantic hairsplitting (as indeed, they often are), but it is this need for preserving opportunities that delineates negative liberty in a political context. Berlin and almost all negative libertarians recognize the need for laws if liberty is to be preserved; absolute negative liberty would result in chaos, thus jeopardizing not only other things of importance to humans—security, justice, fairness—but freedom as well, in that I must spend so much time defending what I have that I am prevented from seeking other things that I want. Laws can restore a balance between my liberty and others' equal liberty. But even given the need for law and political society, negative liberty requires "a certain minimum area of personal freedom which must on no account be violated. . . . A frontier must be drawn between the area of private life and that of public authority."[23] Thus, regardless of the technical or semantic differences among negative-liberty theorists over the definitional requirements of "restraint" and the role and meaning of "choice," the strong individualism of negative-liberty theory ensures that restraints on liberty are seen as external to the self and, moreover, that they contain an inherently conflictual character, because individuals' desires and interests inevitably collide with them.[24]

Positive-liberty theory challenges, or at least "expands," the negative conception of liberty in at least three ways. Most obviously, it concerns itself with the "positive" provision of the conditions necessary to take advantage of negative liberties, such as providing wheelchair access to buildings or scholarships for education. The definition of barriers as external impediments is too narrow; for instance, freedom of education is rather hollow if you cannot afford tuition or get into the building where instruction is offered. Adopting a more contextual and communal notion of the self, positive liberty is able to view individual conditions such as disability, as well as social conditions such as poverty, as barriers to freedom that can be overcome by positive action, that is, the provision of conditions the individual cannot create on her own. This might not seem like a noteworthy enhancement of negative liberty. After all, since Berlin wrote his original article, various negative-liberty theorists have endorsed different versions of this idea and incorporated it into their own conceptions of negative liberty. Particularly popular is the effort to expand the notion of "external barrier" to include generalized social conditions such as poverty. I will discuss some of these arguments in the following section; but even if this first challenge of positive liberty has been taken up successfully or even appropriated by negative liberty, it sets the stage for the remaining two ways in which positive liberty differs from its counterpoint, and these are far more significant.

One of these is positive liberty's focus on "internal barriers": fears, addictions, compulsions that are at odds with my "true" self. According to positive liberty, we can have "second order desires," or "desires about desires. We experience our desires and purposes as qualitatively discriminated, as higher or lower, noble or base, integrated or fragmented, significant or trivial, good and bad."[25] Because of these conflicting capacities, it is not enough to experience an absence of external restraints, because the immediate desires I have may frustrate my true will. For instance, while trying to quit smoking or to combat an eating disorder, an argument with my department chair triggers a craving for a cigarette or an entire bag of Oreos. Positive liberty says that if I were to give in to these cravings, I would be not just weak-willed but unfree, because I am violating my true desire, on which I have reflected at some length (and after all, smoking or binging will not resolve the dispute with my colleague, so we cannot even argue for a trade-off between competing goals).

It follows from the notion of internal barriers, however, that others may know my true will better than I, particularly when I am in the grip of these self-destructive desires: as you snatch the cigarette or Oreo from my lips, you are preserving my true self from false desires, and enhancing my liberty. This is often called the "second-guessing" problem, because others claim to know what you want better than you do yourself. It is the most troubling aspect of positive liberty: determination of the will by others, and specifically by the state. The classic instance is Rousseau's general will; since the laws embody the true will, he says, then by forcing me to obey the law the state is only "forcing me to be free," that is, to follow my true will, whether I know it or not. This is the nightmare that Berlin particularly argued against in "Two Concepts of Liberty," with good reason. But what Berlin and other negative-liberty advocates seriously underplay is the idea of an individual having *conflicting* desires and a *divided* will. That is clearly the sentiment behind the claim that the compulsive binger or addicted smoker is unfree: I really want to quit smoking, but the stress is pushing me to cheat. Similarly, perhaps my husband broke my leg because he was trying to keep me from meeting my cocaine supplier; I've been struggling for months to kick my addiction, but she called me at a particularly vulnerable point. In both of these cases, I want two mutually exclusive things—to smoke or take drugs and to quit—and most people would probably have to agree that quitting would be a better choice, a choice that would be more consistent with my continued freedom; indeed, one that would liberate me, and hence the choice I really prefer to make. So it is at least an open question whether the person who prevents me from pursuing my addictions impedes my liberty or enhances it. For this reason, Taylor calls positive liberty an "exercise concept" of freedom: people must exercise their full capacities if they are to be considered free.[26]

The notion of internal barriers to freedom generally raises the greatest hostility to the idea of positive liberty, precisely because it seems to indicate that others can prevent me from doing certain things which *they* think will violate my deepest desires and highest purposes, or force me to do other things which *they* think will help me realize these purposes. Berlin thus argues that the two key notions in positive liberty are self-mastery and rationality: in order to be my own master, I (or my intellect) must control, or at least not be under the influence of, anything that is "not me." But what is "not me" may often include my own emotions, feelings, desires, physical sensations, and so forth: freedom is defined as what I would want if I were perfectly rational. Since people frequently betray rationality and desire the wrong things, however, an independent external force, usually the state, must ensure that I follow my true will. The idea, subscribed to by Hegel and (many believe) Rousseau, of an objectively true, higher-order desire stemming from a true self which others can know better than I entails that I do not need to be able to identify the desire as mine for it to be genuinely mine; because it is the state's will, the common good, the *Geist* or general will, it is my higher will by definition, whether I realize it or not. Berlin thus defines positive liberty as a paradox: to coerce X to do A because it is for her own good is a logical impossibility, because if it is for her own good, then she really wants it and therefore is not being coerced.[27] He therefore maintains that internal factors should not be considered relevant to the concept of freedom.

However, most positive-liberty theorists do not share Berlin's interpretation. Charles Taylor, for instance, argues that a focus on internal barriers to realizing my higher desire does not entail external mechanisms to direct me to it. His account of the "divided self" is indeed quite individualist: in his examples, the subject always seems to know that he has a higher and lower desire, and is struggling to achieve the former. He offers this example: "spiteful feelings and reactions which I almost can't inhibit are undermining a relationship which is terribly important to me . . . I long to be able not to feel this spite. As long as I feel it, even control is not an option, because it just builds up inside until it . . . bursts out."[28] In this example, he is aware that he is destroying himself, and the higher-order desire is one he can identify and identify with: "I long to be free of this feeling . . . as I lash out at her with my unbridled tongue." In what Taylor calls the "self-realisation" view, direction toward the higher desire must be done individually, because individuals have different higher purposes and goals.

Taylor's account has the merit of avoiding the "totalitarian menace" of second guessing. But just like Berlin's argument that positive liberty's emphasis on higher desires inevitably leads to state control, Taylor's argument that I can and must be able to identify higher desires as mine oversimplifies positive liberty. Its individualism brings us full circle to the very atomism that Taylor critiques in negative-liberty theory. For instance, even though Taylor's spite is expressed in the context of a personal relationship, and particularly when he is interacting with a specific other person, rather than alone in his study, he describes the feeling as emerging spontaneously from within himself, the highly individuated subject, without any attention to the context within which it has developed or exists: Where does the spite come from? Why does he feel it? And why spite rather than, say, withdrawal or self-pity or sadness? What are the criteria for determining the "importance" of the relationship? What does the "almost" mean when he says he "almost can't inhibit" his spiteful feelings? Is there a specific reason, hidden in that space between "almost" and "can't," that prevents him from controlling his spite? For instance, perhaps the relationship isn't really "good" for him, not in accord with his "true" interests, and spite is his subconscious's way of telling him this.

On this view, the question of which desire is "higher" and which "lower" is somewhat up for grabs. Just as Taylor sees that the relationship is more important to him and wants to stop his spiteful behavior, so could he then identify the spite as in fact protecting him from the relationship; but then what's to stop him from saying that such justification of spite is simply a more sophisticated way to rationalize his fear of commitment?

And so on, in an endless stream of second-guessing.[29] Such a possibility certainly allows for, and even requires, articulation of his preferences and desires by the individual himself, as Taylor argues; but it also demands a working-through of history, relationship, and context, all of which are subject to and even necessitate the assessment and input of others. Understanding the self presupposes the existence of language, of a conceptual vocabulary, a system of signs with which to formulate and represent my own experience to myself; and it requires others with whom I can be in conversation, to analyze and determine what desires are really mine, and really better for me.[30] This raises the question of where to draw the line between the internal self and the external world, because our self-understandings, our desires and choices, as well as the barriers we experience, always need to be understood in context. If individuals exist in contexts, then they—their feelings, desires, thoughts, wills, preferences—cannot be understood outside of those contexts, as abstract and self-contained units. Without such specificity of context, the individual too is unspecified, an abstraction. In this regard, Taylor's argument displays, even as he himself ignores, the inherently social dimension of internal barriers and the relationship between internality and externality.

Acknowledging this relationship leads to the third way that positive liberty challenges negative liberty, though it is an aspect that most theorists of freedom do not recognize: namely, the "social construction" of the choosing subject of liberty, of the person who is supposedly having desires and making choices. How is it that I have the desires I have? Why do I make the choices I do? If it is possible to say that we can have conflicting desires, and if it is possible to rank these desires as better or worse, more and less valuable, then the issue of who I am comes inevitably into play: What *is* my true will? What *do* I really want? Such questions invite us to consider the social construction of the choosing subject, of the individual agent who has desires and makes choices within specific social, historical, and institutional contexts. The idea of social construction is that human beings and their world are in no sense given or natural but the product of historical configurations of relationships. Our desires, preferences, beliefs, values—indeed, the way in which we see the world and define reality—are all shaped by the particular constellation of personal and institutional social relationships that constitute our individual and collective identities. Understanding them requires us to place them in their historical, social, and political contexts. Such contexts are what makes meaning possible; and meaning makes "reality."[31]

But of course the context that women and men live in is one of patriarchy, sexism, and male privilege—as well as racism and white privilege, capitalism and class privilege, and so forth. If we are socially constructed, feminists have argued, male domination has played an important part in that construction; its laws, customs, rules, and norms have been imposed by men on women to restrict their opportunities, choices, actions, and behaviors. Hence, to those who say that women are more "caring" than men, we could reply that that is because they have always been required to take care of children and men; to those who maintain that women are naturally irrational, we could respond that that is because they are denied access to education; to those who assert that women and girls are not naturally assertive in the classroom, we could also say that that is because they are often not called on or are ignored when they speak.

This construction of social behaviors and rules comes to constitute not only what women are allowed to do, however, but also what they are allowed to *be*: how women are able to think and conceive of themselves, what they can and should desire, what their preferences are, their epistemology and language. If a man beats his wife repeatedly and tells her that she's stupid and ugly and that she deserves to be beaten; if she calls the police but they just tell the man to cool off and walk around the block; or if she has left him, but he has hunted her down, or threatened to hurt her family, or come to her office and behaved violently there, resulting in her dismissal, she may eventually start to act in ways that facilitate the batterer. For instance, she may begin to believe that there is no escape, so why bother trying? She may find that going limp during a beating reduces the injuries she receives; but at the same time it makes it easier for him to hit her. Or when she perceives that he's getting angry, she may trigger an outburst by picking a fight, so that the attack does not catch her by surprise. It is difficult for most nonbattered people to make sense of such choices—it looks like she is not really doing anything to help herself—but the choices she has made have been constructed for her through a system of male privilege that tacitly condones domestic violence even though we claim that it is unacceptable. In this sense, these rules and norms of patriarchy are not simply external restrictions on women's otherwise natural desires; rather, they create an entire cultural context that makes women seem to choose what they are in fact restricted to.[32]

Social construction thus shares some features with "adaptive preferences": the notion, as Elster in particular develops it, that my preferences become shaped and formed by the options that are available.[33] Certainly that could explain the woman with an extremely controlling husband watching her every move who has convinced herself that she does not really want to leave the house. Similarly, "oppressive socialization"[34] is an apt description of women who have come to associate violence with love because they have never experienced any other kind of relationship. Like theories of socialization and adaptive-preference formation, the notion of social construction allows us to engage questions that most contemporary theorists avoid, for example, the possibility of "internal" barriers to liberty. It simultaneously opens up the possibility that the inner self—our preferences, desires, self-conceptions—is constructed by and through outer forces and social structures, such as patriarchy, colonialism, capitalism, and so forth.

However, social construction is more complicated and deeply layered than either socialization or adaptive preferences. Socialization, for example, is seen as something that is done to people by particular other people; it is seen as at least quasi-conscious and intentional, and often damaging. Socialization is thus conceived as specific psychological and behavioral responses to conditions that could be changed or avoided. It thereby assumes an essential, natural self underlying these oppressive conditions which would emerge if they were removed. The concept of adaptive preferences similarly assumes this natural self by positing that the preferences that have been adapted to circumstances are not what the individual truly wants. Hence, every one of Amartya Sen's examples of adaptive preference involves someone who is clearly oppressed—the "hopeless destitute," the "subjugated housewife"—and who would have other desires but for the conditions oppressing them.[35] Granted, Sen most frequently writes about freedom in the context of dire poverty and oppression in Asia and North Africa, the millions of "missing" women resulting from a disproportionately large female mortality rate, which he attributes to sexist neglect of female children "in terms of health care, hospitalization, and even feeding."[36] I by no means wish to deny the force of such arguments, nor the possibility that people can adapt their preferences to extremely oppressive conditions. But the idea of social construction is aimed at understanding much less overt forms of social production; it is something that happens to everyone, men as well as women, rich as well as poor, at all times and in multiple ways. By suggesting that people are *produced through* social formations, and not simply *limited by* them, the idea of social construction thereby calls into question the assumption of what is genuine or true to the self and what is false. As Kathy Ferguson puts it, "It is not simply that [we are] being socialized; rather, a subject on whom socialization can do its work is being produced."[37] The social constructivist argument that the context in which women's desires and preferences are produced, expressed, evaluated, and either granted, denied, or ignored altogether, is a patriarchal one does not mean that women are simply "unfree." In developing a critique of naturalism and a theory of how women are who they are because they are socially constructed by patriarchy, feminists have been able to note the ways in which desires, preferences, agency, and choice are as socially constructed as are the external conditions that enable or restrain them. But at the same time, if social construction characterizes our entire social identity and being, if everyone is always and unavoidably socially constructed, then not only our restrictions but our powers as well must have been produced by this very same process. Who we are—the "choosing subject"—exists within and is formed by particular contexts; the ideal of the naturalized and unified subject utilized by most freedom theory is thus deeply problematic and simplistically overdrawn. The contexts in which we live, patriarchal, sexist, racist, and classist though they may be, have produced women's, indeed everyone's, agency. Yet, while they "empower" women and make their agency possible, they often simultaneously put restraints on women's freedom not suffered by men. This duality of social construction permits, even requires, a more complicated engagement of the question of freedom.

This might suggest something of a paradox, for it seems to imply that nothing need—or can—be done about social construction. If women or the poor happen to be constructed in ways that make them different from wealthy white men, so what? How can feminism claim that this construction is worse than any other construction of identities? Do we not end up with the helpless relativism of a deconstructive poststructuralism? I believe not. Social construction suggests that the dichotomy between negative and positive liberty, and between internal and external restraint, is itself artificially constructed; and moreover that this construction can be seen as motivated by particular power structures that favor men over women. The fact that these power structures themselves were socially constructed, in a seemingly endless devolution, does not prevent feminists from acknowledging the ways in which power operates within any given social context and to make political evaluations of those operations. For instance, in a society where resources for battered women are a low funding priority, where courts and police openly disbelieve women who report abuse, where relatives and friends fail to help and protect them, shame, guilt, feelings of helplessness and/or desert are predictable responses. But they are not just "internal" feelings that come from the self as an isolated entity. Rather, they are social expressions and manifestations of public policy and attitudes, political structures and decisions that reflect particular, even if frequently unrecognized, values and relationships of power that privilege some and disadvantage others. Similarly, in a society that pays poor women a bare subsistence subsidy for raising children, that requires them to reveal the most intimate aspects of their personal and sexual lives in order to gain such help, that demands that they enter the labor force even at the cost of foregoing education, that considers them as "cheats" if they try to rise above subsistence poverty by working on the side, "public assistance" is likely to have an impact on the self-conceptions of recipients, in the form of shame, anger, feelings of powerlessness, or victimization, or some combination of these. But to "blame" welfare mothers for these self-conceptions ignores the generative source of such feelings, which are, arguably, reasonable responses to extreme situations produced by a set of power relations and values that are constructed to privilege some over others.

Social constructivism thus reveals that a focus on external barriers will be weakened without attention to the internal ones, as well as to the larger social, institutional, and cultural context in which such barriers are created and operate. We must acknowledge the *interaction* of "inner" and "outer" and see them as interdependent in meaning and in practice, in order to interrogate the social construction of the choosing subject, the subject of liberty. This interaction does not result in determinism—the view that since there is no way not to be socially constructed, there is no way to change ourselves, because humans cannot control social formations like "patriarchy" or "racism"—but rather provides the means for identifying not only the ways in which power relations are structured but why it is so difficult to see those relations and that structure.

## Freedom as Political, Not Philosophical

The issue of social construction will be developed more fully in chapter 3; the perhaps more controversial question of whether social constructivism actually informs positive-liberty theory, and the relationship of social constructivism to the modern history of liberty theory, will be considered in chapter 2. But for now, I merely want to note that the possibilities of social construction and the focus on the internal aspects of liberty—desire, will, and identity—and how they both facilitate and block freedom is, in my opinion, the most important contribution of Berlin's typology: it offers two different conceptions of the free self and a conceptual language of the "external" and "internal" factors of freedom. Although Berlin rejected the latter, and although many freedom theorists place internal and external in a dichotomous relationship and deny or ignore the more complicated potential that positive-liberty theory offers us concerning social construction and the inner self, Berlin's conceptualization makes it possible to see this potential and offers a vocabulary for a more complex understanding of freedom that is more conducive to feminist concerns.

Certainly, Berlin's typology has been challenged by many, and some would suggest that couching a discussion of liberty in its terms is misdirected. For instance, Gerald MacCallum argues that there are not "two concepts of liberty" at all but rather only one, consisting of a triadic relationship between agents, objects of desire (including desired actions and conditions), and preventing conditions. "[F]reedom is thus always *of* something (an agent or agents), *from* something, *to* do, not do, become, or not become something."[38] Theorists of negative and positive liberty are each "attending to, or emphasizing the importance of only one part of what is always present in any case of freedom,"[39] and what they are really arguing about are various values which they believe are important to political society and social relations,[40] not about freedom per se. Freedom as a political practice can be structured with a particular content according to particular values, but that can never negate the basic philosophical truth that its conceptual meaning is constituted in a triadic relation.

MacCallum's argument is important for the ways in which it identifies, with brutal honesty, the politicalness (or normativity) of the supposedly philosophical (often semantic) debate about freedom. Neither positive nor negative liberty is usually embraced simply on the grounds of its philosophical consistency or compelling logic. Rather, politics is always at issue. Indeed, as Gray implicitly suggests, MacCallum himself obscures his own political leanings: the triadic formula that he sets up is already biased in favor of negative liberty, because his idea of "reasonableness" and the role he ascribes to "rationality" all presuppose a negative-liberty framework. His negative-liberty bias allows him to dismiss variants of positive liberty as confusions of the question of liberty rather than as genuine dimensions of it.[41] But even if we grant MacCallum's point, this does not counter the notion that positive and negative liberty are two significantly different visions of freedom. It is precisely *because* of the political nature of liberty that the positive/negative typology provides an important theoretical division, one that defines general parameters for two orientations toward ontology and epistemology. To borrow from Rawlsian terminology, MacCallum may be correct that we have one *concept* of liberty, but we do have two *conceptions*, negative and positive, and they differ at fundamental levels.

This suggests three reasons for retaining the typology, not to perpetuate the often semantic arguments about how to define freedom, but as an important normative tool for framing its central issues. The first reason is that, debates and challenges notwithstanding, the typology of positive and negative liberty has in fact dominated theoretical discussions of freedom. Prominent theorists as diverse as Stanley Benn, Ian Carter, Diana Coole, Richard Flathman, John Gray, Quenten Skinner, Hillel Stiener, and Robin West all acknowledge the centrality of the typology to liberty theory.[42] Though individual theorists such as MacCallum may disagree with Berlin's typology, they seem unable to escape it, and it has retained a powerful grip on philosophical thinking about liberty. Second, this grip is due, to a significant degree, to the decidedly—if often overlooked—*political* character of the typology. I agree with some critics that Berlin's formulation is overdrawn and simplistic. He clearly had Cold War political motivations for his categories: he wanted to ally positive liberty with bad-guy communist dictatorships and negative liberty with good-guy Western democracies. But that Berlin manipulates philosophy to the ends of politics should not lead us into the trap of separating the two, and of missing the impact of the concepts *as* political and not "just" philosophical. The two concepts of liberty, as he articulates them, reflect two different—though perhaps equally problematic—conceptions of a person: one as innately separate, individualistic, unconnected, rights oriented, even antagonistic; the other innately connected, communitarian, even selfless, concerned with responsibility. Depending on which view of the subject one takes—or more precisely, where on the continuum between these two extremes one's conception of the subject lies—a variety of conclusions follow about the relation between state and society, society and individual; in short, political values. In this, the typology suggests that freedom is not just about "who we are" but also about "what kind of world we want to live in." Many critics such as MacCallum who want to reject the typology altogether fail to recognize these issues as central to freedom, and this failure may explain why political philosophers keep getting drawn back into Berlin's framework.

Finally, and perhaps most importantly, both positive and negative conceptions inform popular understandings of liberty: after all, most of us can understand, in an everyday sense, how the cheating smoker and cocaine addict are both free and not free. This is because the typology does in fact say something very important about freedom. Both variants of freedom are centrally about making choices. Choice is a complex process of negotiation and relationship between what we commonly call "internal" and "external" factors; between will, desire, and preferences, on the one hand, and forces that not only inhibit or enable the realization of such desires but also contribute to or influence the formation of these desires, on the other. It is precisely in this notion of internal and external barriers to liberty that I think the positive-negative typology is the most powerful, and at the same time most problematic. Negative liberty emphasizes the role of external barriers, while positive liberty highlights the internal; and indeed, I believe that this is the key dividing line between the two models. Those, like MacCallum and Orlando Patterson, who focus on Berlin's differentiation between "freedom from" and "freedom to" to illustrate its incoherence (because every "freedom from" is automatically a "freedom to") miss the more important point of this external/internal divide.[43]

Indeed, a great deal of contemporary freedom theory fails to acknowledge the politics involved in arguments over freedom and instead tends to focus on somewhat semantic debates over the meaning of freedom, and particularly what constitutes a "barrier" or "restraint." The distinction between being "unfree" and "unable" sits at the heart of contemporary theorists' consideration of what counts as a barrier. A "restraint" by definition is something that makes me unfree, but "inability" is seen as something intrinsic to myself or the world, part of nature or naturally caused.

As Phillip Pettit argues, freedom involves more than "nonlimitation," because intentionally placed limits on freedom are of greater moral and political concern than are those that occur naturally or through no one's fault.[44] Accordingly, negative-liberty advocate Richard Flathman requires that barriers must be "obstacles deliberately placed or left by other intentional or purposive agents."[45] The requirements of intentionality and purposiveness, Flathman suggests, eliminate from consideration impediments that are not deliberately placed but are nevertheless socially generated and constructed, such as poverty and lack of employment opportunity or inhibitive social norms for women. Rather, these are part of our "form of life," basic background conditions that must be taken as given. In a footnote, Flathman does potentially allow "social arrangements as impediments to liberty if they are alterable or remediable by human agency," but only if they are conducive to a "charge of responsibility for deliberate interference, not merely . . . causal influence."[46] There must be an identifiable moral agent who can be held accountable, and that agent must have used her agency—that is, acted deliberately, intentionally, purposively—in erecting the barrier to others' freedom.

In Berlin's initial formulation, of course, restraints had to be seen as deliberate in order to count as such; the mere incapacity to do something did not constitute unfreedom to do it unless someone else caused the incapacity. Though Berlin later expanded this notion to include "alterable human practices" which bar *possible* choices,[47] thus suggesting that obstacles need not be deliberate, they still had to be attributable to specific humans who could be held accountable for them. Parent, however, argues that Berlin may go too far in this modification. For Parent, physical force or other overt coercion is required to constitute a restraint.[48] Though Parent rejects Flathman's requirement of purposive action, and thereby allows for natural events to serve as barriers, this apparent expansion is counteracted by his strict requirement that unless something is impossible, I am free to do it. Barriers to freedom must be objectively assessable, not subjectively contingent; a battered woman, for instance, may be afraid to leave her abuser, but this fear does not in itself make her unfree to leave. After all, "consider the many individuals who have performed actions, started movements, and initiated reforms knowing full well that their doing so would cause others to inflict severe, sometimes unjustified punishment on them."[49]

Ian Carter, by contrast, suggests that intentionality is not relevant to the existence of a barrier, though identifiable agency is.[50] This might allow us to identify a rapist who claims he "didn't mean to hurt" his victim, or a sexual harasser who thought he was simply paying his secretary a compliment, as interfering with women's freedom even if such men did not intend to do so. Another way of expanding the notion of restraint, "the responsibility view," involves focusing less on how barriers are set in place and more on their possible removal: I may not have closed the door to the room in which you are now locked, but the fact that I can let you out without serious risk to myself means that I am morally responsible for doing so, even though I am not causally responsible for your predicament. By not letting you out, I interfere with your freedom.[51] This view rejects the notion that obstacles need to be deliberately placed in order to count as restraints on freedom, for the notion of moral responsibility transcends causal responsibility: just because I did not create an obstacle does not mean I may not be morally responsible for removing it. This view of barriers to liberty can be seen as extremely expansive as well as highly political, for what constitutes a barrier will turn on our views of moral responsibility. So as David Miller suggests, a socialist will view a capitalist as responsible for the unfreedom of workers.[52] One could, therefore, see poverty as a restriction on liberty if one developed an economic theory that identified a definite class of people who were able to alleviate the poverty.

Indeed, the question of poverty and whether "economic inequalities constitute constraints on freedom"[53] is one that a number of freedom theorists take up. It holds potential for feminist inquiries into the possibility that sexism or patriarchy presents a barrier to women's freedom, but this potential is largely unrealized, because of the individualist framework freedom theories deploy. For instance, because Kristjansson separates moral from causal responsibility in the responsibility view, social conditions such as poverty can be viewed as a constraint on freedom, but only "to the extent that identifiable people can be held accountable for it through their negligence, violation of positive duties, etc."[54] Such precision cannot be achieved, however, even within a socialist framework: at best, a generalized *class* of people can be shown to benefit disproportionately from the existing structure, and even they are only responsible for participating in it, not for changing it, which as individuals they may not be able to do. But this undercuts the socialist's claim at the root.

Similarly, Miller maintains that the standard of moral responsibility should be construed fairly narrowly, and he retains the individualist idea of assignable agency in two senses. First, he rejects the idea of collective responsibility except insofar as we can isolate and identify individual agents within a collective "who contribute to the outcome intentionally or in dereliction of duty."[55] Noting that the person who adds the final straw that breaks the proverbial camel's back is responsible insofar as he knows others have added *their* straws, he concedes that "I bear my share of responsibility of the resulting injury to the camel." However, "the difficulty in such cases is likely to be finding out who could reasonably be expected to have foreseen which outcomes," a dim prospect at best, according to Miller. Hence, one cannot hold a collective responsible to a greater degree than the individual members. At the same time, however, the assignable-agency criterion can also restrict the scope of a barrier; for instance, a capitalist will not see his own activities as restricting his workers' freedom but rather as augmenting it, by offering them various choices.[56] Thus, Miller limits responsibility to a relatively direct relationship; otherwise, he says, the notion of restraint grows far too large.[57]

Benn and Weinstein, whom Kristjansson credits as originators of the responsibility view, similarly consider poverty as a potential barrier to freedom,[58] only to take away with one hand what they give with the other. Their well-known example of a shopkeeper who sells eggs rather than giving them away is used to counteract notions of social responsibility that extend beyond purposive individual agency. Because "the general framework of property relations is taken to define the normal conditions of action," and the shopkeeper is an individual agent who has not caused the background conditions that lead to the eggs' price—as would be the case if he owned the only shop in the neighborhood and raised his price with the express purpose of exploiting his customers—then the shopkeeper cannot be seen as interfering with liberty.[59] Because of this individualism, the shopkeeper is the focus of inquiry and therefore let off the hook. It may be true that the egg merchant in this example is not himself a "restraint" on my desire to eat eggs, but the lack of money is, and the possibility that poverty is a barrier to freedom requires inquiry into the social conditions that create that lack. By directing our focus to the price of eggs and rejecting the claim that it is a barrier, Benn and Weinstein can claim that there is no barrier at all, when it may instead be the case that the blockage exists elsewhere, and would be revealed by broader notions of economic and social responsibility.

In Benn's subsequent book on freedom, he seeks to pursue the issue of economic and social structures as barriers to liberty by considering economic exploitation. Exploitation requires both "that there is no reasonably eligible alternative and that the consideration or advantage received is incommensurate with the price paid. One is not exploited if one is offered what one desperately needs at a fair and reasonable price." This definition is certainly compatible with a broad understanding of barriers and social responsibility. But Benn goes on to argue that restraints must be the product of "some rational being or beings" who "can be held responsible for them, for bringing them about or permitting them to continue."[60] For his example, however, he uses Esau and Jacob, not worker and capitalist, that is, a relationship of two specific individuals rather than of two social groups and categories. This presents an almost willful denial of the broader potential of his argument. Indeed, in my view, Benn misconstrues the point of the parable altogether, which is not to illustrate exploitation; insofar as he limits Esau's freedom by stealing his birthright, Jacob betrays the love and trust that a brother is supposed to feel and display and violates his responsibility to his brother.

So even the responsibility view of restraints persists in its dependence on the overly individualized self and insists on an assignable agency of particular and identifiable individuals who, if they do not purposely place barriers in the agent's way, are at least morally responsible for failing to remove them. By contrast, Gray argues that restrictive conditions such as poverty do not have to be caused intentionally, nor by identifiable agents, as long as they are avoidable (e.g., if "mass unemployment . . . resulted from misguided monetary policies whose application was in no way inevitable"), or at least remediable by human action.[61] This allows for collective, rather than merely individual, responsibility. But at the same time, Gray also maintains that determining whether social conditions are avoidable or remediable is extremely difficult, if not impossible, and gives up on the idea fairly quickly. For him, as for the other theorists discussed so far, even when negative-liberty theory seeks to accommodate positive-liberty theory's expansion of the concept of barrier to include generalized social conditions, the strong individualism that persists in these efforts dooms them to failure. For when considering large social forces such as poverty in a capitalist economy, intentionality and assignable agency are generally impossible to locate; indeed, they are in some ways definitionally excluded, because a much broader set of theoretical assumptions is required, such as those found in socialism. Indeed, the focus on defining terms such as "barrier" rather than on the political and normative implications that follow from particular social relations is what allows this methodological individualism to persist. Poverty is a political and social condition, not a semantic one, and it affects classes of people, not isolated individuals.

Gerald Cohen seems to adopt this more political understanding when he argues that poverty restricts individuals' freedom. Wealth is not simply a resource that some people happen to have, and which happens to make those people freer, according to Cohen. Rather, he seeks a more systematic understanding of poverty and wealth. "My argument overturns the claim that a liberal capitalist society is, by its very nature, a *free* society," he says, for all societies and economic systems "have structurally different ways of inducing distributions of freedom." In capitalist societies, that distribution is determined by "the distribution of money."[62] Indeed, the notion that wealth does not determine freedom is an "illusion" forged by the very ubiquity of capital's determination of freedom, much as the supposed "naturalness" of property that the social-contract theorists posit (as will be shown in the following chapter) creates the illusion that inequalities of wealth are the result of individual choices and abilities rather than of power. But according to Cohen, "a property distribution just *is* . . . a distribution of rights of interference." Hence, poverty is deeply political; indeed, it constitutes *"social relations of constraint"* whereby some are free to act and others are not.[63]

Such a broad understanding of the constraints that poverty produces as a social force, and particularly as a social relation, has the potential to broaden the concept of a "barrier" to liberty to include general social forces that lack identifiable agency and intentionality. But like the other theorists discussed here, Cohen is drawn back into individualist ideals and qualifies his arguments. He maintains that capitalism per se does not interfere with poor people's freedom; rather, "to lack money is . . . to be *prey to* interference" by particular individuals who have more power (relative to the people whose liberty they interfere with) within a capitalist system.[64] For instance, if I cannot afford to buy a sweater, he suggests, the department store clerk (or, more accurately, the store security guard) will interfere with me if I try to leave the store with the sweater without paying for it. The "interference" with freedom is located in, or exercised by, particular individuals; once again, it is identifiable agents, not economic systems, that interfere with my action.[65] What Cohen's account leaves out, however, is the notion that the clerk's or security guard's actions are themselves constructed and determined by the contextual framework of capital in which the possibilities for action are set. Just as the shopper is prevented by the security guard from taking the sweater without paying, so the security guard is prevented by his supervisor from letting the shopper take the sweater (he would be fired, at the least). And his supervisor is prevented from overlooking the guard's infraction by the store owner, who would likely dismiss the agency if he discovered its laxity. And the store owner could even be seen as restrained by a moral imperative to keep the store going so that people like the sales clerk can continue to have jobs and feed their families. All of the actions and choices made by these individuals may be self-consciously "theirs," in the sense that the guard does not want to let the shopper take the sweater, the supervisor wants a vigilant employee, the store owner wants a well-run security force guarding his store. It is not necessarily the case that capitalism is overtly forcing these individuals into certain choices. However, these choices and actions are, nevertheless, conditioned and constructed by and within the context of capital; and insofar as capitalism is not a force of nature but an economic and political system that distributes freedom along with economic resources, as Cohen maintains, then that context itself may be conceptualized as at least a significant, if partial, source of the shopper's unfreedom.

Certainly, as Cohen himself argues, the conclusion that poverty restricts freedom does not in and of itself mean that capitalism is "bad," or that it must be rejected in favor of socialism; socialism can produce its own set of constraints on freedom. But even if we decide that capitalism is desirable, Cohen would say, we still need to acknowledge the ways in which freedom for the poor is limited. As he admits, however, this final assertion is a conceptual claim, not a normative one—"no normative claim has been defended, or even asserted" in his paper—much less a political one. It is a claim about the meaning of freedom, and whether poverty fulfills the criteria of "interference." By contrast, I suggest that the *politics* of unfreedom—whose freedom is limited and whose is not, whether certain groups of people (for instance women or racial minorities) are systematically poorer than other groups (such as white men)— are central to conclusions about the *concept* of freedom. Like the other theorists considered here, Cohen's individualist focus undermines the ability to accomplish what he—and they—originally set out to do: namely, consider poverty as a barrier to freedom.

Amartya Sen is a notable exception to this individualism, for he pays a great deal of attention to the ways in which poverty as a social force inhibits people's liberty. Poverty involves "deprivation of basic capabilities, rather than merely . . . low income." Wealth and income are not goods in themselves but rather means to other things, such as food (freedom from starvation) and health care (freedom from morbidity). Sen argues that by negatively affecting the capabilities of individuals, poverty can deny substantive freedoms to do specific things and thus undermine any formal or process-oriented freedom they may in theory possess. Thus "economic unfreedom," though not the only freedom, is nevertheless key, for "extreme poverty can make a person a helpless prey in the violation of other kinds of freedom," such as political freedoms.[66] Other kinds of freedoms he identifies, such as health care, are of course directly "economic" only in some contexts; in the United States, for instance, health care is privately administered and therefore requires health insurance, usually through employment benefits or out-of-pocket expenditures (or sometimes both). But even socialized medicine, which guarantees rich and poor alike access to care, requires a certain level of GNP for a nation to afford the technology and medicines necessary for adequate health care; and as Great Britain has demonstrated, those rich enough to go outside the public system generally receive better and prompter care. Sen argues for the importance of evaluating substantive freedoms on a "factual base" that considers the "real opportunities" individuals have: not just the doors that are open, as Berlin puts it, but whether one can actually go through them. Thus famine should be considered "in terms of the loss of entitlement—a sharp decline in the substantive freedom to buy food"; illness and mortality resulting from inadequate (access to) health care should be seen in terms of a denial of entitlements to life.[67] I will return in chapter 7 to Sen's arguments about the role of equality in freedom, but here it is enough to note that Sen's consideration of poverty as a barrier to freedom, in contrast to the other theories I have discussed, raises the question as to whether the negative-liberty concept of external barrier can be expanded to include broad social conditions such as poverty. He clearly demonstrates a strong alliance with liberal principles, and the conception of freedom to which poverty poses a barrier is expressed in the negative-liberty terms of making choices and expressing preferences that are not the product of or adapted to oppression. And of course he also gives a great deal of attention to political freedoms. Yet Sen also asserts that substantive freedom is as important as procedural freedom, and an important concept he develops along with "agency freedom" is "well-being freedom," which shares positive-liberty values.[68] But Sen is much less interested in whether he should be labeled a positive or negative libertarian than in the political and economic conditions that set the terms for people's lives, their capabilities and freedom to achieve their own welfare. He is concerned with understanding the political conditions in which particular situations of freedom evaluation are made; and poverty, he maintains, is a decidedly political condition.

## FEMINISM AND FREEDOM

Sen's argument is significant for feminism, because if generalized conditions like poverty can be established as a barrier to freedom, perhaps patriarchy can be similarly established. And indeed, it is not coincidental that Sen is one of the very few mainstream theorists to develop a theory of freedom that gives a central place to the specific forms of oppression and unfreedom that women experience. He identifies these forms of oppression as the political products of cultural, historical, and economic forces rather than as simply part of the cultural landscape, a "normal background condition."[69] Feminists frequently point out ways that customs, practices, and beliefs that men and women have accepted as "normal" in fact encode deeply sexist attitudes that restrict women—and often men as well—in illegitimate, unjustified, and unnecessary ways. If context sets the terms for understanding claims of freedom, and if women's choices, opportunities, desires, and options exist within a context of patriarchy or sexism, there is good reason to believe that sexism itself can be a barrier to freedom. That is, not just individual sexist acts perpetrated by particular individuals, but the entire cultural construct that assigns greater value to men than to women, that provides more options to men and supports men's pursuit of choice more than women's—in short, what many feminists alternately call male privilege or patriarchy—can restrict women's freedom. But this is a restriction which the mainstream conception of restraint and freedom, focused as it is on intentionality, identifiable

agency, and purposiveness, can never see. For instance, the theorists discussed here would most likely agree that an individual sexual harasser or
abuser or rapist interferes with individual women's freedom but would
not regard as barriers to freedom the social conditions that allow such
things as rape or abuse to happen in the first place, and make the arrest
and conviction of the perpetrators of such actions difficult. As Benn maintains, "the mere possession of . . . power [what he calls "power against"]
without its being exercised [what he calls "power over"] would not be
enough to make the other unfree";[70] the fact that men can rape women
and beat up their wives, frequently with impunity, does not matter, it is
only when a woman is raped or beaten up that her freedom can be said
to be limited.

But consider a woman's decision to go out at night. Most men have the
power to rape at least some women, a "power against" women which
women do not reciprocally have against men. Most men do not exercise
this power, and many would be horrified at the suggestion that they do
so, but it is a power that pervades the culture nonetheless, making many
women afraid to go out at night alone. Even if they have never themselves
been raped or attacked, the fear still inhibits them. Such women are made
unfree by such power and the fear it generates; the existence of power
against, though not actually exercised at a given moment, has translated
into a generalized and constant power over. Could we say that while
women may "feel" unfree, they are wrong, that they are "in fact" free,
that their fear is irrational and misplaced? Some, like Katie Roiphe and
Christina Hoff Sommers, suggest that statistics on rape are inflated, and
that women's perception of unsafety is not justified.[71] But even granting
their claims—which are at best controversial, given that the rape figures
used in many studies are not made up by feminists but are provided by
the FBI and other state-run, and supposedly patriarchal, institutions—the
fact remains that rape is an act perpetrated against individual women,
and there is no way to predict accurately whether a particular woman
will in fact be raped in a given situation.[72] The notion that women simply
need to avoid overtly unsafe situations is further belied by the experience
of acquaintance rape; and even stranger rape often occurs in women's
homes and during the day, rather than in dark alleys at night. And even
if it did only occur in such stereotypical contexts, doesn't telling women
to simply avoid those situations—say, jogging in Central Park at night—
restrict women's liberty, and do so more than men's?

We could say, following William Parent, that women are "in fact" free
because no one is physically restraining women, no laws bar them from
going out, no one literally waits outside the door with a gun. After all,
the famous Central Park jogger *did* go jogging in Central Park, so it is
contradictory to say that she was unfree to do so.[73] Women go out all the

time, afraid or not, so it is absurd to say that the fear of rape inhibits them. A related position is taken by Camille Paglia; she says that in order to be free, women have to face up to the risks of adult life. Just as a man risks being mugged in New York City at night, a woman risks rape. Indeed, she suggests, risking rape is part of the deal of liberation: you cannot have one without the other.[74] As Benn asserts, even if "power against" is actually used, it is not determinative of unfreedom:

> If Alan has the power adversely to affect Betty's interests and successfully threatens her, he has exercised his power over her. But if the power he has against her is insufficient to support her claim that she acted under duress, her excuse that she was in Alan's power would fail. For when assessing excuses, one looks not only at Betty's preferences but at standards governing the course that she might reasonably be required and expected to choose, whatever her actual preferences.[75]

On a feminist reading, however, this sounds like the "reasonable man" view often drawn on in rape cases. For instance, if Alan said he had a knife but in fact did not have one, should Betty have then fought back to prevent her rape? Does the fact that she did not fight mean that, in fact, she wanted the sex and hence was not raped? Or let's say Alan and Betty were on a first date and drinking heavily; and Alan forced Betty to have sex, or she was too inebriated to resist effectvely. Do we say that Betty should not have been drinking and therefore is responsible for what happened to her? Did she "ask for it" by getting drunk in the first place, and compromising her ability to resist? If so, then is Alan not guilty of raping her, by definition? Or do we say that rape is excusable because Betty was in fact free to avoid it?[76]

As many theorists note, the simple existence of cost does not make one unfree: if Betty has a gun and could use it to prevent her assault, she must choose between two terrible options, shooting Alan or being assaulted, but the point is that she has a choice, can exercise a counterpower, and is thus free. And "power against" can be countered by other "powers against": self-defense courses and Take Back the Night marches can empower women; advocacy for tougher sentencing and more woman-friendly evidentiary procedures in rape trials have made prosecution more possible for women; sexual harassment policies can give women rights of redress against harassers. But the difficulty of building such counterpowers in the first place, not to mention using them effectively, suggests something more systemic about barriers to women's freedom than is captured by the requirement of assignable individual agency. Indeed, such difficulty stems precisely from the normalization of masculine power, which ensures that the dominant culture will resist women's counterpowers, and indeed depends on such resistance. The semantic focus of Benn's argument pre-

vents us from seeing the politics of the situation: supposedly neutral standards of reasonableness are stacked against women in a systematic way
because of the background condition of patriarchy that provides men
with greater power.

Philip Pettit potentially offers a more feminist-friendly approach to liberty with his argument that freedom should be defined in terms of "nondomination." In contrast to Benn, Pettit holds that a person can be dominated by others without their actual interference. "Even if the others don't
interfere in his or her life," Pettit maintains, "they have an arbitrary
power of doing so: there are few restraints or costs to inhibit them." Such
domination is a function not merely of individual behavior but of background social conditions as well; "an employee may be dominated by an
employer in a tough labor market, a wife by a husband in a sexist culture,
or an illegal immigrant by the citizen who gives them a job and a living."[77]
In fact, Pettit says, in such examples, the employer, husband, or citizen
does not actually *need* to interfere, because those background conditions
pressure the employee, wife, or immigrant to limit their own behavior.
Freedom, therefore, cannot be defined as merely "noninterference," because people can dominate others without interfering; freedom also requires "nondomination."

Despite the apparent social understanding of power that his recognition
of domination offers, however, and despite his acknowledgment of the
restrictions such power may impose on liberty, Pettit, like the other theorists discussed here, undermines the potential of his argument by falling
back on an individualistic framework. There are two particular ways in
which this individualism stands out. In the first instance, Pettit posits a
conscious awareness of unfreedom; in his examples, the dominated person always seems to be aware of her or his domination, and such awareness affects that person's choices and actions. Accordingly, a dominated
person "will not be able to speak out in a forthright and free way—or act
on a basis that such speech might justify—but must always have an eye
out for what will please the powerful and keep them sweet." Hence, "The
price of liberty is not eternal vigilance but eternal *discretion*"—a term
that particularly connotes conscious effort and control.[78] For instance,
battered women often seek to placate the batterer by doing what he demands and saying things to soothe his anger. But of course, nonbattered
women may similarly seek to please their spouses and in doing so may
frequently subjugate their own desires to their husbands'. This leads to
the second instance of Pettit's individualism, though it is even subtler than
the first. As I mentioned previously, Pettit claims that domination can
occur without any interference at all; for instance, Mrs. Bridge is not
beaten, but because of social norms of masculinity and femininity, she
restrains her own behavior in ways that her husband expects. But wait:

how does my example of Mrs. Bridge attest to Pettit's individualism? Indeed, does it not attest to the power of patriarchy, which does its work regardless of what Mr. Bridge does?

Not in Pettit's concept of domination, which ironically pays little attention to the social forces that *enable* such domination. It is as individualistic as his claim that discretion is the price of liberty. For Pettit assumes that since the individual does not *notice* the interference, and since no particular individual is engaging in identifiably interfering behavior, then interference simply does not exist. Such an assumption is unwarranted, however. Considering domination as a social force suggests that domination is often effective precisely because the interference that power makes possible is not noticed. Indeed, the more effective social ideologies are in creating subjects who conform to restrictive norms—for instance, women who stay with their abusive partners because they believe that women are responsible for making relationships work—the less aware of interference individuals, both the dominated and the dominator, will likely be. But such lack of awareness does not mean that interference is not exercised. Even within the terms Pettit offers us, there is a certain illogic and counterintuitiveness to his assertion that domination can exist without interference. For unless there is some actual interference, some material instances of the power the dominant figure (what he calls the "dominus") has *to* interfere, the power of domination will weaken. If the dominus *never* interferes with the actions of the dominated, the vigilance and self-restriction of the dominated will wane, boundaries will be tested and stretched. If such tests are not met with resistance by the dominus, then domination can no longer be said to exist. Hence (to return to the example I used in my discussion of Benn), if all men refrained completely from assaulting women, men's "power against" women would diminish, if not vanish entirely.

The fact that some men do assault some women, however, ensures that interference occurs all the time in patriarchal society; just because an individual woman has never been raped does not mean that reading about other women's assaults in the newspaper will not "interfere" with her freedom to go out at night. Like Benn, Pettit seems committed to saying that women's fear of going out at night is a function of domination ("power against"), but not of interference ("power over"). But this misses the feminist point that the "power against" women that patriarchy gives to men *constitutes* a kind of interference. This interference is not individually located, nor does it even have to be expressed by any given individual man, and yet it works to restrict women both as a group and individually. Consider, for instance, that women in Afghanistan continue to wear the *burqa* even after the Taliban have been deposed, because they fear that violence against them may continue. Though the religious police have been removed, the possibility that others may seek to interfere with women's freedom by criticizing or assaulting them for uncovering their faces causes them to continue to wear it. The effectiveness of their domination is a result of the past interference with women's movement, and an expectation of possible future interference as well, even when the interference is not actually occurring. (As of January 2002, for instance, there have been no reports of violence against women who have removed the burqa, though many women are still wearing it because they fear the assaults will be renewed).[79] The trauma of such past violence creates a framework for perception that continues to interfere in women's lives and choices even though such interference is not exercised by particular individuals (indeed, even though such individuals are presumably gone). But at the same time, such fears are not unchangeable; if the women who have removed the burqa continue to be unmolested, if women gain more social status and economic power, presumably such fear will diminish, and more women will abandon the burqa for less restrictive (and uncomfortable) forms of veiling.

Thus, we need a more complicated understanding of the relationship between domination and interference, and between social forces and individual action, than Pettit gives us. I am arguing, against Pettit, that domination always requires interference; there has to be a *reason* for the fear that motivates the self-vigilance of the dominated, even if the dominated is not fully aware of that fear, or of being dominated. Social norms do not come into being by themselves, and they cannot persist without people's actively calling on and deploying them. So the domination that might result from such norms cannot persist without individuals' acting within larger frameworks of cultural meaning to interfere with other individuals' self-conceptions, desires, and choices. But at the same time, the power of norms, practices, and meaning far exceeds the grasp and control of any individual, so that this power can be used and called into play without the explicit awareness of anyone, either dominus or dominated. I believe that Pettit's individualism keeps him from recognizing this feature of domination. That is, he wishes to hang onto the individualist conception of freedom, wherein interference always requires an agent who acts intentionally and purposefully. Because of that, rather than seeing that interference is often systematic and socially produced, and that individual actions take place within larger social structures that make those actions possible and give them meaning, Pettit maintains that we can have domination without interference. That is, the only way for him to claim that freedom can be restricted without intention and purpose being exercised—a claim which I obviously support—and yet retain individualism is to reject "non-interference" as the defining feature of freedom. While such a solution makes a welcome advance over some of the other theories I have critiqued here, in the end it really begs, rather than resolves, the question of freedom from a feminist perspective. It fails to provide a framework for understanding how it is that social forces like patriarchy are able to restrict women's freedom. Such a framework requires the rejection of individualism as a guiding principle.[80]

In a negative-liberty model, the systematic nature of power, domination, and interference could be revealed by expanding the concept of a barrier, as various theorists discussed here suggest; but this would then require a reformulation of "agency" to acknowledge the ways in which individuals operate within systems and structures and are responsible for contributions to power imbalances without necessarily intending or realizing it. Sexual violence is a good example of this problem, for it is on the one hand pervasive and systemic (it is overwhelmingly women who are targeted for rape) and on the other hand arbitrary and random (all kinds of women are raped, young and old, regardless of race or class, in a broad variety of circumstances, thus making formulaic solutions like "avoid X to avoid rape" impossible). Although rape is a specific and individual act—even when a woman is "gang raped," we tend to consider her raped repeatedly by a number of individuals, she is not seen to be raped by a collectivity, much less by patriarchy—individual rapists live and operate within a cultural context that makes rape a conceivable and even acceptable act, that in effect "enables" the action. The failure of police to arrest and courts to convict is compounded by the stigma of shame that plagues rape victims; this shame stems in part from the intimate violation of the assault, and particularly from the fact that the assaulter's pleasure comes directly from the victim's pain, disempowerment, and humiliation.[81] But the acceptability of rape also stems in part from patriarchal ideas of sexuality, both men's (rape is an inevitable outcome of men's sex drive) and women's (the twin images of angel and whore, which are invoked to justify consideration of women's moral character and sexual history in judging whether to blame the victim).[82] Indeed, the vanishing point of rape comes at the pinnacle of patriarchy, in that the rapist's belief that what he is doing is simply "having sex," that "normal" sexuality for him involves women's subordination, humiliation, and injury, and that women "really" want such treatment depends on and operates from the obliteration of women's human subjectivity. If women are not people, if they are only objectivized projections of male desire, if masculine perspectives dominate the account of "what actually happened," then "rape" by definition does not occur. Such views of women fail to challenge—indeed, are unable to challenge—the very existence of rape as a practice; they do not question why men rape or make that question the focus of women's unfreedom. Feminists thus seek to challenge patriarchy by claiming that rape is unacceptable, to make the streets safe for all. Without such wide-sweeping challenges, the very real barriers to women's freedom are invisible.

Thus, many "expanded" negative-liberty theories have serious flaws that may stem in part from a failure to concretize and specify the experiences of people who are inhibited by political and social conditions such as sexism, or racism, or poverty. Yet it is for this very reason that an expanded notion of external barriers is necessary to a feminist understanding of freedom. In considering gender, once we expand the notion of an external restraint we open the door to asking how external factors shape the internal self, how restraint and opportunity form and influence desire, preference, and choice. Accordingly, I will be operating from an understanding of freedom that advocates the need to see the relation between inner and outer factors of freedom. Like classic negative-liberty theorists, I maintain that the ability to make choices and act on them is the basic condition for freedom. However, like positive-liberty theorists, I maintain that choice needs to be understood in terms of the desiring subject, of her preferences, her will, and identity. For subjectivity exists in social contexts of relations, practices, policies, and institutions that affect and shape desires, will, and identity. Recognizing the inadequacies of the negative/positive typology, I maintain that it can nevertheless yield useful insights into freedom from a feminist perspective.

## Defining Feminism

That, however, may well depend on what one means by "feminism." If "freedom" is a concept that is difficult to define, because of the unrecognized but *implicit* political battles underlying it, "feminism" is even more difficult to define, because it is the locus of *explicit* political and theoretical debate. I follow bell hooks and define feminism very basically as a political and philosophical devotion to ending the oppression of people on the basis of gender and sex. Hooks argues that the more common definition of feminism, as women's equality with men, traps feminism within the terms of not only masculinist discourse—because men become the neutral standard used to evaluate women's experience, thus erasing gender difference—but racist and classist discourse as well. For which "men" do such feminists want to be equal to? Poor African-American men? Or economically privileged white men? She maintains that a genuinely inclusive feminism should be defined as a struggle dedicated to "ending sexist oppression."[83] Of course, what constitutes "sexist oppression" is itself in need of clarification, but people who are assigned to the social category "women" are the primary, although not the only, victims of such oppression. Hence, feminism is a political value system that has at its heart the empowerment of women to direct their lives. Though this may seem individualistic—and perhaps terminally Western—the notion of "self-direction" here depends on and presupposes the context of community: feminism as I use it here does not entail an abstract notion of choice, but rather acknowledges that all choices occur in contexts. The issue, then, turns on how power operates in various contexts. The focus on context also requires attention to other aspects of identity, such as ethnicity, culture, race, and class; since "women" belong to multiple identity categories, their "gender" and "sex" are defined in terms of these other categories as well. But what makes something "feminist" is its primary devotion to *women*, regardless of how that category is defined by and within different contexts.

In focusing on the relationship between internality and externality, *and* in considering positive and negative liberty as political and normative categories, not just philosophical and semantic ones, a feminist approach to liberty can suggest a way to hold onto the political usefulness of the differing models of self, subject, and politics, and yet in the process develop a somewhat different conceptualization of freedom that transcends the duality even as it borrows from it. Why should feminism be particularly useful to this undertaking? To begin with, despite the fact that feminists would not agree on whether the women in any of the scenarios with which I opened my discussion are free, or in what ways they are unfree, most feminists *would* agree that the question of freedom is extremely important, because women have been denied freedom in most societies throughout the world and throughout history. In the control of their bodies and reproduction, property rights, participation in politics, law- and policymaking, definition of moral values, family and childrearing decisions, and even the construction of language and epistemology, women have historically been restricted—not totally or uniformly by any means, but far more than males of the same race and class. This history of women's oppression thus gives feminism a particularly appropriate edge on the concept of freedom.

Furthermore, feminists should support my desire to hang onto certain aspects of the positive/negative typology, because both positive and negative liberty models inform feminist concerns. For instance, negative liberty's emphasis on individual choice is vital to issues such as reproductive freedom, sexual harassment, and employment discrimination. Feminists who have struggled against centuries of "second-guessing" by men about what it is that "women really want" are not eager to give up on the ideal of negative liberty. Similarly, positive liberty's emphasis on context and community, as well as the internal restrictions on liberty, are also important to feminist issues such as affirmative action and other means to positively provide for the conditions that enable women to exercise choices, as well as efforts to identify the effects of patriarchy on women's identity, psyche, and self-conceptions that may interfere with their ability to formulate choices in the first place.

While the dualistic typology of positive and negative liberty is useful to understanding freedom, however, it is also theoretically inadequate to deal with many questions raised by women's historical and material experience. Throughout history, theorists of both persuasions generally denied women both the "opportunities" and the "exercise" of freedom. Theorists such as Hobbes and Locke, commonly seen as negative libertarians, barred women from public life on the basis of their "natural" inferiority, which meant that they were incapable of rational choice. Women's diminished humanity disqualified them from taking advantage of the "opportunities" of liberal society and required that they be ruled by men. Indeed, women's restraint in the private sphere was one of the things that made negative liberty in the public sphere possible for men. That is, freedom could be defined as abstract choice for men only because women were bound to the aspects of life that are not necessarily chosen.[84] Even Mill, in spite of his remarks against women's subjection, limited women's freedom more than men's by failing to challenge the structural barriers to women's choice. He sometimes extended the notion of what counted as a barrier to include social customs and norms but at other times treated such customs and norms as natural and self-evident. Like Wollstonecraft, Mill suggested that women learn to be irrational by being denied education and trained to engage in trivial pursuits; yet he also seemed to believe that the social role of motherhood and wifehood was naturally ordained.[85] Positive libertarians such as Rousseau, Kant, and Hegel denied women's rationality, requiring them to adopt very particularized and structured roles within the family as a means of guaranteeing the stability of the state. All people could be free only by following their true will, but women were too emotional to know what their true will was. Furthermore, their irrationality confused men and impeded *their* ability to know their true will. So women could "exercise" their greatest freedom only by being restrained in the private realm and allowing men to act for them in the public realm.[86] Yet in both positive- and negative-liberty theories, despite these exclusions, freedom is seen as natural and universal, thus suggesting the virtual erasure of women from the concept of freedom.

In this light, women's experiences provide a powerful basis for highlighting the sexism frequently found in liberty theory, precisely because these experiences often lie at the crossroads of the Enlightenment ideology of agency and choice and modern practices that systematically restrict women. That is why I conduct my analysis of freedom not simply through standard works in political philosophy (which I discuss in chapter 2), but through specific material experiences of women. Such an approach offers a concrete understanding of patriarchal contexts and the paradoxical relation between empowerment and restraint. Accordingly, in chapters 4, 5, and 6 I examine the experiences of domestic violence, welfare, and Islamic

veiling to apply the theory of social construction to the question of freedom. These three experiences are certainly not the only ones which can
be seen to restrict women's freedom, limit their opportunities and choices,
and compromise their self-definitions and autonomy. But by virtue of their
familiarity in everyday discourse, I hope to raise questions not normally
considered in discussions of the freedom or unfreedom of women. For
instance, while a narrow reading of negative liberty such as Parent or
Flathman offers would say that Susan, the battered woman discussed at
the beginning of this chapter, is free to leave if she is not actually being
restrained at the time her decision is made, positive libertarians would
say she is unfree, because she does not understand what is in her best
interest—and both of these responses dominate the common public view
of domestic violence, which alternates between scorn and pity. This
merely perpetuates the internal/external divide, however; the possibility
that battered women actually express agency and choice every day, but
do so within severely restrained contexts that in turn affect their understanding of their options as well as their preferences, is not generally recognized. By expanding the notion of a barrier, we may be prompted to
look more carefully at the social context in which battering occurs: the
(un)responsiveness of state agencies such as police and courts, resources
(un)available to women who wish to leave abusive partners, the impact
of psychological abuse on desire, and beliefs about the naturalness or
normality of male violence.

Similarly, it is commonly asserted that the external conditions of welfare have produced a mind-set of dependency such that women who could
otherwise be productive members of society are instead drains on taxpaying citizens. This situation, it is argued, is bad not just for taxpayers but
for welfare recipients as well, for in order to be autonomous, one must
be economically self-sufficient. What these critics fail to acknowledge is
that welfare makes it possible for women to bring pregnancies to term
and to raise children without dependency on individual men. At the same
time, liberal democrats and many feminists have sought to defend the
welfare state from Republican attacks by attempting to present poor
women as downtrodden victims deserving of middle-class sympathy. Not
only does this perpetuate the disempowerment of women on welfare and
the view of welfare as charitable dispensation rather than a right but it
also fails to recognize the fact that welfare forces women to depend on a
paternalistic state. Both sides of the argument get a piece of the puzzle
right but miss the larger picture, which turns on the ways in which the
state both forms a backdrop for individual choice and action and yet
constructs individuals to make particular choices through an elaborate
system of punishment and reward. Such ambiguity is also seen in the practice of Islamic veiling. Although many Westerners view veiling as positive

proof of women's oppression under Islam, in fact many women choose to wear the veil as an expression of cultural identity and resistance to Western imperialism. Moreover, women use the veil to negotiate and resist patriarchal customs and norms, such as bars to women's paid employment. Yet veiling also exists within the parameters of patriarchy, such that women's choosing it simultaneously expresses their free agency and reinscribes the terms of their oppression.

Considering these problems in light of the social construction argument articulated in chapter 3 makes a more complex reading of freedom possible. The different configurations of choice found in these various scenarios derive from, and in turn suggest, differing levels of power, control, and coercion stemming from a variety of contextual factors. If, returning to my original definition, freedom consists in the power of the self to make choices and act on them, but the self that makes those choices, including her desires and self-understanding, is socially constructed, then to analyze freedom theorists must examine specific concrete situations in which that construction takes place. Viewing freedom as a *political* question requires applying general theoretical conceptions not just to specific events—a sexual assault, losing a job to a less qualified male, being forbidden by religious edict to leave the house, blocked entry to an abortion clinic, coerced sex with your boss—but to the broader contexts that construct both the events and the individuals who participate in them. Women are obviously a diverse group, though perhaps also one group among many. Despite their differences, however, they are nevertheless oppressed throughout the world to varying degrees, ranging from the minimal to the horrific, but always systematically. By locating the problem of freedom in the lived experience of women, and by seeing these experiences as variably situated in contexts that may share certain elements of male power but also differ significantly from one another, the complexity of freedom becomes particularly apparent. It is true that when we pit women's real-life situations against abstract and often abstruse theoretical formulations, existing conceptions of freedom are revealed to be gender biased and inadequate for understanding women's lesser freedom, or even unfreedom. But I do not explore domestic violence, welfare, veiling, and other material experiences simply to establish that women are less free than men. Rather, the goal is to explore how the social and personal construction of gender through concrete experiences influences theoretical perceptions and representations of the world, and how these representations in turn create experience. The specific political issues and concrete conditions of women's lives, such as battering, welfare, veiling, heterosexism, sexual harassment, rape, or abortion, are less important in defining "the problem of freedom" than they are in providing touchstones for understanding what is *problematic about* freedom.

What this suggests is that a feminist conception of freedom requires a detailed political analysis of patriarchal power in the particular contexts in which "freedom" is in question.[87] Such an analysis would include the conditions in which women live, the way power is utilized and executed by individual men, social institutions, and state agencies, and the effects of these conditions and this power on both the options that are materially available to women and their subjective understandings of those options. Individual women's desires, the choices they make, and the reasons for those choices—both the reasons they understand themselves to have and the reasons they may not be able to see, precisely because desire has been constrained and produced in particular ways—are all important to a feminist understanding of freedom. Recognizing that all choices, and our very subjectivity as choice makers, exist in contexts requires that we be self-conscious and critically aware of the contexts we live in, draw on, and utilize in making our choices, but such awareness is in circular fashion conditioned by the social formations that have constructed us. Hence, in chapter 7 I attempt to explore how to escape, or at least subdue, this apparent circularity so that awareness may expand and positive reconstruction proceed. In the process, I show how the feminist analysis of patriarchal power and contexts I have provided in the foregoing chapters is not only deconstructive but productive as well, not just critique but a positive vision of alternative possibility.

## Why Not Autonomy?

Before turning to that analysis, one question remains, and ironically (given my earlier criticisms of the semantic orientation of many freedom theorists) it brings us back to questions of definition. My criticisms of contemporary freedom theory, combined with my concern with the internal aspects of freedom, suggest the importance of autonomy to my conception of freedom. Cass Sunstein suggests that freedom and autonomy are somewhat interchangeable.[88] In particular, the traditional conception of autonomy as self-rule overlaps a great deal with both negative and positive conceptions of liberty. It shares the extreme individualism of negative liberty, defining itself in terms of absolute freedom from any influence of others,[89] and at the same time the extreme sense of self-control that often characterizes positive liberty, the notion of a rational, reflective, self-ruling agent who is concerned not just to choose but to make the best choice, the right choice. As Emily Gill puts it, autonomy involves "the capacity to govern oneself . . . the freedom to pursue what one judges to be good but also the ability to define this good in one's own manner."[90] At the same time, several autonomy theorists explicitly identify positive liberty with autonomy; John Christman calls autonomy positive liberty's "identical twin," and Joseph Raz similarly allies autonomy with positive liberty.[91] Many other autonomy theorists, though not explicitly asserting such alliances, nevertheless develop similar accounts of autonomy that focus on "the inner self," and control over the self, which echo central positive-liberty themes. To the extent that I maintain that social constructivism is suggested by positive liberty and urge the importance of the internal to a conception of freedom, this might prompt the question of why this book is devoted to freedom rather than autonomy.

It is certainly true that there are many shared concerns and features of autonomy and the conception of freedom that I develop here. Autonomy is fundamentally about capabilities, specifically about the ability to assess one's options, reflect critically about them, and make choices that allow one to exert some control over one's life. Thus, both freedom as I conceptualize it and autonomy are concerned with the inner workings of desire and will; both allow for the possibility of differentially evaluating desires and declaring some desires to be more consistent with autonomy or freedom than others; and both, hence, are forced to confront the paradox of "second-guessing." Additionally, because of the focus on such internal elements, both autonomy and my approach to freedom turn on the conception of self: a theorist's conception of "who we are" will be central to her conception of what selves need for freedom or autonomy, what conditions define the parameters of possibility for its achievement. And some recent work on autonomy, particularly in the feminist vein, has argued for a "social self," whose capacity for self-understanding must be understood in the context of community, family, and other particular and personal relationships.[92]

But there are also important differences between the two concepts, and these lead me to retain freedom as my subject. Some theorists argue that one cannot be free unless one is autonomous; unless one knows what one's true desire is, one cannot pursue it. For instance, Wright Neely maintains that "to be free . . . means there is an absence of restraints (positive or negative, internal or external) standing between a person and the carrying out of that person's *autonomous* desires."[93] Others maintain the reverse, that freedom to do what one wants is a precondition of autonomy, of figuring out what it is that one wants to do. "Freedom is necessary for autonomy," says Robert Young; "that is what freedom is for," argues Jennifer Nedelsky, "the exercise of" autonomy.[94] Freedom is thus both broader and narrower than autonomy. According to some theorists, such as Flathman, freedom is narrower, because it refers only to actions and is therefore event-specific; claims of freedom cannot be made about generalized conditions, only about specific actions.[95] An "unfree person" is unfree because she is prevented from doing many things, but it is those specific blockages that define unfreedom. As MacCallum argued, "[F]reedom is thus always *of* something (an agent or agents), *from* something, *to* do, not do, become, or not become something."[96] By contrast, autonomy is a characteristic of persons and thus must be considered historically over the life span of an individual.[97] As Dworkin puts it, "freedom is a local concept, autonomy a global one."[98] At the same time, other theorists maintain that freedom is broader than autonomy, because freedom is seen to cover a wider array of possibilities, ranging from the absurd (freedom to eat chocolate versus vanilla ice cream) to the most serious (freedom from incarceration for criticizing the government). By contrast, autonomy is reserved for consideration of choices that really matter to the individual and her ability to exercise control over her life.[99] Additionally, because freedom is concerned with external blockages to action, it enters at many more access points and involves a much wider range of social relations and institutions than does autonomy, which, being concerned with the inner workings of the will, focuses primarily on the individual in whatever context she happens to find herself.

Indeed, the issue of internality demarcates the most important distinction between freedom and autonomy. Although the absence of coercion and severe restraint is necessary to acting autonomously, autonomy itself is generally conceived in terms that refer to the inner self, the psychological, rational, moral, and emotional capabilities of the individual. Friedman defines it as "acting and living according to one's own choices, values, and identity within the constraints of what one regards as morally permissible." Nedelsky says that autonomy means "we feel that we are following an inner direction rather than merely responding to the pushes and pulls of our environment." Dworkin defines autonomy as a "capacity . . . to reflect critically upon . . . preferences, desires, wishes," an idea Raz echoes when he calls autonomy "a kind of achievement . . . a capacity." Autonomy particularly involves "reflective judgment," "the critical evaluation of desires," "self-discovery, self-definition, and self-direction," "living life from the inside."[100]

Because of this focus on internal aspects, autonomy arguments frequently encode value judgments about desire into their arguments. Distinctions between true and false, higher and lower, and first- and second-order, authentic and inauthentic desires, as well as frequent references to the "true self," the "authentic self," or the "unified self," pepper autonomy writings, even feminist ones.[101] In this, they share a great deal with classic positive-liberty theory, the variants of it that Berlin most feared and which I agree are troubling, the strong "second-guessing" for which theorists like Rousseau are excoriated. So-called procedural accounts of autonomy such as Dworkin and Meyers put forth claim to obviate this dilemma. They maintain that autonomy says nothing about what choices we make but only requires that we are able to, and actually do, reflect critically on our choices. Hence, there can be no value judgments about the specific things I choose, only observational judgments about whether I have reached those choices after adequate reflection. But even these procedural criteria are extremely value laden, echoing the essence of Enlightenment rationality. Meyers, for instance, says that one must not merely be able to offer reasons; one must be guided in formulating those reasons by "firm goals or moral views" rather than "feelings, intuitions, and arguments of the moment." For autonomy "expresses the true self."[102] Dworkin's criteria are somewhat weaker, requiring only that we be able to have reasons for our actions with which we identify; but at the same time "the conditions of procedural independence involve distinguishing those ways of influencing people's reflective and critical faculties which subvert them from those which promote and improve them." The question this begs, of course, is who decides that; Dworkin implies that this is somewhat self-evident, but only because he identifies "hypnotic suggestions, manipulation, coercive persuasion, subliminal influence" and the like as the obvious candidates for "subversion."[103] Indeed, to the extent that most autonomy theorists acknowledge the impact of external influences at all, they are generally described in the same terms of purposeful and intentional agency that freedom theory relies on: manipulation, coercion, oppression, brainwashing. The more subtle influences of social construction, and the ways in which restraint is intrinsically intertwined with production, are not generally acknowledged.

These conceptions of the self, though they may adhere to a feminist conception of self-in-relationship, nevertheless pose problems for feminist theory. For instance, consider, in terms of a "true self," the woman discussed at the start of this chapter, who was trying to get an abortion. External barriers prevented Meg from acting on her preference; as a result, she decided to adjust her life plan to adapt to the reality of these constraints. Here there is certainly an effort to be autonomous, to exert her own presence and individuality on circumstances created for her; Meg has critically evaluated her remaining options and has committed herself to loving her child. Yet her self, her life, follows a different path than the one she intended; she wanted to abort the fetus and was prevented from doing so. But if she achieves success in loving her baby, then which "self" is the true one: the one who was thwarted in obtaining the abortion, or the one who now loves and delights in her baby and is glad that in the end she had it? It is difficult not to say that she is autonomous; yet we can readily make the claim that she was unfree, if we redefine subjectivity and barrier beyond the confines of existing freedom theory. Or consider Young's claim that deep conflict over which projects to pursue means that one is not autonomous, that autonomy requires a "unified self," in the context of sexual assault. Yet, as Susan Brison has argued, in the face of traumatic memory spurred by sexual assault, autonomy may in fact require us to fragment the self, to compartmentalize and avoid aspects of ourselves that would otherwise immobilize and incapacitate us from acting in the world, forging life projects, and moving ahead with life.[104]

As will be argued more fully in chapter 3, the idea of social construction challenges the possibility of an essential "inside," which seems so vital to autonomy theory, and demands that determinations of freedom must consider internality and externality together. Meyers notes that "Since one must exercise control over one's life to be autonomous, autonomy is something that a person accomplishes, not something that happens to persons."[105] But freedom is precisely a combination of self-creation and what happens to you, the internal as well as the external, the combination of and dynamic between the two. If freedom is concerned with the capacity to choose, then social construction requires us to think about the broader conditions in which choices are made. Even if we can say that someone is "manipulated" into making a particular choice, we need to consider the social conditions that made such manipulation possible and that made this choice appear to make sense.

I will return to some of these points in chapter 3, but it is sufficient for now to note that there are significant differences between my approach to freedom and most theories of autonomy, even feminist ones. This is not to deny that feminist arguments about autonomy make valuable contributions to a feminist approach to freedom and that I draw on them here. Most importantly, they have brought attention to the need to reconfigure autonomy rather than reject it. As with freedom, the critique of mainstream accounts of autonomy as masculinist could yield the conclusion—one which some feminists have drawn—that feminists should reject the concept of autonomy altogether. By recognizing that the problem with autonomy is not the concept itself, but rather the conception of it that follows from an individualist and naturalist construction of the self, feminists have been able to begin the kind of rethinking that I here suggest is also necessary to the concept of freedom. But while the areas of concern overlap, freedom prompts somewhat different questions than autonomy. Indeed, freedom is, rather appropriately, less conceptually constrained. I agree with those who argue that freedom is a precondition for autonomy, not the other way around: if there is such a thing as a "true" self, or "authentic" desire, then in order to determine what that might be, women must be freed from the multiple, intersecting, and overarching barriers that pervade patriarchal society. In this, I seek to push freedom further than autonomy seems able to go.

## Chapter Two

# THE SOCIAL CONSTRUCTION OF FREEDOM
# IN HISTORICAL PERSPECTIVE

IF MY CLAIM that social construction is fundamental to the concept of freedom is not self-evident in contemporary theories of positive liberty, the suggestion that it is an essential element for the canonical figures might seem even more dubious. Indeed, those most obviously identifiable as "freedom theorists"—the social contract theorists like Hobbes, Locke, and Rousseau, for whom freedom was a central concern—based their accounts of civil government and the social contract on elaborate theories of human nature, of which freedom and equality were the fundamental building blocks. Others, such as Kant and Hegel, may have given less attention to human "nature" per se but nevertheless posited certain "spontaneous" and essentially "true" characteristics of man; and even those, such as Mill and Marx, who came the closest to explicit recognition of social construction, ended up falling back on quasi-naturalized assumptions about what would follow from the elimination of false and perverting social structures: in Marx's case, the elimination of capitalist exploitation would liberate man to true individuality within community, whereas for Mill the elimination of ignorance and restrictive laws would produce citizens who could recognize Truth.

Yet I maintain that various forms of what we might call social construction in fact play a significant role in the major conceptions of freedom that emerged from the Enlightenment. Indeed, not only is social construction relevant to these theorists but it complicates the very separation of internal and external which the dominant understandings of freedom presuppose. In particular, the avoidance of the internal matters that I identified in contemporary theories of freedom, which were concerned with defining "choice" in terms of available options rather than in terms of subjective desire and "barriers" in terms of externality (even when such efforts required a vast expansion of the relevant terms), is not supported by the historical foundations of the concept of freedom. The four theorists I consider here—Locke, Mill, Rousseau, and Kant—all concern themselves with the inner workings of desire and will. Indeed, they are concerned with the social construction of desire and will; in a persistent tension between free choice and right choice, these theorists seek to construct men so that they will want to choose what the theorists think they should choose. Gender is a significant element of this social construction; for in all of these theories the subject of liberty is male. Examining the place of gender in their writings helps reveal not only the social constructedness of that subject (in contradiction to the naturalist language the theorists frequently use) but also the ways in which internal and external factors of freedom constitute and shape one another.

## LOCKE: AN EDUCATED FREEDOM

This analysis begins with Locke, one of the earliest of the modern figures to put freedom at the core of his theory. Though freedom for Locke is importantly defined in what are generally considered negative-liberty terms—that is, in terms of property rights, rights to self-preservation, rights of conscience and religious toleration, representative government, and safeguards against tyranny—reason is a key element as well. The logic of natural law means that liberty cannot be absolute, cannot be "license."[1] There are limits posed by "the bounds of the laws of nature," which prevent men from making certain choices: we should not take more than we can use and must leave enough for others; we are not permitted to kill ourselves or sell ourselves into slavery, nor kill others except in self-defense; we must respect others' property and their ability to accrue property through labor. But this does not mean that natural law "limits" us or provides barriers to our desires;[2] for God created people so that they would not normally want to do the things which natural law forbids. For instance, the proviso that people should not take more than they can use before it spoils is a moral rule that follows the natural law that we preserve mankind, but it is also a rational one: people do not in fact want more than they can use, for spoilage represents a waste of labor, and hence a waste of property, thus contradicting the whole point of acquisition in the first place. So even if men lack the "right reason" that allows them to see the laws of nature as the will of God, normal, everyday reason should motivate them, out of rational self-interest, to act in accordance with the laws anyway.

Reason thus demarcates the limits not only of what I am permitted to do but also of what I (should) want to do. Indeed, like Kant, Locke intimates in a number of his works that people who do not access their rationality are not following their true will. Thus Locke says in the *Essay Concerning Human Understanding* that "Without Liberty the Understanding would be to no purpose; And without Understanding, Liberty (if it could be) would signify nothing . . . he that is at liberty to ramble in perfect darkness, what is his liberty better than if he were driven up and down, as a bubble by the force of the wind? The being acted by a blind impulse from without, or from within, is little odds. The first therefore and great use of Liberty, is to hinder blind Precipitancy; the principal Exercise of Freedom is to stand still, open the eyes, look about, and take a view of the consequence of what we are going to do, as much as the weight of the matter requires."[3] Similarly, Locke rejects the principle of "vox populi vox dei" because the majority of people do not use their reason and may hence agree with all sorts of evil propositions. Although "reason is granted to all by nature, and I affirm that there exists a law of nature, knowable by reason," not everyone accesses this reason, because some men have a "defect in nature" or are "nurtured in vices."[4] Locke distinguishes reason, which he defines as "that faculty of the intellect by which it articulates discourse and deduces arguments," from right reason, which constitutes "some definite practical principles from which flow the sources of all virtues and whatever might prove necessary to the proper formation of character" (*Questions* 99). The possibility that some might not even have access to basic reason, let alone "right reason," is a primary justification for the formation of the social contract. The question of who is able to display the reason which Locke asserts is essential to freedom is an important matter in defining who are the political actors, and hence free.

Yet right reason does not manifest itself spontaneously. Locke maintains that it requires careful development through scholarship—particularly Latin, Greek, philosophy, and mathematics—and broad reading, for exposure to a wide variety of ideas.[5] This kind of learning meant that right reason was something that only the educated—which in Locke's day meant a relative minority of people, including most obviously the wealthy but also members of the emerging bourgeois middle class and the clergy— could achieve. C. B. Macpherson, in his famous thesis of "differential rationality," maintained that Locke attributed different natural abilities to people by virtue of their class and that poverty was a sign of natural irrationality.[6] Locke certainly associates wealth with reason: property was a sign of rationality, or more specifically of an individual's ability to access, develop, and use the reason that God gives to all (or to most). Though "God gave the World to Men in Common," he specifically "gave it to the use of the Industrious and Rational . . . not to the Fancy or Covetousness of the Quarrelsome and Contentious." Land in its uncultivated state was useless; thus "God, when he gave the World in common to all Mankind, commanded Man also to labour, and the penury of his Condition required it of him" (*Second Treatise*, 332–33). I must be industrious not just because God wants me to but because God has made me rational enough to see its necessity and desirability. If I am not industrious, I am failing to employ my reason; and the less evidence of industry I have, namely, property, the less rational I must be. Though it wasn't necessarily the case that all people in the upper classes were fully rational, they were more rational than "the laborer or artisan of a great city such as London," who in turn was less defective in rationality than the "artisan of a country town," who was in turn superior to the agrarian day laborer. On the bottom were the unemployed, beggars, and those on parish relief (*Second Treatise*, 339).

In contrast to Macpherson's thesis, however, I suggest that for Locke these differences are not natural but rather socially constructed by and through the exigencies of economic and class inequality. In *Of the Conduct of the Understanding*, Locke says that the difference in rationality between the rich and the poor is a practical matter, not one of nature. Nature may "give first rise" to reason, but "it is practice alone that brings the powers of the mind as well as those of the body to their perfection" (*Conduct* 14). The wide range of scholarship necessary to the development of right reason required time that the laboring classes did not have. If they were industrious, however, the poor could develop enough reason to see the wisdom in obeying the law and tacitly consenting. Hence, Locke's recommendations for reforming the parish relief system involved strict work requirements: beggars were to be punished by forced labor; those who requested parish relief were instead to be employed by members of the parish at "less than the usual wage"; and children were to be put in working schools—basically wool factories—which would also free mothers from child care responsibilities, so that they could work as well.[7] Though such measures originated under Elizabethan poor law to reduce the costs of supporting and managing the poor,[8] Locke was more concerned with creating new habits of industry. The true evil that needed to be rooted out, according to Locke, was not poverty per se, but irrationality, which leads to poverty.

Thus, it wasn't that the poor *couldn't* reason but rather that they *wouldn't*, due to their lack of practice and the corrupting influences of the mean material conditions of their lives. "Try in men of low and mean education," Locke challenges his readers, "who have never elevated their thoughts above the spade and the plough, nor looked beyond the drudgery of a day labourer. Take the thoughts of such an one, used for many years to one track, out of that narrow compass he has been all his life confined to, you will find him no more capable of reasoning than almost a perfect natural" (*Conduct* 21). Nature had little to do with this; rather, what people did within the contingencies of life into which God placed them determined their level of reason. Through labor, laborers would develop reason sufficiently to know that working hard is the right thing to do, that work is key to achieving as much contentment out of life as their lot will allow. They would become sufficiently rational to follow their leaders and obey the law, even if they were not rational enough to give express consent to the social contract.

Those express consenters, the leaders of civil society and presumed descendants of the parties to the original contract, by contrast, needed to have right reason developed in its full capacity, and that required a carefully executed education. Indeed, much as industry was aimed at developing the character of the poor, so the education required to attain right reason involved the building of character long before learning philosophy, mathematics, Latin, and Greek. The point of education is to habituate children to the correct behaviors, values, and attitudes: "The great thing to be minded in Education is, what *Habits* you settle."[9] The fact that reason is a natural capacity is what makes Locke's "white paper" theory of education possible; but as with all good paintings, the canvas must be primed. Locke asserts that "great Care is to be had of the forming of Children's *Minds*, and giving them that seasoning early, which shall influence their Lives always after" (*Thoughts* 138), and most of his recommendations aim to build a strong foundation for the acquisition of civic moral talents. In this, Locke is concerned with the internal aspects of freedom, particularly identity and desire. The goal of education is the mastery over inclination, and the disciplining of desire is thus key: "Children should be used to submit their Desires, and go without their Longings, even *from their very Cradles*. The first thing they should learn to know should be, that they were not to have any thing, because it pleased them, but because it was thought fit for them" (*Thoughts* 143). Parents must teach children to "stifl[e] their Desires" and "master their Inclinations" (*Thoughts* 210). Or more precisely, they must learn to want the right things. The cornerstone of education is thus to make children subservient to the parents' will. Though the goal of education is self-discipline or self-mastery, this can only be achieved *via* submission.

Locke's theory of education thus suggests a complicated notion of individuality and freedom that does not, indeed cannot, exist naturally but must be developed through social institutions and processes. Through education, a child should develop the best "Habits woven into the very Principles of his nature" (*Thoughts* 146). What is "within" us is put there by education and other outer forces, including parents and tutors. As Mehta points out, Locke is extremely concerned with charting the inner landscape of individuality: the minds, thoughts, feelings, and preferences, in short, the basic elements that make up the liberal individual. Because of the "malleability of the mind," it can easily turn to waste and evil, but it can also be turned toward productivity and virtue by the proper education. Accordingly, education must begin at an extremely young age, and children should be formed in their individuality even as they learn language and before they have a well-established sense of themselves. Focusing on the very young has the power of "making whatever is habituated *appear* natural."[10] This education must therefore be undertaken in the family.[11] Because the family is the locus for love and affection, parents can be expected to have greater concern for their children's welfare than hired teachers; hence, even tutors within the family must be supervised by parents.

The fact that education is to take place in the family would seem an open invitation to educate girls alongside boys. Locke indicates in some of his correspondence that girls can and should be educated, and girls are explicitly included in some of his educational prescriptions, such as those concerning diet, loose clothing, cold, wet feet, and physical punishment for obstinacy. But Locke admits that the overt point of his book is to turn boys into gentlemen and notes that many of his recommendations "will not so perfectly suit the Education of *Daughters*" (*Thoughts* 117). So girls, like laborers and the poor, are largely excluded. Part of this is likely due to social custom (his biggest concern for girls seems to be preventing sunburn), but part is also due to his ambiguity over whether females have the ability to access and utilize the rational faculty. Locke's views on women's rationality have long been debated. Whereas some feminists, such as Lorenne Clark, have argued that Locke denied women natural rationality altogether, other scholars, such as Rogers Smith, point out that Locke never actually says that in the *Two Treatises*.[12] It is safe to say that Locke believes that women are *less* rational than men, but as with laborers, whether this is by nature or prescription is less clear. Smith is correct that the *Two Treatises* suggests a rough equality between the sexes, and indeed Locke implies women's rationality through his reiteration of the fourth commandment (why would God grant both parents equal respect if they were not equally rational?), as well as his provision to women of a right to separate from their husbands once their children have grown up (indicating that women are capable of living on their own). But Locke's other works are less generous to women. In *The Reasonableness of Christianity*, for instance, Locke explicitly says that laborers and "those of the other sex" can only understand "simple propositions," suggesting a natural limitation on reason.[13] But as noted earlier, in *Conduct* he attributes class differences to the pragmatic realities of laboring life, raising the possibility that females, who must run a home and manage servants in addition to bearing and raising children, are similarly disadvantaged. The fact that most of Locke's educational recommendations are explicitly for boys and are acknowledged to be inappropriate for girls suggests that he believes girls should not be *allowed* to develop reason to the same degree as boys, rather than that they are naturally irrational.

Women's inferior powers of reason would logically be linked to their inability to hold property, which is, in circular fashion, key evidence of rationality.[14] And it would be linked to their civil status as imperfect members of the social contract, whose consent must be tacitly inferred rather than expressly taken.[15] Indeed, the links between women and workers on these two issues of consent and property, so central to reason and freedom for Locke, suggest a two-tiered conception of freedom that centers around the social construction of reason and freedom through the social institution of civil law. That is, at least among the propertied "gentlemen" who are the intended targets of Locke's *Thoughts*, the private sphere produces subjects of positive liberty through education; it produces people who can use "right reason" and make correct choices. The point of such education—and of the positive liberty it produces—is to create individuals ("perfect members") who can make good laws. These laws, in turn, produce and safeguard negative liberty for everyone else by protecting them from arbitrary and absolute power. (And indeed, insofar as laborers and other "imperfect" civic members do not receive formal education, they are thereby produced as subjects of negative liberty.) Hence, although Locke's primary governmental concern is to guard against tyranny, whereas his primary concern in the (at least bourgeois) family is the education of sons, these two concerns are complementary. The public sphere produces a negative liberty that can be enjoyed in the private sphere, in the form of rights of property and person, just as the private sphere produces a positive liberty that is expressed in the public sphere, through the creation of good laws passed by right-reasoning, well-educated gentlemen. Law is, therefore, the nexus of positive and negative liberty for Locke: the development of rationality and goodness in the private sphere creates men who will make the right choices for the public sphere by passing good laws that define the parameters of right. Thus Locke says,

> *Law,* in its true Notion, is not so much the Limitation as *the direction of a free and intelligent Agent* to his proper Interest, and prescribes no farther than is for the general Good of those under that Law. . . . that ill deserves the Name of Confinement which hedges us in only from Bogs and Precipices. So that, however it may be mistaken, *the end of Law* is not to abolish or restrain but *to preserve and enlarge Freedom. . . . where there is no law there is no Freedom.* (*Second Treatise* 347–48)

On my reading of Locke's two-tiered conception of freedom, perfect members of civil society—educated, propertied white males who have developed right reason—would determine the laws to which the rest of us tacitly consent, thereby establishing our subjection to law as freely chosen, and also ensuring that our lives are circumscribed only by laws that are rational and in keeping with the laws of nature. Consent can be inferred only because express consenters—again, for the most part, propertied white males—use right reason, so all civil laws they make and policies they choose will cohere with the law of nature and "the light of reason," which less rational, tacitly consenting laborers and women would follow if they could. By taking on the duty of creating virtuous laws based on right reason, the educated and propertied minority thereby attains positive liberty, whereas everyone else would reap the benefits of that reason and its application in law by living under a government that provides negative liberty property rights and allows them to pursue their interests. As I mentioned earlier, in the *Essay*, Locke argues that liberty and "understanding" are interdependent. When this argument is combined with his overt admission of the limited reasoning abilities of laborers and his more ambiguous comments about women's reason, Locke implies that women and the poor can never enjoy freedom at all, for they seem to lack the "understanding" that is essential to liberty. But if Locke deploys a two-tiered understanding of liberty as I am suggesting, then perhaps he means that liberty and understanding do not necessarily have to coexist *in every individual*. That is, the two parts—"understanding," which is linked to reason, the essence of freedom in the positive sense; and "liberty," defined now in negative-liberty terms as the absence of external impediments to choice—must certainly fit together, as Locke argues in the *Essay*. But perhaps the interdependence of understanding and liberty can be seen in a communal rather than individual sense: if a sufficient number of well-educated property owners have adequate understanding, and if they are empowered to make the laws, then the rest of us can be free. Just as Locke argues that "understanding" protects us from "blind Precipitancy," so does he maintain that law protects us from "Bogs and Precipices." On this reading, then, even if a large percentage of individuals do not themselves have understanding or reason, following the law will allow them to live as if they had it.

This resolution may work better for landless workers than it does for women, however. Without education, neither women nor workers can ever be subjects of positive liberty and right reason. But whereas laboring women, like laboring men, simply do not have the resources for such education, bourgeois women have them under their very roofs and are explicitly denied access to them. Furthermore, as beings confined to the private realm, bourgeois women, unlike poor women who work for wages, are never subjects of the negative freedom of property rights either, for the property that supports them belongs to their husbands. Indeed, bourgeois women are arguably even excluded from property in the person—Locke's well-known idea that labor is property which I can add to things in nature to create "goods and Estates" (*Second Treatise*, 328–29)—since everything that women work on in household production is already owned by their husbands or other male relatives. The only things they could be said to produce through nature, namely, children, are explicitly designated by Locke as the property of neither parent but of God.

Whether it is a result of nature or practice, this differential rationality for the poor and women impacts on Locke's vision of freedom, for the realm of the internal demarcated by his attention to right reason and intellectual development is what sets the foundation for the external realm of political liberty. The two vicious circles of gender and class are at least overlapping, if not concentric, for both are excluded from political power and freedom because of a lack of rationality, a lack which is constructed by the failure to provide them with the same education Locke prescribes for propertied white men. If Locke bifurcates freedom into public and private components, then the truly "free" individual must partake of both parts, which neither upper-class women nor laborers—male as well as female—could ever do. Whereas Locke may have been ambiguous on whether differential rationality in women and the poor was natural or socially constructed, however, it is clear that the different relationship of women to public and private that Locke posits is clearly not a result of nature, but rather of social practice, economic inequality, class structure, and gender hierarchy.

## ROUSSEAU: A "WELL-REGULATED" FREEDOM

This pattern—different kinds of freedom in different spheres marked by gender and class—is reiterated by other theorists for whom freedom is a central concept, particularly Rousseau. Of all the modern canonical figures, he is the one most explicitly aligned with positive liberty by contemporary theorists. Indeed, his central notions of the general will and "forcer d'être libre" are precisely the ideals which Berlin seeks to undermine in his attack on positive conceptions of liberty.[16] Additionally, Rousseau's notions of moral freedom and the explicit attention he pays to education suggest that internality is far more important to his understanding of freedom than is externality. And, perhaps not coincidentally, Rousseau is among the most explicitly sexist of political theorists, the theorist that feminists most love to hate, because of his views that women's nature disqualifies them from public life. Yet the social construction elements of his theory present understandings of freedom and subjectivity that feminists should find helpful; they facilitate a reading of Rousseau that challenges the notion that he necessarily or uniformly takes the absolute ends of political virtue as the measure of freedom but rather allows for the recognition of the importance of personal choice, and an understanding of the self that is somewhat fluid and contextual.

Rousseau posits a "natural freedom" in the state of nature that is based primarily on force and demonstrates clear affinity for negative-liberty ideals: the freedom to do whatever one physically can, limited by the physical laws of nature such as gravity and, more significantly, the superior strength of other individuals. It is the inequality among men that produces conflict and thereby stimulates the development of passion and reason. Because the early, primitive state of nature is sparsely populated, it is easy to get what one wants from nature, and the wants themselves are few ("food, a female, and sleep").[17] When population increases and people are forced to interact, natural inequality of strength becomes apparent, competition for resources increases, and desires or passions strengthen accordingly. It is this strengthening of the passions that stimulates the development of reason; where the strong systematically satisfy their passions at the expense of the weak, the reasoning powers of the weak must develop to compensate, or they will die off. Through the development of reason, cooperation emerges because it is seen as a strategic advantage in, for example, capturing a large animal such as a deer (*Origin* 78). Such cooperation, which is not "natural," even though men are still in the state of nature, but rather learned through experience and reason, gives rise to regularized interaction in organized societies. But this cooperation also brings about the means to further entrench inequality and domination, for as our ability to satisfy our desires increases, the desires themselves proportionately multiply, and we become more "enslaved" to our passions as the development of property and economic inequality erodes the possibilities of natural negative freedom: "Each became in some degree a slave even in becoming the master of others; if rich, they stood in need of the services of others; if poor, of their assistance" (*Origin* 86). This forced dependence prompts people to seek a new kind of freedom, namely, civil or political freedom through man-made laws that supposedly apply equally to all but in fact simply institutionalize social and economic inequality; thus, "all ran headlong to their chains, thinking they secured their freedom" (*Origin* 89).

Rousseau's solution to this institutionalized inequality and unfreedom is to reformulate civil society in terms of a new social contract that puts equality and moral freedom at its heart. This equality is expressed in three ways: the contract must be agreed to unanimously, must provide for a participatory legislative politics, and must ensure relative material equality among citizens. These different forms of equality are important because of the problem of power: rather than alienating part of your liberty to a person—a monarch or parliamentary representative—you alienate all of your freedom to every other member of society, and every other member does likewise to you. The alienation is total, reciprocal, and impersonal. A society marked by such equality can be said to have a will which by definition constitutes the will of its members: a "general will." Yet because these members are not just parts of the organic whole but also are individuals with particular needs, desires, and preferences, people's wills can be divided. Because of the "dual character" of citizens of the polity—they are at once the legislators who create the law and the subjects who must obey it—Rousseau argues that both the particular and general wills are "my" will. However, because Rousseau insists that moral freedom—obedience to a self-prescribed law—is needed to make man "master of himself," then citizens cannot achieve freedom without the assembly. That is, people cannot be morally free if the participatory form of government is jeopardized, for then the laws I must obey are not those I have made for myself as part of the legislative assembly. Because of this, the general will is more important to me—a "higher" will—than my particular will. Hence, if I advocate a law that runs contrary to the interests of the community, I jeopardize my own freedom by misconstruing my true will. Disobedience does far more harm in jeopardizing the stability and legitimacy of the democratic polity—the only political form and process within which freedom is possible—than I do good in pursuing my particular will. Since both wills are mine, the evaluation between wills does not inhibit my liberty; indeed, since the will that prevails under Rousseau's formulation is the will that is more important to me, my own higher will, my freedom is enhanced.[18]

Such reasoning is more consonant with Berlin's version of positive liberty than Taylor's, because it relies on the state and the majority—sources outside the self—to decide what my true will is, but clearly Rousseau believes that this struggle must go on within every individual citizen himself. As he demonstrated in the *Origin of Inequality*, nature is not a static essence but a dynamic process. Thus Rousseau posits human nature as containing numerous possibilities, and different potential qualities will be developed in different social contexts. In order to be sure that citizens can see the general will, therefore, it is vital to create the environment that favors the "good" capacities. That is why we have to work so hard to get the right social order, so that the right natural capacities are developed and the harmful ones repressed. Thus, in the *Social Contract* Rousseau argues both that the general will is equivalent to the majority will and that it is "unalterable, true, and pure." Not only must we choose the right answer and select the best laws; we must also *choose* the right answer and *select* the best laws. Virtue or "political right" must coexist with voluntarism and majority rule; each is useless without the other.[19]

This is why education is so vital to Rousseau's construction of the social contract. In the *Emile*, he maintains that the purpose of education is to create a virtuous man, and thereby a potential citizen. As he says in *Political Economy*, "there can be no patriotism without liberty, no liberty without virtue, no virtue without citizens; create citizens, and you have everything you need." But at the same time, "To form citizens is not the work of a day; and in order to have men it is necessary to educate them when they are children."[20] The *Emile*, which was written at the same time as

*The Social Contract*, is Rousseau's effort to show how this should be done. By leading them to virtue, education gives men the necessary foundation on which to build virtuous political institutions and pass virtuous laws that are in conformity with the general will. Accordingly, as for Locke, education seems to be less concerned with academic subjects than with character. The good citizen must not be limited by self-interest, which can only yield the "will of all," not the "general will." Hence, a central task of education is to "transport the *I* into the common unity, with the result that each individual believes himself no longer one but a part of the unity and no longer feels except within the whole."[21]

Rousseau argues that man has no innate knowledge of the good, but he does have an innate tendency to love it when reason reveals it to him. Yet at the same time, that very same reason that reveals the good also counters the tendency to love it, because reason fuels self-interest and alienates us from compassion, hence from truth. Virtue thus cannot be established by reason alone; faith and love are also important. Thus, the tutor must develop all of Emile's faculties, his sentiments, particularly compassion, as well as reason. The tutor must make Emile "fear nothing" and give him the "finest habits," so that he is not subject to any negative qualities or constraints; or rather, the constraints he experiences should be those of virtue, which of course are not constraints on his true will but actually enhance his freedom. And indeed, the whole point of education is to produce a "well-regulated freedom" (*Emile*, 92). Virtue is key to the moral freedom of the general will and therefore of the individual, for without virtuous individuals who subsume themselves in the general will moral freedom cannot exist.

Yet this virtue is under constant threat, even in Rousseau's social contract, because of the persistent tendency of private interest to overcome the general will. Thus, in the assembly, Rousseau does not allow citizen-legislators to discuss and debate proposals, but only to announce publicly what their view of the general will is and cast a vote, because Rousseau fears that informal groupings will arise around particular interests and corrupt the citizen's virtue. This might seem to suggest that, once learned, virtue can be protected only by the individual's vigilance over himself. But in fact, virtue cannot be sustained in solitude, and so an important part of Emile's education consists of pairing him off with a woman who can preserve, protect, and inspire his continued virtue. Of course, a more accurate, though subtextual, message might be that Emile must learn about women to protect himself against the dangers that they pose to his moral freedom. But either way, it can be argued that the "subject" of this education, and hence of liberty, is a (heterosexual) male, though its "object" may be, importantly, female.

It is significant that women are a key element of the citizen's education, for Rousseau's comments on women are also important to recognizing the social constructive elements of Rousseau's theory. It is commonly recognized that Rousseau is extremely critical of women throughout his work, though often in a backhandedly complimentary way.[22] And despite the absence of references to women in *The Social Contract*, Rousseau places women and gender at the heart of his theory of politics by placing them at the heart of his theory of education. Once again, virtue is key. But whereas the virtuous man is independent, autonomous, and self-controlling, the virtuous woman is dependent, servile, self-inhibiting. While nature gives women "modesty and shame," it does so to counterbalance the animal sexuality it also gives them. Context is vital to this balance: just as men's greed will dominate in contexts of despotic or representative government, but their *pitié* and identification with the general will can bloom in democratic assembly, so will women's natural animal sexuality be overdeveloped in Paris (accompanied by the loss of maternal feeling), and their equally natural shame, modesty, and maternal affection surface in the country. Many feminist commentators have noted the apparently self-contradictory picture Rousseau has painted of women's nature; women are modest yet brazen, weak yet powerful, helpless yet dangerous, pure yet sexual, superhuman yet subhuman. But it is precisely the contradictory remarks that Rousseau makes about women's nature in this book that make visible the contextual quality of human nature: nature contains many conflicting potentialities, and different ones will be developed in different contexts. Hence, the right contexts must be carefully created and maintained—by the Great Legislator in the public sphere, by parents and tutors in the private—to make sure that the "bad" elements of men's and women's natures do not surface.

Accordingly, Sophie must be educated in the womanly virtues to ensure that her sexual nature is regulated, and this is to preserve her own freedom as much as her future husband's. Though in book 5 of the *Emile*, it often appears to many readers as if Sophie is spontaneously virtuous, particularly in comparison to the Parisian women excoriated in book 1, in fact she is virtuous because her parents have done such a good job of bringing her up. As Sophie says, "O my mother, why have you made virtue too lovable for me? If I can love nothing but virtue, the fault is less mine than yours."[23] As Sophie approaches marriageable age, however, Emile's tutor conveniently steps in periodically to refine and hone her earlier training so that she will ably perform her civic and wifely duties of guiding Emile toward virtue and the general will. Both Emile's freedom and Sophie's are realized through the general will, but they do not achieve this freedom in the same way. Specifically, while Emile must pass laws in the assembly that both men and women must obey in order to be morally free, Sophie's task is to keep her husband on the path of virtue so that he will choose the good laws. The home, with women at its heart, is the repository of virtue to which men retreat from the pressures of self-interest, corruption, and vice. This is not to say that women tell men what to do, or even that men and women discuss politics at all. Indeed, to bring politics overtly into the home would corrupt it. Rather, coming home from the assembly confused and torn between the particular and general wills, a man sees his wife at the hearth with several children sitting at her feet[24] and is reminded of the essence of virtue. Her soft words and gentle touch, her modesty and manners, reveal to him the truth which he must put into law. Sophie and Emile form a complementary "partnership" through which, acting together, both can achieve freedom and without which, acting alone, each is doomed to unfreedom.

Of course, skeptics might say, some partnership! For Sophie can sustain this virtuous example, and thus moral freedom, only if she subverts herself to her husband. If moral freedom for Emile entails obedience to a self-prescribed law, moral freedom for Sophie entails obedience to Emile. Thus, virtuous women "must first be exercised in constraint, so that it never costs them anything to tame all their caprices in order to submit them to the wills of others" (*Emile* 369). Women must learn such behaviors; they do not come naturally. On one level, this is no more paradoxical than male citizens having to choose the laws they must obey; Sophie has chosen her "master," whom she must obey. The demands of moral freedom are not easy, Rousseau suggests, and require not only careful crafting of both the social structures and the individuals who make them up but constant vigilance as well. Jean-Jacques's project is to mold Emile by bringing out certain features and characteristics that lie deep within him and stifling others. By manipulating Emile into learning very specific lessons, he turns Emile into his own particular ideal of manly virtue. Hence, Emile would seem to be as carefully constructed and controlled as Sophie.

But of course the outcome is quite different, for gender plays a decidedly unbalanced role in this construction of the citizen. The male citizen's dependence on law is "impersonal" and thus does not contradict freedom, but Rousseau explicitly rejects "personal" dependence—dependence on another *person* (for example, a husband)—as inherently contradictory to freedom. Yet that is precisely the nature of Sophie's dependence on Emile. This is because of the remarkable power Rousseau attributes to women in the home and specifically in the bedroom. Indeed, it is in the realm of sexuality where women's freedom finds its surest footing and poses the greatest challenge. Rousseau openly acknowledges that women are sexual and desire (heterosexual) sex and that they are able and likely to act on their desires by seducing men. Though Paris salons supposedly run contrary to women's true interests, because they encourage women in vice,

Rousseau suggests that this is so only indirectly; his focus is on the danger to children of being farmed out to wet nurses, and to men of becoming virtual sex slaves to women who would "drag men to their deaths" (*Emile* 359). It is not so much a concern with women's characters as with men's—their helplessness in the face of female sexuality, their pathetically weak wills, which are unable to resist sex—that justifies Rousseau's conclusion that in order to make men free and autonomous, women must be restrained. For "natural" freedom—the only kind of freedom such animal passions can serve—is inevitably enslaving, "the impulse of mere appetite" (*Social Contract* 178). Moral freedom, obedience to self-prescribed law, must entail chastity for single women, monogamous marriage, and an elaborate structure of behavior that grants moral and civil powers to men that will counterbalance the natural powers of women. Thus, to say that women are dependent on men implies a more passive role for women than Rousseau actually constructs. If women do not play the role of moral guardian and pristine temptress just right, deftly manipulating men and pushing them where they should go without letting them know they are being pushed, Rousseau's carefully laid structure falls apart. Hence, Rousseau derides women who aspire to the manly virtues of independence, autonomy, and action; by pursuing these, women lose the power they could have over men (*Emile* 363).

Thus, though women are not merely "passive" subjects vis-à-vis the state, waiting for men to be the actors, in a sense women are in a worse position, because their active role and power lie, paradoxically, in their being subservient; their only hope for freedom is to subject themselves to their husbands, to deny their natural powers and give up their voice. Women can partake in only one part of the moral-freedom equation: they can and must obey the laws, but they cannot make the laws they are to obey. The subject of moral liberty is male. Rousseau has no difficulty allowing women to be the subjects of natural freedom; like men, women can and do make choices all the time, express and pursue their desires. As in Locke's theory, women may be able to exercise negative freedom in the private sphere, while men exercise positive liberty in the public. But that is exactly the problem in Rousseau's view: it is women's sexual desire—insatiable, dangerous—that is at once the hallmark of their own natural freedom and the destroyer of men's. There is an unavoidable— and to Rousseau's mind, unacceptable—zero-sum outcome. Even worse than zero-sum, women's natural freedom destroys men's moral freedom, for men ensnared in the quagmire of necessity and physicality will be unable to discern the general will, let alone put it into practice. Instead of going to the assembly, they will go to the salons and theatres, thinking that they are acting freely but instead merely ensuring their servitude. The maleness of the subject of liberty for Rousseau is thus inescapable; for even if women destroy men's natural and moral freedom through the exercise of their own natural freedom, they thereby destroy their own hopes of genuine liberty. Only men's freedom "counts," in a sense, because only it can yield moral freedom; only if men are empowered to choose the good can they, and thereby women, be truly free. But this is so only because women are constructed—indeed, must construct themselves—so carefully to create that possibility.

## KANT: AN INTELLIGIBLE FREEDOM

Like Rousseau, Kant also takes up the theme of women having to be taught to express qualities that are supposedly natural. Indeed, it is in his views of women that Kant's social constructivism is revealed. Because of Kant's focus on the noumenal realm and things-in-themselves, he might not seem a logical candidate for such a claim, but the similarities between Kant's and Rousseau's conceptions of freedom are worth noting. In fact, Kant was considerably influenced by Rousseau, and particularly by his idea of obedience to self-prescribed law.[25] Additionally, Kant's theory makes important contributions to contemporary understandings of freedom; his notion of the categorical imperative has, in particular, influenced later conceptions of positive liberty, while his advocacy of liberal forms of government and individual rights has helped to shape the negative-liberty tradition.[26] Indeed, it is to Kant that we can attribute the terminological invention of positive and negative liberty.[27]

Admittedly, as Allen Wood suggests, Kant's treatment of liberty is highly "metaphysical,"[28] largely because of his belief that humans occupy two worlds, the phenomenal and the noumenal; in other words, the "sensible" world, the world of sense objects, in which we physically live and the world of "things-in-themselves," things as they are in their essences, which cannot be observed or experienced but only known a priori. The noumenal is the "intelligible" realm, the realm of ideas, and exists only in and through reason. In the phenomenal realm, our knowledge is grossly incomplete, we can "know objects only as they affect us; what they may be in themselves remains unknown" (*Groundwork* 118), but in the noumenal realm, ideas come from me alone and not in response to objects in the sensible world. True freedom is possible only in and through the noumenal realm, through a priori knowledge and the use of reason to understand things-in-themselves. In the phenomenal realm, the sense objects of the natural world cause us to think, act, feel, and desire in certain ways, by virtue of the natural laws of the physical world: we are determined. If we are caught in causal chains that determine us and our behavior, then to break free we must enter the realm where we are not determined by previous events. The reasoning mind is the way in which this freedom is achieved. If we are to be free, the will, rather than desire, must determine our actions.

Maxims are the way in which the will can exercise its rule, through laws that I lay down for myself. They provide guideposts, reminders, and boundaries for my sensible tendencies to act on my desires. Not only must I follow these maxims, but as for Rousseau, I must make the rules that I follow; if I simply followed the rules that others set down for me, I would be acting heteronomously. The idea of an imperative carries the idea of a maxim further, to that of a universal law. While a maxim may apply to me alone, an imperative goes beyond my individual circumstances and experience. If I satisfy a heteronomous desire, I treat myself as a means to an end, rather than an end in itself. An imperative extends this treatment to other people as well. Because of this "universalizing" character, imperatives carry more moral force than maxims. That is, though true freedom exists in the noumenal realm, our bodies are located in the phenomenal realm, with physical needs that determine us. Freedom thus involves the struggle to get beyond that and attain the "holy will," by which we are guided only by reason to do only that which is good and true. The purpose of imperatives is to help keep us as close as possible to this will, and hence as free as possible (*Groundwork* 81). But Kant distinguishes further between "categorical imperatives," in which an "action is represented as good in itself, and therefore as necessary, in virtue of its principle, for a will which of itself accords with reason," and "hypothetical imperatives," which are conditional, actions that "would be good solely as a means to something else" (*Groundwork* 82). The categorical imperative—"Act as if the maxim of your action were to become through your will a universal law of nature" (*Groundwork* 89)—is one of Kant's most famous legacies. It is, for Kant, the surest guide to moral action and the free will; if I measure what I will against the categorical imperative, I can assess whether what I will is good in itself, and hence whether it is really what I will. Thus, like Rousseau, Kant locates freedom in law and morality. Freedom is the expression of will, the "power to act *in accordance with [the] idea* of laws" (*Groundwork* 80).

Reason is necessary to this process, for only a rational agent can perceive what the law should be and establish it. Freedom thus consists in rational behavior, which is the true expression of the will. What makes behavior rational, however, is its conformity to moral law.[29] We can be free only by doing our duty, but I must will myself to do it; I cannot be forced to do it by another and still be free. Whereas Rousseau relies on the state or collective to determine my true will, thus displaying some affinity with Berlin's construction of positive liberty, Kant's conception is closer to Taylor's individualistic conception, where the individual knows he has a divided will and continually struggles to achieve the higher will and subdue the more basic, lower order desire. Only if I am successful in this can I be free.

Kant's conception of freedom would seem to be fairly securely locked into a kind of naturalistic worldview: the phenomenal realm is marked by natural desires, the noumenal realm by reason, which is not only "spontaneous" but also deals with timeless truths that transcend cultural particularity. At the same time, however, such spontaneity is not so spontaneous in a fair number of people: rationality is not utilized by "an apprentice in the services of a merchant or artisan; a domestic servant (as distinct from a civil servant); a minor; all women, and in general, anyone whose preservation in existence (his being fed and protected) depends not on his management of his own business but on arrangements made by another (except the state). All these people lack civil personality." These are what Kant calls "passive citizens"; they must obey the laws, but they do not make them, because such people are not economically independent, which is an important criterion "for active participation in political affairs."[30] For the apprentice and the child, of course, and possibly the servant, the possibility of future economic independence holds out the possibility of active citizenship, but only if their irrationality is situational rather than essential. Indeed, the notion of passive citizens raises the question of whether their irrationality is natural or a product of situation. And this distinction, in turn, leads to the further question of whether rationality and irrationality might be socially constructed.

The answer to some degree depends on who you are: if you are a woman, perhaps your irrationality is natural and irremediable, but if you are a young boy, your irrationality can be changed through education. Education is vital to the categorical imperative, and hence to freedom, for it helps "develop [man's] tendency toward the good. . . . Man can only become man by education," an echo of Rousseau.[31] But Kant also echoes Locke: since "the first endeavor in moral education is the formation of character," this process is best begun in childhood. One can learn "facts" later in life, but character, or the abilityy to "act in accordance with maxims," must be established at a young age (*Education* 84); "moral training" is of the utmost importance, for it "aims at freedom" (*Education* 66). Indeed, there are quite a few similarities between Kant's prescriptions and Locke's, such as cold baths, not dressing too warmly, sleeping on a "cool and hard bed," and avoiding "too warm foods and drink" (*Education* 37–38). As surprising as it may seem for a philosopher so closely associated with the mind/body dualism, Kant links the body with the mind here, not only making numerous recommendations for care of the body, such as unrestrictive clothing, but also insisting that "physical education of the mind" must complement "moral training" (*Education* 66). Reason, of course, is the ultimate tool for a child's pursuit of morality and freedom, so Kant advocates teaching children how to think rather than "breaking" them like a horse or demanding rote learning (*Education* 20). Children must do right because they have developed their own maxims about right and wrong, and not merely from habit or from fear of punishment (*Education* 77). At the same time, however, it is essential that children be governed by rules, for only this will develop their character and their ability to follow their own maxims once formed. Obedience "to his master's commands" prepares the child for obedience "to what he feels to be a good and reasonable will." The former lesson of obedience prepares him to be a citizen who must obey laws that are inconvenient, such as those requiring payment of taxes; the latter prepares him to exercise a moral will. These lessons must be taught through the use of discipline and "natural opposition" (*Education* 57), which most effectively takes the form of disapproval, as both Locke and Rousseau maintained. Rather than punishing children, parents and teachers should show "contempt" (*Education* 84) and "humiliate the child by treating him coldly and distantly" (87–88).

Such an education would seem to prepare children to think for themselves; but the rules that they are socialized to follow are surprisingly conventional. For instance, Kant declared that paying debts is more important than giving to those in need (*Education* 104). And his remarks about sex, as feminists have noted, border on hackneyed. Girls, of course, are nowhere mentioned in this book; and despite references to "parents" participating in their children's education (about which he seems rather dubious, preferring public education [*Education* 25]), women are mentioned only twice and in passing, once to declare that fathers must be responsible for shaming children when they lie, because mothers tend to view lying as a sign of cleverness (*Education* 91); and once to suggest that the best way to prevent boys from masturbating is to channel their sexual interest toward women (*Education* 118). He indirectly refers to women as well when he says that education should prevent boys from becoming "effeminate," which is the opposite of hardiness (*Education* 44). One is left to assume that girls need not be educated because they are not rational; they are incapable of independence and therefore permanently passive citizens. But Kant is actually rather ambiguous on the question of women's rationality, in some places indicating that women are naturally rational, in others that they are naturally irrational, in yet others that they have the natural capacity for rationality but should not develop it. For instance, in his discussion of sex—a major challenge to freedom, because it involves treating people as means to the satisfaction of phenomenal desire—Kant maintains that men and women alike "are still *rational* beings,"[32] and this rationality enables them to see that monogamous marriage is the only way to contain and order sexual desire (which cannot be eliminated because the future of the species requires it). Monogamy not only introduces "reciprocity" into the use of others as means but constancy as well, "for in this way each reclaims itself and restores its personality" (*Metaphysics* 97).[33]

Such reciprocity stems from the notion that men and women are each superior to the other in different ways; man "by his physical strength and courage; the woman . . . by her natural talent for gaining mastery over his desire for her" (*Anthropology* 167). Like Rousseau, Kant believed that women had a natural talent for dominating men, but while Rousseau believed this power lay in raw sex, Kant locates it in love and women's shrewd manipulation of men's emotions. "Loquacity and emotional eloquence" are women's tools of "*domestic warfare*" (*Anthropology* 167). Yet, as with Rousseau, this apparent power and equality mask a gross inferiority. Despite his claim that "marriage is a relation of equality of possession" (*Metaphysics* 97), Kant also claims that "If a union is to be harmonious and indissoluble . . . one party must be *subject* to the other" (*Anthropology* 167). Kant says, "there can be only one person who coordinates all occupations in accordance with one end, which is his" (*Anthropology* 172). Of course, this ruler must be the man; "the woman should *reign* and the man *govern*; for inclination reigns and understanding [reason] governs" (*Anthropology* 172). Whether men's superior reason justifies their superiority, however, or their superiority is established in order to prevent women's reason from being deployed is ambiguous. In *Observations on the Feeling of the Beautiful and Sublime*, Kant says that men and women both have "understanding," but women have "a *beautiful understanding*, whereas [men's] should be a *deep understanding*, an expression that signifies identity with the sublime," or reason.[34] Given that reason is necessary to morality, this distinction might not bode well for women's virtue, but Kant insists that women have a "beautiful" virtue. In contrast to men, who obey the categorical imperative because reason tells them they must follow the universal law, women are naturally inclined to the good because of their "strong inborn feeling for all that is beautiful" (*Observations* 77). "Nothing of duty, nothing of compulsion, nothing of obligation!" (*Observations* 81) sways women to the good.

Thus, it might seem that women are constitutionally incapable of the reason which directs men to the categorical imperative, and hence to freedom: "I hardly believe that the fair sex is capable of principles" (*Observations* 81) Kant notes. "Her philosophy is not to reason, but to sense" (*Observations* 79). Hence, Kant derides the scholarly woman, who "uses her *books* in the same way as her *watch* . . . which she carries so that people will see that she has one, though it is usually not running or not set by the sun" (*Anthropology* 171). That these passages seem to contradict those cited earlier, which affirmed women's capacity for reason, may be explained in terms of Kant's prescriptive vision. The struggle to follow duty and live in the noumenal realm is very difficult for most men. By contrast, women, in following their natural inclinations to beauty, have an easy path. And this, Kant says, is appropriate to the particular role that nature has given to women, namely, "the cultivation of society and its refinements" (*Anthropology* 169). Accordingly, "Laborious learning or painful pondering, *even if a woman should greatly succeed in it*, destroys the merits that are proper to her sex." Such a woman "might as well have a beard" (*Observations* 78, my emphasis). Since "the beautiful understanding selects for objects everything closely related to the finer feeling," then "A woman therefore will learn no geometry. . . . The fair can leave Descartes his vortices to whirl forever without troubling themselves" (*Observations* 78–79). Similarly, Kant says that though "woman, by her nature, is sufficiently glib to represent both herself and her husband, even in court" she should never do so; "just as it is not woman's role to go to war, so she cannot personally defend her rights and engage in civil affairs for herself, but only through her representative" (*Anthropology* 80). While this "legal tutelage with regard to public transactions" supposedly gives women more power in the domestic realm—for reasoning men will "respect and defend" the "right of the weaker" (*Anthropology* 80)—it would seem clear from this account that women not only are, but must be passive citizens. Rather than being *unable* to reason, Kant seems to be arguing that women *should not* reason, indeed that they should not even develop their natural capacity to reason, for it will corrupt and compromise the "beautiful" understanding needed to complement men's "deep" understanding, or reason.[35]

Kant thus intermingles naturalism with prescription and common prejudice. Though he dismissively chides women for their conventionalism—"'what the world says is true, and what it does, good' is a feminine principle that is hard to unite with character in the strictest sense of the term" (*Anthropology* 171)—Kant himself draws on every standard cliché of sexism and articulates a conception of beauty that is even banal: women are naturally attracted to the "elegant and decorated," "adornment and glitter," "pleasantry and . . . trivialities . . . [that] are merry and laughing" (*Observations* 77); beautiful women have "regular features" with "colors of eyes and face which contrast prettily" (*Observations* 87), a "pretty appearance" (*Observations* 90), and a "fine figure, merry naivete, and charming friendliness" (*Observations* 94); they display "agreeableness" (*Observations* 87), "sly coyness" (*Observations* 88), and "delicate feelings in regard to the least offense" (*Observations* 77). These qualities are hardly what one expects from a vision of the beautiful that is to complement the "sublime" of reason. They are extremely conventional, yet Kant tries to pass them off as objective truth, knowledge that he has discovered on his journeys through the noumenal realm of reason.

As he argues in *Education*, a natural ability to reason does not guarantee the natural use of that reason; it must be learned and developed. However, in women such learning is contrary not only to their own interest but to the interests of mankind in general. As Nancy Tuana argues, for Kant, "Women, although potentially capable of moral agency, are . . . to be educated in such a way that they will be unable to actually achieve it"; women should be educated not in reason but in "domesticity," in being wives and mothers.[36] "The principal object is that the man should become more perfect as a man, and the woman as a wife" (*Observations* 95); woman's beautiful understanding is far from an end in itself, but rather serves the greater end of man's perfection as an end in *him*self. And because morality and reason are inextricably linked to Kant's conception of freedom, women's subservience is a necessary condition for the development and exercise of men's reason, and hence for their freedom. That is, it is only because women safeguard the beautiful that men can occupy the realm of the sublime; it is only because of women's subservience that the family can impart morality and reason to children; it is only by women's unfreedom that men's freedom can be sustained. Could Kant support a dual conception of freedom, with privileged men enjoying positive liberty while everyone else has to be content with negative? Kant certainly provides for a republican government that is marked by the predominance of rights (to "*freedom* . . . as a *human being*; *equality* . . . as a *subject*; *independence* . . . as a *citizen*"[37]) and classically liberal values such as freedom of expression. The "passive citizens" that he mentions may be able to achieve a limited form of negative liberty. The problem with this, however, echoes the similar problems in Locke and Rousseau; women are excluded even from these freedoms by virtue of the requirement that they be subservient to and dependent on men, and even if they could attain it, such freedom is not particularly valuable.

This configuration obviously involves the treatment of women as means, not ends, which puts Kant in the position of violating his own moral imperative. He tries to get around this by arguing that *nature* has made woman as she is; and the idea that nature is immoral (or at least amoral) because it treats women as means, not as ends in themselves, would be perfectly consistent with Kant's theoretical framework, since nature is the core of the phenomenal world, and hence the fulcrum of determinism. But if, as I have suggested, Kant's argument is motivated, not by women's "nature" per se but rather by his beliefs about what women should and must be for the end of men's freedom, then Kant not only treats women as means rather than ends but enjoins all men to do so. Women are thus constructed as unfree subjects; but that must logically entail that men are equally constructed as free subjects, through education as well as their role in politics as active citizens. Not only is the subject of liberty masculine, but freedom itself is a function of social constructivism.

## MILL: A UTILITARIAN FREEDOM

Of all the modern theorists who focus on the issue of liberty, John Stuart Mill would have to be the most sympathetic to my project. Not only was he a champion of women's rights and freedom, he quite explicitly rejects naturalism and deploys something close to a social constructivist approach. Yet Mill, too, exhibits many of the tensions illustrated more overtly by Kant, Rousseau, and Locke, particularly in his development of a two-tiered conception of freedom that divides along lines of class and gender. Though he seeks to grant certain women a kind of liberty in a more consistent fashion than the other theorists discussed in this chapter, he too designates the subject of liberty as male.

Most readers of Mill are familiar with his famous passage that "what is now called the nature of women is an eminently artificial thing—the result of forced repression in some directions, unnatural stimulation in others." A dominant theme in *The Subjection of Women* is that women are how and who they are because of a patriarchal culture that made them. Restraints on liberty can thus come from the very structure of society itself, which can both limit and enhance capacities; and it can prevent people not only from acting on certain desires but from having such desires in the first place.[38] Mill is known for his feminist arguments that women are fettered by laws that prevent them from voting, from obtaining education, and from pursuing professions. They lose control of their property upon marriage through coverture and are subject to violence and abuse from their husbands. Mill even goes so far as to say that marriage is a (indeed "the only") legal form of slavery (*Subjection* 482–85). These restrictions make women economically dependent on men and forestall their ability to formulate life choices and act on them. But even more significantly, Mill suggests, such external restrictions produce effects on women's character. If women are beings who are not taught to think rationally but rather are encouraged to indulge in useless activities and gossip, then it is not surprising if women develop into beings who seem to want no better than they get. Women's self-sacrificing characteristics (516), their absorption in "small but multitudinous details" and trivia rather than intellectual questions (540), their "disinterestedness in the general conduct of life—the devotion of the energies to purposes who [*sic*] hold out no promise of private advantages to the family" (566), their reluctance to complain about or press charges against abusive husbands, and even "to beg off their tyrant from his merited chastisement" (485–86)—all these traits are a function of what society makes of women, of the attitudes, self-conceptions, beliefs, and values it requires women to adopt. By contrast to the woman of superior abilities (like Mill's wife, Harriet Taylor), who can rise above such confining social strictures, the average, uneducated woman is completely vulnerable, even helpless against such vast social forces. For the average woman has so internalized the tyranny of "common public opinion" as to be its "auxiliary"; the critical and analytical abilities that might allow her to see through it have atrophied so atrociously (if they were ever developed at all) that she seems incapable of even questioning, let alone rejecting, it. Such arguments suggest that removal of external barriers to women's equality may not be enough; social norms and attitudes must change *within* women in order for women's or men's freedom to be achieved. Women must learn to desire other things than what current convention dictates.

Though the social constructionist element is most apparent in *Subjection*'s consideration of women's plight, in fact it pervades all of Mill's thought. This might seem surprising on its face, for Mill is often seen as offering the classic notion of negative liberty; indeed, Berlin draws on him several times in formulating this conception.[39] One of the key themes in *On Liberty* is the importance of people's being able to pursue their desires and act as they wish without interference from other people or from government: "The only freedom which deserves the name, is that of pursuing our own good in our own way, so long as we do not attempt to deprive others of theirs" (*Liberty* 17). The need to be independent, to differ from one's fellows, to think for oneself, are for Mill the essence of human liberty. Particularly by focusing on conscience, thought, and speech as the essential dimensions of human freedom, Mill shows that he operates from an exceedingly individualist notion of the subject and individual desire. He loathes the mediocre masses who conform to common opinion and fail to think for themselves, for this makes way for the antithesis of individual liberty, namely the tyranny of the majority. Mill's critique is not that people "choose what is customary, in preference to what suits their own inclination," but the much stronger, scathing criticism that "It does not occur to them to have any inclination, except for what is customary." Hence, "the danger which threatens human nature," he writes, "is not the excess, but the deficiency, of personal impulses and preferences" (*Liberty* 68).

But the context in which Mill's individuals live is a social one, not (merely) an individualistic one. Ideally, the members of a society should have a common interest in seeking the truth, in creating laws that reflect the common good and that treat all (or almost all) members with equal respect. Hence, Mill valorizes the "eccentric" not because of individualism per se but rather because difference is so vital to the productive confluence and interaction of ideas, an interaction which in turn stimulates individual mental processes. It is only through a social process of democratic exchange that the end of individual freedom of thought and expression—namely, "Truth"—can be attained. Individuals on their own, without the opportunity to exchange their ideas with others, will not likely achieve truth, he says; thus, society and social relationships are essential not only to the greater good but to the individual's well-being and liberty. Even regarding freedom of expression, the highest and apparently most individualist form of liberty, Mill argues against censorship (whether by government or by custom and majority tyranny) not because of "natural rights" but because of the danger to truth, and thereby to society. After all, he asks, what if a censored view is actually correct? Or if it contains some portion of truth? Even his market argument for freedom of expression depends on a social view of humanity: that is, if a view is wrong, then challenging, discussing, and ultimately rejecting the view through reasoned discourse will help us affirm—or reaffirm—the views that are true and good. So, for instance, women should not be legally excluded from education or professions because men believe they are incompetent; if they are incompetent, then they will fail, and laws shutting them out from these endeavors will be unnecessary. The market, not government, should decide the truth.

Mill's theory of utility offers similar notions. Mill came to reject the individualist variant of utilitarianism put forth by Bentham and James Mill and adopted instead a more social notion of utility, the version that we find in Hume and which Rawls later called "rule utilitarianism."[40] Bentham's axiom "pushpin is as good as poetry" suggested that utility is a matter only of quantity, that the *amount* of pleasure I obtain from playing a simple game is more important than the intellectual quality of my pursuits. But Mill sharply disagrees, arguing that utility should be a matter of quality, because some kinds of desires and preferences are more valuable than others: "better to be a human being dissatisfied than a pig satisfied; better to be Socrates dissatisfied than a fool satisfied" (*Utilitarianism* 140). In particular, the mental pleasures are superior to the physical (138), "a sense of dignity, which all human beings possess in one form or other" and which is vital to human happiness, is "in some, though by no means in exact, proportion to their higher faculties" (140). Presumably, then, satisfaction of one person's desire to hear Mozart might produce more utility than satisfying ten people's desire to hear Lawrence Welk.

But how does one decide which pleasures are superior? On the one hand, Mill offers a democratic solution: people who have experienced two pleasures are more competent to judge between them than are people who have experienced only one of them, and so "all or almost all who have experience of" two pleasures must prefer one for it to have greater utility. But he also says

> If one of the two is, by those who are *competently acquainted* with both, placed so far above the other that they prefer it, even though knowing it to be attended with a greater amount of discontent, and would not resign it for any quantity of the other pleasure which their nature is capable of, we are justified in ascribing to the preferred enjoyment a superiority in quality, so far outweighing quantity as to render it, in comparison, of small account. (*Utilitarianism* 139, emphasis added)

This clearly suggests an antidemocratic element, not only because a vaguely defined "quality" of pleasure can supersede the majority's preference, but because a standard of competency can be self-fulfilling. It is not enough simply to have heard Mozart and Lawrence Welk; one must be competent in music appreciation for one's preference to really count. Indeed, a preference for Lawrence Welk could be taken as *evidence* of one's incompetence. Mill acknowledges that it is easy to lose sight of the higher pleasures and prefer the lower ones: "Capacity for the nobler feelings is in most natures a very tender plant, easily killed." Most people "addict themselves to inferior pleasures, not because they deliberately prefer them, but because they are either the only ones to which they have access, or the only ones which they are any longer capable of enjoying" (*Utilitarianism* 141). But it follows from this that most people are not in fact "competent" judges: if they only have access to the lower pleasures—a population which for Mill would include the majority of laborers, the poor, the uneducated or less educated—they cannot evaluate the higher. (Indeed, Mill's formula systematically favors the educated, professional, and wealthier classes, for their range of experience will of necessity be larger than that of laborers and the poor.) And if they are no longer (if they were ever) capable of enjoying the higher—if, after hearing Mozart, they still prefer Lawrence Welk—they are similarly disqualified as judges, because their preference indicates an impoverished sensibility.

Mill thus distinguishes between what people want, what they think will make them happy, and what they should want, what actually will make them happy. It is precisely because the majority of people do not have elevated or educated tastes that Mill advocates the utility of certain practices and rules, even when it might appear, in some instances, that following the rule yields little utility for the individual concerned. "The rules of morality for the multitude, and for the philosopher until he has succeeded in finding better," will guide us in deciding which things produce utility and which do not (*Utilitarianism* 157). Such "secondary rules"—keep your promises, respect others' property, tell the truth—are guides to the "first principle" of promoting happiness and minimizing pain, for following such rules will, in most cases, produce greater happiness. The tension between utility and freedom is thus unavoidable: Mill emphasizes individual choice and freedom as the absence of external obstacles, but he also is afraid of what people will choose without guidance. His theory of utility tries to provide such guidance but conflicts with the strong notion of individual liberty of conscience and thought that is generally attributed to Mill. Utility is in fact central to Mill's theory of liberty; "I regard utility as the ultimate appeal on all ethical questions," he says in *On Liberty*, "but it must be utility in the largest sense, grounded on the permanent interests of man" (15). Indeed, liberty is a *means to utility*. The point of freedom is to achieve truth, and if truth is key to people's wanting the right things and making the right choices, then it would seem not only that freedom serves the end of utility but that freedom is the paramount utilitarian value. Because we often want the wrong things, Mill has to figure out a way to safeguard our freedom from those misguided desires.

Education is an important way in which this can occur; it will produce better-thinking citizens who are more likely to approach the truth, and thus less likely to think solely of themselves and their immediate short-term interests and pleasures. Though Mill never wrote a treatise on education, as Locke, Rousseau, and Kant did, various of his essays reveal a theory of education that echoes these other theorists in important ways. Perhaps due to the extremely intense education his father gave him,[41] Mill seemed to believe that people were the products of their environments, that a better environment produced better people, that they were, as I have put it, socially constructed. For Mill saw his own acquirements under his father's educational regime as nothing remarkable, not the result of any particular talents or intelligence on his part: "what I could do could assuredly be done by any boy or girl of average capacity and healthy physical constitution." Rather, the credit was to go to the time and attention his father took to bestow this education on him.[42] Hence, an important point in Mill's *Autobiography* was to show "how much more than is commonly supposed" can be achieved through a more demanding education; and as Collini suggests, the *Autobiography* "reads more like Rousseau's *Emile* than his *Confessions*."[43]

Mill defines education extremely broadly as "whatever helps to shape the human being; to make the individual what he is, or hinder him from being what he is not";[44] what education should produce is people who can think critically and independently, but also "effective combatants in the great fight which never ceases to rage between Good and Evil,"[45] that is, people who will prefer the higher pleasures, eschew mediocrity and conformity, and seek the truth. But if education includes many aspects of experience, then social construction would seem to take place in those many aspects as well. Though in *On Liberty* and *Subjection*—as well as in "The Negro Question"—Mill views the social production of desire and identity as a negative force, a result of oppression that squeezes out hope of accomplishment or elevation, his views on education seem to suggest the possibility of more positive construction of individuals. Garforth maintains that "environmental influence is a constant theme throughout his writings"; the "associationism" that Mill inherited from his father— the notion that ideas come from sensory experience, and ideas that persist must come from repeated experiences—meant that he favored nurture over nature in his understanding of education and human identity. As he says about women, what is "natural" is difficult to discern, given the powerful constructing forces of poorly organized and run social institutions (like schools), not to mention the frequently mind-deadening requirements of industrial labor. In an echo of Locke's *Conduct*, Mill suggests that a "day labourer who earns his wages by mere obedience to orders may become a good artificer in his particular manual operation, but his mind stagnates. He is not paid for thinking and contriving but for executing," and so a nonthinking automaton is what society gets. Much like Rousseau, Mill seems to hold that what is "natural" to humans is both good and bad, and education must encourage the development of the former and the atrophy of the latter. His method of education, like Locke's, therefore involves the formation of the right habits, for as Garforth notes, "repetition . . . is essential to the formation of associations."[46] Thus, even though the end product of education should be free-thinking citizens, rather than minds "hopelessly filled full with other people's conclusions," and a university should be "a place of free speculation," his prescription for what should be taught in universities, as well as in the common schools, is quite rigorous and demanding, and the outcome of such free thinking should be fairly consistent agreement on ethical and political issues, or at least disagreement within "reasonable" parameters.[47]

Given Mill's broad definition of education, however, schools are not the only location of learning and stimulation; indeed, law and government themselves are key educative tools, at least as Mill would like to design them. At the same time, education is the key to political power, for Mill's theory of representative government advocates universal suffrage, in part on the premise that people with a vote will have a stake in thinking through the issues they are voting on. However, recognizing that there is no guarantee that a vote will make every individual mindful of the common good, Mill also develops a system of plural voting, where those who score highest on standardized tests of knowledge would receive more than one vote. Since the shortsighted, self-interested, and intellectually unstimulated masses constitute a majority, and the superior, public-minded peo-

ple a minority, the latter must be given an advantage in determining policy. Mill undercuts his proposal when he suggests that, until an
educational and state-administered testing system is in place, plural votes
should go to those in the professions—not because of income (he rejects
money, particularly inherited money, as the basis for political power) but
because they are likely to have received the best education and thus to
think about the common good rather than narrow self-interest. Despite
the class elitism and naivete evident in this proposal, however, Mill intends plural voting, combined with universal suffrage, to ensure a balance
between wisdom and populism, without allowing either to dominate systematically: the wise will prevail if they convince a sufficient minority of
the general population, but if the majority of single voters is large enough,
their will may prevail, despite the plural votes of the wise and the learned.
He does not entrench the power of the educated, because even their superior views of utility must be challenged periodically, if for no other reason
than to force them to defend their position and to reaffirm its truth. At
the same time, however, wisdom must be given a leg up, by giving the
educated more than one vote. Though people must choose for themselves,
Mill also wants to increase the odds that, as a society, they will make the
right choice.

Education is also key to women's liberation, for not only is it essential
to their intelligent participation in politics, not to mention to their entry
into the professions, but to the performance of their roles as wife and
mother in a more utilitarian fashion. Utility is a major theme of *Subjection*; women must be granted equality and freedom both for their own
happiness—which counts in the calculation of utility (*Subjection* 576)—
and because men themselves will be better off if they have more intelligent
and better-educated wives. Mill claims that "a man married to a woman
his inferior in intelligence finds her a perpetual dead weight, or, worse
than a dead weight, a drag, upon every aspiration of his to be better than
public opinion requires him to be" (*Subjection* 568). By contrast, educated wives can provide men with intelligent conversation and spur them
on to continual improvement. Furthermore, as better, more intelligent,
and more fulfilled mothers, such women will be able to create a new gener-
ation of thinking citizens, for they will educate their children to be similarly analytical and stimulating (*Subjection* 560–61). Beyond the family,
removing barriers to women's participation in the public sphere would
result in "doubling the mass of mental faculties available for the higher
service of humanity" (561) in political office or professions such as medicine or law, and will thereby improve the quality of politicians, doctors,
and lawyers. The increased competition would also stimulate the current
available applicant pool—namely, men—to improve themselves.

It is perhaps not surprising that Mill's utilitarian arguments, rather than his arguments for liberty, prevail in his case for gender equality. Indeed, the tension between liberty and utility in his writings is particularly evident in the *Subjection* where, after his exhaustive argument for removing legal barriers to women's participation in the economy, and their right to compete in the marketplace, he maintains that most women will not in fact enter the labor force, but will choose the "career" of wife and mother (*Subjection* 522–23). Mill's arguments at the end of chapter 2 can be read in several ways. On the one hand, given the rigors of nineteenth-century housekeeping, women's participation in the paid labor force would be extremely burdensome, leading to what is now called the double day. In arguing that it is enough to end the subjection of women that they have the *capacity*—the educational skills and the opportunities, unimpeded by legal barriers—to earn their living, he provides women with power in their marriages by providing an exit option that can effectively forestall husbands' domination and abuse, a problem with which Mill was particularly concerned (*Subjection* 523). But on the other hand, Mill's failure to at least think about the necessity of restructuring the family can be read as patriarchal, and indeed as once again exhibiting a strong class bias. For the double day of which he speaks would be particularly relevant to working-class women; professional women could afford to hire other women to do housework and child care (*Subjection* 523). An important, though subtle, theme in his work is that only upper- and upper-middle-class women can really qualify for full "liberty of choice" and hence for "equality" with men. Like the plural voter and the experienced judge of qualitative utility, upper-class women can be trusted to make the right choices, unlike the vast majority of women.

Furthermore, this passage illustrates the central tension in Mill between radical individualism and social constructivism. Although he challenges claims about women's "nature" and points out that women are *constructed* by social norms to be inferior, he then leaves it to women to pull themselves up by their own bootstraps, individualizing both blame (for those who do not meet his ideal) and ability (for those who do), giving little attention to the ways in which women are likely to fail or succeed because of class background, not to mention race. On the contrary, Mill seems to think that, though spared domestic violence and disrespectful husbands, economically privileged women are in fact *more* restricted than women from the laboring classes: "Society makes the whole life of a woman, in the easy classes, a continued self-sacrifice; it exacts from her an unremitting restraint of the whole of her natural inclinations, and the sole return it makes to her for what often deserves the name of martyrdom, is consideration" (*Subjection* 570). In this sense, while Mill may be advocating a quantitative equality in freedom for all women by removing legal barriers and providing them with economic possibilities, there is a decidedly qualitative difference in the unfreedom of women of different classes. In the lower or "laboring" classes, Mill's goal of gender equality focuses on ending the brutality of domestic violence, on increasing men's respect for their wives, and on making women better wives and mothers through education. The removal of external barriers is probably all that is needed to "liberate" such women from their oppression. By contrast, the goals for upper-class women are to end coverture, to facilitate economic and professional opportunities, and to end socially restrictive attitudes that hinder the development of women's talents and intellectual abilities. The focus is less on simple external obstacles than internal ones: the prejudiced attitudes of men must be changed, and women's intellectual and professional abilities must be developed. Like Locke, Rousseau, and Kant, Mill differentially constructs freedom along class and gender lines. But Mill's explicit acknowledgement of women's social construction leads him into an even deeper problem of inconsistency.

### Conclusion: A Masculinist Freedom

This admittedly brief sketch of four modern theorists suggests several things about the concept of freedom. First, it reveals that although many contemporary theorists might tend to categorize each of these figures as either a positive or a negative libertarian, in fact all four theorists develop theories of freedom that depend deeply on both conceptions. All demonstrate a concern with both the external conditions of and barriers to freedom and the internal factors of freedom, namely, desire, will, self-understanding, and self-definition. In this, we can see that Berlin's typology is not particularly accurate as a description of conceptions of liberty within the modern canon. But his categories are helpful in the ideas they provide *about* freedom: they give us a conceptual vocabulary and ideational language with which to differentiate the various aspects of freedom, desire, will, restriction, capability, and power. The typology provides a useful and reflective vocabulary for identifying the tension in these theories between the theoretical need to define freedom as a universal concept and the political need to exclude most people, including laborers and women, from its expression and enactment.

This tension leads to the second theme developed here, that the notion of social construction is central to the concept of liberty even as far back as the seventeenth century, despite common readings of these theorists in naturalist terms. While the humanism of the Enlightenment and the desire to reject divine right and patriarchal theories of government led theorists to emphasize the human ability to make choices, these same theorists were simultaneously afraid of what such choices would be. As a result, they are all concerned with the double aspect of choice: making one's own choices for oneself, but at the same time making the right choice. The only way to resolve this tension was to create citizens who would think about and see the world in a particular way. Theoretical moves such as "tacit consent" and the "general will" were probably motivated by such an effort, but more practical recommendations for methods of social construction, such as rigorous education, plural voting, or poor law reforms, were also instrumental to addressing this tension.

Third, I have shown that gender is a key element in revealing the importance of social construction in these theories, for women's differential relationship to these recommended practices and their situation within the family present the most serious challenge to the claims of naturalism by tripping these theorists up on some of their most obvious inconsistencies. By undercutting the naturalist reading, and suggesting that freedom is developed in ways that are both richly complex and self-contradictory (the latter because of the effort to define freedom as a value primarily for men), I have made the case that understanding women's relationship to the concept of freedom is vital to an accurate interpretation of these theories. The fact that the subject of liberty is male suggests important insights about the ways in which freedom is defined and conceptualized, not as the universal concept it is claimed to be, but rather as one that derives from, and is intended to apply to, the experiences of a particular group of people, namely, propertied white men. Moreover, if attending to the treatment of women in these theories reveals the relevance of social constructivism, and if women's unfreedom is a function of their social construction as inferior beings who must reside primarily in the private sphere, it logically follows that men, too, must be socially constructed. The portrayal of men as "naturally free and equal" is, thus, a ruse to hide the masculinism of freedom.

These findings can be applied to other theories in the modern canon as well, of course. Hobbes, for instance, who is often taken to be the classic example of a negative libertarian,[48] defining freedom as "the absence of external impediments to motion," also demonstrates a significant concern about the choices people might make. He thus binds them to an absolute sovereign who can make the right choices for them, but does so through blatant second-guessing. Given that human life is "nasty, brutish, and short" in the state of nature, anyone voting against the social compact "is not to be understood as if he meant it." Accordingly, "as well he that *Voted for it*, as he that *Voted against it*" gives consent to the compact. Similarly, foreshadowing Locke's ambiguity about law's relation to freedom, Hobbes declares that law will "direct and keep [people] in such a motion, as not to hurt themselves by their own impetuous desires, rashnesse, or indiscretion as Hedges are set, not to stop Travellers, but to keep them in the way."[49]

Even more noteworthy perhaps is that Hobbes deploys a social constructionist argument; he maintains that the sovereign must not only preserve his rights of dominion but also educate his subjects so that they *understand* these rights, as well as understand why it is in their own interest to acknowledge them. Law in and of itself is not enough to maintain the grounds of these rights, but understanding those grounds is vital. For instance, Hobbes says, if I do not understand the logic of prohibitions against rebellion as necessary to my primary interest in peace and security, then I will seek to rebel whenever an opportunity presents itself. Accordingly, citizens are to be *taught* not to prefer a neighboring country's form of government, nor "to desire change" of any kind; and not to challenge or dispute the sovereign's power. They are also taught legalistic variations of the Ten Commandments (in which God is not portrayed as a superior power to the earthly sovereign).[50] Women are similarly constructed to obey. In the state of nature, women are completely equal to men and do not marry, there being "no matrimonial law"; but in civil society women are subordinated to men in marriage. Since women are as strong and smart as men according to Hobbes, they have no reason to acquiesce in this subordinate role, nor can they be consistently conquered by men, so this subordination must be actively created by the sovereign. Women are a significant source of instability in the state of nature; in "Quarrells of competition," men "use violence, to make themselves masters of other men's persons, wives, children, and cattell," and rape is a way for men to attain dominion over another man's property. And, of course, women produce children, who can become natural confederates if women choose to "nourish" them, so men seek dominion over women to gain dominion over children. Thus, once the social contract is formed, it then makes sense for the sovereign to write laws establishing father-right. Such laws secure peace by establishing territorial or property rights over women and the products of their bodies, namely, children.[51] Women's consent to subordination within the family would thus not have to be given expressly; it would be "deduced" from their original consent to the sovereign. That is, like men, women enter the social contract to obtain security and to end the "continual fear of death." But unlike men, women are subject to a further level of subordination, precisely because of the greater threat they pose to the stability of the social contract. Hence, once again, women lose their own freedom to enhance the freedom of men: within Hobbes's zero-sum formulation of liberty, the smaller the "environ" or "certain space" within which women can move, the larger the space for men.[52] The sovereign determines those spaces by "matrimonial law," and Hobbes indicates that in most cases the sovereign will see the necessity of making those laws such that husbands have power over wives. In Hobbes, just as men begin in a radically free state of nature and end up under the most repressive of political regimes, so women begin in a position of radical freedom and equality and end up in the most repressive of patriarchal families. But this trajectory is constructed by Hobbes; it is not predetermined by women's nature.

At the other end of the continuum, Marx similarly illustrates the three insights that the foregoing critical analysis has revealed. Though I will speak in greater detail about Marx's contribution to social constructivism in the following chapter, a few points are worth noting briefly here. Marx is generally taken as a positive libertarian, for he clearly considers systematic and institutional phenomena, particularly capitalism, to be the key barriers to freedom; moreover, the nature of capitalism's restrictive quality is the way in which it constructs workers to desire what capital wants, even though such desires dehumanize the individual. But after the revolution, the freedom that Marx envisions is almost liberal. A significant objection to capitalism is the way that it takes choices away from workers, and hence the ability to control their own lives. It is after the restrictions of capitalist exploitation have been removed that individuals can be free to express their natures and do as they wish, fishing in the morning and philosophizing in the evening. "Only in community"—the community formed once the division of labor is ended—"is personal freedom possible," because then the "individual" has "the means of cultivating his gifts in all directions."[53] At the same time, though, Marx's failure to recognize the contributions of women's work in the home to capital and the role of women in communist society, particularly the double day that will result from Marx's failure to address the gendered division of labor in the family, suggests that this free individual, the subject of liberty, is male for Marx as well.[54]

The maleness of the subject of liberty thus coheres with the role and importance of social construction in the concept of freedom, for claims of freedom's naturalness conflict with the patriarchal political need to restrict women's freedom. The free subject must be defined as uniquely masculine. But saying that the masculinity (or masculinism) of the subject of liberty is a social construction is not saying that liberty and its subject are a purely linguistic fiction: social construction, as will be discussed in the following chapter, produces not only ideological and discursive conceptualizations but material manifestations of those conceptualizations. That is, as much as social construction involves discursive categories, actual living men and women must be created to meet these linguistic and ideological definitions. That is an important reason behind not only the justifications and structures of political power but more actively constructive practices and institutions, such as education. They seek the creation of male citizens who can reinforce and reproduce the very power relations that presumably justify them. A significant part of those material power relations involves gender stratification, a system of gender that constructs freedom to serve the political needs of men of a particular race and class. Such a construction of freedom and the subject of liberty as masculine undermines the foundational assumptions and claims of the naturalism of freedom and will pose serious problems for women facing situations of oppression and restriction, as the following chapters will show.

## Chapter Three

# FEMINISM AND FREEDOM: THE SOCIAL CONSTRUCTION PARADOX

ALTHOUGH in contemporary scholarship social constructivism is much more common in fields other than political theory—particularly sociology, literary theory, psychoanalytic theory, philosophy, and history—its importance to modern and early-modern canonical figures has important implications for political theory. Indeed, it ironically points to some of the internal tensions that I identified in the theories discussed in the previous chapter. As I noted in the introductory chapter, the central idea of social constructivism is that there is no such thing as "human nature"; human beings, their social structures, institutions, relationships, and so forth are the product of sociohistorical configuration. If claims for human "nature" or for knowledge of timeless or universal truth about the human condition are actually particular, time- and culture-bound ways of "seeing" humans, then the "natural man" of social-contract theory, for instance, with his natural freedom and equality, should really be seen as the construct of particular individuals located in particular times and places: specifically, of bourgeois white males at the dawn of capitalism and liberal representative democracy. This does not mean that liberalism is "wrong" per se, of course, only that it is not what it says it is. Developed in part as a response to absolutist political authority and emerging political movements for parliamentarian and representative government (motivated in turn by largely economic considerations),[1] the emphasis on the individual as the unit of analysis and freedom as noninterference by government is an understandable reaction to contemporary historical and political conditions. But it is not the only possible reaction to them, and that is where social constructivism plays its arguably least controversial card. If there are several different possible reactions to apparently timeless questions and problems (such as whether tyranny is bad), then not only do we need to look further to understand why *this* reaction (liberal individualism) occurred at this particular time and in these particular conditions, but the status of this particular reaction must be reevaluated as well. It is no longer inevitable or natural but contingent and historically specific. Thus, it is not that social constructivism rejects individualism or negative liberty out of hand; rather, it points out that calling these conceptions natural and timeless obfuscates their origin and meaning, decontextualizes and dehistoricizes them, and hides their biases thereby. In such hidden biases lie the dangers of totalizing representation and the erasure of men and women of color, white women, workers, and the poor.

Social constructivism thus suggests that the values that we hold in the modern era, the meanings we give to words like "freedom," "justice," "equality," "selfhood," "person," "citizen"—definitions seemingly settled for at least two centuries, settled in a way that systematically excluded large segments of the population of the West—are in no way essential or natural but rather the product of particular social formations and relationships that have developed through time. At the least, then, social constructivism affords political theorists a vital notion of contestation and suggests that we must continually and critically reevaluate our own assumptions in order to understand that what we have called natural is not necessarily so. This feature fits very well with one of the central enterprises of political theory as an intellectual and pedagogical field, namely, the project of getting ourselves and our students to think critically, to analyze, evaluate, and form judgments. By enabling the rejection of theoretical arguments about women's supposed "natural" proclivities as patriarchal efforts to disempower and constrain women, social constructivism also provides a point of entry for historically excluded groups—like women—to participate in the existing discourse. The claim found in political theory from Plato to Rawls that women's primary identity and role lies in the family, for instance, is seen as less a function of nature than of patriarchal ideological power. Social constructivism allows feminists to critique political claims of naturalism and thus to challenge the supposed universality and timelessness of political theory's core concepts.

Social constructivism particularly challenges mainstream freedom theory's dominant definitions of purposeful agency and identifiable blockage. For instance, when Benn defines heterarchy as a condition in which one loses the ability to challenge the beliefs that have been "implanted" by others—a condition he wants to distinguish from "mere socialization," an unavoidable aspect of social relations[2]—it is important to note that women are precisely "socialized" to be submissive and men to be violent, women to be deferential and men to be assertive, women to think of the self in terms of relating to and caring for others and men to think of others in terms of how they relate to the self. Certainly, some instances fit the stronger imagery of "implanting"—for instance, when a severely controlling man, through repeated physical, emotional, and psychological abuse, convinces his wife that she is worthless, that she deserves to be beaten, and that there is no escaping him—but "implantation" is not an appropriate description of most women's experience. Socialization is much harder to resist and change, let alone even to identify and understand, precisely *because* it lacks an identifiable agent as its source: What is there to struggle against in socialization? Who is there to resist? As Connolly notes, "The conative dispositions people have are themselves shaped in part by the concepts, beliefs, and roles they internalize from the society in which they are implicated. . . . the more successful a group is in maintaining ideological hegemony the less liable it is to the charge that it has limited the freedom of other groups."[3] Indeed, where sexism is normalized, barriers can become completely invisible, falling out of the range of contestability altogether. Yet it is precisely here that a feminist theory of freedom must struggle to define itself.

As I have already argued, going beyond socialization to social construction requires examination of not only constraints on belief and self-conception—difficult enough to define and articulate by their very nature, for the individual experiencing the constraints often does not realize that she has them—but the contexts in which claims of freedom and unfreedom are made. "Internal barriers" are neither individualistic nor strictly internal; they reflect, and work interactively with, a social context that determines the limits of the conceptually possible. Both individual and collective beliefs and self-conceptions are "embedded in the very fabric of the social order."[4] Such a notion goes beyond socialization to a much broader and deeper consideration of the production of social contexts, as well as the production of individuals who occupy and are shaped by those contexts. To repeat Kathy Ferguson's insightful comment, "It is not simply that [we are] being socialized; rather, a subject upon whom socialization can do its work is being produced."[5] The process to which she refers, on my reading, is the social construction of the choosing subject.

## SOCIAL CONSTRUCTION AND POLITICAL THEORY

The importance of social construction to feminism does not deny the deep contestation over how social construction operates, who does it, and what it means for who we are as subjects, for all of those aforementioned central concepts in political theory (justice, freedom, democracy, and citizenship) as well as for feminist questions of gender, sexuality, the sexual division of labor, and reproduction. This contestation, I believe, is based in part on the generally unacknowledged fact that there are actually several "levels" to the idea of social construction. The first level is what might be called "the ideological misrepresentation of reality." Marx, for instance, talked about how capitalism inverted the truth of material reality so that, for instance, exchange was seen as more important than use; competition, rather than cooperation, was seen as the essential condition of production; and relationships between people took the form of relationships between things. In this inversion, ideology is more than simply party dogma;

it is a picture of reality that comes to dominate lived experience by distorting it. Similarly, feminists have argued that women's experience and "nature" have been misrepresented by patriarchy. We are virgins, we are whores; we are asexual mothers, we are sexual temptresses; we are helpless and weak, we are demonically strong. All of these platitudes about women's nature, as contradictory as they are, fail to recognize women's humanity, their membership in society, their differences from each other, and not just from men, their individuality and their commonality. They reduce women to simplistic and exaggerated caricatures.

The ideological misrepresentation of reality is the most common understanding of social construction; it is what most people (or at least most nontheorists, and indeed many theorists) mean when they use the term. "Social construction" is taken to mean something artificial, something actively created by particular social forces and norms; "constructed" implies "false." The term "socialization" is often used in this sense: the implicit assumption is that if we were not socialized, or socially constructed, we would be more natural, real, or true. Many feminists, in particular, commonly use the term "social construction" to indicate that women act or think in certain ways because they have been socialized by patriarchy; they consider socialization as a force of oppression. Judith Lorber, for instance, in developing a "new paradigm of gender . . . *as a social institution*," asserts that gender "is produced and maintained by identifiable social processes and built into the general social structure and individual identities deliberately and purposefully." Indeed, she echoes here the terms of individualist freedom theory I discussed in chapter 1, where barriers to freedom are defined somewhat reductively in terms of indentifiable agency; and her chapter on "the micropolitics of gender" is devoted primarily to a discussion of professional women's barriers to success.[6] Paul Benson similarly examines the "oppressive socialization" of women by patriarchal standards of physical beauty for women. Many women, he maintains, perceive these standards as oppressive and coercive because they realize they will not succeed—in either the job market or the marriage market—if they do not meet them. Other women, Benson maintains, have "internalized" these standards and so do not perceive themselves as oppressed; but this complete internalization signifies that they are even more oppressed. As a result, these women experience "diminished autonomy."[7]

Given the pain that these standards have inflicted, particularly as seen in such profound disorders as anorexia, such arguments help identify the hidden power of social forces. But they also have obvious problems from a feminist perspective. For one thing, second-guessing seems unavoidable: a woman who enjoys using makeup by definition exhibits diminished autonomy, because she has internalized patriarchal standards. Yet consider the Miss America pageant, which many feminists over the years have pointed to as the logical extreme of such sexist standards. Certainly, a woman who has entered beauty pageants, endured the rigors of competition, and as a result won scholarships, a degree of fame and wealth, and/or a springboard start to a career in the performing arts would have to be considered autonomous by Benson's own definition of critical competence in rational reflection.[8] Or consider drag queens, transsexuals, or transgendered individuals, for whom deployment of such standards of "feminine appearance *is* a necessary ingredient of [their] personal worth," contrary to Benson's claims.[9] Second, underneath such arguments as Benson and Lorber make is an implicit assumption that if patriarchy would just leave women alone, women would be okay. Beneath that is a further assumption that women could be *not* socially constructed at all, that there is some true identity and set of interests that women have as women—an essentialist or naturalist thesis which, ironically, most feminists would consciously claim to reject. Thus, this understanding of social construction, though important to feminism, is flawed and limited.

But social construction actually goes much deeper than a surface socialization: the construction of social behaviors and rules takes on a life of its own, and becomes constitutive not only of what women are allowed to *do*, but of what they are allowed to *be*. At this second level of social construction, which I call "materialization," how we think about, talk about, interpret, and understand social phenomena produces material effects on the phenomena themselves. Once again, we can refer to Marx, because he notes that capitalist ideology not only distorts the reality of the relations of production but actually produces those relations and constitutes empirical reality: workers become alienated from their labor, from each other, from themselves, and are reduced to the exchange value of their labor. Similarly, social constructivism suggests that the degree to which women live out patriarchal ideology—for instance, by withdrawing from responsibility for politics and declaring that politics is for men— is dependent on the ideology's success in creating them concretely. As both Mary Astell and Mary Wollstonecraft argued (a century apart from each other), if you deny education to women on the grounds that they are irrational, they will in fact never develop the skills that are defined as constituting rationality.[10] Even a physical sense of the body becomes constructed through social and linguistic practice. In practices ranging from Chinese foot binding to female circumcision to cosmetic surgery, we see interpretive discourses (e.g., that women are dainty and delicate creatures who are physically unable to fend for themselves) producing the reality they claim to describe (e.g., crippled women who cannot run).

This concrete dimension of social construction—the intersection between ideological notions and categories, and the way that individuals actually live their lives—is significant for contemporary feminist politics and for a feminist interpretation of freedom. Guided by concerns such as pornography, domestic violence, prostitution, sexual discrimination, sexual harassment, rape and abortion, feminists argue that such social expressions of male domination have produced and codified customs and rules that restrict women's opportunities and choices; women cannot be doctors, for example, if they are denied access to medical schools. Further, according to the logic of social constructivism, such gender restrictive customs and rules affect not just actions but self-conceptions, including desires and preferences; women should *want* to be nurses rather than doctors, because it is more appropriate to essential femininity. As Benson's "oppressive socialization" argument suggests, women's understanding of what it means to be a "woman" becomes constructed, shaped and defined by and through these other social formations and phenomena. But whereas theories of oppressive socialization claim that patriarchy perverts a supposedly natural reality, materialization involves the production *of* reality. Social construction in this sense comes full circle: from *misrepresentation* of material reality, a reality at odds with the ideology that claims to describe it, to *creation* of the very social phenomena that it claims to describe. Women's identity and experience are concretely formed by the requirements and limitations that patriarchy has imposed on the material conditions of women's lives and the theoretical understanding of that experience that patriarchal ideology allows. On this level, social construction is not at odds with material reality; it actually produces it. It *creates* women's reality; it "constructs" women's lives in the most active sense of that term.

But even this "reality" must be seen, interpreted, and understood in the way that patriarchy needs if it is to be effective. For instance, it is not enough to bar women from medical school, or even to produce a preference in women for the nursing profession; nurses must also be socially devalued vis-à-vis doctors in order for this construction of women to result in the perpetuation of male privilege. This dynamic interaction between individuals and society—between self-understandings and cultural beliefs, individual preferences and social practices or institutions—leads to the third "level" of social construction. At this level, construction of reality takes root in our very language, where it establishes the parameters for understanding, defining, and communicating about reality, about who women are, what we are doing, what we desire. Sociological literature refers to this as "the social construction of meaning" and refers to the importance of how we talk about, interpret, and give meaning to things in the world. People, relationships, practices, rituals, and so forth do not have independent existences but rather become meaningful for us through interpretive frameworks. Particularly important is what sociologists call "the social construction of social problems." In their classic article, "Toward a Sociology of Social Problems," Kitsuse and Spector talk about how particular social phenomena get defined *as* problems, and how this is a culturally and historically defined process. Foucault lodged a similar argument in *Discipline and Punish* and *The History of Sexuality*: the way problems get defined *as problems* affects how we think about and see the world, how we define reality.[11]

At this level of social construction—what I will call "the discursive construction of social meaning"—theorists otherwise as varied as Foucault, Derrida, and Lyotard all say (revealing their common Saussurian legacy) that language is not merely the medium through which meaning is communicated; it is constitutive of meaning itself. As Gayatri Spivak says, "We know no world that is not organized as a language, we operate with no other consciousness but one structured as language—languages that we cannot possess, for we are operated by those languages as well."[12] Spivak's point is that language does not merely influence us; it constitutes us. As Judith Butler puts it, "language is not an *exterior medium or instrument* into which I pour a self and from which I glean a reflection of that self"; rather, language constitutes the self.[13] Language sets the conceptual parameters not only to what we think or know (or think we know) but to what it is *possible* to think or know. For without words, we could not have ideas: not only could we not communicate them to others but we would be hard pressed to articulate them to ourselves as Wittgenstein argued.[14] By extension, then, the people having those ideas—"thinking subjects"—are themselves constructed by and through language. We can only be the kinds of persons that our context and language allow. As Stanley Fish argues, there is no "text," no reality independent of and prior to interpretation: "interpretation is the only game in town."[15]

Why should language be important to this process however? Indeed, given that Marx apparently has displayed both aspects of social construction—that ideology distorts reality and that it produces the very conditions it describes—why is it necessary to consider the linguistic dimensions of social construction, which require us to invoke "postmodern" theory (and, as some would say, complicate things unnecessarily)?[16] If we confine ourselves to the first two levels of social construction, we might conclude that men are the constructors, women the constructed, just as, for Marx, capitalists are the constructors, the proletariat are the constructed, who must shake off both the distortion and the created reality. On this view, because our conceptual and material world have been formulated and developed by masculinist perspectives, women are not only often unable to act on their desires but even unable to *formulate* desires, preferences and wills in their own terms, rather than in terms defined and limited by the values of patriarchy. The first two levels invoke a determina-

tive notion of power as domination, or "power over"; the first level of
social construction adheres to the "two faces of power" theorized by
Bachrach and Baratz, which involve forcing someone to do something
you want (or preventing them from doing something you don't want)
them to do.[17] Proscriptions against women's education or women's entry
into certain professions utilize this kind of power: they prevent women
from pursuing options simply because men do not want them to. By contrast, the second level of social construction invokes the "third face of
power" that Steven Lukes articulated, where you may actually get the
other person to want to do what you want them to do, or to think it is in
their interest to do so, even though it objectively is not.[18] For instance,
one could argue that when patriarchal norms convince women to abandon higher education in order to be full-time wives and mothers, women
apparently want to do something that runs contrary to their interests by
making them dependent on men. Presumably, on this view, no woman
would want to be a full-time homemaker once her awareness or consciousness of this situation is raised.

   These conceptions of power depend on notions of interest and of pre-
formed and independently existing subjects. As Peter Digeser describes it,
the first two faces of power (which he combines into one "liberal" conception of power) assume that the mandated course of action runs contrary
to the other person's interests, and favors your own. The third face of
power—the radical conception of power—retains this notion of interests,
but claims that there are objective interests which the individual may not
realize or recognize as her own, but would recognize if this power did not
operate.[19] This kind of power constructs desires in subjects but does so in
a way that retains the concepts and categories discussed in chapter 1 as
essential to most standard conceptions of liberty, namely, intentionality
and purposiveness.[20] By contrast, the "fourth face of power," which characterizes the third level of social construction, engages a different understanding of power, and thereby of freedom. It is not just desires that are
constructed but the entire being of subjects, the individuals who can have
desires, formulate wants, and make choices. Rather than a "mechanism
of repression," that particular agents exercise over others,  power in this
sense is "everywhere." Moreover it is "productive," and is linked to
knowledge or truth. As Foucault puts it:

> In any society, there are manifold relations of power which permeate, charac-
> terize and constitute the social body, and these relations of power cannot
> themselves be established, consolidated nor implemented without the pro-
> duction, accumulation, circulation and functioning of a discourse. There can
> be no possible exercise of power without a certain economy of discourses of

truth which operates through and on the basis of this association. We are subjected to the production of truth through power and we cannot exercise power except through the production of truth.[21]

Foucault does not see power as a dualistic hierarchy, with people at the top constructing those on the bottom, while remaining themselves free from such construction; it is not that men construct women, whites construct people of color, capitalists construct workers. Rather, we are all constructed and constructing, simultaneously and at once. Power should not be conceptualized as a vertical relationship, Foucault suggests, but rather as a circulatory mechanism: "power circulates" through all of us as we are caught in an inescapable web of social relations.[22] Power operates as a "discursive field," which Foucault and Lyotard visualize as a net. We all exist in the net; we live at the "nodal points" of the intersecting lines of the net, from which our power is sent out and through which we receive the effects of others' power.[23] As Nancy Fraser puts it, power is not "a property that could be possessed by some persons or classes and not by others; power is better conceived as a complex, shifting field of relations in which everyone is an element."[24] Thus we are all, "always already" socially constructed, because power is "always, already there," it is not brought into being or exercised by specific individuals over others. Rather, we are all players in the field of power, and we are all played upon as well.[25]

In this, Foucault suggests that power and freedom are not opposed, as they are for Digeser's "liberal" and Lukes's "radical" conceptions of power, and indeed, as they are in most of mainstream Western political theory. For such an opposition suggests, as Digeser notes, "that we could jump outside our social skin to some unsituated arena where power . . . had no play."[26] When feminism portrays social construction as something bad, an expression of power as oppression, the postmodern asks, But what is the alternative? Just as there is no way, in Foucault's view, to be outside power, there is no way out of social construction, no way to be a person and not to be constructed. The idea of "them" constructing "us" is therefore too conspiratorial—or too conscious and active—for men are socially constructed as well as women; they are as much the products of power as they are its agents. The idea that we have been constructed to be a certain way suggests that we are worked upon by another, but if all of us are "always already" constructed and constructing, if we participate in such constructions on a multiplicity of levels and in a variety of ways continuously and constantly, in a "discursive field" of power, then the activity of construction is not something that one necessarily—or even usually—engages in consciously or actively. Indeed, though we all engage in it through specific and particular actions, most of us are unaware of the degree of our participation, or even that we are participating at all. Social construction happens constantly and unobtrusively, in an everyday sort of way, as systems of power, privilege, and oppression replicate themselves through the daily and apparently innocent actions of well-intentioned people who may not be aware of the social significance of their actions.

Another, even more compelling reason why we cannot leave our understanding of social construction at the first two levels is the self-contradictory assumptions it makes about the "subject" of social construction. The claim that men construct women, and that such construction involves an oppressive socialization that patriarchy imposes on women to give them false desires, implies that women can only be persons if such construction does not occur. This view not only tacitly embraces a radically individualist account of "free will," much like that found in the state-of-nature theory of which feminists are so critical, but also suggests that women's desires, wills, and psyches are unaffected in their "essential being" by sexism. It would lead us to maintain, for instance, that women's desires to be mothers are either false desires constructed by patriarchy or true desires that exist naturally despite patriarchy. Both claims simplistically reduce women's desires for children, which are neither biologically natural nor necessarily false consciousness. They would also obviously contradict the second level of social construction: if women are constructed by patriarchal ideology such that we become what it creates, then how can this "person," this "inner core" uncorrupted by patriarchy, exist? The point is, it cannot. As Diana Coole argues, "there is no essentially free subject whose project of liberation would be to throw off the shackles of power that constrain it."[27] And as Nancy Fraser suggests, if "power is in our bodies, not in our heads," then we must eschew "the view that given the appropriate objective material conditions, the only or main thing that stands in the way of social change is people's ideologically distorted perception of their needs and practices."[28]

The conception of social construction implicit in the third level has an additional feminist advantage in that it suggests that men, too, suffer from patriarchy, and they have nothing to lose but their chains in giving it up. It is not that men are the problem and feminism the solution; rather, the problem is patriarchy and we all suffer from it.[29] By recognizing the broad-ranging and far-reaching effects of social construction in our very epistemology and language, the third level of social construction can help those men who feel alienated from feminism because it seems to blame them for women's problems. It can clarify that it is not men per se that feminists are critiquing but the structure of patriarchy, "not . . . some property contained within men but . . . the conventions of power and privilege *constitutive* of gender within an order of male dominance."[30] This realization could help to stimulate such men to start working with women toward resistance of that structure. Social constructivism thus provides a theoretical framework within which a barrier to freedom can be acknowledged even in the absence of assignable agency and also helps us to understand the interaction of "inner" and "outer," to see that "who we are" is a function of the construction of social forms and practices.

## DISCOURSE AND REALITY

If the third level of social construction does all this, however, then why not simply talk about social construction in those terms and leave the first two levels out altogether? If the Marxian materialist versions of social construction, particularly level one's "distortion of reality," is so flawed, why do we need it? And doesn't level three always already incorporate level two? That is, isn't the materialization of and through discourse part and parcel of the discursive understanding of social construction? Unfortunately, the answer is "no," because the phenomenon of "linguistic monism" is still alive and well within postmodern and poststructuralist theory. For instance, if, as Fish asserts, "interpretation is the only game in town," then where do these interpretations come from? From other interpretations, says Fish: more specifically, from an "interpretive culture" that (for lack of a better word) "evolves" historically. As Drucilla Cornell puts it, "All there 'is' are social systems. Systems transform themselves and we who are encompassed by systems are transformed with them."[31] There is nothing "real" underlying the assumptions we have about the world, our intellectual framework for understanding and interpreting "reality"; there are just "other assumptions," all the way down. Other postmodern theorists, such as Lyotard and Derrida, similarly provide fodder for critics' worries about the primacy of discourse and the resulting dissolution of identity into relativist nihilism, as many feminists have noted. If discourse is everything, the common objection runs, then there is no "reality." But then what about the pain and suffering women and other oppressed groups endure? And what happens to feminism if the concept "woman" is simply a discursive entity with no real-presence component that experiences rape or domestic violence? In short, as Butler herself asks, "what about the materiality of the body?"[32] These questions pertain not to social constructivism per se but to the broader tensions between feminism and postmodernism that have been discussed and debated for the past twenty years. But they boil down to a concern with the materiality that the first two levels of social construction represent: the exploitation of women's labor in the home, the discrimination that they experience on the job, their lower pay scales, the violence they suffer, all seem to evaporate if language becomes the primary focus of analysis.[33]

Butler herself actually rejects such criticisms as simplistic—or perhaps reactionary—modernist misreadings and maintains that a poststructuralist vision of social constructivism does not entail linguistic monism. She and Denise Riley argue that postmodernism does not reject the possibility of "woman" as an existence; it simply questions the supposed unity of "woman" as a social category. They say this questioning in itself does not mean that the concept "woman" disappears. Or rather, they suggest, the argument that it does disappear through such questioning should be seen as the result of modernist efforts to retain dualism and hegemony: questioning the category "woman" and positing its multiplicity is a threat only if one requires "woman" to be a unified and universal category.[34] And yet ironically, many postmodernists—particularly poststructuralists—at least tacitly require precisely that when they position women as "sidebars" to the "real" subject of analysis, to wit, men. The Derridean casting of woman as perpetual "Other," for instance, as "a space—an excess of signification . . . rather than as an identity or a sex"—may, as feminists like Alice Jardine assert, provide a powerful challenge to the hegemony of truth claims; but it also, as Rosemary Hennessy points out, "denies feminism's specificity as well as the specificity of other social movements organized around the social construction of difference."[35] In addition, such radical questioning of the meaning of the category "woman" produces a self-contradiction, by ignoring the temporal, cultural, and historical location of postmodern theories. At least implicitly, it takes away the political power of feminism as a critique from "women's" perspective; it ignores the particular ways in which women are oppressed—battery, rape, unequal pay, prostitution—in short, "the concrete material grounds for oppression."[36] It also glosses over the difference between "feminine" and "feminist," the former embodying a state of being that gets represented and constructed in particular ways, the latter being a political positionality that stems from experience linked to identity. The notion that, as "Other," women have no position from which to speak in a sense surrenders to patriarchal power and denies the ways in which women act all the time—in short, it contradicts central tenets of social constructivism. Indeed, though Butler herself claims to attend to such questions of materiality in *Bodies That Matter*, she fails on these very grounds. While her first chapter suggests that she will recognize the body as concrete entity, in the remainder of the book she restates the arguments of *Gender Trouble*. That bodies exist in discourses, she suggests, does not mean they do not exist, only that such existence cannot have a "reality" outside of discourse. But this is a rather weak argument, which begs rather than answers the question of "the body." This question implies precisely the possibility of meaning not fully contained by discourse, which Butler will not allow; or more precisely, since she ostensibly wants to entertain the possibility of the body as concrete, the logic of her framework will not allow it. In this sense, for Butler as for Fish, "interpretation is the only game in town"; she enacts the very linguistic monism that she claims to critique.[37]

As Jean Grimshaw notes, "the danger in some 'deconstructionist' theories . . . is that they seem to leave no space for the material struggles or ordinary aspirations of women."[38] Indeed, as Drucilla Cornell points out, theorists cannot reduce the subject to discursive contextuality without self-contradiction; the "assertion that critique is foreclosed by an all-encompassing context, demands an appeal to a stand beyond context."[39] Even Connolly's theory of freedom, so indebted to poststructuralist ideals of the constructedness of individual desire, nevertheless pins important aspects of freedom on an "ideal of the autonomous person whose central projects are as nearly as possible 'his own,'" an ideal which presupposes some "genuine" core self that lies underneath or beyond its social construction.[40] Thus, although deconstructing the distinction between the individual and the social is vital to feminism's need—and ability—to challenge the false ideal of the unified self, feminists must also hang onto the concrete and empirical consideration of women's lived experience as an important ingredient in political struggle.[41] Viewing power as a "discursive field" where we are all constructors and constructed denies—and even conceivably excuses—the very deliberate and coercive power used by many men against women in situations of domestic violence or sexual harassment, as well as in public policies concerning abortion, reproduction, and welfare. Though women may act within given practices, and though no particular set of men may have constructed those practices any more than particular women have, these practices can be historically and culturally identified as male-produced. Indeed, sometimes specific men *can* be identified as having constructed them—for instance, the politicians who designed welfare reform, the Taliban rulers who sanctioned beating up women who did not wear the burqa—but that does not mean "men" as a universal category produced them. Male privilege and power make it possible for men to establish and participate in practices without making that establishment or participation evident even to themselves.

Indeed, one finds this invisibility of male privilege even in Foucault, the theorist cited most often as a founder of social constructivism and most frequently invoked by feminists. In volume 1 of *The History of Sexuality*, Foucault's critique of the medicalization of sexual perversion and the social construction of sexuality through repression is illustrated by a story of an adult man, a farm hand, who "obtained a few caresses from a little girl" and played a game he calls "curdled milk." This man, who was then "persecuted by town officials," was engaged, according to Foucault, in a "petty" activity, an "everyday occurrence in the life of village sexuality." These "inconsequential bucolic pleaures . . . become the object not only of a collective intolerance but of a judicial action, a medical intervention, a careful clinical examination, and an entire theoretical elaboration."[42] But feminists—as well as men and women who have been the victims of childhood sexual abuse and incest—want to ask: For whom are these pleasures "inconsequential"? Aside from the fact that Foucault conveniently violates his own recommendations about genealogy and historicity—we never learn what counts as a "caress," nor exactly what the suggestively named game of "curdled milk" entails—the perspective of the little girl is completely obliterated.[43] It is a phallocentric construction of sexuality and, furthermore, one in which Foucault disingenuously hides his own moral framework and value system. Indeed, there is a double contradiction: his central notion that power merely "circulates" suggests an inevitable moral neutrality about the use of power, despite his claims to the contrary;[44] yet here Foucault clearly portrays sex per se, regardless of its form, as good and liberatory (or at least harmless)[45] and the reaction of the town officials as bad and oppressive. This would seem to contradict the notion of power as circulatory mechanism, and at the same time to reveal its deep embeddedness in a particular, though not honestly articulated, value system.

In volume 2, *The Use of Pleasure*, Foucault seems to offer a potential recognition of and answer to this problem (though in discussing a different historical epoch), by acknowledging that sexual codes in ancient Greece were "an ethics for men. . . . A male ethics, consequently, in which women figured only as objects. . . . it was an elaboration of masculine conduct carried out from the viewpoint of men in order to give form to *their* behavior," not to women's.[46] But again it is only a code specifically "for men" if one forgets about women as subjects to begin with. Although Foucault recognizes a gendered hierarchy, in which men control themselves but women are controlled by men, he simultaneously argues that in spite of these differentials, there is a "symmetry" between men and women, because of "principles and laws to which they are both subjected in the same way."[47] Thus Foucault notes that "[t]he pleasure that one takes by force is much less agreeable than that which is freely offered. It is the latter pleasure that the wife can give her husband," so "the mistress of the household will always be preeminent over the other women of the household."[48] But this is "true" solely from men's perspective; there is never any attempt to discern what this might mean for women themselves. In the first place, it is not obviously true that pleasure taken by force is less agreeable; indeed, the logic of gender subordination would seem to contradict that, not to mention the logic of rape, where it is precisely the woman's powerlessness and unwillingness that produces pleasure for the attacker. But even granting Foucault's claim, while it is true that some women (and only wives of free male citizens, it should be remembered; Foucault pays no attention to class issues here) may have been able to use sex and their ability to produce male heirs and future citizens to their own advantage, it is also true that in a context where women already have minimal amounts of power, and where their provision of pleasure is part of their civic obligation (to maintain the family and produce citizens, both key to the success of the polis, according to Aristotle), talk of women's giving pleasure "freely" seems disingenuous at best. Indeed, the distinction between "free" women and "slave" women seems to disappear: in order to *be* "free," women have no choice but to serve men's sexual pleasure—in an eerie echo of Rousseau.

These textual examples support my claim that it is important to acknowledge and work with all three "levels" of social construction. Level three reveals the depth of social construction, that it is not simply a superficial socialization process but takes place in our very language, epistemology, and ways of understanding our identity. But levels one and two link discursive understandings to the physical, visceral reality of oppression. One should imagine "levels" in quotation marks, however, because these are not really three entirely distinct processes, one leading to the next in linear fashion. Rather, the three dimensions are intricately intertwined and interdependent. After all, if the epistemology and language available to us are themselves, at least in part, patriarchal constructions premised on women's subordination, then, as Adriana Cavarero argues, "Woman is not the subject of her language. Her language is not hers. She therefore speaks and represents herself in a language not her own, that is, through the categories of the language of the other. She thinks herself as thought by the other."[49] The alienation of women from language, constructed as a reflection of male experience and privilege, means that women have little opportunity within the dominant conceptual frameworks and discourses to critique existing conceptions of women, let alone existing sexist practices, customs, and laws. The language and categories of knowledge available to women are structured to express men's experiences and desires and to obscure, ignore, and deny women's experiences and desires. "Reality" for women becomes constructed as a specifically male reality; but it is, de facto, women's reality as well, because it *is* (the only possible) "reality."

But this does not mean that women are simply victims of men's constructive power. Rather, male power takes on a character that is independent of individual male action and yet at the same time founds and enables men's specific acts and patterns of behavior. As Sharon Marcus argues, patriarchy constitutes various "scripts." For instance, she argues that the prevalence of rape is significantly due to the social construction of femininity that makes women freeze, not resist or fight back, and not protect themselves. In the patriarchal rape "script," women equate rape with annihilation and death, and see the rapist as all-powerful, the penis as indestructible, and rape as inevitable. These beliefs support patriarchy, because they not only disempower women but fuel the rapist's own perceptions of himself as powerful. That is, "The rapist does not simply *have* the power to rape; the social script and the extent to which that script succeeds in soliciting its target's participation help to create the rapist's power." But in order to see "rape as a *process* of sexist gendering," we have to "understand rape as a language" rather than "as the fixed reality of women's lives" or "an identity politics which defines women by our violability."[50] Discourse does not constitute or substitute for the event; rape is a "fact" that "actually" happens to women, and to take linguistic forms as "metaphors for the rape itself . . . occludes the gap between the threat and the rape—the gap in which women can try to intervene, overpower and deflect the threatened action."[51] But discourse is an important framework for understanding and reacting to events. Indeed, by changing the discourse we can re-see and redefine the event: "To understand rape in this way is to understand it as subject to change."[52] In particular, by seeing rape differently, women who are attacked may be able to respond differently and defend themselves more effectively. Changing discourse is thus a vital entry point for changing the social construction of rape, and thereby of women as victims and men as predators. Material changes and discursive changes occur interactively and complementarily.

Thus the three "levels" of social construction I describe do not translate into an image of a three-storied building with a spiraling staircase, but rather something resembling a painting by M. C. Escher. In Escher's paintings, we seem to have stairs that lead up or down, but they really lead up only to end by leading down, appearing first right-side up and then upside down—appearances which in turn will change depending on one's position vis-à-vis the picture. In the same sense, the different levels of social construction lead into and out of one another, and whenever we try to position ourselves within them, we may find that in fact we are standing on our heads.

Awareness of these different levels and their relation to one another helps reveal that all three levels are present in most social constructivist theories, even those that ostensibly appear to operate at only one of the three levels. Take, for example, Catherine MacKinnon, who can be seen as one of the foremost advocates of the position that social construction is something that men do to women, and it is both bad and false. Specifically, she is generally read as arguing that men create, construct, define, and police women's sexuality through the implementation of power structures that serve men's sexual and psychological interests. Pornography—which she links with other practices, such as domestic violence, rape, prostitution, and sexual harassment—provides a discourse on sexuality that fosters and facilitates men's power over women. More precisely, it defines women as not only subordinate but freely subordinate, that is, as freely choosing their subordination—a clever combination, she suggests, of the sexual slavery she asserts is common to male fantasy and the modernist liberal ideology of the democratic state based on consent. MacKinnon says that the patriarchal discourse takes on a life of its own and becomes reality; "women" are defined in language as creatures who wish to be raped, beaten, and humiliated. Women themselves take on this meaning as well, she argues, as evidenced by women who are in the pornography or prostitution businesses without apparent coercion, or by battered women who have the opportunity to escape but do not take it. It is not only that women are "defined" as such beings by a "discourse" that lies outside of us. If that were the case, women could, in theory, simply step back from masculinist discourse and reject its definitions (after all, it's "only language"). Rather, this definition has concrete effects, experienced as violence, as rape, and even according to MacKinnon, as pornography.[53]

Indeed, more than that, she asserts, language *is* concrete, it does not merely have concrete "effects." MacKinnon's strong version of social construction—what we might call "social-construction-as-domination"—depends on the totality of masculine domination, not only in deed but thought and word as well. Accordingly, in direct contrast to Marcus, she marks no differentiation between what physically happens to a woman in a film and the film itself. A "snuff" film in which women are actually murdered has the same status as a big-budget Hollywood film in which high-tech special effects allow murders to be simulated without (what most people would consider) physical harm to the actors or actresses. And both of these have the same status as a blue-jeans ad provocatively displaying a woman's posterior or an advertising billboard displaying a badly bruised woman who claims to be "Black and Blue by the Rolling Stones and I love it!" MacKinnon says that the "physical harm" of the murder in the snuff film is the same as its representation. More strongly, she claims that the "physical harm" of the murder in the Hollywood film is no different from the "physical harm" to a woman murdered by her spouse who has been (subconsciously?) "influenced" by a film that "only represented" such a murder. And neither is the "physical harm" produced by the Rolling Stones billboard different from the "harm" to a woman beaten by a boyfriend who has taken such advertisements as daily micro-reinforcers of a more general and pervasive cultural belief that it is men's prerogative to hurt women.[54] In all of these, MacKinnon asserts, the "rep-

resentation" is as bad as the "real thing." Indeed, there is no differentiation between the two, because the "representation" *becomes* reality; it
becomes definitive of a world in which it is not only acceptable, but even
a positive good to brutalize women. This is most fully realized in snuff
films, where the supposed distinction between representation and reality
collapses completely.

But here again, we see the intertwining of the three levels of social construction. For though MacKinnon might wish to deny it—and certainly
many feminist postmoderns would too, since MacKinnon for them is the
quintessential reductive humanist or liberal feminist—the Foucaultian elements in her argument are pronounced. Like Foucault, MacKinnon suggests that discourse and action are one, or if not exactly one, then so
intimately intertwined that they cannot be separated coherently. Accordingly, in Mackinnon's framework, legislative prescriptions to protect pornography actresses more completely from physical injury, leaving in place
the bigger-budget special effects Hollywood murder, in which the actress
is not "really" harmed, deny that the latter has an equally powerful and
harmful epistemic and political—and hence physical—effect on women's
freedom. As Foucault might say, the dominant discourse of pornography
"disciplines" women through the "tyranny" of its "globalizing" effects.[55]

At the same time, Foucault's and Butler's emphasis on discourse—their
level-three orientation toward social construction, which we might call
"social-construction-as-everywhere"—demonstrates more overlap with
MacKinnon's view than either seems to want to acknowledge. For instance, Foucault and Butler argue that even the most intimate and supposedly "internal" aspects of our being, such as our sexuality, must be understood in terms of the historical relations and actions that have imported
meaning to our bodies.[56] In his three-volume *History of Sexuality*, Foucault performs a detailed analysis of how ideas of sexuality—and hence
sexuality itself—altered in different historical contexts. Obviously, if sexuality were "natural," a concrete "given," this alteration could not occur.
As Butler says, "If sexuality is culturally constructed within existing
power relations, then the postulation of a normative sexuality that is 'before,' 'outside,' or 'beyond' power is a cultural impossibility and a politically impracticable dream, one that postpones the concrete and contemporary task of rethinking subversive possibilities for sexuality and identity
within the terms of power itself."[57] Foucault and Butler do not mean to
separate "sexuality" as a political identity from physical pleasure and the
body that feels it: bodies, they argue, are socially constructed, because
they, too, enter language and are subjects of discourse. Biology itself
would seem to be socially constructed, since it exists, is studied and understood, in the context of discourse. The "concrete reality" of a body does
not have that "reality" independent of how we see it, think about it, talk

about it, write about it. Even our physical sense of the body is constructed through social practice, as Foucault and Butler have explored in the case of the transsexual Herculin Barban. Thus, the meaning of "who we are" is, in every sense—sexual, physical, biological, generic, racial, economic—constructed through and by context; as speaking, thinking subjects, our subjectivity is socially constructed. There is no "self" outside this "power."[58]

But this, of course, is the very same position taken by those who focus on the second level of social construction: that ideology is materialized into concrete reality, a point that Butler herself actually emphasizes in the final chapter of *Bodies That Matter*. There, Butler argues for a strategy of political resistance through adoption of the term "queer," which involves an ironic parodying of the dominant conception of homosexuality, and derives its power from the fundamental belief that heteropatriarchy misunderstands and misdescribes who and what gays are.[59] But as the first level of social construction suggests, the notion of misdescription presupposes a further notion of what gays "really are." Despite her rejection of a prediscursive material reality—which might suggest a commitment to level three as the only meaningful sense of social construction—Butler's concluding arguments about the use of the term "queer" as an empowering political positioning tacitly rely on the first two levels of social construction as much as the third: heteropatriarchy distorts the reality of gay identity, and simultaneously produces it, makes it real, through homophobic and heterosexist practices, laws, and policies. But both the distortion and the (re)creation are premised on the underlying assumption that homosexual identity is prior to, or outside of, such discourses.

## THE SOCIAL CONSTRUCTION OF FREEDOM

This detour into postmodern theory may leave the reader asking what all this has to do with the concept of freedom. The answer is that social construction affects two key aspects of freedom: choice and subjectivity. Social construction sets the parameters for choice, in two senses. First, it determines what choices are available; customs, laws, and practices make certain options possible and foreclose others. For instance, the United States' funding policies have made space travel possible, but illnesses such as diabetes still ravage the lives of millions of children and adults; the technology of our military weapons produces guided cruise missiles, but millions of people throughout the world starve to death each year; scientists can fertilize an ovum in a test tube and select an embryo for implantation that has a specific genetic composition desired by the parents, but millions of women in the United States and abroad are forced to bear unwanted children every year because of the lack or ineffectiveness of birth control and the unavailability of safe abortion. Oftentimes, we tend to accept the options that are available with a shrug—if other options are not available, then they are just not available; the limitations we face are a function of nature, or the inadequacy of knowledge. But social constructivism requires us to consider the "why" of availability, and funding policy decisions are an important factor. After all, space flight at one time was considered to violate the laws of physics, but in fact it simply shows that our previous understanding of physics, and of humans' physical limitations, was inadequate. History has shown time and again how increased knowledge overcomes obstacles that were previously seen as insurmountable and inevitable, and the latter half of the twentieth century showed us that public funding is vital to speeding up the process of developing knowledge.

As a function of the social choices that we make, the fact that certain options are available and others are not is thus a social construction in the most obvious, tangible sense. The availability of options relates most obviously to the concept of restraint or barrier, which is also socially constructed in this same sense. In some cultures, for instance, women are prohibited by law and custom from having sexual relations with men of their choice; they are forbidden from pursuing education or professional careers; birth control and abortion are outlawed. Since such barriers are culturally variable, they would appear to be socially constructed in the most obvious sense. They are not "natural" or "inevitable" but rather reflect cultural assumptions of how women should behave and, derivatively, of the social meaning and significance of femininity, that is, what it means to be a "woman" in particular contexts: in short, the ideological construction (or misrepresentation) of reality. But choices are discursively constructed as well; whether particular social formations are defined as barriers, what social arrangements seem "natural," what possibilities can be imagined, are historically and culturally variable, pertaining more to language and differing understandings of reality. Hence, women who choose to wear the chador or head scarf as a mark of cultural membership, or to demonstrate a solidarity of political resistance, may not view cultural sanctions against those who do not veil as a barrier to their liberty. By contrast, Westerners who read about the enveloping burqa that Afghan women wear (not to mention the Taliban beating up women for showing their ankles) will be likely to assume that veiling restricts women's liberty. Similarly, Western women who view cosmetics as a boost to their self-esteem, or as a fun expression of individuality, can be viewed in other cultural contexts (or within other frameworks in the West, as Benson illustrated) as enslaved by sexist exploitation of their sexuality. Rather than concluding from such differences that claims of freedom and unfreedom are simply relative, however, and thus unavailable to those outside a specific context, social constructivism provides a conceptual vocabulary for interrogating various contexts in order to understand how barriers are created, understood, and defined by and within specific contexts, and hence how options and choices are created, understood, and defined.

Accordingly, social construction also relates to the conditions for making choices and to the understanding of what counts as a choice. That is, not just the choices or options available, not just the variable interpretations of the significance of those options, but the very meaning of the concept of "choice" itself is defined and articulated differently in different contexts. Some choices, though apparently voluntary, may be seen as illegitimate; indeed, they may not be seen as choices at all. For instance, many Westerners assume that any veiled Muslim woman is veiled because she is oppressed, that no one who had a choice in the matter would choose to be covered in such a manner. Hence, the agency of women who choose the veil is negated. Many people would also consider the choice of a battered woman to stay with her abuser similarly illegitimate, assuming that a woman in an abusive relationship has so little sense of self that she cannot possibly know what she really wants. Because of culturally variable—though generally masculinist—conceptions of the "self" who is the choice-making subject, women's choices may be delegitimated and ignored. Or conversely, women may be seen as making a choice when they have been forced in a particular direction, such as when politicians characterize single mothers on public assistance as "welfare queens." Not just women's actual choices and how they interpret them, but the conceptual parameters of what "counts" as a choice, are constructed by and through language, cultural norms, and patriarchal assumptions about what it means to be an individual and a person.

Understanding how choice is socially constructed similarly requires a consideration of desire. As argued in chapter 1, the meaning of freedom cannot be left simply at the "objective" level of options available but must include consideration of subjective preferences, or desire. The social construction of desire, however, is even more complex and difficult to discern. What we desire will always be influenced and shaped by social context; desire is itself socially constructed. And yet desire may be the most "internal" aspect of liberty. Certainly, some desires must be universal—to drink when we are thirsty, for instance, is a basic biological urge, all humans will die if they do not consume liquids. However, even "biological urges" are socially mediated responses to socially constructed contexts and stimuli: Why do people in different cultures find different things beautiful and ugly? Why are men and women often sexually aroused by different kinds of stimuli, and why does this vary among cultures? Why do people from different cultures desire and enjoy different kinds of foods and flavors? All of these preferences are "biological"—I like salmon because it tastes good to me—but they are also socially situated—if I lived in a culture that eschewed oily fish or was strictly vegetarian, this same fish might well repulse me. Or conversely, consider the taste for whale blubber among Inuits, a food that most people in the mainland United States would balk at. Such taste preferences are not simply cultural prejudice: wherever we grow up, certain kinds of tastes develop in response to cultural practices, available foods, and moral beliefs, and we have physical responses to foods that are culturally mediated and produced. My preferences, tastes, desires, and wants are thus socially constructed at the second level: they materialize into "biology."

Of course, most desires and preferences are not even biological in this sense, and hence are even more strongly subject to social construction. And yet they may be no less difficult to analyze in terms of the relationship between internal and external. For instance, if a battered woman desires to stay with her abusive mate, how should that desire be evaluated and understood? Should it simply be taken at face value, because feminism is dedicated to respect for women's autonomy and therefore must oppose any effort to second-guess their desires and choices? Should it be rejected, because violence and living in oppressive conditions are by definition antithetical to freedom? Our answer to such questions will turn on our ability to understand the ways in which that desire has been constructed. What are the social-contextual conditions that led the woman to formulate this desire, and does uncovering those conditions allow a reconsideration and reevaluation of that desire from a critical perspective? For instance, does her desire stem from her economic dependency, because her husband forced her to quit working so that he could exert greater control over her? Does it stem from skepticism that the criminal justice system can protect her? Does it stem from love for him and faith in his claims that he will never hurt her again? Are some of those reasons for her choice more legitimate than others, and if so, why? Understanding the social context for choice, and how individuals' particular histories lead them to particular desires, is important to evaluating the freedom of choices that are desired and made, but it is also important to understanding the meaning of the desires that motivate the choices in the first place. Women's desires— for security and safety, for love, for independence, for their children's happiness, for a successful marriage, for economic well-being—are the result of many social forces and factors. And yet different women in similar situations may want radically different things. What are the "external" factors that account for these different desires, and how can they be identified? How can their influence on these particular desires be traced? Answering these questions requires a detailed explication of circumstance, the Foucaultian "archeology" and "genealogy" that allows for in-depth but specifically located analysis.

The problem with such analysis, of course, is that when dealing with social phenomena like domestic violence or welfare, feminists want and need to come up with broad-based understandings of social construction that can account for the ways in which large numbers of otherwise very different women are treated in the same way, and to establish that this sameness is part of the social construction of femininity. That is, individual women are constructed through broad social categories of gender, as well as race, class, and sexuality. In order to understand individual desire we need to locate desires in the broader contexts of social categories that are also socially constructed. As Wendy Brown puts it, "while gender *identities* may be diverse, fluid, and ultimately impossible to generalize, particular modes of gender *power* may be named and traced with some precision at a relatively general level."[60] It is important to a feminist understanding of freedom that we be able to understand how "patriarchy"—not just unique individual circumstances, but broad social forces—constructs women as desiring subjects. If we acknowledge that not just particular actions within given practices, or even particular practices within given contexts, but entire contexts themselves can present barriers to women's freedom, then under a contextual theory of freedom it would follow that some contexts will be better and freer for women than others. Certainly, we always live in contexts, and those contexts always socially construct the people who live in them. But the contexts that construct the choosing subject are not necessarily neutral in a relativist sense. Rather, contexts contain conditions that empower some people and restrict others.

What I have argued in the past several paragraphs may once again sound like level-one social construction—something that men do to women, not seeing how men themselves are similarly constructed. But my argument must be understood in the context of the complicated understanding of power that Foucault has brought to critical theory. Recognizing that no specific group—not even wealthy white males—has control over the system of patriarchy and male privilege through which social construction operates, we can still point out that certain positionalities have more and less power within the grid. For instance, as Foucault points out, doctors have more power over patients than vice versa, but that does not mean that the doctor controls the medical practice in which he operates (as managed care made clear to most Americans at the end of the twentieth century), nor that the patient is powerless and does not affect the doctor's construction in turn. But Foucault also wants us to realize that the doctor does have *more* power than the patient within the medical setting, that the power the doctor has is often intertwined with "domination," or what Benn called "power over."[61] The same can be said about men and women; that (holding steady for race and class for the moment) although women participate in the construction of reality daily in myriad ways and on multiple levels, under patriarchy men have more power to participate in affecting the terms of social construction. Through their individual actions they can access and perpetuate the privilege that larger social forces give them. Social construction differentiates, and yet sees the connections, between the individual sexist actions of particular individuals—the local or "micro" forces—and the larger, "macro" social structures that make those actions possible. When a man rapes a woman, he does not "construct patriarchy," but his actions derive their power from, and in turn contribute to, patriarchal power. He participates in the construction at the same time that his actions are made possible by the construction and by his positioning within the network of patriarchal power. Indeed, as Marcus implies, what makes individual acts of sexual violence so powerful is precisely their location within this larger construct of gender and sexuality. That is why Marcus suggests that changing the discourse of rape is key to women's ability to successfully resist its practice.

It is in this much broader sense that patriarchal contexts can be seen as socially constructed barriers to women's freedom and personhood, for the social and political structures of patriarchy are premised on women's subservience to men, on the denial and obliteration of their humanity. Hence, the reason that such strategies as Marcus articulates—that is, for changing the "script" of rape—have such potential is that they challenge the broader contexts within which rape occurs as a means to disempower the singular and immediate event. Far from accepting contexts as given and focusing on particular practices within the context, such strategies challenge the context by challenging the assumptions that underlie the practices, and in that way changing the practices themselves. Feminism allows us to deconstruct the "self-evident" and "natural" claims of modernist ideologies as the social constructions of particular times, histories, contexts, classes, races, and genders. And this recognition enables us to make comparisons: a woman who is not abused is freer than one who is; a woman who is able to obtain an abortion when she wants it is freer than one who cannot; a woman who can be open about her sexuality without fearing professional repercussions is freer than one who must hide it. These evaluative conclusions are explicitly political: social construction is about power, and hence about politics.

## THE PARADOX OF SOCIAL CONSTRUCTION

The importance of contexts for freedom suggests two somewhat opposing points: on the one hand, because our conceptual and material world has been formulated and developed by masculinist perspectives, women are restrained at a fundamental level, even in our epistemology—in how we know what we know, in the parameters of what it is possible to know, in the linguistic possibilities for imagining and naming alternate possibilities and choices. If freedom involves the ability not only to pursue my desires and preferences but to define myself, and hence my desires and preferences; if such definition must logically require a context in and through which such definition and my "self" can occur; and if this definition is more difficult for women within a masculinist epistemology and language, as it is for people of color within a white epistemology and language, and lesbians and homosexuals within a heterosexual epistemology and language—then this greater difficulty means that women and other "excluded others" are less free within these respective contexts, and within the terms of white masculinist discourse itself. In this light, the very contexts within which women live pose constraints on freedom. The "strong evaluation" central to positive-liberty theory needs to be reconceptualized so as to be applied to contexts themselves, and not merely to individuals or even to conditions, situations, or actions *within* those contexts.

On the other hand, however, language, meaning, identity, and choice are made possible by whatever context exists. If self-definition and the construction of meaning always take place in and through language, it follows that women have participated in that language and responded to it throughout history with our own practices. We are who we are because of our contexts, even if it is a patriarchal one, and hence those contexts make freedom possible. How can women reject patriarchal discourse if we have participated in its construction and it makes us what we are? Indeed, if patriarchy constructs us all, men and women alike, to a totalizing extent (as Foucault puts it) that includes language and epistemology, how can we ever know that we are constructed? How can women ever think (let alone "know") that we are not what patriarchy says we are? How can we ever figure out who "we" are or what "we want" if the language and concepts we must use are antagonistic to the enterprise we seek to carry out, that is, are themselves barriers to women's freedom? How is it possible to talk about "women" outside of the conceptual vocabulary patriarchy provides?

Jacques Derrida articulates this very paradox in *The Margins of Philosophy*. He argues that deconstruction can occur in one of two ways. First, it can occur "internally" to a particular construct or system, "by using against the edifice the instruments or stones available in the house, that is, equally, in language." But in this "internal" strategy, "one risks ceaselessly confirming, consolidating, *relifting*, at an always more certain depth, that which one allegedly deconstructs." The second, "external" strategy, requires that we "decide to change terrain, in a discontinuous and irruptive fashion, by brutally placing oneself outside, and by affirming an absolute break and difference." However, this strategy involves a dual risk; not only "inhabiting more naively and more strictly than ever the inside one declares one has deserted," via the *illusion* that one has achieved an "external" position, but also *"the simple practice of language ceaselessly reinstates the new terrain on the oldest ground."*[62] That is, Derrida suggests, one *cannot* place oneself outside of the context one seeks to deconstruct, because one cannot accomplish such deconstruction without language, and without the context which gives language meaning; and yet one *must* do so in order to see that we are constructed by it, and that such construction is so total and "totalizing."

Similarly, the argument that patriarchy involves an epistemology and language that pervade women's very being, their self-conceptions and desires, is powerful and persuasive; and yet its totalizing effects paradoxically allow women no possibility of seeing themselves in any other way. For such an argument must either be made within the context of patriarchy, in which case its claims cannot logically make sense; or by a radical attempt to step outside of patriarchy, which blinds us to the ways in which we still support and reinforce it. Feminists need the idea of social construction to deconstruct our identity within male-dominated cultures, to identify the ways in which patriarchy has limited not only our options and choices but our self-conceptions. It is only through a notion of social construction that we can critically engage in all its complexity the complicated and multilayered imbrication of women in the choices we seem to make "freely" and yet which are structured for us through systems of power over which we have little control. Yet social constructivism also appears to make such deconstruction impossible by taking away the politicalness of identity; it undermines the possibility of our existence as "women," let alone as "feminists."

One answer to this apparent paradox is that the reality that is shaped and limited by patriarchy can never be totally subsumed by it, so that women always interact with and in it to create a reality that is somewhat at odds with the ideology. For instance, if patriarchy prevents women from becoming educated and instead requires women to learn embroidery, it would seem that patriarchy inhibits women's liberty on a variety of levels, most grandly by preventing them from developing reasoning skills and learning about the world. But at the same time, while embroidery may be discounted as a frivolous occupation by patriarchal discourse, it also provides the opportunity for artistic creation, space for contemplation that may yield profound insights about the human condition, or conversation with other women that, even if it is correctly labeled "gossip," may lead to relationships of solidarity and the communication of alternate (or even "subalternate") knowledge, as de Beauvoir suggested.[63]

A second answer is that patriarchy is not the only "macro" structure that constructs us. Systems of race and class, to name only the two most obvious, also operate conjointly with gender, and at times conflict with and contradict one another. Hence, a wealthy white woman may have powers within white patriarchy that a poor black man does not have. Race and class can work to compound the effects of sexism, as we see particularly in social practices like public assistance, but they can also work to ameliorate or even counteract their effects as well. Indeed, none of these systems can be said to work linearly; for example, it is not always the case that a wealthy woman is freer than a poor man, or that a white woman is freer than a black man, nor is it the case that all women are less free than all men. Similarly, there are considerable differences among women themselves. These differences often cleave to lines of race, class, and sexuality, but not always; the lines are not determinative. In this sense, "totalization" takes on a different meaning than is commonly assumed. If we imagine a box filled with round balls, we can cover the balls "totally" by pouring concrete into the box, solidifying the balls into permanent place within the box. Or, we could put a cloth over the box, completely covering the balls but maintaining space between the balls, which permits them to rotate, move, and shift when the box is jostled. Though many people assume that Foucault intends the first sense of "totality," I believe that the second sense is the only one consistent with his writings. For in this latter sense, if the context in which we live (the box) is shifted or altered, we, and our possibilities of action and self-definition, can similarly change our position in the context, our understanding of who we are and what we want, of what we can and desire to do.

Finally, acknowledging the disparities in powers of production and creation *within* the processes of social construction allows us to identify, locate, and name the ways in which men have power to define women, and to see that gender is a broad system, interactive with yet distinct from other systems like race and class, within which women are constructed. For instance, noticing that most instances of domestic violence are cases where men hit women, or documenting that women are the primary recipients of welfare, or that women are excluded from the public realm and economic power may not in itself produce any sort of analytic or moral conclusions about freedom; but it does provide the basis for asking different kinds of questions about the workings of those systems, and about the assumptions underlying them, that can produce a clearer understanding of freedom. While recognizing that we all participate in social construction, identifying disparities in this process yields a further recognition that we participate unevenly, that such disparities are systematic, and that there is a loose pattern to how social construction takes place.

These ways of engaging the question of freedom through social construction are what lead me to focus on the practical problems of domestic violence, welfare, and Islamic veiling. These very concrete experiences are central to women's lives within patriarchy, and they are central to women's liberty within patriarchy as well, in both the negative and positive senses. In the following chapters I will show the ways in which these experiences are part of larger practices that cohere with patriarchal society and values and yet provide contexts for women's agency, subjectivity, and choices. These social phenomena show that the arguments for expanding the concept of external barrier, and along with it the concept of negative liberty, are justified and needed. But they also illustrate the ways in which individual women, and along with them cultural meanings of womanhood and femininity, are constructed so as to foreclose certain choices and possibilities altogether. And in this, these three phenomena demonstrate the need to look at internal barriers and the ways that the inner self is constructed by a productive and oppressive externality. The experiences discussed here reveal that choices are so deeply, fundamentally, and complexly constrained and constructed for women—even more than they are for men—that the conventional understandings of liberty and of constraint found in the positive/negative debate are inadequate to address women's experiences.

*Chapter Four*

# INTERNAL AND EXTERNAL RESTRAINT: THE CASE OF BATTERED WOMEN

ON ITS FACE, domestic violence might seem an awkward place to begin an argument that all three levels of social construction are needed to understand women's freedom, for physical abuse would seem to be a clear-cut case of domination. For instance, has Susan, the abused woman from chapter 1, made a "free" decision if she returns to her husband? The answer might seem a rather straightforward "no." Susan's sister Sarah certainly thinks Susan is unfree; she wants Susan to press charges. The pattern of Susan's husband's behavior—violent attack followed by flowers, gifts, and apologetic messages in which he promises to change—is by now familiar to Sarah. In fact, this is the third time in two years that Susan has decided to return to her husband after a violent incident. Sarah thinks Susan should go to the battered-women's shelter and take advantage of its resources, such as psychotherapy and job training. Sarah believes that Susan's reluctance to leave her husband is grounded in fear of being alone, of not being able to make it on her own, and an even greater fear that she deserves the abuse. But Sarah has been unable to get Susan to admit to such feelings, let alone to realize that they are unfounded. The local battered-women's advocacy group is now lobbying the state legislature for a law mandating arrest and prosecution for domestic violence. This would guarantee that the abuser is put in jail whether or not the woman pressed charges herself. Sarah supports this effort and sees it as Susan's only hope to be free of abuse.

It seems obvious to feminists and nonfeminists alike that violence is the quintessential barrier to freedom, particularly from the negative-liberty perspective. The use of physical force in the state of nature was the major limitation on natural man's freedom and motivated the move into civil society via the social contract. Laws were instituted to protect men from other men's interference, thereby preserving more securely in society the very same freedom—albeit in a more limited degree—that man sought to enjoy in the state of nature, but which natural law could not sufficiently sustain. Admittedly, as I argued in chapter 2, Rousseau and Kant went further with the notion of law and its relationship to freedom, but it would be difficult to imagine even the sexist Rousseau praising a citizen for beating up his Sophie, even after she reveals her affair with another man.[1] Such a view of violence as a straightforward external barrier would probably exclude a social construction argument altogether: violence simply prevents me from doing what I want. But of course positive liberty is relevant as well; for violence is similarly irreconcilable with realizing the true self. Indeed, Sarah's advocacy of mandatory arrest, by taking choice out of Susan's hands in her own best interest, shares positive liberty's tendency to second-guess. And since emotional and psychological abuse generally precedes, and always accompanies, physical abuse, a more complete understanding of domestic abuse would have to include inner barriers. But even allowing for this, it might well seem that the only level of social construction involved here would be the first, the ideological misrepresentation of reality—social construction as domination, power as "power over."

It is my contention, however, that domestic violence illustrates in a particularly complicated way the interaction of the three levels in the social construction of choice and the choosing subject. Domestic violence presents a particularly strong insight into the social construction of choice: not only what a woman's possible options are, which "doors" are "open," and how those options are materially constructed through social relations that produce and constrain economic, political, and social power and opportunity, but also what the conceptual parameters are to different definitions of choice, how certain actions are or are not considered "genuine" choice, and hence, how individuals are constructed as "choosing subjects" along lines of gender as well as race and class. To defend this claim, however, we need to understand battering in a larger context than an individual relationship between a man and a woman, even if such relationships are its starting point.

Saying this does not exclude the possibility of female-on-male violence or lesbian and homosexual battering. The latter two will be discussed further on in this chapter, but I should explain why I focus primarily on male-on-female domestic violence here, since it might seem to skew my argument in favor of the conclusion that patriarchy underwrites the social phenomenon of domestic violence. The main reason for my focus is that the prevalence of female-on-male violence is extremely difficult to gauge, for few reliable and broad-ranging studies have been done on it. In 1978, Suzanne K. Steinmetz argued that there was a "battered husband syndrome," suggesting that "the percentage of wives having used physical violence often exceeds that of the husbands."[2] It was immediately argued that Steinmetz misread her own data, which did not support her claims.[3] She also failed to account for differentials in strength and resulting injury; men were rarely injured in the incidents she counted, while women were often severely hurt.[4] She therefore similarly failed to acknowledge that because of differences in strength and injury, men are not afraid of women or intimidated by their violence. Such inequities exacerbate the dangers to women while creating a mask of mutuality and a myth of women's power that doubly protects men.[5] Even so, subsequent studies by some of the pioneers of research into family violence, such as Murray Straus and Richard Gelles,[6] though more nuanced in their claims about husband battering, were subject to similar methodological criticisms. More recent studies from the National Violence Against Women survey (NVAW), the National Crime Victimization Survey (NCVS) from the Bureau of Justice Statistics (BJS) (both of these studies included FBI Uniform Crime Report data), and the National Family Violence Survey (NFVS) suggest that females do commit violence against male partners, though these studies differ considerably in their numerical findings. In 1992 NCVS found that 7.6 per 1,000 women were assaulted annually by an intimate partner in comparison to 1.4 men (in addition to 1 per 1,000 women sexually assaulted versus no numbers for men), whereas the NVAW survey in 1996 found 3.2 per 1,000 women raped or sexually assaulted by an intimate and 44.2 women and 31.5 men per 1,000 physically assaulted. NFVS reported (for 1985) that men and women were equally assaulted, at a rate of 11 to 12 percent.[7] The National Alcohol and Family Violence Survey, which depended in part on NFVS data, reported even higher overall rates of intimate violence than these other studies, and indicated that more men than women were intimately assaulted.

As Patricia Tjaden and Nancy Thoennes point out, however, it is once again difficult to interpret such discrepancies because of differences in sample design and interview techniques. (For example, NFVS asked "how many times in the past 12 months has violence been experienced?" whereas NVAW asked "whether" violence had occurred; NVAW counted only victims' experiences, whereas NFVS counted perpetrators' experiences as well.) Tjaden and Thoennes made a significant observation, however, that the more serious the assault, the greater was the rate of male-on-female violence in comparison to female-on-male assault: whereas "women were two to three times more likely than men to report that an intimate partner threw something at them . . . or pushed, grabbed, or shoved them," they were "7 to 14 times more likely to report that an intimate partner beat them up, choked, or tried to drown them, or threatened them with a gun."[8] This is not to say that women do not sometimes inflict injuries on men, despite average disparities in size and strength, but since most men are stronger than most women, it is not surprising that more women are injured. Furthermore, it does seem at least ironic that one of the key traditional foundations of masculine claims to superiority—superior physical strength—is suddenly forgotten in the effort to undermine one of the key movements to fight women's oppression and destabilize patriarchal power. Claims that feminists misrepresent the reality of domestic violence and that men are victimized as frequently as women, if not more so, are at least suspect. Indeed, claims of reverse victimization are a classic defense maneuver of abusive men, who often divest themselves of responsibility for their violence by shifting blame onto women. After all, men have dominated research agendas in universities since the advent of contemporary social science, so the fact that feminist research into woman battering has initiated a backlash interest in husband battering—along with severe criticisms of feminists for failing to put husband battering at the top of their agenda—should similarly be viewed with skepticism.

At the same time, however, female violence against male partners should not be uncritically dismissed: after all, the National Violence Against Women survey found higher rates of both male and female intimate assault than the other studies. Even taking the NCVS's lowest estimate of 1.4 men per thousand victimized by assault, and even if the majority of these assaults are self-defensive or noninjurious, that still leaves room for the possibility that some men are seriously abused in unprovoked, aggressive attacks by their female partners. Furthermore, precisely because of socially constructed definitions of masculinity, it is possible that men do not report serious assaults by their female partners because of the fear of ridicule and social stigma; and there are no shelters for battered men from which numbers could be anonymously obtained. So even if husband abuse exists relatively infrequently, it is still a serious problem that should be of concern to feminists. Why to feminists? Because even if committed by women, such violence is still a function of patriarchy, of the ways in which gender relations between men and women are constructed by and through power. Sexism may create stigma for male victims as much as it does for female victims, even if the specific features of that stigma differ by gender. Such stigma may prevent policymakers and legislators from recognizing the seriousness of female-on-male battering, because it threatens an idealized image of masculine power, just as female victimization was denied for many years because confronting it posed an implicit challenge to masculine power and authority within the family. Indeed, patriarchy may actually motivate female-on-male violence, not because women are seeking to assume a masculine role but rather because the unequal distribution of power under patriarchy constructs families into institutions where justice does not operate, where mutual respect is not expressed. Despite the power of gender role socialization and identification, the patterns of behavior and interaction that children observe between their parents is not reductively gendered; an adult woman who as a child observed her mother abused by her father may understandably have considerable anger and fear that translate into violence against her partner when under stress, just as a man who grew up in similar circumstances might, for instance, be afraid of his own masculinity as a potentially destructive force and hence not defend himself against attack.

Such patterns are not the dominant norm, however. Most of the statistical studies that I will discuss below—studies conducted by the United States Department of Justice, the American Medical Association, and many international organizations, all which could be labeled "feminist" only by extreme, misogynist ideologues—found that the vast majority of intimate assaults are perpetrated by men against women. It is the seriousness of this situation that determines my focus. Even Straus, Gelles, and Steinmetz, despite their questionable claims about husband abuse, maintain that violence is least likely to occur in egalitarian marriages.[9] And inegalitarian heterosexual relationships overwhelmingly favor men. Men have resources often not available to women: economic and earning power (men are paid more than women in part because they are men), legal power (men as a group make laws and social policy because they hold the vast majority of official decision-making positions), and social power (male privilege is a normalized dimension of most societies throughout the world). But the dominance of norms cannot negate altogether the possibility of contrary patterns. As many feminists are wont to insist, women have always exercised power throughout history. The most troubling aspect of studies claiming the prevalence of husband abuse is not the assertion that women may be violent but rather the patent intent to erase gender from consideration altogether; to put forth the view that violence is simply "one person attacking another person," which somewhat naturalizes and justifies violence as an inevitable dimension of human relationships. Though the effort to attain gender neutrality is a recognizable and important strain of contemporary feminism, the *apparent* gender neutrality of such arguments instead displays a misogynistic tone and agenda that seeks to discredit and delegitimize feminist efforts to recognize that relations of gender are structured by and through power. That not all persons identified as masculine wield this power, and that some persons identified as feminine access it, does not change its fundamentally gendered character: the power is built on social categories of male and female that subjugate the latter to the former and allow the use of violence as a legitimate mode of reinforcement.

Thus, I take an open-minded position on the possibility of husband abuse; though I clearly believe that the power of male privilege in all other aspects of social life makes it extremely unlikely that it is as prevalent as wife abuse. Whatever the possible prevalence of violence against men, the rich accumulation of data on violence against women affords a complex and nuanced understanding of the workings of power in patriarchal societies, and the ways in which such power constructs freedom. The point of focusing on *woman* battering in this chapter is thus not to establish reductive claims that women are victimized by men, that women are only victims and men only predators, or that women are completely unfree because of domestic abuse. Rather, it is to provide a window of understanding into the dynamics of power as they operate through intimate relationships within the context of patriarchy. This context constructs women's—but also men's—choices, freedom, and subjectivity in ways that perpetuate power inequalities; and these inequalities in turn feed into and set the terms of such constructions. Analyzing the contextual dimensions of domestic violence can help enrich our understanding of the social construction of subjectivity and choice.

## BATTERING IN CONTEXT

Violence against women in the home is a pervasive phenomenon that, despite its long history,[10] has only recently gained broad public awareness. In the 1980s and 1990s, hundreds of articles and books were published on the subject in a variety of disciplines, and passage of the Violence Against Women Act in 1994 brought national notice to the problem in the United States. Despite this popular and scholarly attention, however, there is considerable disparity in defining the problem and solving it. As I just indicated, estimates on numbers and percentages of women who are battered vary considerably, depending in part on how violence is defined, calculated, and measured, how surveys are conducted, the time frame involved (e.g., "lifetime" versus "annual" assessments) as well as the particular samples in the study.[11] Moreover, methodological differences across various nations and cultures produce results that are not directly comparable, and the dominance of United States figures, models, and theories in global research on woman abuse may not produce accurate results.[12] But even within the United States, figures range from less than a million to over six million, and from 11 percent to as high as 73 percent. It is commonly estimated that a woman in the United States is abused every fifteen seconds.[13] Many researchers agree that anywhere from a quarter to a third of all women are abused by their intimate partners at some point in their lives. These numbers do not include the even more common phenomenon of psychological abuse. The overwhelming majority of these numbers reflect attacks on women by their male intimate partners or ex-partners, though lesbian and homosexual battering occur at statistically significant rates as well.[14] This violence begins at an early age: the American Medical Association found that one in five female students reported physical or sexual abuse by a dating partner, and several other studies report a surprisingly high incidence of teenage dating violence as well.[15] A study of the

National Crime Victimization Survey conducted by the Bureau of Justice Statistics documents that "the highest rates of intimate violence affect women ages 16 to 24," although "females at every age are much more likely than males to be murdered by an intimate."[16]

Many of these numbers are extrapolated from limited samples, but even the most conservative numbers, coming from the FBI Uniform Crime Reports and the Bureau of Justice Statistics, indicate that substantial numbers of women are abused annually by intimate partners. The FBI draws on data from the National Incident-Based Reporting System and does not directly provide numbers of battered women (although racially based "hate crimes" are designated as a specific category of analysis), but reports that of 420,272 violent criminal offenses committed in fourteen states, 23 percent were committed within "family relationships." Approximately 43 percent of these were committed by spouses, and in 71 percent of these incidents the victim was female.[17] These numbers were virtually identical to those reported in a similar study in 1995 (46 percent and 73 percent respectively).[18] But this latter figure (percentage of female victims) would include daughters, sisters, and other female family members. Moreover, though FBI figures include "common law spouse" as well as legal spouses, they exclude "boyfriend, girlfriend, ex-spouse, ex-boyfriend, or ex-girlfriend,"[19] which according to a number of researchers are important categories to include in intimate violence, not only because of teenage dating violence, but also because batterers may begin, continue, or escalate violence after a relationship ends.[20] Furthermore, the Bureau of Justice Statistics estimates that only half of all incidents of domestic violence are reported to the police.[21] Thus, the FBI's numbers must be considered somewhat conservative. The BJS produces separate statistics through its National Crime Victimization Survey, "which gathers data on criminal victimization from a national sample of household respondents," and estimates national percentages on the basis of this data. BJS found that 840,000 women were abused nonlethally by their intimate partners in 1996—this time including ex- and not-married partners—a figure down from 1.1 million in 1993. Of approximately 1,800 murders by intimates (down from 3,000 in 1976), three-quarters of the victims were female.[22] An update on that report conducted by a different group of BJS statisticians established that in 1998, 876,340 women were victimized by current partners (former partners were not taken into consideration) with approximately the same statistics for intimate homicide as in 1996.[23] The Violence Against Women Office of the Department of Justice puts the number somewhat higher, at 1.3 million, which they claim translates to 22.1 percent of U.S. women, in 1996. Moreover, they find that women are much more likely to be injured when assaults or rapes come from intimate partners rather than from strangers.[24] Twenty-one percent of women in the United States were the victim of violent crime perpetrated by an intimate in 2000.[25]

Internationally the numbers are similarly significant. Though comparisons among countries are severely hampered by different gathering methods and definitions of violence, it is estimated that one in three women worldwide is the victim of abuse, one in four during pregnancy.[26] According to a study published by the Johns Hopkins School of Public Health, between 1982 and 1999, 21 percent of women had been the victim of abuse by a domestic partner in Switzerland, 20 percent in South Africa, 46 percent in Ethiopia, 47 percent in Bangladesh, 16 percent in Cambodia, 40 percent in India, 27 percent in Mexico, 28 percent in Nicaragua, 34 percent in Egypt, 67 percent in Papua, New Guinea, and 29 percent in Canada.[27] Hageman-White reports data for women's victimization by partner or intrafamily violence in Europe at rates ranging from 1 percent in Denmark (by "current partner"—adding "past partner" brings the figure up to 8 percent) to 45 percent in Finland ("by past cohabiting partner").[28] Adelman reports that "in Israel one out of every seven women is battered by their male partners."[29]

What is domestic violence, however—or "intimate partner violence" (IPV), as the U.S. government now calls it? In general, domestic abuse is divided into several broad categories, including physical (punching, kicking, shoving, hitting, slapping, restraining, using a knife, gun, or other weapon), sexual (rape, coerced sexual acts, as well as genital injury), property related (punching a wall, breaking household objects, taking or destroying objects of particular value to the woman, injuring or misusing pets), and psychological (threats, insults, insistent demands, yelling, and intimidation).[30] These can be combined, obviously, and often are, such as when a batterer shouts insults at a woman as he beats her up (psychological and physical abuse), when he beats and rapes her (physical and sexual), or when a man puts his fist through a wall immediately next to a woman's head and says "Next time I won't miss" (property-related and psychological). Thus, these categories suggest more separation between various kinds of violence than is actually the case, but they are meant to emphasize that domestic violence is diverse in its dynamics and particular forms. However, the dominant characteristic of all domestic violence is that one partner forces the other to "live with a constant sense of danger and expectation of violence."[31] According to many scholars, intimidation and fear are the goals of abusers.[32] In this, it is obvious that psychological abuse is the dominant mode that colors the other categories, in both a direct sense, because it accompanies and precedes physical and sexual abuse, and a broader sense, as an integral part of the more tangible forms of abuse. Being assaulted or seeing one's pet tortured does not just have a psychological "component" which is "often" present: such acts themselves have profound psychological effects, inextricable from the physical acts. Accordingly, "everyday life for a battered woman is not necessarily one of dramatic beatings and continuous physical damage. It is more likely to be filled with threats and fear. . . . the most damaging aspect of being a battered woman may be the uncertainty that accompanies life in such an environment."[33]

Indeed, fear of a repeat of violence or of retaliation against family members is the second most often cited reason why heterosexual women stay with abusive mates.[34] Economic dependence or lack of economic resources is another major factor cited by many researchers, and indeed, although domestic violence crosses all economic strata, poorer women are more likely to suffer IPV.[35] While economic dependence could be attributed to "internal" factors (e.g., a woman just did not want to finish school, or chose to be a housewife rather than work outside the home because she believed she would be more fulfilled in the former role), battered women often do not work and lack employable skills because the batterer prevented them from working or studying during the marriage.[36] Women who have been disabled by abuse may be unable to find work because of the disability.[37] Furthermore, for a woman who leaves her abuser, finding a job that pays enough to support herself and her children may be very difficult, given—in addition to educational limits—sexual discrimination in employment opportunities and pay scales, discrimination that is often severely compounded for women of color.[38] In many cases, alimony is no longer awarded to women who secure separation or divorce, particularly in "no fault" states, and those who obtain court orders for child support often do not succeed in actually collecting it.[39] Alternately, women who have well-paying jobs may lose them because of harassment from their partners that causes missed days, lateness, or workplace disruption. Or a woman may have to quit her job because her place of employment is the one place where the batterer knows he can find her.[40] Finally, a woman may have nowhere to go: relatives may be unable or afraid to take her in, since batterers are likely to threaten or attack those who assist their victim, and since threats against the woman's family are a common strategy of psychological abuse. Battered women's shelters are too few to meet demand, and inadequately funded, and women can generally remain at these shelters for only four to eight weeks. Affordable housing that is also safe is often extremely difficult to locate, particularly given women's lack of economic resources. Homelessness is thus often the plight of battered women, and significant proportions of families in homeless shelters are victims of domestic violence.[41]

At any rate, leaving the abuser does not always end the violence; though a woman has a greater likelihood of being hit again if she remains, her risk of being *killed* goes up if she leaves.[42] In what Mahoney calls "separation assault," leaving may precipitate violence "to block her from leaving, retaliate for her departure, or forcibly end the separation."[43] The Violence Against Women Office reports that more domestic violence "starts" during the marriage than after termination, but does not track violence that continues after separation (since divorced and separated spouses are left out of the Uniform Crime Report's definition of "family" violence). Tjaden and Thoennes find that although more women separated from male partners *report* violence, "only 6.3 percent of rape victims and 4.2 percent of the physical assault victims said their victimization *started* after the relationship ended."[44] By contrast, Harlow, also operating out of the Department of Justice, asserts that ex-husbands perpetrate more attacks and inflict more injuries than any other category of abusing partner, including current boyfriends or husbands.[45] And in a 1998 study conducted in Washington, D.C., by the American Medical Association, "45.3% of divorced/separated women reported an injury from an intimate partner"; compared to never married women, "divorced or separated status was associated with an almost three-fold increase in the risk for reported IPV . . . and a four-fold increase in the risk for injury from IPV."[46] Even if women who remain are overall at greater risk of assault than those who leave, however, the likelihood of retaliation could induce a woman not to press charges or leave. After all, battered women are confronting, not statistical averages, but the likelihood that they themselves will be injured or killed by their particular abusers, and these perceptions must be highly individualized. The reason that battering "works" as a method of controlling women, according to Tifft, is precisely the terror it inspires. The psychological manipulation involved in convincing the woman that there is "no way out" of the relationship is important to the abuser's goals of power and control.[47]

These are all arguably "external" barriers to liberty, but there are other reasons why women stay with abusive mates that most people would consider internal barriers. For instance, women who as girls observed their mothers being beaten by their fathers, or who were themselves abused as children, may internalize a belief that violence is a "normal" expression of love.[48] This may particularly be the case for abused children who are too young to have the conceptual vocabulary to define what is happening to them; as they learn language, the concept of love becomes constructed for them in a way that can accommodate violence.[49] But a history of child abuse is hardly necessary for women to see jealousy and possessiveness as evidence of the depth of a partner's love, or to see violence as the result of their own failure to "be the perfect partner . . . so that the violence in him would no longer emerge."[50] Rather, socially constructed discourses of romantic love make a man's controlling behavior, such as frequent phone calls to see what a woman is up to, or insisting that a woman quit her job to devote more attention to him and the home, seem like "endearing" features that demonstrate his deep care and concern for every facet of her life.[51] Love also may persuade women who believe an abuser's promises of reform and displays of remorse and affection to choose to stay or return, in a state of what is sometimes called "learned hopefulness." Indeed, "hoped partner would change" may be the number one reason why battered women, both heterosexual and lesbian, stay in their relationships.[52] Women who have left often return to batterers because of feelings of loss or loneliness or of responsibility for the relationship, particularly if the batterer is an alcoholic or substance abuser.[53] Similarly, women may hold traditional values about women's and men's roles and the stigma of divorce.[54] Even when women resort to the police or to battered-women's shelters, they may often "not feel that they [have] severed the relationship" but rather that they are simply seeking intervention that would get him to stop his abusive behavior.[55]

Though some of these emotional states and beliefs likely predate a woman's involvement in an abusive relationship, it is not surprising that abuse creates its own intrapsychic manifestations. Lenore Walker has identified a "battered woman's syndrome" which is caused by the pervasiveness of abuse. Based on Seligman's research into "learned helplessness," Walker postulated that after repeated incidents of violence and the continual uncertainty of how the abusive partner will behave, battered women become unable to perceive "exit options."[56] Women, particularly those who have been raped or sexually assaulted by their partners, may feel intense shame which may make them reluctant to come forward at all, or even to admit to themselves, let alone anyone else, that they are battered women.[57] Depression, feelings of low self-worth and the accompanying belief that she somehow deserved to be hurt, or guilt and the belief that she provoked the violence, are all too common and may keep women from leaving their abusers.[58] Thus, some battered women even defend or excuse their spouses or refuse to testify against them in court, in an attempt to convince themselves that they are in control: if the violence is not his fault but hers, then perhaps she can control the conditions under which it happened.

### THE THIN (BLACK AND) BLUE LINE: INSTITUTIONAL CONTEXTS

Attributing women's failure to leave an abusive relationship to individual material factors, such as economic dependence and fear of violence, thus ignores the complex emotional and structural factors that take away many of a woman's choices, both objectively (she has few alternatives) and subjectively (she *feels* as if she has no alternatives at all). But at the same time, focusing on emotional and psychological states rather than material conditions locates the problem of violence exclusively in individual pathologies and locates the solution in therapies directed at changing individual personalities. Simultaneously, it excuses others from responsibility for helping victims by reducing IPV to a matter of preference—if it wasn't what she wanted, she would leave, so she must get something out of it—in a perversion of liberal relativism. Hence, social constructivism requires us to consider the ways in which intrapsychic phenomena are produced and shaped by external forces and conditions, to consider not just the violence itself but the social context in which it occurs. This context is one that tacitly condones and even supports violence against women even as it expressly declares it to be wrong, through the social construction of gender. This construction takes place in a myriad of institutions and social relationships in ways both overt and subtle, at all three levels. The first level, however—social construction as domination and ideological misrepresentation—is the most evident.

Consider, for instance, the police, who are not only the first but the most frequently called-on helping agency for battered women. Although the BJS reports that half of domestic-violence victims report the assault to law enforcement, and that, according to victim reports, police respond to 90 percent of calls for assistance in such cases and arrive within ten minutes 60 percent of the time,[59] other studies find that police routinely fail to arrest abusive male partners, particularly in poorer and nonwhite areas, displaying dismissive attitudes toward "family disputes" and women complainants.[60] Until the mid 1980s, many states and jurisdictions lacked any formal policy regarding domestic abuse, and those that did had policies against arrest. Police may be reluctant to investigate domestic-violence complaints for a number of reasons. Many police consider domestic violence a "private" affair—an attitude shared by one out of every six victims of domestic violence and by one-third of victims who did not call the police.[61] But police are also aware that domestic-violence intervention is highly dangerous to police officers. Accordingly, police have tended to take on conciliatory roles, suggesting that the man needs to "cool down" by taking a walk around the block, viewing scratches or other marks on the man as evidence that the violence is mutual, or failing to see that the woman's fear of her abuser motivates her reluctance to press charges. Police may more actively discourage arrest by explaining to women the implications of pressing charges: the loss of the husband's wages, the likelihood of his quick release on bail, the onerous process of making statements, signing warrants, and appearing in court. Such conditions have changed in some places in the past ten to twenty years, largely due to class-action suits brought against police departments for failing to protect women who were severely battered or murdered by their partners.[62] As of 2001, very few states lacked domestic-violence statutes of some kind, and "mandatory arrest" laws have been instituted in twenty states and the District of Columbia since the mid-1980s. Such statutes require police to arrest for "probable cause," which is established by witness testimony, visible injuries, or property damage that indicates a crime has been committed. Without such policies, the victim herself must press charges, which she is often reluctant to do for fear of retaliation, loss of income, or contact with the criminal justice system in general, or because of feelings of guilt and responsibility for her attacker's behavior.[63] The issuance and enforcement of restraining orders has grown in the past ten years as well.[64]

But such changes in law, public policy, and official attention, while encouraging in theory, have had disappointing practical effects on reducing domestic violence. As many feminist legal scholars have pointed out, sexist implementation and enforcement still hamper battered women's efforts to be free of violence. Ferraro maintains that police use discretion in interpreting the requirements of mandatory-arrest statutes such that arrests are made in a minority of cases, and that sexist and racist attitudes guide police responses to IPV.[65] If women are able to separate from their partners, men can respond by stalking, attacking women at their place of work, making threatening phone calls, or taking legal action to obtain custody of children. Though stalking laws have also been enacted in some states, they are for the most part extremely difficult to enforce, since stalkers often operate in stealth.[66] Orders of protection are, moreover, often openly ignored by batterers, who know that enforcement is problematic. While such orders can be used as evidence that a woman sought to leave her abusive partner and will thus strengthen the case for prosecution of a batterer after an attack, they often do not effectively prevent attack. Furthermore, domestic violence is a not uncommon problem among police themselves.

Such attitudes and behavior certainly display the first level of social construction, much like battering itself, because they prevent women from accessing state power to protect them from others' interference with their liberty. The power exercised over women involves obvious gender discrimination that fails to see accurately and respond appropriately to violence against women. But the broader context in which police operate ensures the materialization of the reality they encode. For instance, police who discourage a battered woman from pressing charges by pointing out that the abuser will be released on bond or bail in a few hours may not be trying to intimidate the woman or to save themselves the hassle of having her change her mind later on; they may actually be helping to protect her by warning her about the legal system's failure to take male violence against women seriously. For instance, in Ferraro's Arizona study, despite the mandatory-arrest statute, "city and county prosecutors did not increase prosecutions, and judges did not sentence batterers to jail," thus making arrest ineffectual. Hirschel and his colleagues found that prosecution followed arrest in only 35 percent of cases, and of those, few were sentenced to additional jail time.[67] Prosecutors allow battered women more discretion in deciding whether to prosecute than is normally permitted for violent crime, even in jurisdictions with "no drop" prosecutory policies. While such discretion apparently increases women's control, and respects many women's belief that domestic violence is a private matter, it also makes women more vulnerable to ongoing threats from their attackers.[68] If a case makes it to court, judges may abuse discretion by trivializing the violence, construing it as mutual, discounting the woman's testimony, giving greater credence to the man's version of events, or excusing the man on weak grounds.[69] Anecdotal evidence abounds in scholarly literature and the popular press in which judges dismissed and trivialized women's complaints, released batterers who subsequently killed their partners, or revealed the woman's location to the batterer, even when she was living in a battered-women's shelter and despite the fact that such disclosure could jeopardize the shelter's federal or state funding.[70]

Whatever the reason for such biases, they routinely work against women as well as children. On the apparent belief—and despite evidence to the contrary—that wife abuse and child abuse are unrelated, judges routinely grant child custody to male abusers, or at least grant visitation rights that prevent the woman from moving away, forcing her to have continued contact with the abuser. Such actions are mandated in eighteen states by "friendly parent" statutory provisions, whereby parents must "allow an open, loving, and frequent relationship between the child and the other parent."[71] States have such provisions as part of legislative initiatives to promote children's "best interests," ignoring that children who see their mothers abused are routinely injured either directly—because spouse abusers often abuse children as well, or because the child has sought to prevent the father from hurting the mother—or indirectly, through the transmission of "intergenerational violence."[72] At the same time, other judges believe that battered women must be unfit mothers because they are abused, even though children, like women, are more vulnerable to attack at the time of separation.[73] Indeed, some judges have used the fact that a batterer has violated a restraining order as evidence that the *mother* is unfit. At the same time, women who seek to move away in order to escape their batterers, and thus protect their children by protecting themselves, are seen as acting against the best interests of their children, which are supposedly served by joint custody, despite the fact that living in a different city from a former abusive partner reduces the likelihood of repeat violence.[74] On the assumption that a woman is moving out of selfish or vindictive motives, courts may even respond by shifting custody to the abusive husband, or abusive men can exploit such assumptions to discredit their female partners in efforts to obtain acquittals or to gain child custody, often as a way to further control the (former) partner.[75] Thus, either a woman leaves her abuser—and possibly town—to protect herself and her children, in which case she may lose custody to the batterer, or she stays and remains vulnerable to further abuse in which case she may lose her children to foster care.

Such double standards affect women in other ways as well. Though Greenfield and his colleagues show that about one-third of women who are victims of nonlethal intimate violence "actively defended themselves against the offender" by "struggling, shouting, chasing or other means without a weapon (30%) or with a weapon (4%),"[76] women who resort to physical means of self-defense are judged by male-defined legal standards that ignore women's differences. For instance, the "equal force" requirement of the law of self-defense fails to take into account that a woman's lesser strength may require a weapon to equalize force, and the "imminent danger" requirement fails to account for such inequities of strength as well as for a history of past abuse. Women who hit their batterers in self-defense may be arrested even when no injury was done to the man, and judges will then treat domestic violence as mutual.[77] At the same time, women who resort to killing their spouses are treated more harshly than men. Although abusive men who kill their wives or girlfriends receive widely differing bail judgments and sentencing, often benefitting from a "domestic discount" (e.g., a murder charge dropped to manslaughter) because "killing out of anger . . . decreases moral blameworthiness," women who kill their abusers are generally arrested without bail, charged with first-degree murder—frequently on the grounds that they were taking "revenge," or perhaps wanted to collect on an insurance policy—and given heavy sentences, including a higher proportion of death sentences.[78]

The various aspects of the legal system are not the only institutional barriers women face. Medicine also impacts strongly. Ptacek found the very same patterns in the medical as in the criminal justice systems, and both mirrored the patterns displayed by individual batterers, such as blaming women for the abuse and denying or trivializing the violence.[79] A study in the *Journal of the American Medical Association* estimated that "approximately 20% of emergency department visits for trauma and 25% of homicides of women involve intimate partner violence."[80] Yet emergency medical personnel screen for IPV in only 6 to 10 percent of cases, fail to inquire into the cause of injuries, or accept patently false explanations ("I fell down"), which may result in inappropriate prescriptions for pain-killers and tranquilizers that could put women at greater risk of attack. They often view battered women's injuries as minor, and thus of lower priority compared to car accident or shooting injuries, and consider domestic violence a psychological problem.[81] At the other extreme, several states have instituted mandatory reporting of suspected cases of abuse to the police, regardless of the woman's wishes, which will likely cause some battered women to refrain from seeking medical aid.[82] When women are treated for abuse at a medical center, child neglect or abuse reports are often filed on the basis that wife abuse harms the child. As valid as such assumptions are, these reports are filed against the mother rather than the abuser, since she is the parent presenting for treatment. Such a report can then be used by the abuser against the woman in a custody battle.[83] Similarly, religious institutions replicate the same patriarchal power that other institutions display. Although women contact clergy more often than any other source of help except the police, clergy have been found to rebuff women's requests for help with responses ranging from biblical injunctions that women should be subservient and proclamations that divorce is a sin, to efforts at reconciliation that involved talking to the women in the presence of their abusers, leading two authors to declare that "clergy had the highest negative influence in counseling battered women."[84]

Not only formal institutions like law and medicine, but broad social categories such as race, class, and sexuality are significant social formations for understanding battered women's freedom and restraints. As many researchers attest, domestic violence is a phenomenon that occurs to women with a remarkable degree of similarity across race and class. Although some studies show that domestic violence occurs in some minority communities at a greater rate than others,[85] when studies control for income level, racial differences may disappear.[86] Yet race may affect the specifics of battering. For instance, although more victimized African-American women tend to call police than white women, those who do not involve law enforcement may refrain not because they are afraid of their abusers or believe that the matter is private, as is the case with white women who do not call the police, but because they do not wish to subject themselves or their abusers to the racism of the U.S. criminal justice system.[87] If they do call the police, they and other women of color may also be censured by the broader community as "traitors to the race."[88] Community norms in Latina and Asian communities may present further sanctions on women seeking security, such that leaving the spouse entails leaving the community.[89] And of course some women are married to undocumented workers and are thus afraid to call the attention of legal authorities.[90] Legislative efforts have been made to change the requirement that immigrants remain married to U.S. citizens for a minimum of two years if women can substantiate domestic violence, but the conditions for proof of victimization are such that many women cannot meet them. Furthermore, language barriers and illiteracy will make it difficult for some immigrant women to find out about available resources, let alone take advantage of them, as well as make communication with police and prosecutors difficult. Finally, cultural norms from their country of origin may influence women not to see the criminal justice system as an appropriate remedy, or even to identify battering as anything but a normal part of marriage.[91]

At the same time, attention to culture often denies the specifically gendered dimensions of racism. In what is known as the "cultural defense," men who have killed their wives argue that country-of-origin norms which allow men to kill their wives for violating their "honor" mean that the premeditated intent required for murder is absent.[92] Obviously, this does not only occur in the United States; according to a United Nations Commission on Human Rights report, honor killings have been reported in Bangladesh, Brazil, Ecuador, Egypt, India, Israel, Italy, Jordan, Morocco, Pakistan, Sweden, Turkey, Uganda and the United Kingdom.[93] In some of these countries, the practice is fairly common; in Pakistan alone, one thousand women were killed in 1999.[94] But in North America, at least, the significant factor in such cases when they are brought to court is that such rulings do not reflect observations of cultural norms which judges are viewing impartially; rather, judges play an active role in turning cultural prejudices into law, in violation of women's safety and their right to freedom from violence. Indeed, as Sherene Razack notes, in the North American context, white judges' acceptance of the "cultural defense" is a particularly pernicious form of racism; "dominant groups too readily adopt the cultural differences approach, relieved not to have to confront the realities of racism and sexism."[95] "Cultural difference" becomes an excuse for allowing sexist behavior: it provides "white patriarchs" a basis for dismissing violence against women of color by permitting alliance with "brown patriarchs" to supersede the legal protection of women.[96] In this, Razack argues that "women and children who are victims of violence do not stand in relation to culture as do their assailants."[97] Women's experience of violence becomes not only subservient to the "higher" dictates of "culture" but thereby invisible; "culture" is defined as that which excludes women. In this, men of color accept the dominant imperialist and colonizing values of white Western culture, with women as the colonized. It is not merely that white court systems are being racist in failing to understand nonwhite cultures, nor that women's experience of culture is "different," but that whites may *use* "culture" and racism to *express* sexism, and men of color thus ally themselves with white men to solidify their power over women of color. In a similar vein, Uma Narayan notes the phenomenon of Westerners focusing on dowry murders in India but on nonlethal domestic violence in the West, constructing non-Western cultures as inherently violent *as cultures*; such imbalance promotes the idea that non-Western women experience "death by culture," whereas Western women are hurt either by individual men or by patriarchy.[98] Such deployments systematically exclude women from the constitution and meaning of culture, hide sexism behind cultural relativism, and deny that patriarchy is itself a cultural construct.

The impact of racism on domestic violence can be even more blatant and direct. For instance, James and Elsie Zion maintain that white disruption of Navajo culture has directly led to domestic violence.[99] Because Navajo culture values equality between women and men in marriage and the community, domestic violence was not traditionally common. Furthermore, family units were structured to protect women from abuse; for instance, couples lived with the wife's family, in part to forestall abuse, and mothers played an active role in condemning spousal assault and defending women victims in Navajo mediation councils. Indeed, traditional Navajo community norms explicitly view spousal abuse as unacceptable, as violating gender equality and hence disrupting the community's ability to function. Consider, for instance, Navajo views on women's adultery: "If your wife [commits adultery], do not abuse her or get jealous of her. She has this privilege; she is a human being. You have the choice of leaving her or staying with her regardless of what she does."[100] Divorce was traditionally a readily available option for either partner in the face of marital discord and particularly allowed women to leave abusive husbands quickly and easily. Beginning in the nineteenth century, however, these cultural norms were dismantled by whites through the "introduction of individualism and the individualistic norms of paternalism and patriarchal rule" as well as the "disruption of traditional lifestyles and economies."[101] Whites violated gender equality by outlawing traditional divorce, assigning property allocations to male heads of households, and insisting on negotiating with a "head man" of the tribe, never with female tribal leaders. New economic incentives were based on the white (patriarchal) ideal of the male head-of-family wage earner, which often resulted in the couple's having to leave the wife's family home and in the dissolution of Navajo communities. By these means, whites played a direct and very active role in *creating* domestic violence as a new cultural norm among the Navajo. A similar phenomenon is implied, but not directly analyzed, in the film *Once Were Warriors*, where dislocation of Maouri tribes and the tribal heritage of a warrior people—which sublimated violence through carefully controlled ritual with a strong mental discipline— resulted in poverty and male violence against women and other men.

Racism also affects the battered-women's movement, sometimes overtly but often indirectly, as well-intentioned actions produce disastrous results for women of color. For instance, battered-women's advocates may not wish to highlight cultural differences in domestic violence, either to undercut racist stereotypes that domestic violence is a problem only for minorities or to ensure funding from white male legislators who are primarily worried about white, middle-class women. Similarly, Kimberle Crenshaw relates the story of a Hispanic woman who was denied entry to a shelter because she could not speak English, which would prevent her participation in a mandatory support group. When it was suggested that her son could translate for her until a Spanish-speaking battered-women's advocate could be found, they rejected this, "*since it further victimized the victim.*" The fact that this woman had been living on the street for two days, too afraid to return home, and had been mugged twice during that time, seemed to be less important than providing the "proper" form of "empowerment,"[102] in a caricature of positive liberty. That such shelter policies are well intentioned and that shelter workers who follow them are oblivious to their effects on minority women does not, Crenswhaw suggests, lessen the racist impact.

Heterosexism and homophobia can present additional obstacles that some battering victims face. Police may refuse to respond because they view gays and lesbians as deviant, and violence as simply one more permutation of that deviance. Like women of color who view the criminal justice system as racist, lesbian and gay victims may not want to expose their partners—let alone themselves—to a heterosexist legal and judicial system. For lesbians in particular, friends may be reluctant to believe the victim because of cultural and political values of the "lesbian nation" (the notion that lesbian relationships are egalitarian and peaceful) in an echo of demands for cultural solidarity made on women of color.[103] Family members may not know about the victim's sexual orientation or may disapprove, making appeal to them problematic. By contrast, gay men may view violence between men as normal. Additionally, shelters are exceedingly rare for battered gay men. And women's shelters may be reluctant to accept battered lesbians, because of homophobia on the part of staff or of other residents; admitting lesbians may be seen as disruptive to the recovery process of the majority of shelter residents. Additionally, the lesbian batterer may likely know where the shelter is, and indeed, if the victim tried to defend herself, may plausibly demand admittance to the shelter herself, putting shelter staff in the position of deciding who is the batterer and who is the victim.[104]

## Constructing Violence

Such institutional, social, and cultural settings reinforce the batterer's authority as well as the message that a battered woman is up against something more than a single abuser in the social construction of her choices. Rather, the abuser derives his power to restrict his partner's freedom from the set of ideological beliefs and norms that constitute the basic tenets of patriarchy: male superiority, women's subservience, men's property rights in women, lesbians' and minorities' "social deviance." Control at the individual "micro" level by individual batterers works interactively and complementarily with the social "macro" level of courts, police, and medicine to socially construct battered women's choices, desires, and freedom. Such control is not a coincidental byproduct of social structures, but rather motivates and founds them. Social construction as domination and ideological misrepresentation—the batterer's violence, his claims, endorsed by police and judges, that violence is the victim's fault and that she deserves it—bleeds into materialization as it creates a situation in which there is, as abusers often say to their victims, "no way out." Because police fail to arrest, women stop calling the police; because courts do not convict, women become reluctant to press charges or testify; because emergency personnel either fail to help adequately or report abuse to state agencies, women stop seeking medical attention; because friends and relatives tell them, along with the rest of society, that women are responsible for making relationships work, and because battered women themselves share these beliefs and hold themselves responsible for the welfare of their batterers, battered women are ashamed of their abuse and do not tell anyone about it or ask for help. Similarly, the misrepresentation that IPV is more common among minorities, the notion that people of color are "animals," produces a material reality wherein racial minorities are treated differently by the legal system. In the effort to survive violence in such a context, women will respond with a variety of strategies: they may deny that it is occurring, or rationalize it or claim responsibility for it as a way to claim control, or go limp during a beating to minimize injury.[105] All of these strategies help women survive, but they feed into men's power to hit women. From the institutional and social treatment battered women experience, they learn that society, at least tacitly and often overtly, condones the violence perpetrated against them, and they must thereby define themselves by and within that context. They thus become what their batterers tell them to be. Institutions reflect individual sexism, and in turn make it possible. If domestic violence happens because it works, it works because social structures grant and support men's social power; and this power, in circular fashion, supports, normalizes, and condones such violence.

This, however, leads into the third level of social construction, the discursive construction of social meaning: how men and women see and define themselves, the available vocabularies for understanding and recounting their experiences, their way of perceiving reality. The way that batterers, their victims, other people, and social institutions think and talk about gender relations and violence affect lived experience and cause certain social formations, and not others, to make sense or appear "natural." Thus Barnett and LaViolette note high correlations between battering and patriarchal beliefs that men "own" their wives or partners, that a man has the "right" to "discipline" or "punish" his woman, to determine whether she can work, to decide if she can leave home at night, and "to have sex with [her] even if she does not want to."[106] Yllo and Straus also found that the more patriarchal norms and beliefs held by a man, and the more strict they were, the more likely he was to abuse his female partner, and the more severe the abuse was likely to be.[107] And Michael Smith, in a comprehensive empirical study specifically aimed at measuring the correlation between patriarchy and wife abuse, concluded unequivocally that "wife beating results from adherence by battering husbands to an ideology of family patriarchy."[108] Such attitudes are not limited to abusive men, however: in Ewing and Aubrey's random sample study of 216 people, 60 percent agreed that if a battered woman was really afraid of her mate, she would leave him, and 40 percent saw battered women as partly to blame for their plight.[109] In her study of 422 North Carolina women, Genteman found that although "nearly all respondents reject norms which approve of wife beating . . . a substantial minority (18.8%) accepts the idea of situations in which beatings are justified," for example, if the woman flirts with another man, is drunk, nagging, or having an affair. "Over 20% blame the victim for her beatings."[110] In other countries this figure is higher; in Ghana, for example, over half the women and 43 percent of the men said that a man was justified in beating his wife if she used contraception without his consent.[111] And in rural Egypt, 80 per cent of women surveyed said that beatings were particularly justified if a woman refused to have sex with her husband.[112]

The discourses of patriarchy are thus not merely utilized by individual batterers, but, more importantly, provide the contextual setting in which their abusive behavior, and others' interpretation of and reaction to such behavior, occur. Indeed, the notion of "battered women" is itself a social construction, a social trope that embodies a set of discursive social meanings about gender and gender relations, male privilege and power, the appropriateness of violence and control within the institution of marriage (or its surrogates) and the relationship of various categories of social identity to state power. These discursive meanings together help constitute and produce the specific experiences of battering that various women live through. But they also construct how others, ranging from agents of the state (police, judges, district attorneys) to neighbors and family members to strangers who read about the latest murder by an intimate partner in the newspaper, read and interpret such events and the individuals who experience them. "Battered women" are constituted as "other" by non-battered individuals who do not wish to consider the possibility that IPV is one end of a continuum of normal (heterosexual) interaction or who do not want to acknowledge possibilities for such violence within themselves. By considering "battered women" as a unique category set off from what is normal, distance is placed between the violence that potentially underwrites all relationships in heterosexual society and these particular instances of its concrete expression. These constructions form the backdrop against which victims of IPV experience and understand their own abuse as well. Blaming victims becomes the discursive maneuver to suppress collective awareness of the violence within the social context of patriarchy.

The power of such constructions to shape battered women's existence and define its meaning operates even within feminism. For instance, how does my own deployment of the term "battered women" throughout this book shape and reinforce patriarchal assumptions about IPV, even as it seeks to challenge them? As Donileen Loseke argues, even shelter workers, the feminist women on the front lines of the fight against domestic violence, deploy discourses that are defined and shaped by patriarchy. Battered women, Loseke maintains, are constructed as helpless by feminists within the shelter movement; they are seen as completely alone and trapped, "pure victims" of male violence as well as of traditional beliefs about gender roles and the shame of divorce. Similarly, domestic violence is defined by "shelter feminists" and policymakers as extreme physical violence that follows a longstanding pattern of repetition and escalation. This construction marks women who physically defend themselves and/ or engage in mutual violence as "undeserving of help"; a woman who is slapped once or twice every year is not considered a "battered woman," because a certain level of violence, indeed of male-on-female violence, is accepted as normal.[113] Furthermore, by constructing domestic violence as a pattern of extreme and horrendous assault, leaving the abuser becomes the only possible solution to ending the abuse, and not leaving is unimaginable. Indeed, the fact that "shelters" are seen as the focal point of the battered-women's movement reinforces the construction that leaving is the only option compatible with independence, and that "independence" is the only acceptable goal. Social constructions beget further social constructions by shifting the parameters of discourse to limit the range of alternatives which it is possible to imagine. Loseke points out, moreover, that focusing on the extremes of domestic violence leads to policy outcomes that are self-defeating. For instance, since domestic violence is likely to become more extreme the longer it continues, she argues, it might make sense to devote resources to helping women at a much earlier stage. Such help can be offered, however, not to mention sought, only if the social construction of "battered women" changes to incorporate the varied and nuanced range of experiences within interpersonal relationships. If "shelters" are seen as the appropriate response to domestic violence, women suffering at less extreme levels will not seek help; indeed, they will not see themselves as suffering from "domestic violence" at all.[114]

The fact that shelter workers and other feminists engage in these constructions is not to say that they secretly or even subconsciously endorse patriarchy. Rather, it is to highlight the ways in which social construction exceeds the grasp of the individuals who operate within discourses, even when they overtly seek to change those discourses. Certainly, by pointing out the tensions within such constructions of domestic violence, feminists seek to provide more complicated and nuanced understandings of the "empirical events," the concrete instances of woman battering. But such accounts are always already filtered through discursive categories of sex, race, class, age, property, and family that set parameters to *any possible* account of the "empirical events." When someone is labeled a "battered woman," the social images the label conjures up, and the discourse that frames those images, "transform the heterogeneity of lived experience into the homogeneity of social types." The fact that "wife abuse and the battered woman are socially reproduced each time a social member evaluates a specific, unique practical experience as that of 'wife abuse' " means that all of us, no matter how well-intentioned, inescapably participate in the social construction of domestic violence.[115]

The implications of the relation between discourse and event for women's freedom are significant. Women's desires, preferences, and self-conceptions are constructed by and through the macro forces of patriarchy—discourses such as law, medicine, cultural tradition, religious and moral belief—and the specific micro actions that individuals take through institutions such as the family or the courts. Individual circumstances and choices are expressions of larger social formations interacting with the specificity of particular subject positions within them. For instance, consider "learned helplessness and hopefulness." Though noting that some individuals are more prone to develop learned helplessness than others, Walker also notes that those who experienced strict sex-role socialization or childhood abuse are particularly prone to it. She also shows that the more severe the violence, and the more active the control a batterer exerts, the more likely a woman is to develop battered-woman syndrome. It is, as she points out, learned through the repeated experience of relatively random violence which the victim can do nothing to avoid or escape. That helplessness is *learned* is often ignored by both courts and mental health professionals who interpret battered-woman syndrome as a dysfunction but male violence as a normal expression of the dominant patriarchal discourse. The fact that these discourses of patriarchy prevent those with power and authority from hearing the stories that women tell of their experiences in turn shapes how women themselves understand those experiences.[116]

"Learned hopefulness"—the notion that victims stay with their abusers because they hope (s)he will change—even more complexly stems from the interaction of internal and external factors located in the dynamics of abuse. Through the "cycle of violence" that characterizes most abusive relationships—the "tension building" stage, characterized by verbal abuse, jealous outbursts, "minor" violence or destruction of property, followed by the "acute battering" stage, the climactic eruption of the man's violence in a relatively serious beating, and the "honeymoon" stage, characterized by profuse apologies, lavish gift giving, loving atten-tion, and promises that the violence will not be repeated—victims of IPV develop ways of seeing their lives and experiences that not only facilitate their own domination and the misrepresentation of the reality they are living but feed into the materialization of those representations to make them real. If acute battering shocks a woman because the violence seems out of character, alien to the man she married, the honeymoon stage makes her feel that the relationship has returned to normal, that the "real" man she knows and loves has reemerged.[117] The violence may even take on a surreal character rather than appearing as a cycle or pattern. It is in this stage that women learn hopefulness, for the batterer appears to recognize that what he did was wrong; and so she believes his displays of remorse and his promises to change. Indeed, hoping and perhaps even expecting that the previous outburst was his last, she does not see herself in a "stage" at all, but rather embarking on a new status quo of harmony and stability. Hope becomes an important way to cope with the state of uncertainty produced by this pattern of violence alternating with tender-ness and remorse. But the batterer's apologies typically turn into rational-izations—I wouldn't have hit you if you weren't mouthing off/if you had my dinner ready/if you hadn't embarrassed me in front of my friends—and the woman internalizes the blame. The "honeymoon" gets shorter and less loving, and indeed often becomes characterized simply by the cessation of violence;[118] and the batterer requires his partner to swallow her anger or other self-defining emotions and instead appear forgiving immediately.

The social isolation that batterers often demand (that the woman not go out, see her friends, or spend so much time talking to her family), or even engineer (insisting that he drive her everywhere or accompany her whenever she leaves the house), contract the woman's social context and framework to the world of the relationship. When combined with the failure of response on the part of external agents on whom she calls for help and validation, ranging from friends and family to police and courts, the internalization of blame leads to beliefs that if she has provoked the violence, then she should be able to prevent it by changing her behavior. Women thus learn to be (or at least to act) hopeful as a way to cope with their helplessness; and their victimization becomes the primary evidence or mark of their agency: they "choose" not to leave. As Memmi argues, the more complete and effective a system of oppression is, the less aware of it *as* oppression its victims are. A truly successful system of oppression will encode itself into the worldview of the colonized, become reality, and construct their inner visions of themselves, social and political relations, nature, the world.[119] Women's reality becomes materially constructed through the violence and its contextual and discursive framework.

This construction results not only in the restriction of options for women but in the meaning of choice itself, in what is viewed as a choice and what is not. For battered women, returning to an abusive partner is viewed as a choice by police, doctors, and indeed most nonbattered people. Yet male abusers are seen as acting unfreely in a myriad of ways. Men who enter therapy as a condition of women's returning to them are seen as not acting freely; in reference to a male therapist for abusive men, Pagelow writes, "Only once has a man voluntarily come to him for help to curb his violence; in the other cases, men come to him because *their wives either left them or were threatening to leave.*" Similarly, Larry Tifft notes that "there are few men who enter counseling voluntarily; most enter via court order *or as a condition of 'getting her back.'*"[120] While some men are ordered by courts to enter therapy, Pagelow and Tifft—both strong feminist analysts of IPV—are here referring to situations where battered women make men's therapy the condition for returning. Thus, in the very moment of women's setting boundaries and asserting themselves, men are seen as coerced because they have to choose between two nonideal options. By contrast, women are seen as free to choose when their options are severely constrained: either leaving the abuser but living in poverty and the fear of him finding her, or staying with him and continuing to be beaten. Even men's violence is often not viewed as a choice: men routinely blame their violence on alcohol, on women's "nagging," late or unsatisfactory meals, or other supposed deficiencies, even as they speak of a "right" of punishment and ownership, or say they are "teaching her a lesson" and "showing her who's boss," demonstrating that a desire to control, rather than alcohol or mental disability, motivate the violence. Mental-health professionals may support men's claims of choicelessness by asking battered women what they did to trigger the violence, even suggesting that physical beatings are men's way of equalizing the imbalance of power created by women's "superior verbal resources."[121] Such discursive constructions of abuser and abused thus both create and invert lived reality. How we culturally, linguistically, and epistemologically define and understand "choice," "choosing," and "subjectivity" allows abusive men to represent themselves as victims, but materially and systematically restrict women more than men. Indeed, these constructions disqualify women from the category of "choosing subject" altogether.

This aspect of social construction suggests that the violent actions of individual men, like women's responses, need to be understood in the larger context of patriarchy. The notion that external factors, controlled by the abuser, construct internal factors in the abused must incorporate the degree to which men are constructed by the same social conditions of patriarchy, and must acknowledge that domestic violence actually fits certain standards of normal masculinity. Barnett and LaViolette point out that "12% to 40% of all men can be classified as physically abusive. . . . It is not simply a case of sick people gravitating toward each other."[122] Although feminists may use such findings to support claims that men are by nature a predatory class who seek to victimize women, these statistics might also suggest the opposite: that men are constructed by gender norms, as well as class, race, and other social formations. Indeed, and ironically, to think of social construction at only the first level, in terms of men's domination of women, denies women's agency altogether, and emphasizes men's agency in a way that risks dehumanizing them in turn. After all, as Towns and Adams illustrate, many batterers display classic personality traits of idealized masculinity; women are attracted to this ideal because it fits the script of gender relations and romantic love.[123] Masculine gender identity, which for heterosexual men involves being attractive to women, similarly propels many men to this idealized masculine personality. Thus, although it may appear that women are attracted to abusive men, in fact they are attracted to an ideal personality type; and this idealized masculinity in turn "attracts" individual men to violence and abusive behavior. Similarly, women's feelings of hope and responsibility are not necessarily caused by violence per se; rather, they are constructed through the broader discourses of romantic love and gender identity. Women's emotional life and the social meaning of love are themselves social constructions that form the context in which violence occurs; they are what make it possible for a batterer, acting as an individual agent, to construct his partner's (perception of) reality. The social constructions of romantic love, idealized masculinity, and women's social responsibility for men's emotional lives provide the discursive context for batterers' anger and frustration, remorse, appeals to sympathy, and shifting of blame. Hence, just as "The enigma of battering relationships and why women remain in them begins with the long journey of learning to be female in this culture,"[124] so is learning violence and adapting to it key to the social construction of masculinity. The individual men who embody these personal characteristics cannot be understood outside a larger context of patriarchal gender relations.

Conversely, social factors that constitute the limiting conditions of patriarchy cannot be considered in isolation from the social and emotional constellations of particular families, nor from the highly individualized psychological effects on different people. For instance, studies on "intergenerational violence" maintain that men who were abused as children or observed their fathers hit their mothers are more likely to become batterers themselves.[125] Donald Dutton theorizes that abusive men suffer from borderline-personality syndrome, as well as from posttraumatic stress disorder, like their victims. While women's stress may be caused by men's violence, men's stress is caused by an earlier childhood trauma which, triggered by some otherwise innocuous behavior of their partners, provokes a violent reaction.[126] Even more significantly, Dutton argues that "the biggest childhood contributors to wife assault, in order of importance, are: feeling rejected by one's father, feeling a lack of warmth from one's father, being physically abused by one's father, being verbally abused by one's father, and feeling rejected by one's mother."[127] Domestic violence, on this account, is the interactive result of the individual and the social; the construction of individual personality through cultural constructions of gender. Without relying on a direct causal relationship, we may reasonably assume that in cultures that associate masculinity with aggression, this developmental predisposition to a violent marriage "script" may strongly influence the roles each partner plays. Similarly, "feeling a lack of warmth from one's father"—Dutton's second most important indicator of domestic violence—is bound to be a widespread phenomenon in cultures that require men to participate very little in child-rearing and to repress emotion. Individual batterers have not created this script any more than individual victims have. Indeed, many battering men know no other way to conduct their intimate relationships. They may not even be able to identify that what they are doing is seeking power and control; they may think that they are simply doing what men are supposed to do. Indeed, borrowing from Philip Pettit's idea of "elusive selves," battering men may be just as unfree as battered women. Pettit defines an "elusive self" as a self that does not have a clear sense of identity or boundary and that displays an inability to "live up to past commitments"—a definition that may describe many abusive men. It is possible that some batterers, when apologizing for their behavior and lavishing their partners with gifts in the "honeymoon" stage, engage in diabolically duplicitous behavior that purposely seeks to lull their partners into a false sense of security. But it is much more likely that such men are not keenly aware of how their behavior is inconsistent, even self-contradictory, and displays a gross discontinuity of selfhood and intentionality. Such men would seem to be, according to Pettit, just as unfree as are the women they abuse; if the women are unfree because they are dominated by men, the men are unfree because they are unable to articulate to themselves, much less to others, a coherent set of meanings and ideals consistent with democratic participation.[128] This does not mean that batterers do not know that violence is "wrong"—as is evidenced by the profuse apologies typically following early incidents of abuse—nor does it mean that experiences such as child abuse predetermine or excuse their abusive behavior, for other men with similar backgrounds do not become batterers, and abusers clearly display awareness and intentionality in their actions. However, *why* they make the choice to use violence depends to a significant degree on a justificatory background which legitimizes their desires for power and control and helps make rational sense out of those desires. The "wrongness" of violence may conflict with their understanding of their roles and entitlements as men in ways they are not able to fully comprehend, but such background narratives can serve as smokescreens to hide from themselves what it is that they are actually doing. This may be one important reason why it is so difficult to get men to stop violent behavior: the apparent privileges of power and control that battering gives to men feeds into a broader understanding of masculinity and male privilege that men are reluctant to give up—at least unconsciously, though often consciously as well—even if such violence is, in the long run, self-defeating to men's ability to critically assess their desires and understand their options.[129]

Social constructivism thus suggests that even when men appear to be actively constructing women through violence, the situation is never that straightforward. To use Marcus's term, domestic violence follows a patriarchal "script," and specific violent incidents are micro-enforcers of this script.[130] For instance, even if we see learned helplessness as a rational response to terror rather than a pathological personality disorder, a woman who has given up on escape is easier to control. Scripted ideas that women ask for abuse, or that they do not press charges because they do not really mind it, or that they are pathological codependents may misrepresent reality, but they also reinforce men's power and control over women and create the concrete conditions of their victimization. How to change the script of men's entitlement, power, and independence, of women's status as objects, helplessness, duty to care, ties to relationship, and economic inequality is an important question for feminists concerned with freedom, because it produces ways of altering a materiality that otherwise seems fatally determined. Viewing domestic violence as a script also may help us understand how some women are able to stop the abuse, for example, by threatening to leave or by having their partners arrested, actions which may interrupt the script of feminine victimization. Interrupting this "script" could help shift the dynamics of domestic violence and provide women with new choices and new ways to see themselves and their choices.

## RECONSTRUCTING FREEDOM

The third level of social construction thus reveals the depths of women's unfreedom: how totalizing is the construction of women's desires, opportunities, self-perceptions, relationships, and choices. But it also yields a way to enhance women's freedom; by changing discourses we can effect material relations, the ways in which women's experience is materialized, which will in turn make misrepresentation and domination more difficult to enact and sustain. Creating new ways of thinking about, talking about, and conceptualizing freedom can produce new material possibilities for women, new options as well as new ways of perceiving, understanding, choosing, and enacting options, new ways of understanding desire.

For instance, Martha Mahoney argues that the intractibility of IPV is related to a discursive and conceptual dichotomization of agency and victimization, freedom and unfreedom. "Victimization implies the one-way exercise of power, harm without strength; agency implies freedom from victimization."[131] Such a definition of "victim" can lead to the failure to see battered women as agents, such as when killing an abuser in self-defense is viewed as insanity or learned helplessness,[132] or going limp is seen as passivity rather than self-protection. The result is a focus on exit as the only option for women: if agency and victimization are opposed, and if battering victimizes women, then women cannot be free agents within the context of a battering relationship. This focus on exit, however, ignores the many barriers to women's exit I have described, as well as the possibility that exit may further victimize women, such as when they become homeless or lose custody of their children. Furthermore, despite the fact that it is feminists who have forced us to recognize that battered women have in fact repeatedly and creatively struggled to leave abusive partners, the focus on situations where women are prevented from doing so has the unintended effect of making women appear as victims, and only as victims, thus reinforcing the patriarchal script. Women are thus trapped in a vicious circle created by a combination of physical violence and language, of power, materiality, and discourse.

In order to break out of this circle, Mahoney suggests a redefinition of agency as "acting for oneself under conditions of oppression" rather than as the absence of oppression.[133] This definition requires us to see that violence is both an action of particular individuals (not all women are battered) and a structural component of patriarchy (but any woman could be). Redefining agency in this way makes it easier to understand why the conceptual vocabulary and epistemological assumptions of the existing discourses skew our inquiries to emphasize certain questions (Why didn't she leave?) while obscuring others (Why is he violent? Why did no one help?). In turn, this discursive reconfiguration makes it possible to see the efforts of battered women to get restraining orders, to move out of state, to get divorces, or to defend themselves as movements to create freedom within a context of oppression. Conversely, it makes it easier to identify women's complicity with patriarchy through choices and actions: the battered woman's mother who tells her to work it out for herself, the white heterosexual shelter worker who denies access to a lesbian or a woman who speaks no English, the upper-middle class nonbattered woman who scorns battered women for their weakness in staying with an abusive mate all participate in the support of patriarchal power without themselves "causing" it. The choices that they make within the constricted parameters of patriarchy express women's agency within a context of oppression, but simultaneously undermine it. While it would serve no feminist purpose to declare women's agency where they in fact have none—or by implication to emphasize women's agency to the point of implicitly holding them responsible for their victimization—it is equally problematic to deny this agency altogether. Both errors are unavoidable by-products of the failure to see the interaction of individual, institutional, and discursive oppression.

Of course, as I suggested in chapter 3, changing discursive "scripts" such as Mahoney identifies is a problem of infinite regress: how can one see a different way of conceptualizing the relationship between victimization and agency, oppression and freedom, constraint and choice, unless it already exists in discourse? One answer I suggested there was that the totalizing effects of the dominant discourse are not determinative but inevitably allow for movement within its framework, and that, as a result, more than one discourse operates on the social construction of meaning at any given time. By drawing on multiple discourses at their points of conflict, the dominant discourse can be shifted and altered. For instance, lesbian battering might seem to challenge the notion that "patriarchy" motivates the violence that restricts women's freedom, because the cultural and discursive context for lesbian relationships is one that tends to value equality, in direct contrast to the inequality of heterosexual IPV, and no men are involved in the relationship.[134] Indeed, lesbian battering often contradicts the standard pattern of heterosexual battering, for many lesbian batterers are smaller than their victims and more closely allied to stereotypical "femme" roles. Furthermore, while dependence tends to increase the likelihood of violence in lesbian relationships, as in heterosexual ones, the direction of dependency inverts the heterosexual pattern; that is, lesbian victims often make more money than batterers, and indeed, the batterer's economic dependence on her partner contributes to the violence.[135] Instead of challenging the linkage between patriarchy and battering, however, a feminist understanding of the discursive meaning of lesbian battering *reveals* particular dimensions of patriarchy that are present, but perhaps not so obvious, in heterosexual abuse. For instance, the notion that it is the batterer, not the abused partner, who is dependent would fit Mahoney's "separation assault" theory, where the woman's departure triggers the most severe violence in the man. Some men's extreme jealousy and possessiveness make better sense if viewed in terms of their dependence on women and their fear of such dependence, which is culturally at odds with norms for masculinity. The notion that abusive men are afraid of intimacy, and that their violence expresses the need to control what they are dependent on, viz., women, is a less obvious, but no less important, dimension of the cultural construction of masculinity within patriarchy. Indeed, Horsfall notes the paradox: "Male batterers render patriarchy audible and denote that the system of power is not so thoroughly in command. . . . If both men and women were well adapted to the patriarchal structures, men would have no need to exercise their superior physical power." The batterer's recourse to violence is "a sign that these [patriarchal] relations are under duress."[136]

Similarly, race and racial discourses can provide different ways of understanding domestic violence than the dominant white discourse. For instance, consider the deterrence effect of arrest on IPV recidivism. In the 1980s arrest was thought to be the best deterrent to repeated violence, following a study conducted in Minneapolis that compared recidivism among batterers who were arrested to that among those to whom police offered conciliation measures. But efforts to replicate that study in the late 1990s in five other cities showed that arrest produced only "modest deterrent effects."[137] That same study, however, showed that although "white batterers committed about 35 percent more acts of aggression against their victims than did African-Americans and other minority suspects . . . . minority suspects were 30 percent more likely to have a subsequent *officially recorded* incident of aggression than were white suspects."[138] In other words, though a higher proportion of IPV assaults are committed by white men, a higher proportion of black women who experience violence at the hands of their partners report the assault to the police (a finding confirmed by BJS).[139] Thus, it may be the case that arrest is relatively effective in reducing recidivism among African-American abusers, which in turn encourages black women to call the police when attacked. This higher figure could be a by-product of racism, of course, in that police may be more likely to arrest a black man than a white man when called by an IPV victim, thus again sending contrary messages to black and white women about the effectiveness of calling the police, as I have already discussed. But the fact that black women might succeed in halting abuse by having their abusers arrested may simultaneously interrupt the script of female victimization and provide white women with a different way of seeing their situation, as well as a reason to pursue not only arrest but effective prosecution. Indeed, as Mahoney notes, the dominant discursive formation of victimhood—which women frequently have to adopt in order to gain the sympathy of police, judges, and jury, but which also works against them—may be premised on racist stereotypes or ideals of white femininity. She points out that women of color may have less trouble reconciling personal strength with the fact of being oppressed or battered; hence, the dichotomy that a woman is either assertive *or* battered is a myth that "reflects white middle class norms about the family."[140] Attention to race can thus reveal that women of all races are harmed by white-dominant racist constructions of "femininity."

The battered women's movement, and the shelter movement in particular, may provide the most powerful alternative discourses, despite my earlier discussion of the ways in which shelters may at times depend on, replicate, and reinforce patriarchal discourse. The fact that shelters and the battered women's movement operate within contradictory and hostile patriarchal belief systems, linguistic and epistemological frameworks, and conceptual vocabularies does not negate the ways in which shelters and battered women's organizations often help women to achieve safety and freedom from violence. And this is *precisely* because of the focus in domestic-violence policy on the provision of "shelter." Without contradicting Loseke's insights that the concept of "shelter" reinforces the imagery of battered women's victimization and helplessness, it is also important to note that the protection from violence that "shelters" provide is instrumental in giving women the space to reject their victimization and reconstruct their agency. If the context of patriarchy itself imposes restraints on women's freedom, shelters can provide an altogether different context: a woman-only and woman-defined context where violence is unequivocally condemned, where women can see themselves not as weak and deserving of abuse, but as strong and capable precisely because they have survived and coped with abuse, and because they took the difficult step of leaving their homes to seek out the shelter. Mary Ann Dutton argues that the feminist approach to therapy available in shelters, which aims to empower women to see their options realistically, as well as to struggle to increase and maximize those options, is vital to battered women's ability to see beyond the intensely limiting context of their abusive relationship and to envision a different way of living and responding.[141] At the same time, what occurs in the professional's office may be even less important than what occurs between battered women in the community of the shelter, where women can compare experiences and come to see the violence they have endured as part of a larger social phenomenon and not simply a result of their own inadequacies.[142] Such community, marked by equality among women, including staff, has an added benefit where battered women take part in collective decision making and responsibility for the shelter's daily operation. Shelters that treat women as agents by pointing out that they can, as Mahoney put it, act for themselves under conditions of patriarchal oppression can help women develop different conceptions of themselves as well as different understandings of the violence they have experienced. Such reconfigured narratives and normative frameworks produce safe spaces within the larger patriarchal context. In such spaces, individual women can reclaim and rename their experiences, and this process can in turn yield a shift in the larger discourses of gender relations and the meaning of masculinity, femininity, and love. If the patriarchal context itself poses a barrier to women's freedom—to their protection from violence and control by others, to their ability to define themselves, explore alternate possibilities, and make choices in at least the same terms available to nonbattered persons—then achieving women's freedom requires a change of context. Shelters provide this in a literal sense, a physical space of safety in which emotional, psychological, and discursive spaces can be developed and deployed. This space, though temporary, begins the process of freedom: even one visit to a shelter provides some women with the power they need to end their partner's violence, or the self-validation to leave for good at a later date.[143]

At the same time, of course, the risk of romantic idealization here is considerable. As I have already indicated, racism and heterosexism exist among shelter workers and residents alike, thus challenging how "different" this new context and discourse can be from the patriarchal one it seeks to supplant. Moreover, as Brückner shows in her research on shelters in Germany, the early feminist ideals of radical equality that characterized the shelter movement in the 1970s have given way to an increased professionalization and hierarchy in the twenty-first century, largely because women traumatized by violence were not necessarily able to make the radically new choices and decisions that were expected of them. Although I will argue in my concluding chapter for the importance of equality to a feminist notion of freedom, the German experience that Brückner details raises important questions about the relationship between freedom and authority. For instance, in one shelter Brückner studied, the staff decided to exclude residents from a decision to admit a Moroccan woman in the interest of countering residents' hostility toward foreigners. Identifying many such examples in the everyday functioning of the shelter, Brückner highlights an ongoing tension between messages of empowerment and self-determination on the one hand, and the perceived need to determine residents' choices for them on the other. Similarly, the "therapy trap" Brückner identifies—the emphasis on psychotherapy rather than social supports—derives from an image of battered women "externally and internally occupied by patriarchy" and leads to an effort "to uproot this occupied wrong self, thereby liberating the real" or "nonpatriarchal self,"[144] thus "forcing" women to be "free."

Mandatory arrest similarly poses a paradox of forcing on women the conditions in which their freedom and autonomy can develop. Mandatory arrest and no-drop prosecutorial policies certainly protect women from the abuses of official power which put women at risk, as earlier discussed; and women who are not permitted to drop charges against their abusers are at decidedly lower risk of subsequent abuse than women who choose to drop charges. As domestic violence clearly shows, when the state, under the liberal rubric of nonintervention and protection of family privacy, fails to arrest and prosecute domestic abusers, it in fact intervenes most intrusively and violates women's privacy most egregiously. As Tifft notes, simply "criminalizing the batterer does not change the social-organizational or cultural context within which battering takes place." Rather, what is needed are community-based programs that coordinate efforts between police, prosecutors, judges, shelters, and medical personnel, and mandatory arrest and no-drop prosecution are often key elements in such programs.[145] But at the same time, such policies take away choice and control, just as battering does; choice is important to a battered woman's ability to feel in control, the thing she has least in IPV and the thing she needs most. And indeed, although women run lower risks of repeated abuse when no-drop policies are in force than when they are permitted to drop charges and do so, the lowest rates of recidivism are seen when women are allowed to drop charges but do not do so.[146] Choice thus enhances freedom the most, even as it jeopardizes it the most.

The tensions I have identified—between seeing domestic violence as a social formation constructed by and through discourses of gender, and a function of material obstacles such as economic inequality and discrimination by the legal system; between recognizing violence as a systematic expression of institutionalized male privilege and identifying the specificity and difference of experience for each individual woman; between external and internal forces and factors—means that freedom cannot follow either a positive- or negative-liberty model. Yet my discussion here has clearly borrowed from important ideas each model suggests about individual differences, choice, abilities, resources, and relationships. Feminist discursive interventions in domestic violence help make us more aware of the dominant discourses that construct battered women and indeed all women, and specifically the exclusion of women's humanity from the conceptualization of freedom. Recognizing that the "subject" of liberty is male enables us to be more self-aware and critically analytical about the choices we make. In keeping with negative-liberty ideals, battered women must themselves decide whether to separate from their abusers; nobody else can make this decision for them. Paradoxically, however, because of the trauma of violence, a battered woman may not realistically be able to do this, a phenomenon which battered women's syndrome identifies. Women's exercise of agency and freedom thus requires the help of others; the positive-liberty focus on the potential for others to help one realize one's true self and desires is important to retain.

Social constructivism makes it possible to formulate a feminist theory of freedom by bringing together these two otherwise conflicting models of positive and negative liberty. Social constructivism allows us to see how social institutions, practices, cultural values, and roles create pictures of reality and languages for interpretation that influence an individual's behavior and self-understanding. But at the same time, it is crucial to note that individuals are not determined by such constructions, that various possibilities of movement, agency, consciousness, and choice exist within the parameters of language and culture, that multiple contexts coexist with which individuals can identify and ally, and that we create and participate in these constructions in more and less active and conscious ways. Moreover, although we exist within large social formations, in which all knowledge, desires, and options are constructed for everyone, some people systematically have more power than others, including power to affect the social formation itself as well as conditions within it. As long as we are blind to the restrictiveness of the framework in which women live and battering occurs, we will continue to attribute agency and freedom to women when they in fact are responding to fear of imminent physical injury (such as when it is assumed that a woman's failure to flee her abuser must mean that the abuse was not really so bad), and overlook choice and agency when it is exercised (such as when a woman's acquiescence to the batterer's demands is seen as capitulation rather than negotiation). Recognizing "the congruence of expectations between [male] batterers and society at large"[147] may help unmask the ways in which battering is about power rather than sexism per se, while at the same time helping us understand the gendered dimensions of this power—and hence of freedom—more fully.

## Chapter Five

# WELFARE AS A PROBLEM FOR FREEDOM THEORY

IT COULD be argued, of course, that domestic violence provides too easy a case for the argument I am making about freedom. Because violence frequently involves palpable, physical coercion and is often cited as the clearest example of a restraint on freedom, as noted at the start of the previous chapter, the challenge is not to establish *that* women are made unfree by IPV, but rather *how* they are unfree in ways that are not obvious. By contrast, welfare is something that, according to the dominant discourse, some women freely, if not eagerly, pursue, because it provides "money for nothing," that is, a source of income not related to labor, even the labor of housewifery and raising children (particularly since such women are not married). At the same time, according to that same discourse, such choices do not make women free; rather, they become entrapped by their own laziness and greed into a system that robs them of the independence and autonomy necessary for freedom.

The connections between domestic violence and welfare are at one and the same time intuitively obvious and difficult to articulate definitively. Just as statistics on the frequency of domestic violence in the general population display considerable variety, as I showed in the previous chapter, so is it difficult to achieve agreement on the incidence of domestic violence among welfare recipients. This is partly due to the varieties among states in the administration of welfare policy, but it is also due to the reluctance of welfare recipients to report information about domestic violence, for reasons ranging from the mistaken belief that welfare still forbids a "man in the house" and that benefits can be taken away even from a woman who is dating a man, to anxiety about being declared an unfit mother, to a more generalized fear or resentment of further state intrusion into a private life that is already substantially controlled by the state. As I explained in the previous chapter, although battering happens across all economic classes, poor women are more vulnerable, not only experiencing a higher incidence of domestic violence, but also having access to fewer resources to escape or stop it. Studies conducted in various states have reached similar conclusions: about two-thirds of women on welfare have been victims of domestic violence, and about 20 to 30 percent are abused annually.[1] As the Personal Responsibility and Work Opportunity Reconciliation Act (PRWORA) has taken hold on the concrete realities of women's lives, domestic violence has posed considerable extra burdens on women receiving welfare, particularly requirements to participate in wage labor. As discussed in chapter 4, battered women are vulnerable to their partners' interference with efforts at economic independence, and even to attack in the workplace.

Yet freedom was an important political and theoretical theme in the debates over welfare reform in the late 1990s, particularly in the United States. Arguably, of course, freedom has always been a subtext, if not an overt issue, for women on welfare. In both Europe and the United States, the forms of public assistance commonly called "welfare" can, at least in theory, be seen as a series of programs developed as a resource to empower citizens, to enable them to liberate themselves from certain restrictive conditions such as poverty, unemployment, poor health, and the economic uncertainties of old age. For women in particular, welfare programs such as Aid to Families with Dependent Children (AFDC) in the United States and maternal benefits in Europe were conceived as means for providing women with a certain degree of financial independence from individual men, particularly women who faced destitution after widowhood or abandonment, or who needed to escape from abusive marriages.[2] Yet many feminist scholars have revealed that this "liberation" was always at least dubious, if not an outright failure, entailing many more constraints and restrictions than powers and freedoms.[3] In practice, welfare often seems more about institutionalizing social control over women than "liberating" them from economic destitution or "empowering" them to be economically independent. Feminists agree that "being on welfare" (in U.S. parlance) involves strict and intrusive scrutiny by the state over women's sexuality and mothering, as well as their participation in wage labor. Moreover, the small payments made to welfare mothers, as well as the form it often takes—subsidized rent in housing that is often substandard, food stamps rather than cash, work assignments in low-grade, unskilled labor—often makes welfare extremely punitive, restricting women's options and freedom of action in many ways. Exploring the ways in which freedom was and is discursively deployed in welfare reform and how the discourse of welfare both misrepresents women's lived reality and produces material effects in the form of public policies can illuminate another aspect of social construction that IPV suggests only indirectly. Though for both issues, law provides an essential discursive framework for freedom and restraint, battered women's contact with legal discourse is generally funneled through police and the courts, while welfare recipients encounter state power in other forms and arenas, namely, social policy and the bureaucratic state. As Kathy Ferguson has argued, women's contact with bureaucratic state agencies provides an even greater degree of normalization than the criminal justice system, because of the status of their regulatory power. Certainly, IPV brings the state into the home and personal relations, as I have shown in chapter 4. Welfare policy, however, does so not at moments of crisis but in its regulation and construction of the everyday aspects of personal experience that most people take for granted. Its effects are thus that much more pervasive, for bureaucracy engages in a "feminization" of its subjects, it produces them as subordinate, dependent, and submissive by apparently protecting them from the most overt forms of domination, such as abject poverty and homelessness, while creating its own forms of less obvious domination—in the case of welfare, the regulation of sexuality, reproduction, family structure, and labor market participation. Although such feminization affects men receiving public assistance as well, women's unique position as primary caretakers enables welfare to be administered through intense surveillance techniques. As opposed to Social Security or unemployment compensation, where many, if not the majority, of the recipients are men, it is the fact that women are the primary beneficiaries of welfare that motivates and legitimizes the construction of state power in this way. As Wendy Brown puts it, bureaucracy "creates *feminized* subjects while it excludes or colonizes *female* subjects." By this, I take her to mean that state policies rely on, and in turn promote, reductive and harmful constructions of gender that ignore the lived experience and needs of actual women. And as she observes about this process of state regulation of women's lives, it is perhaps less the case that the bureaucratic state attempts to regulate a preexisting and essential femininity by making it *possible* for women to continue in mothering roles even when the role of wife has been disrupted than that it produces and constructs this femininity, particularly by creating and reinforcing the norm that women *should* be mothers. Yet paradoxically, in welfare reforms that took place in the 1990s, this role is taken as a social given which the state must oversee, regulating how such roles are to be played and expressed and what that role means, not only for femininity, but for the different classifications of women who are filling those roles.[4]

## WOMEN'S FREEDOM AND DISCOURSES OF WELFARE

I begin this discussion by returning to Greta's story from chapter 1, the woman who had to decide whether to go on welfare. With three small children, including one infant to support, she did not believe it was sensible to remain in her job; her wages were low, and her prospects of advancement not very promising. She would have been happy to return to secretarial work, but since she quit her job when she married, most businesses underwent the computer revolution, so her former secretarial skills were sorely out of date. Without money to enter computer training programs, she was disqualified from most secretarial positions. Furthermore, her child care arrangements were not very satisfactory; she was paying her neighbor Georgia, who has been on welfare for years, to look after her children. But Georgia's house was extremely dirty, and she watched a lot of soap operas, so Greta did not entirely trust Georgia to give her children the careful supervision Greta herself provides. She decided to bite the bullet and apply for welfare. After eighteen months on AFDC, though, she was able to land a job as a shipping clerk for UPS that paid quite a bit more than minimum wage. Greta was doing somewhat better economically, but the job was not full-time and did not provide benefits, so when her middle child developed a serious case of asthma the following year, she had to quit and go back on welfare so that she could qualify for Medicaid. When the boy's health stabilized, she landed another job but she had to quit after six months, because once again it just did not pay enough to cover her child care expenses and the costs of her son's medication.

When she returned to welfare this time, however, the Personal Responsibility and Work Opportunity Reconciliation Act (PRWORA), more commonly known as welfare reform, had been passed by the U.S. Congress and signed into law by President Clinton. The PRWORA replaced AFDC with Temporary Assistance to Needy Families (TANF), which denationalized welfare as a program by turning funding over to the states in the form of block grants, along with a great deal of discretion to construct welfare programs and policies and to decide how payments would be made, and under what conditions. States were now to decide eligibility criteria, benefit levels, and specific work requirements. PRWORA did set some broad parameters, however, with which states had to comply, time limits and work requirements being among the most central. PRWORA specifies a five-year lifetime limit for the receipt of welfare benefits and a two-year consecutive limit, after which recipients must begin to participate in wage labor in order to maintain a portion of benefits, such as food stamps or Medicaid.[5] States have instituted various specific approaches within those parameters. In some states, after only two months of receiving benefits, regardless of the age of their children, recipients must engage in community service labor, generally called "workfare." Workfare was a provision originally included in the bill, though many states have not enacted it, and some have extended the period in which recipients may receive benefits before engaging in workfare. Other states have created exceptions to work requirements, and some have allowed certain kinds of educational training to count as fulfillment of the work requirement for a limited period of time. Such variability in policy is exacerbated in states in which decisions about welfare programs are made at the county level. Other federal parameters set by PRWORA involved the establish-

ment of long-range goals for family structure and reproduction, such as
the reduction of abortion and out-of-wedlock births and increasing rates
of marriage. Various states pursued such goals by structuring benefits to
favor married couples, putting "family caps" on benefit increases after the
second child, and mandating child support and recipients' cooperation in
locating noncustodial parents. But time limits and work requirements
were the dominant focus of welfare reform and PRWORA; the rubric of
"personal responsibility" in the bill's title emphasized the need for welfare
recipients to "get off the dole" and be active contributors to the economy
and civil society.

Greta was lucky: she lives in West Philadelphia, and Pennsylvania is a
state that allows welfare recipients to fulfill the first year of work requirements through vocational training. This allowed her finally to acquire
word processing skills, and she was able to land a job that paid almost
ten dollars an hour. But the job is located in the Philadelphia suburbs, it
takes her an hour each way to commute by bus (she cannot afford a car),
and in the morning she has to start out before all her children have left
for school. Through a patchwork of assistance from neighbors and relatives, she has been able to provide supervision for her children before and
after school; and fortunately, since the youngest entered first grade this
year, she no longer has to worry about half-days. But the after-school
supervision for her children has posed the greatest difficulties. The two
arrangements she has worked out have each in turn failed. First, Greta's
aunt, who looked after Greta's children in their own home, was hospitalized. So Greta had to return to her neighbor Georgia, who was fulfilling
her work requirement at home by looking after other children along with
her own two. But Georgia was discovered drinking while caring for the
kids. Greta has had to miss work several days running while she searches
for another arrangement and is in danger of being fired. Also, although
she is very lucky to have a benefits package with her job, it has extremely
high employee copayments, and if her son gets sick again and needs to be
hospitalized, she is not sure how effective the coverage will be. Finally,
Social Services has not yet been able to track down her husband for mandatory child support. Even though Greta would receive very little, if any,
of this money, her social worker is complaining that Greta is not doing
enough to assist their office and that her eligibility for future benefits is
threatened.

The question of Greta's freedom is on the surface somewhat straightforward, at least from the first level of positive liberty—the provision of
enabling resources—or even from an expanded negative-liberty model
that viewed larger social formations as barriers to freedom. For what
keeps her from economic independence and security for her family, from
living the life that she wants to live, in the way she wants to live it, is a

lack of resources that the economically privileged take for granted. For instance, the job training and vocational-education programs that the state permitted her to use for her first year of work requirements helped her obtain a better job that paid a reasonable salary with decent benefits. But other resources are sorely missing, and their absence seriously compromises her ability to live freely and autonomously. For example, national health insurance—which many of the Clinton proposals for welfare reform originally presupposed, before they were gutted by conservative Republicans—would liberate Greta from worrying about her child's health and how to pay for the services he needs. Transportation funding—either in the form of an individual subsidy to help her buy and maintain a car or improved public transportation from the city to the suburbs—would give her greater time to spend with her family or simply to take care of herself. Subsidized and standardized professional child care would not only free her from having to construct her own patchwork of care but could ease her worries about the quality of care in which she leaves her children. Some of these freedoms would be material, such as greater income, but others are less tangible, such as a reduction of worry, leaving the mind free to "imagine" the self and envision alternative future directions in which she might take her life.[6]

But at the same time, Greta has made a number of choices in her life that have led her to where she is. As her mother points out, she clearly chose to stop working and chose to be economically dependent on her husband. And she makes choices every day about how to negotiate the demands of her job and the needs of her children. But by locating those choices in their context of patriarchal social and economic relations, as I argued in the previous chapter, we see that choice is not enough to establish freedom, for the parameters of choice have been determined by and through power structures in which Greta is not entitled to participate. However, Greta is not the only person in this story, and many would point out that PRWORA was not really setting its sights at someone like Greta, but rather at someone like Georgia. Georgia has been on welfare for years; she complains about not having enough money, but she owns several televisions and watches them for large portions of the day, attending to her children in rather careless ways. She sees Greta's need for child care as a way that she herself can get a little extra money, but she does not take her caregiving responsibilities very seriously and she pretty much ignores Greta's children, as she does her own. Moreover, although Georgia is legally required to report all the income she earns, she has not done so, and has not told Greta that she hasn't done so.

Many feminists will be rolling their eyes right now, if not groaning in outrage, at my portrayal of Georgia; she is certainly the stereotype on which welfare reform is based. Certainly, contemporary antipathy toward welfare, and the birth of the Republican reform movement, had its basis in the image of the "welfare queen," which arose well before the mid-1990s; indeed, it dates back to the Johnson administration, continued through that of Richard Nixon, and culminated in the language of race and class antagonism favored by the Reagan administration. The welfare queen, who is usually black and sits at home watching television while the welfare checks come pouring in, having baby after baby as a way to fill her coffers, is shiftless and lazy, but clever enough to manipulate the system and rip off taxpayers. Indeed, she feels an indignant sense of entitlement to the support she receives from the tax dollars of hard-working (white) Americans.[7] This vision has persisted, with some (male and female) members of Congress going so far as to call welfare recipients "wolves" and "alligators." Many, including members of the Clinton administration, talked frequently in terms of a "culture of welfare."[8]

But in the 1990s debates over welfare, the welfare queen also began to intermingle with a contrasting, though no better, and certainly no less stereotypical, image of the pathological dependent: maybe not everyone on welfare was evilly ripping the system off, but those who weren't were being victimized by their own reliance on the system. In the rhetoric surrounding U.S. welfare reform in the 1990s, conservatives repeatedly hammered home the argument that welfare is a "dependency," an unhealthy state from which recipients should want to free themselves. This dependency robs welfare recipients of rationality, so that they cannot even see the mess they are in, cannot see that welfare is precisely what is keeping them down. Indeed, politicians have likened welfare to drugs, and the language of addiction has been an important subtext, if not an overt theme, in antiwelfare rhetoric. This supposed pathological dependency has left welfare recipients basically clueless concerning the fundamentals of living an independent life. Lacking skills, even the most rudimentary ones, such as how to get up on time and how to dress for work, they are unable to obtain even the most basic minimum-wage job, let alone to keep one should they get it. They lack the desire to work, not only out of a sense of entitlement to other people's money—a sense that, like the drug addict's, is completely irrational and cannot be argued with—but also out of simple ignorance about how the working world operates, and a low self-esteem that prevents them from even trying to find out. And they certainly don't know how to raise their children, so it is outrageous to subsidize them for that purpose.[9] Thus, welfare is like a drug, which makes its victims unable to cope with life's most basic tasks and particularly disables them from seeing that they *are* addicted and from taking action to break the habit. (Indeed, in keeping with the narcotic theme, perhaps one could argue that the latter image of helpless incompetent could have emerged out of the former "queen" image, following the stereotype of the street-smart drug dealer who sells to support his habit and who becomes taken over by his addiction, turning from evil manipulator to hapless victim.)

Many feminists have rebutted these stereotypical images, showing that they are based on racist as well as sexist misconceptions, and pointing out that many welfare recipients are white,[10] that most recipients stay on welfare for less than two years, that they often work for wages to supplement benefits or cycle between welfare and work, and that welfare is often seen as a last resort in a "crisis" situation such as divorce, a child's serious illness (because the low-wage jobs women often have do not provide health insurance), or the need to escape from an abusive partner.[11] If Georgia is real at all, feminists argue, she represents an extreme minority of welfare recipients, not, as conservatives claim, the average welfare mother. Feminists have also sought to highlight the larger discursive framework in which welfare reform has taken place and the background against which it is set, challenging assumptions that the middle class and wealthy are "independent" of state support even though they may receive Social Security, Medicare, and income tax deductions for home ownership, dependent children, or even businesses.[12]

I agree that Georgia represents a minority of recipients, but I also maintain she is real, and indeed that she is, as some conservatives claim, the living product of welfare. Both Greta and Georgia represent different typologies of "the welfare mother," the symbol of welfare, but both have been constructed by and through the discourses of welfare. By denying or ignoring people like Georgia, feminists have been unable to engage the social construction of welfare subjects and as a result have been limited by the existing dominant discourses on welfare, which prevent the imagining and constructing of a truly reconfigured feminist vision of welfare. That Georgia exists should not be a surprise, after all. When women are expected to raise their children on an income below the subsistence level, when they must endure intense personal scrutiny in order to get it—and from an agency that is often too burdened to provide meaningful personal guidance or assistance—we should not be surprised if they resent these requirements and seek to get around them or try to escape their depressing existence through alcohol, drugs, or television. But the dominant welfare discourse maintains that such behavior displays personal failings or weaknesses on the part of welfare recipients, rather than constituting reasonable responses to unreasonable situations.

Of course, this observation applies to men as well; both women's and men's understanding of reality and the self is itself shaped and limited by the power relations of race, gender, and class, which set the parameters for what we can say and think, the alternative possibilities we can envision, and hence, what we *can* desire and how we *can* think of ourselves as choosing subjects. After all, men have also been powerfully affected by welfare reform. In particular, welfare reform's emphasis on marriage deploys deeply sexist (and at least tacitly racist) attitudes about men: the reason that there are so many children born out of wedlock is not merely that women are immoral but that men are unfaithful, deceitful, and unreliable. Indeed, a dominant conservative theme in welfare reform was that tying men more closely to the family was key to ending women's dependency on welfare; in a distorted mirroring of Rousseau's argument that ending the corruption of women was the way to make men better fathers, it might seem that contemporary conservatives believe that reforming men is key to the reformation of women.[13] But such discourses about men and masculinity have obvious effects on women. Because women are socially assigned primary responsibility for child care and are thus the major recipients of TANF, they are materially impacted by policies aimed at changing men's behavior as fathers and husbands. But more broadly, discourses of masculinity cannot be disentangled from those of femininity; policies aimed at redefining men's identity and roles in the family will inevitably affect the identity and social role of women as well.

Hence, welfare once again demonstrates the duality of social construction—specifically, that while men are socially constructed, as are women, they are constructed precisely to have more power than women. Hence, although poor people of both genders are impacted by welfare reform, it is women, and particularly single mothers, who were the overt targets of reform and who, as the major recipients of AFDC, are by far impacted the most by its transformation into workfare and TANF. Once again, social construction is not merely a "local" phenomenon; the social construction of welfare subjects is not the product of recent welfare discourse in and of itself, acting in a social vacuum. Rather, what makes its impact so significant is the ways in which specific local phenomena like welfare policies emerge within a larger context of much broader socially constructed categories of gender, race, and class—constructions that have gone on for decades and centuries, slowly growing, and evolving in response to changing local phenomena. In this sense, the immediate experiences of welfare participants are filtered through the light of these larger experiences and categories of meaning.

## Freedom Theory and Conservative Discourse

PRWORA was the result of many months of political wrangling between liberals and conservatives in a political climate that was generally hostile to welfare. The measures it introduced have by many accounts drastically reduced welfare rolls, but the reasons offered for such reduction vary widely: reform advocates claim that individuals on welfare, aided by a strong economy, have moved into jobs that hold the promise of continued economic independence, whereas reform critics insist that poor women and men have been pushed off welfare prematurely, because administrators have misinterpreted the rules or because recipients misunderstand the rules and do not apply for benefits to which they are entitled.[14] From a feminist perspective, however, the institution of welfare reform under PRWORA was very problematic, for it displayed certain kinds of ideological and political biases that cleaved to lines of gender and race as well as class. It is clear that poor single mothers were the primary beneficiaries of AFDC and hence were most affected by its transformation into TANF. For all its failings, AFDC did provide a kind of "entitlement" to poor mothers raising children, but under TANF, welfare has become much harder to obtain, and much further away from the "right" advocated by welfare activists since the turn of the twentieth century.[15] More immediately, whatever the long-term outcome might be, TANF has put incredible strains on poor single mothers, who are now forced to work in minimum-wage jobs with little hope for advancement and few benefits while receiving inadequate state support for child care or transportation to better-paying jobs.

Such inequities might seem to have more to do with "justice" than "freedom"; but as John Rawls (1971), perhaps unintentionally, showed us, principles of freedom are central to questions of justice.[16] And indeed, what seems "unjust" to feminists about welfare is precisely the way in which it arbitrarily restricts some people, particularly poor single mothers, while allowing others who receive much larger subsidies, such as corporations, a great deal of freedom. This is particularly the case when one considers victims of domestic violence who are on welfare. Though welfare in theory provides women with the single most important resource for self-protection—economic independence—in practice welfare often makes battered women even more vulnerable to IPV. For instance, women who manage to escape their abusers by moving to a different city or state are caught by welfare reform's requirements that they assist the state in collecting child support payments, for such assistance may reveal to abusive men the location of their (former) wives or girlfriends. As I explained in chapter 4, work requirements similarly may make abused women more vulnerable to violence, since abusers can find women at work even when they are living in shelters whose locations are carefully guarded secrets. Or abusers threatened by their partners' efforts toward economic independence can undermine them by disrupting the workplace and getting them fired. Other aspects of welfare reform, such as "bridefare," which may make it financially unfeasible for women not to marry or to divorce their abusers, similarly may undercut battered women's attempts to gain security and independence.[17] But these measures place obvious restrictions on all poor women, battered or not.

The relevance of freedom to welfare goes beyond the immediate restrictive effects on women, however, to the framework within which welfare discussions take place. I will focus here primarily on U.S. welfare reform, because despite the fact that welfare "retrenchments" are occurring throughout the modern industrialized states,[18] with the possible exception of Great Britain and Germany, no other "welfare state" has staged the kind of elaborate ideological debates that took place in the United States throughout the 1990s. British Prime Minister Tony Blair denounced a "workless class" bred by state welfare policies in terms similar to the U.S. discourse of a "culture of dependency," six months before the British parliament voted to cut funding for unemployed single mothers in need of assistance and to begin means testing for benefits for the sick and disabled. Under the conservative Christian Democrats, Germany provides far more generous welfare benefits than the United States, but does so on the overt premise of keeping women in the home raising children.[19] Such discourses afford a different, but no less fruitful, avenue for analysis of the relationship between welfare discourse and freedom.

But the United States discourse on welfare has been the most overt, if not effective, in socially constructing welfare as public policy and welfare recipients as its subjects. Conservative Republicans have claimed the bulk of the credit for welfare reform, and the debate has often been pitched as a clear-cut fight between right and left, with "reform" measures being pushed by conservative Republicans who meanly seek to punish the poor and "resistance" efforts being led by ultraliberal Democrats and others on the left who, despite years of criticizing the inadequacy of AFDC, have fought to preserve it as the last, best hope for single mothers.[20] The relationship between this discourse, the policies that have emerged from it, and the ways in which these policies are enacted in practice have raised important questions relevant to women's freedom. In particular, the dominant discourse of welfare reform in the United States, by capturing a particular strand of freedom theory, has forced feminists into a reactive stance that not only ignores key dimensions of women's construction by and through the welfare state but also cuts off fruitful avenues toward an effective political strategy. The Right has particularly appropriated the "internal" dimensions of liberty, viz., desire, will, and identity. As a result, reforms have taken a form that some of its proponents, particularly Newt Gingrich (at the height of the visibility he gained through his "Contract with America," which significantly propelled reform), likened to "tough love." Getting people off welfare is in their own best interest, because it is in the interest of their liberty and self-respect, and the only way to get them off is to force them off. Family caps, workfare, and time limits will all, to borrow Rousseau's infamous phrase, force them to be free.

Indeed, these measures resonate deeply with positive-liberty theory, particularly the notion that others can know your "true will" and "best interests" better than you, which raises the hackles of liberals and feminists alike. Wendy Brown has argued that "the Right's monopoly on positive discourses of freedom" has produced the Left's rejection of freedom as a bourgeois illusion;[21] but I maintain that instead, the Right's capture of positive-liberty discourse has pushed feminists into the negative-liberty camp. Feminists devote most of our time and attention to the important task of pointing out how reforms are taking choices away from women. Particularly significant are restrictions on choices in reproductive freedom through family caps, as well as financial bonuses paid to poor women who agree to have Norplant implanted under their skin. Women's choices in marrying are also limited by policies such as so-called "bridefare," which permits married mothers to care for their children full-time but requires unmarried welfare recipients to work, in an overt effort to "encourage" women to get and stay married. Women's choices are also restricted in pursuit of education and employment, particularly when recipients are not permitted to count education toward work requirements, or are even required to quit school in order to take mandated unskilled jobs.[22] Indeed, since "work first" programs require a recipient to take "any job," which effectively prevents women from trying to develop a rational career plan that would offer financial remuneration and opportunities for advancement, welfare reforms can be seen as preventing women from developing long-term, autonomous life plans. From a feminist perspective, welfare reform, in its rush to get women off welfare, no matter how, seems to seek to punish women simply for being unmarried and poor. Mink's labeling of the PRWORA as "a moral straightjacket, conceived and enacted to . . . intensify the disciplinary function of social policies affecting poor women" clearly articulates the notion that reforms seriously undermine women's freedom and autonomy.[23]

Feminist efforts to reveal the punitive and restrictive character of these "reforms" are vital work and have helped modify some of welfare reform's worst effects. For instance, feminists have successfully lobbied in several states for the "Family Violence Option," which allows battered women to delay work requirements in recognition of the increased risk employment may put them in.[24] Such efforts are important and have made differences in women's lives. But they reflect a reactive, defensive strategy against the constraints of welfare reform, which means that the terms of the discourse are still dictated by the Right. The fact that many (though not all) feminists seem to have taken a largely negative-liberty perspective, focusing on the harms to women that reforms bring about, poses a challenge to feminists concerned with welfare, because it has cut off important parts of the spectrum of freedom theory and pushed us into positions that may not be strategically best for women. The concern is that underneath these important feminist efforts may lie a basically individualist impulse: women's entitlement to welfare payments is often cast as an individual right, without attention to the larger issue of why it is that women are the ones who care for children. There is often inadequate attention to how the choosing welfare subject is constructed, how her choices and desires come into existence, what it is that women on welfare want, how they formulate those desires, and how they would like to see those desires fulfilled and realized. After all, it is not simply that we happen to have mean-spirited, racist, sexist legislators in office, and all we need do to fix welfare is vote them out. Some, even many, legislators may be all those things: they are not just innocently responding to an objective reality. But they also are the expression of a social context of racism, classism, and sexism that pervades the very fundamentals of the "reality" that we live. Social constructivism differentiates, and yet sees the connections, between the individual sexist actions of particular individuals—the local or "micro" forces—and the larger, "macro" social structures that make those actions possible. Though the first level of social construction suggests that welfare discourse may be a false patina that blinds us to truth, it will also materialize its own ideology and become the "truth," shaping not only concrete social relations and experiences but how we think and talk about those relations in defining reality.

Hence the so-called "hard core" of welfare—long-term recipients like Georgia—which many feminists tend to ignore and the Right tends to exaggerate, may in fact be a product of welfare, just as conservatives claim. Neither an independent existence to which welfare is an innocent response, nor a complete figment of the right-wing imagination, it is the materialization of discourse, a discourse that may arise out of ideological misrepresentation but which manifests itself in the concrete conditions in which poor women live. Consider the following account in the *Philadelphia Inquirer*, for instance: according to the Pennsylvania Department of Public Welfare, of the 25,800 welfare recipients statewide who were the first to face the two-year cut-off deadline in March, 1999, 70 percent had been on welfare for three years or longer, and 40 percent had received assistance for more than seven years.[25] These numbers are indeed disturbing, regardless of whether one is liberal or conservative, because public assistance is a key indicator of poverty. But looking more deeply at these statistics reveals that the recipients in fact cycle on and off welfare, as feminists have argued. Heidi Hartmann and others of the Institute for Women's Policy Research have established through quantitative analysis that women do not simply go on welfare and stay there. Rather, they use a variety of strategies for supporting themselves and alternate public assistance with periods of working.[26] According to the IWPR research, the typical seven-year welfare recipient is like Greta: she goes on welfare for two years because, say, her husband left her after the birth of her third child; then she gets a job for a year, then goes back on welfare for another nine months because she was laid off; then gets another job, but has to quit fourteen months later, because her low-paying job provided no health coverage for her sick child.

This cycling phenomenon was not mentioned in the report, nor in the *Philadelphia Inquirer* article; rather the fact that the women included in the Pennsylvania report behaved precisely as IWPR predicted was revealed in response to my specific question about this issue in a telephone conversation with a Commonwealth of Pennsylvania "Information Specialist." This person, however, knew of no detailed figures that would show precisely what percentage of the seven years these recipients actually received benefits. But since many more people read the *Philadelphia Inquirer* than reports from the IWPR, much less from the Commonwealth's Department of Human Services, people's beliefs about welfare are formed by this misleading information, and "welfare" as a program is constructed accordingly. This presentation of apparently conflicting "facts" thus suggests that the discourse of welfare dependency is not simply an ideologically driven conservative discourse but a supposedly neutral bureaucratic one that constructs the welfare subject in this way. Moreover, it creates an ideological dichotomy in which the construction of welfare subjects becomes the prize in a discursive tug of war. The Right (and welfare bureaucrats) focus on the idea that 40 percent were on welfare for seven years, such that people like Greta become represented as being on welfare for seven uninterrupted years because of personal failings. A more accurate picture of Greta's situation, however, is not one of dependence but one of entrapment: she has tried, and succeeded, in getting off welfare several times but is always forced back by the structural factors of poverty, compounded by gender, motherhood, and perhaps race. And indeed, she has tried to use welfare to maintain her independence but failed, not through her own fault but through welfare's structural perpetuation of poverty. The question then becomes not how do we change her psychology but how do we change the structural factors—such as poor pay, no national health care insurance, and inadequate affordable child care—that make it so difficult for her to work.

Thus, the focus on "seven years" distorts the reality of welfare experience and constructs the welfare subject as pathologically dependent. But the feminist temptation to focus on the notion that most women cycle on and off welfare and combine welfare with employment is also somewhat reductive of the problem. Feminists are rightly angry about the Republican sleight-of-hand that takes the image of "the hard-core dependent" as the template for describing all welfare participants and have with some success rebutted it. But often, feminists end up rejecting it altogether, and that is a mistake; it risks romanticizing welfare recipients as completely capable but downtrodden, victims of the patriarchal machine. Welfare reform offers a contemporary version of a discursive construction that has existed since the welfare state originated;[27] Greta becomes the "deserving" poor and Georgia the "undeserving." Reform is aimed at Georgia, because, in the conservative view, she is the one who needs to be changed, but Greta will not be on public assistance for long anyway, because she is diligent and responsible, so she will not degenerate to Georgia's state. Indeed, reform will help diligent, earnest, deserving poor women like Greta by providing job training. Feminists have critiqued this ideological misrepresentation of welfare mothers and welfare reform as willfully denying the difficult and even untenable position it puts Greta in, by failing to provide the social supports that she needs, like child care, in order to be successful at paid employment. Such critique has been important, but it tells only part of the story; feminists need to focus on Georgia as well.

Lucy White attempts such a refocusing of welfare by considering the case of Elaine Presston, a longtime welfare recipient "who readily describes herself as trapped on welfare because she is lazy."[28] Though White's account predates PRWORA, the 1988 Family Support Act required Elaine to attend literacy classes as a condition of receiving AFDC, which also involved participating in her child's Head Start program two mornings a week. After a few weeks, however, Elaine stopped attending her classes, in part because of family difficulties, in part because of "laziness," in part as a test to see if her caseworker would care. Elaine Presston seems to present a self-defeating persona, a woman who does not try to help herself, who is dissatisfied on welfare but does little to take advantage of opportunities to escape it. Indeed, the only thing that seems to capture Elaine's attention is television, which she claims to "love" and which she can watch for hours on end. She also uses drugs.[29] But White also traces a history in Elaine's life of feeling abandoned and uncared for, particularly by a mother who worked when Elaine was a girl in order to support Elaine and her siblings, and by Elaine's teachers "during the first years of court-ordered integration," which made education not only unrewarding but hostile and frightening.[30] Such a lifetime of experiences has produced a sense of futility, but also of anger, since she can see daily on television the gap between her life and that of the white middle class.

White is not saying that feminists should pity Elaine any more than they should shun her, but rather that Elaine cannot be left out of feminist or liberal discourse. Feminists, White implies, do not want to allow real difference into their accounts of welfare reform. Like the battered woman who chooses to stay with her abuser, for any number of reasons that are not visible to the casual or even to the professional observer, women are on welfare for many different reasons and under many different circumstances, and feminists have to address those differences. This requires us to attend to internal as well as external factors. Although shifting attention from long-term recipients to those who already combine welfare with wage work, and who are in the system only temporarily, may be an effective strategy for countering right-wing stereotypes, at the same time it tends to push aside those women who have had the most difficult time getting off welfare. Kathryn Edin, for instance, argues that the longer recipients are on welfare, the more difficult it becomes to escape it.[31] In attempting to respond to the conservative discourse, to create counternarratives to its story of pathological dependence, feminists become captured by its terms and end up ignoring or forgetting the rest of the picture.

Thus, a social constructionist approach suggests that conservatives may be correct when they say that welfare is "the problem," that it creates a "cycle of dependency." Where they are wrong is in the reasons they offer for this cycle. That is, it is not the subsidy itself that produces dependency but the lack of anything else (such as education, training in high-tech skills, or child care) as well as the dehumanizing conditions under which the subsidy is granted (particularly the small amounts, as well as the intrusive state regulation) that trap women in poverty. Feminists have at least implicitly made these arguments before; but they also need to recognize the psychological dimensions of welfare policy, and the construction of the welfare subject. For instance, Lisa Dodson's interviews with women on welfare repeatedly reveal a psychic toll taken by endless waiting, unhelpful and even exploitative caseworkers who refuse to provide advice or guidance, and the contempt that many in social services barely hide for their "clients," leading one woman to say that welfare "is supposed to make you feel helpless, make you feel you are trash." Those conditions—"the little erosions that wear you down into someone you don't want to be"—have helped construct the welfare subject.[32] Other feminist scholars too have documented a lack of self-esteem and confidence, depression, and erasure of identity among women on welfare. Women report feeling "like dirt," "so ashamed I could die," "intimidated," "like a stone" (i.e., emotionless), "a dummy."[33] Faced daily with the humiliation of state surveillance, and particularly of male caseworkers, drug counselors, or public-housing building managers who engage in sexual harassment or even blackmail; the dehumanization of grinding poverty, because assistance is so minimal; the despair of having your efforts to dig yourself out (for instance, by working on the side to supplement benefits) characterized as fraud; the contradictory messages that "good" mothers stay home and care for their children but that single mothers on public assistance who do this are lazy cheats; being reviled by almost everyone not on public assistance, ranging from the grocery store clerk who takes your food stamps to the supposedly "objective" media that launch attacks based on misstatement of fact;[34] the foreshortening of your vision of the possible brought about by lack of education and social isolation—all have profound effects on the construction of selfhood and subjectivity. The fact that the Right has taken this truth and perverted it into a rationale for hatred and persecution should not keep us from understanding the power of the welfare state in constructing women as "dependent welfare subjects."

## THE SOCIAL CONSTRUCTION OF WELFARE SUBJECTS

Once again, this construction happens on all three levels. The first, the ideological misrepresentation of reality, is used to exert the first two forms (or "faces") of power over the poor and claim control over knowledge and understanding. For instance, stereotypes that welfare recipients are lifelong pathological dependents are contradicted by evidence that most welfare recipients remain on welfare for only two years, that they often cycle between work and welfare, and may even have considerable employment histories. The image that dominated in the administration of Ronald Reagan, of Cadillac-driving welfare queens, is similarly belied by the small amounts that AFDC, and now TANF, provide to families, as well as the forms it frequently takes: in food stamps and housing subsidies rather than cash. Just as Marx argued that capitalist ideology inverts the proletarian experience in order to misrepresent it to the proletariat and everyone else, so do we find that conservative patriarchal ideology inverts poor women's experiences to create an image that is at odds with the reality of that experience. But of course, welfare discourse also materializes reality, it creates the material reality it claims to describe. For instance, by using the belief that the welfare system is riddled with fraudulent cheats as a justification for keeping payments punitively small, welfare policy in fact forces recipients to cheat. Kathryn Edin's interviews of women on welfare in Chicago demonstrate that because public-assistance allowances—even accounting for food stamps and subsidized housing—fall considerably short of the cost of rent, food, and other living expenses, many women on welfare are forced not to report money received from relatives, to work under a false Social Security identity, to fence stolen goods, or to sell drugs or sex. As one woman Edin interviewed said, "Public Aid is an agency that I believe can teach a person how to lie. If you tell them the truth, you won't get any help. But if you go down there and tell them a lie, you get help." As another put it, "Public Aid forces you into deceit and dishonesty, things you normally would not think of doing." It is not that these women see themselves as cheats per se but that welfare policy forces them to act in ways that fulfill the stereotype. Indeed, counterdiscourses are deployed by the women themselves. Edin points out that women saw themselves as being torn "between being good mothers and good citizens. In every case, concern for their children's welfare"—that is, trying to obtain sufficient income to care for them through illegal means—"outweighed moral qualms" about "cheating."[35] Similarly, Lisa Dodson writes about female workers in a public school who daily face a variety of ethical dilemmas produced by poverty and the restrictions of welfare reform. For instance, a child with asthma (a disease that has a higher incidence among poor, inner-city children) needs to go home from school, but his mother, attempting to meet work requirements, will lose her job if she is called away one more time. The school workers find a solution that violates official policies and puts the school district at risk; but they employ it in order to protect the boy and his mother from the even greater risk of losing benefits.[36]

Social construction thus forces women to act in ways that can "objectively" be defined as cheating or doing wrong, even if "subjectively" they are experienced as struggling to be a good mother or as doing what must be done. But such acts, and their characterization in public discourse, inevitably affect the internal subjective identity of participants, even if they are not determinative. Thus, this second level of social construction, the materialization of reality, constructs not only the concrete conditions of women's lives but also thereby constructs identity and subjectivity. In Edin's study, indeed, the feelings of shame, low self-worth, and depression that many of her respondents expressed would seem to contradict the interviewees' stated assertions that such behavior is simply a way for them to provide for their children, to be good and strong mothers in the face of adversity. Edin documents feelings of shame and low self-worth not as reasons for *going* on welfare but as the result of *being* on welfare and having to engage in survival behaviors in which these women would not otherwise engage. In this picture, the production of welfare subjects operates on a deeper level, for the empirical reality that these women live impacts on the self-conceptions of even the most self-consciously resistant subjects. Hence, even though women declare that they themselves are hard workers and are struggling to fulfill welfare requirements and make a better life for their children off of public assistance, they simultaneously claim to know of other women who do cheat, who fulfill the stereotype of the lazy welfare queen. Such claims may be an effective way for these women to present themselves to the interviewer or their caseworker in a positive light: by acknowledging the "reality" of the dominant discourse, their claims to be different gain greater legitimacy. But of course, at the same time, such efforts further reinforce the dominant construction of welfare subjects, and thereby of themselves.

This leads to the third level of social construction, for like domestic violence, welfare discourse and policies are mapped onto larger, deeper, and even more hidden discourses of race, class, and gender that have already done substantial amounts of work in the construction of subjectivity. Such constructions not only make it difficult for welfare participants, so directly subject to state power on a daily basis, to resist; they make the general feminist effort to battle welfare reform extremely complicated. For instance, consider the fact that feminists have not been successful in gaining popular recognition of the hypocrisy—or at least contradiction—of Republican "family values" that chastise white middle-class women as "selfish" for working while chastising poor and particularly black women as "lazy" for not working. One obvious reason is that such discourses play off of double standards so commonly accepted that most people, including many feminists, do not even see them as contradictory. The fact that many middle-class working women—including married women—would not even *be* middle-class and able to stay off public assistance if they did not work is completely elided as class becomes the acceptable focus for racist sexism. Particularly in the context of mothering, it would seem that our capacity to accommodate contradictory claims is endless; as psychoanalysts from Freud to Chodorow have demonstrated, mothers never seem to be "good enough," and the mother bashing of both poor, "nonworking" mothers and upper-middle-class "working" mothers that has been perpetrated by predominantly white male politicians demonstrates the generalized ambivalence that Westerners feel toward the mother.[37] And since guilt is the easily exploitable but constant companion to mothers of all races and classes in the West, women themselves are constructed in ways that ensure that any resistance will be overwhelmed. Hence middle-class mothers express ambivalence about working even though they enjoy their jobs, just as welfare mothers critique fellow recipients for their "dependency" and "laziness."[38] This is not to say that such feelings are "false consciousness" but rather to point out that the reason it is *women* who are expected, and put in the position, to feel ambivalent is at least in part a construction of the gendered social relations of childrearing.

Through the discursive representation of welfare recipients and welfare policy, discourses of class, race, and gender become reinforced and subtly reconstructed as they respond to and in turn shape the external material conditions of poor women's, and indeed all women's, lives. This construction takes on a character, as Foucault asserts, that makes it impossible to resist or escape. For instance, much feminist critique that focuses on the ways in which the state inhibits poor mothers' efforts to become independent and raise their children risks a different error of romanticizing wel-

fare recipients, and ignores another powerful scenario in the social construction of the welfare subject, particularly for women of color, as
White's discussion of Elaine Presston revealed: namely, that getting pregnant and going on welfare may well be a reasonable choice. The hope-
lessness bred by poverty, lack of opportunity, disenfranchisement and lack
of political access, exclusion even from a feminist movement in which
"all the women are white,"[39] and middle-class, and unresponsive to your
situation, may likely breed a cynical—even if justifiable—view that you
will be poor no matter what you do; that there is no way out. Indeed,
according to Catanzarite and Ortiz, the measures encouraged by welfare
reform, particularly marriage and labor-market participation, benefit
white women much more than women of color, who seem to be more
heavily locked into poverty regardless of what they do. They found that
although white women not in the labor force were eleven times more
likely to live in poverty than whites who worked full-time, women of
color were only five times as likely to be poor as their employed counterparts, signifying that "white women's work effort had a greater impact
on reducing the risk of poverty than was true for African-American and
Latina women." Similarly, marriage made twice the difference for white
women that it made for women of color; single white women had poverty
rates eight times that of married white women, but single minority women
were only four times as likely to be poor as married women of color.[40]
Certainly, these figures show that employment and marriage can help
some women escape poverty, but at the same time, the fact that women
of color have a very high chance of remaining poor whether or not they
work or marry feeds into the reasonableness of going on welfare rather
than exploring other options. More actively, such conditions could also
likely instill anger, in response to which going on welfare could be a form
of resistance and rebellion, a protest action that suggests a certain degree
of rational calculation, of deliberate exploitation of the system that has
been built on an exploitation of you.[41]

In this scenario, poverty and racism, rather than welfare per se, may
be the primary constructing discourses, but they obviously dovetail with
welfare and gender in powerful and debilitating ways. For of course such
resistance reinscribes these women in the very system of power they aim
to destabilize through their actions: going on welfare as an act of rebellion
does not do anything to change a young woman's status as poor and
powerless. Indeed, it would seem to make her more subject to the regulatory power of the capitalist state; if welfare reform has made nothing else
clear, it is the complete vulnerability of women on welfare to state power,
regardless of the circumstances that led them to it in the first place. Is it
really possible that any attempt to exploit welfare could actually have any
impact on the racist/capitalist/patriarchal system that fuels welfare? Does

not such an attempt simply guarantee the further invisibility of such women in the minimum-wage economy? Indeed, has not their "resistance" in fact been scripted by the structure of racist and patriarchal power?

## FREEDOM, CARE, AND WELFARE RIGHTS

The relevance of such questions to freedom may be subtle, but it is unquestionable, from both a negative- and positive-liberty perspective. Within a negative-liberty framework, attention to social construction allows us to expand the notion of "restraint" or "barrier" by highlighting the ways in which welfare has been structured to inhibit women's liberty, how it presents externally imposed limitations and blocks to the pursuit of things that they may not only want to do but perceive as important to their development, growth, and even survival. A social constructivist approach also demonstrates that the construction of welfare is fed by, and in turn feeds into, understandings of gender and race that are culturally and historically specific, even though they are often claimed to be natural, inevitable, or given. Social constructivism reveals that women are the predominant participants in welfare programs not because they have personally failed to get and keep a job or a man but because it is predominantly women who care for children and other dependents;[42] that women may "cheat" not because they are immoral or pathological but because public assistance does not pay enough to allow them to provide this care; that they do not have wage-paying jobs not because of laziness but because of inadequate opportunities and employment supports like child care and health care. Social constructivism further points out that women's responsibility for care is hardly a fact of nature but of the social relations of production and reproduction, relations that can and must be changed if women are to be able to pursue a full range of human options. It reveals welfare as a social construct that plays off of larger social formations of gender (women should be mothers, they should be dependent on individual men), race (black women are lazy and dishonest, you have to keep an eye on them and make them earn their living), and class (middle-class taxpayers are responsible citizens because they pay taxes; the poor are lazy and irresponsible, because they are poor). These social formations of gender, race, and class are defined independently but in fact intersect and mutually constitute one another (for instance, white, middle-class women should be full-time mothers; black women cannot be good mothers, no matter what, because they are poor and lazy, so they should be forced to work for a living). The recognition of these images *as* social constructions lets us see that they are not natural or essential, but man-made products of racist, sexist, and classist social policies that interfere with women's freedom to lead their lives as they wish.

From a positive-liberty perspective, social construction's relevance goes even deeper, to the formation of the desiring subject. The provision of enabling resources such as education, child care, health care, housing, and transportation would allow women to pursue their goals of economic well-being, familial and professional self-development, and security. The elimination of welfare's stigma, by pointing out that welfare's entrapment is a result of structural limitations rather than participants' personal failings, aids in the removal of certain internal barriers, such as low self-worth, fear, anxiety, and anger. But more than that, social constructivism engages us in a reconsideration of the choosing subject of welfare, of the individuals, predominantly women, who end up in the socially vulnerable role of caregiver. By challenging the inevitability and naturalness of women's role as rearer of children, caregiver for the sick and elderly, and private-sphere care provider for men, social constructivism allows us to call into question the fundamental assumptions about the sexual division of labor on which welfare policies are based.

Thus, the social construction of welfare does not merely involve the construction of the individual women who happen to be its recipients but of other discursive concepts and categories, such as "dependence," "femininity," and "citizen." As Fraser and Gordon have revealed, the "discourse of dependency" has defined and constructed the notion of "dependence" in ways that are fundamentally linked to social constructions of race, class, and gender, and such constructions both legitimate and produce the construction of welfare in circular fashion. Such constructions reveal the interaction of ideological misrepresentation, materialization, and discursive definitions of social categories of meaning. As in domestic violence, women's dependence is constructed both discursively and materially to constitute the limiting conditions of citizenship and personhood. Rousseau argued that impersonal dependence on impartial and universal structures such as law did not compromise freedom; but personal dependence on another person undermined freedom in a central way. Hence, because freedom could be defined as obedience to self-prescribed laws, the free individual is dependent on law, something impersonal, and has himself constructed this law, acting through a collective entity with which he voluntarily associated himself. Women, by contrast, are required to be dependent on individual men in the family; the stability of the state operates by and through a family structure in which women perform caring labor and subordinate their wills and beings to their husbands. Welfare might seem to liberate women from such constructions, and thereby produce the conditions for women's freedom, by enabling women to end their dependence on individual men and instead obtain economic support from the state, by virtue of law. However, this does not occur; welfare policy is constructed precisely to sustain women's personal dependence. In welfare—much as in domestic violence—women are constructed to be personally dependent on individual men, they are defined and demarcated as residents of the private sphere, whose role it is to care for men and children. "Bridefare" is the most obvious expression of this ideal, for it declares that women should be married and directly rewards those who fulfill the patriarchal ideal of the married, full-time mother. But even when women are dealing with supposedly impersonal state agencies, their dependence is constructed in extremely personal ways. For instance, each welfare recipient is assigned a caseworker who has considerable discretionary power to evaluate recipients' adherence to requirements, so the face of the state takes on a personal form, literally. The requirements that welfare recipients must fulfill are, similarly, quite personal; for instance, the paper work that an applicant for AFDC or TANF must fill out is extremely lengthy and requires applicants to reveal considerable details about their lives. By contrast, unemployment insurance and Social Security require extremely little personal information and paperwork. The application process is onerous for welfare but easy for unemployment, and virtually automatic for Social Security. Even PRWORA's work requirements, which might seem to run against this construction of women as naturally dependent, actually reinforces it, through the personal surveillance exercised over them. So-called "job training" that focuses on how to set your alarm clock and dress for an interview rather than providing actual employment skills similarly personalizes welfare dependency by infantilizing women. Indeed, one could argue that one reason that work requirements are so difficult is to force women back into families, to teach them the lesson that marriage is the solution to poverty.

Perhaps the most significant aspect of this personalization of dependency pertains, somewhat ironically, to women's historical role as beings on whom others depend, particularly as mothers. As in domestic violence, the prominence of women's social role as caregivers informs discourses of gender relations and identity and plays a key role in the social construction of women's experiences with and within the framework of state power. Social constructivism allows us to see that women's caretaking roles sit at the heart of welfare debates for both models of liberty, whether overtly or implicitly. This is both problematic and illuminating: problematic, because placing care at the center of welfare debates reinscribes and replicates the dominant discourse of gender relations; illuminating, because it simultaneously has the potential to change the discourse, and thereby the material reality, of welfare policy. Carework has been central to feminist reconfigurations of the welfare state from its earliest days, since it arose in response to a social need to support single mothers; and the fact that women have always performed this carework has highlighted feminist involvement in welfare reform. For instance, Wendy Sarvasy argues that early welfare feminists viewed gender as a socially constructed product of, and foundation for, power. By acknowledging the ways in which gender differences had been constructed through these power inequalities, then not only gender but citizenship, rights, and welfare could be rethought. Sarvasy argues that early feminists believed that focusing on the caregiving work that women typically engaged in was essential to such a rethinking, for it located the particularity of women's experiences within a dialogue of universal access. The goal of securing citizenship for women involved a rethinking of rights such that both particularity and universality, both gender neutrality and recognition of actual gender inequalities, both mothering and paid labor, could be combined in a single vision. Through their social constructivist lens, feminists formulated "a new notion of the citizen-mother as a professional providing a socially supported activity within the context of full political rights," a notion that recognized women's maternal roles without reducing them to those roles, and without falling into the trap of "republican" citizenship, that eliminated women from the public sphere and ensured their dependence on men.[43]

It is significant for freedom that Sarvasy gives central importance to the notion of "rights" in her analysis. Obviously, "rights" are not an exact equivalent to "freedom," but within the history of modern liberal political theory they are seen as extremely close and interdependent. In social-contract theory in particular, the point of rights is precisely to protect liberties: rights are tools to exercise the power of the state in the protection of those liberties. Indeed, in relation to welfare, rights are the only cognate of freedom to which feminists have paid explicit attention and hence provide a useful window onto the tacit model of liberty that underwrites feminist approaches to welfare. The notion of welfare rights for poor mothers is a theme that continually repeats in the history of welfare and has considerable currency today among feminists who have sought to make AFDC/TANF more like other welfare payments, such as Social Security, workers' compensation, and unemployment, which, for all of their problems, are still considered "entitlements" or "rights."[44] Moreover, rights are seen as a tool of freedom, both negative—when feminists argue for greater independence, in the form of more money and less surveillance over women's "lifestyles"—and positive—when they demand more resources such as child care, training for well-paying jobs, better employment opportunities, and transportation to areas offering these opportunities.

However, the focus on rights by feminists is potentially regressive, precisely because of the sexist, not to mention racist and classist, history of rights discourse that feminist theorists have dissected and critiqued. The dominant approach to rights found in negative liberty and classical liberal discourse conceptualizes them as conflictual claims against others. Stemming back at least to the state-of-nature contractarians, rights were conceived as civil—and for some, such as Locke, also natural—grantings of power that applied to individuals exclusively. Individuals were conceived as separate and distinct units their relationships made possible only by chosen agreement (or in Hobbes's case, sometimes by force, which in his view amounted to the same thing).[45] Within contemporary discourse, a right is a "trump," to borrow from Ronald Dworkin,[46] a claim that puts an end to disputes over distribution of resources or conflicting desires, a kind of weapon that individuals can use to beat back the claims of competing individuals. As Wendy Brown puts it, "The motion of rights is to push away or push away from—*against* others, *against* the state, *against* incursions, limitations, or encroachments upon our autonomy."[47] Moreover, the "individuals" at the heart of this negative-liberty vision of rights were for the most part propertied white men, as decades of feminist critique of liberal theory compels us to recognize. Rights were defined, along with other key concepts like property and equality, in ways that not only left out white women and people of color, but depended on their subservience and classified them as forms of property. These concepts all turned on a further conceptualization of individualism that ignored the importance of the relationship and connectedness that women's work in the family ensured.[48] Thus, although deploying rights as weapons for the disempowered may seem an appropriate strategy to take in a time of welfare retrenchment and right-wing demonization of the poor, racial minorities, and women, it is deeply problematic for feminism as well as for welfare.

This point is illustrated particularly well by Elizabeth Bussiere, who argues in a contemporary echo of Sarvasy's historical portrait that freedom was central to the battle of the National Welfare Rights Organization in the 1960s and 1970s to establish welfare rights in the United States. Bussiere argues that this effort failed because of a dedication on the part of the NWRO lawyers, as well as the Court, to a predominantly negative-liberty view of procedural rights, when a positive-liberty view of substantive rights, particularly to a minimum standard of living, was really at the heart of the struggle for welfare rights. Though Bussiere leaves out of her understanding of positive liberty the important dimensions I have articulated here of internal barriers and social construction, her observation about the negative-liberty focus of both lawyers and courts identifies clearly the problem for feminists of embracing the dominant rights discourse. For she argues that although the NWRO and Legal Services lawyers were motivated by the very progressive goals of establishing rights to subsistence income, the strategy they took was patently conservative, construing legal questions as narrowly as possible, trying to move the court only inches at a time, dealing with individuals rather than groups or social categories, and failing to attend to cultural and contextual difference. For instance, in cases involving one-year residence requirements for welfare eligibility, the lawyers argued that such requirements violated a constitutional right of individuals to travel freely between the states—an argument that the Court found persuasive—rather than making a case for subsistence rights based on national citizenship.[49] In practice such an approach—in contradiction to the proclaimed goals of the NWRO—conceived of welfare recipients not as a collective group but rather as a coincidental collection of individuals, who could be protected only through securing rights that each could use individually and separately. Obviously, since the lawyers prevailed, we must conclude that this was a logical legal strategy; and indeed it is a strategy that was again invoked in court cases in Pennsylvania and California in the late 1990s, after welfare reform was well under way.[50] But Bussiere suggests that the use of this strategy is also why the larger goal of establishing welfare rights failed; to achieve that goal, the lawyers would have needed to argue for the right to subsistence, particularly for single mothers as a collective group. The lawyers may have won the battle, but they lost the war, because they sought to empower women and the poor by deploying a discourse that had their subjection at its core, namely, the individualist and combative rights discourse of negative liberty.

Moreover, she suggests, this strategy, with its overtly negative-liberty focus, was at least implicitly a function of the socially constructed gender and race division of labor. For Bussiere notes that the women who made up the membership of the NWRO—98 percent of whom were poor African-American mothers—wanted the white male lawyers responsible for plotting the litigation strategy to utilize "maternalist" arguments in articulating the grounds for welfare rights. According to Bussiere, while the leaders/lawyers believed that the only way to obtain welfare rights was to make single mothers' struggle part of a larger movement for a welfare state, welfare mothers believed that the interests of poor and working-class men would supersede their own interests and preferences if such a strategy were pursued. In seeking rights to subsistence, they sought recognition for the specific work they did in caring for children and for the special problems and difficulties they faced in performing this labor, whether they did it full-time and exclusively or in combination with wage labor.

This construction of rights *through* care might seem counterintuitive given that, at least since Carol Gilligan's 1982 book *In a Different Voice*, the relationship between care and rights has been seen as antagonistic, if not antithetical. Gilligan postulated two different models of moral development: a rights model that defines morality in terms of rules, abstract principles, and a hierarchy of rights-as-trumps and a care model that defines morality in terms of responsibility and responding to need and is based on face-to-face conversation, interpersonal dynamics, relationship, and context.[51] Because of the association of these models with males and females, respectively, Gilligan's argument has led many feminists to challenge the notion of rights as masculinist.[52] But it actually illustrates the ways in which differing and subjugated discourses within the dominant framework can challenge the dominant discourse and open up possibilities for seeing lived experience and imagining public policy, in new ways. Within the context of welfare, however, and particularly of the tensions between women's responsibility for care work and childrearing and the wage labor demands of welfare reform, it becomes apparent that care is a necessary precondition of rights, that what is "wrong" with rights is its rejection of care. Indeed, given the history of racist and sexist exclusion that feminists have long attributed to the notion and practice of rights,[53] what is needed to make a conception of rights truly equitable and accessible to all are the fundamentals of the care model. Rather than opposing care to rights, a conception of rights can be developed *within* a care approach, which is what both Sarvasy's and Bussiere's analyses of welfare activism suggest, at least implicitly.

Consider, for instance, the most common criticism lodged against the care model: that it cannot serve as a general moral theory because the importance of relationship would result in favoritism, whereas rights are impartial. A careful consideration of the care model reveals that it does not in fact reject such central rights values as universality and neutrality, but rather requires their reconfiguration. For instance, in Gilligan's treatment of the "Heinz dilemma" (Heinz's wife is fatally ill, but he cannot afford the medicine that will help her—should Heinz steal the drug?), the girl whom Gilligan discusses ("Amy") never suggests that Heinz should steal the drug because it is his *wife*—someone close to him, whose death would affect him personally—who is sick. Such reasoning would indeed display the favoritism of which critics complain. Rather, Amy says that he should not steal it *at all* (a fact most such critics ignore), but instead should talk with his wife and the pharmacist. In her approach to the dilemma, Amy tries to consider the needs of *everyone* involved, for everyone is equally entitled to a prima facie consideration of care. It is only when details obtained through communication reveal greater or lesser need or ability that determinations of specific and appropriate expressions of care can be made. After all, we never know *why* the druggist will not give Heinz the drug; for instance, perhaps his child is also sick, and he needs the money for her operation. Or perhaps he is facing imminent bankruptcy because of the large chain drugstore that has recently opened in town, and letting Heinz have the drug for free will seal his fate. By sitting down and talking the problem out, as Amy prescribes, such a discussion would presumably be articulated, and from such a discussion can emerge a solution that is fair to everyone. For instance, perhaps Heinz could pay for the drug in installments; or perhaps the pharmacist could help Heinz confront his HMO, which has denied payment for the experimental drugs. (And of course, this does not even get us into the questions of why Heinz's health insurance will not pay for the drug, or why Heinz might not even have insurance, both of which importantly conjoin issues of care and entitlement.) This represents a different notion of impartiality, one that is worked out through more knowledge rather than less, through concrete particularity rather than general abstraction; but it is impartiality, nonetheless. Care may require *particularity*—the need to know concrete details in order to assess the needs of a specific person in a specific situation—but particularity is not the same thing as partiality. If everyone is equally deserving of care, then favoritism does not follow.

What is especially noteworthy about revisioning rights through care is how much it contrasts to the negative-liberty view of rights as antagonistic claims that has characterized the movement for welfare rights. For it is precisely this discourse, with the limits it inevitably sets on how rights can be deployed, and who is entitled to deploy them, that has enabled conservative Republicans to scale back such entitlement programs as AFDC, food stamps, WIC, and Medicaid, as well as to provide tax cuts to the wealthy. As Brown notes in a similar critique of rights, "Insofar as rights operate to distance and demarcate, they are a means of socially organizing us by separating us, using the fiction of our autonomy and independence to produce a social order reflecting it."[54] By emphasizing the conflictual character of rights—which pits the providers of subsidy (taxpayers) against the receivers of subsidy (especially welfare mothers and children)—the claims of welfare rights can be denied, because within this conflictual discursive framework, it is the powerful who decide whether a right exists and whether to honor it. Furthermore, by viewing responsibility as something that *recipients* must develop and demonstrate (because their poverty is evidence that they are irresponsible) but that the privileged need not (because they already have done so, by working and paying taxes), again imparting a conflictual and individualist character to the debate, the conservative denial of welfare rights is greatly facilitated. A kind of class warfare is engaged that reinforces the lines of economic privilege and power, which in turn facilitates the perpetuation of the public discourse of taxpayers as responsible citizens, and welfare recipients as either cheats or pathological dependents.

My argument here should not be taken as an endorsement of rights as essential to a feminist theory of freedom. I believe that a reconfigured notion of rights may support and assist the cause of freedom, but freedom cannot by any means be reduced to rights. Rather, given the ways in which rights discourse intersects with and affects freedom discourse in the dominant schools of liberal political thought, it is important to understand what conceptions of freedom are deployed by rights talk, how rights are used to support freedom, how that shapes the dominant understandings of the concept of freedom, and how a rethinking of rights might help us to rethink freedom also. Similarly, although my claim about the negative-liberty focus of the welfare rights movement might seem to contradict the positive-liberty themes I attribute to the conservative discourse of "dependency," my point above was not that the right-wing appropriation of positive-liberty themes proves the inherent conservatism of positive-liberty theory. Rather, my point was—and is—that feminists need to reclaim its progressive potential. Indeed, the two claims strongly cohere, because the overt positive-liberty orientation of welfare discourse is founded on and feeds into the worst elements of negative-liberty theory, particularly abstract individualism—welfare mothers must "just do it" and pull themselves up by their own bootstraps (a particular feature of "work first" provisions)—and the patriarchal erasure of women's humanity that feminist theorists have traced for decades. As Brown and Wolin both maintain, the conservative discourse of " 'getting government off our backs' actually masked the steady expansion of state power and retrenchment of citizens' rights."[55] It may be for this reason that programs such as workfare do not actually fulfill the criteria of positive liberty. In the supposed interest of "liberating" welfare recipients from the "cycle of welfare," of "empowering" them to become contributing, responsible, taxpaying citizens, recipients are forced to take low-wage, dead-end jobs that provide little, if any, training in skills such as computer programming, welding and construction, or office management that could lead to economic independence. It would be at least ironic to maintain that it is welfare recipients' "true will" to perform mindless minimum-wage labor rather than pursue a college degree that would enable them to obtain higher-paying and more stimulating jobs. Welfare discourse appropriates the most conservative elements of both models of liberty, smuggling the libertarian individualism of negative liberty into an overt positive-liberty framework: the second guessing of positive-liberty theory informs its definition of the welfare recipient's character, while the abstract individualism of negative-liberty theory underpins its rejection of welfare rights.

This recognition, I believe, is why a feminist reconception of rights needs to embrace elements of positive liberty, as Sarvasy (implicitly) and Bussiere (explicitly) both illustrated. It needs to develop a conception of rights that does not merely make "trumping" claims on the state, but rather recognizes the socially constructed sexual division of labor, and specifically how this construction creates a social category called "women"; beings who are forced to "choose" caretaking roles, but nevertheless want to fulfill their prescribed caretaking duties under optimal conditions, such as economic stability. Moreover, the melding of care and rights is significant in its implications for freedom, because it is founded on a recognition of the social construction of motherhood and of women's social roles as caretakers: it is because women care for children, men, the sick, and the elderly that "welfare" in the form of public assistance has had to develop, in response to the tacit recognition of the centrality of that work to the democratic state. But because women are socially constructed as noncitizens by virtue of this very labor,[56] welfare policy has developed in the ambivalent way it has, simultaneously forced to recognize women as entitled to support by virtue of that labor, but never providing sufficient support to fully respect that entitlement or that labor.

At the same time, it is crucial to note that the vision Sarvasy articulates was never realized in practice; the foundation of positive responsibility and the importance of carework to welfare rights was subverted by racist and classist reconstructions of motherhood in the early part of the twentieth century, as Mink argues, and it was denied outright by the NWRO lawyers, as Bussiere documents.[57] Though Sarvasy is careful to argue that early activists sought a feminist welfare state, not a maternalist one, the trope of maternalism was impossible to displace, and maternalism has historically embraced a white, middle-class model of mothering that takes the patriarchal nuclear family as a natural given and simply substitutes the state for the father/husband when he is absent. Because of the larger sexist context of male power, whenever feminists talk about "care," the shadow of essentialism hangs over us, and to make the carework women do the foundation for welfare rights risks reinscribing women in the very same social roles and stereotypes that have fostered and permitted their disempowerment vis-à-vis the welfare state. In this light, the reconstruction of welfare rights in terms of care runs the risk of further restricting women's freedom, rather than enhancing it.

Just as social constructivism can help locate and articulate these problems, however, it can also help prevent this care-oriented reconfiguration of rights from falling into a racist, essentialist maternalism. First, a social construction perspective reminds us that if women are in fact more caring than men, that is to a large degree because they have always been required to perform caring labor. Second, it points out that this historical fact does not negate or delegitimize care as a moral category. That is, by attending to the historical and political context of care, social constructivism forces us to negotiate the contemporary empirical realities of carework; specifically, that women currently do most of it, and that we need to respond to their needs. But it also makes apparent the need to develop a future vision of deontological gender neutrality; for instance, policies that encourage men to partake in child care by ensuring that rights accrue to carework regardless of who does it. By raising the question of *why* it has been women who have always expressed care and been responsible for caregiving labor, we thereby raise questions of how to change that, so that it is not women's exclusive responsibility but rather one that falls on men and women alike. Welfare rights based on women's caring labor would, then, de-gender care: as one might glibly, if not cynically, argue, if the state recognized carework as important and paid it a decent wage, more men might be willing to do it. But more significantly, this vision of welfare rights uses women's historical responsibility for caring labor not as a rationale for their continuing to do it but rather as a basis for understanding its dynamics and how those dynamics fit into, shape, and are shaped by, the larger political and social context of inequality between men and women, between rich and poor, between whites and people of color. By refusing the naturalization of care, we can gain a clearer insight into the sex/gender, class, and race dynamics that construct carework as a practice. Such insight can lead to the institution of welfare policies that more directly address the actual needs of actual careworkers, rather than the assumed needs of abstract stereotypes.[58]

Thus, the social construction dimension of positive liberty gives a more radical potential to the reconfiguring of welfare rights through care. Indeed, in many ways welfare is the perfect issue for this reconfiguring of rights and freedom, for it contains all of the supposedly contradictory elements of the two discourses at once: individual integrity and caring for family; claims against the state and responsibility to and for others; autonomy and a rethinking of the self through relationship. A focus on caretaking will make welfare more woman-friendly and free, at least by providing mothers with greater resources and a wider range of choices in how that care is exercised. A consideration of women's freedom demands that women have as wide a range of choices open to them as possible, whether they desire to give care full-time—in which case larger stipends are needed—or to combine carework with wage labor or to work full-time—in which case women need better pay and opportunities, and better protection from sexual and racial discrimination and harassment, in addition to high-quality child care and transportation.

Of course, the phrase "as possible" is key; once we move from the abstract principled claim that we need to honor, respect, and value care to the actual practices and policies of doing so, issues of cost come to the fore. As positive-liberty theory shows us, freedom can never be about abstract choice but must be located within the contexts of community and relationships that define one's choices. Paying individual caretakers to care for one or two children full-time in an isolated nuclear family is extremely inefficient and costly, leading O'Connor, Orloff, and Shaver to suggest that it is unrealistic to question whether "women's caregiving claims . . . will survive at all," and to argue that welfare must be market driven.[59] Accordingly, I agree with Orloff that provision of care-related supports must be developed in conjunction with work-related supports.[60] This is more than a matter of efficiency, however; it is also a matter of freedom. I am not, of course, endorsing the conservative positive-liberty maneuver that requires women to participate in wage labor under the guise of forcing them to be free. Rather, I mean that "choice" also requires a restructuring of other social institutions, like the family, so that such "choices" about distributing and structuring carework and wage labor are not simply excuses for keeping these burdens on women. The availability of options such as shared parenting between a husband and wife in a traditional family, or living in a nontraditional family structure, in which several adults share responsibility for carework, will increase women's positive and negative liberty not only by providing a greater array of choices to women but also by reconstructing what it means to be the "woman" and "mother" who makes these choices. Whereas negative-liberty ideals show us the ways in which welfare limits women, a positive-liberty focus can reveal how the conditions of sexism and racism within which mothering takes place produce welfare subjects. If, as Butler suggests, "the feminist subject turns out to be discursively constituted by the very political system that is supposed to facilitate its emancipation," then feminists must reconstitute the system.[61] Part of that project involves reclaiming positive-liberty discourse from the right and deploying it to feminist ends. Positive liberty, by directing our attention to the social construction of the individual subject, as well as to the need to understand individuals' desires and abilities in social contexts that enable or restrain those desires and abilities, also requires that we rethink the fundamental conceptual vocabulary that engulfs welfare debates and discussions. In that strategy lies a powerful potential for women's freedom.

## Chapter Six

# EASTERN VEILING, WESTERN FREEDOM?

IT COULD be argued that the conclusion of the previous chapter is somewhat predictable, for unlike domestic violence, welfare is a uniquely Western phenomenon, the explicit product of democratic states that emerged in the late modern era and were founded on and derived from Western liberal conceptions of individualism, citizenship, rights, and responsibilities. By contrast, despite the dominance of U.S. models in measuring and interpreting domestic violence in other countries, domestic violence is a cross-cultural, even universal, problem, one that women have faced in all countries and historical periods (well before the time it was actually called "domestic violence"). Yet my discussion of domestic violence focused primarily (though not exclusively) on a Western, and indeed a U.S., experience, for consideration of law, police, judicial systems, social practices, and gendered belief systems requires some focus in terms of culture, geography, and history if it is to be discursively intelligible. At the same time, my selection of two policy issues that resonate particularly in a U.S. context poses a tacit challenge to the attempt to develop a "feminist" theory of freedom, for "feminism" must appeal beyond U.S. borders to all women. Western feminism has been arguing about issues of sensitivity to cultural specificity and difference for a number of years now. On the one hand, it is clear that context, specificity, and difference are all vital to a successful feminism: if feminism is dedicated to respect for women, and if women, like men, are located in divergent contexts, then the only way to respect women as individuals is to acknowledge and respect those contexts as shapers of the self. Western feminists have worked hard (though not always with success) to resist the cultural imperialism that adheres virtually automatically, regardless of good intentions, to a Western (particularly white) location, to overcome a blindness, born of privilege, to the nuances of gender equity and women's power in other cultures. On the other hand, however, some maintain that the cultural relativism to which this earnest effort to show respect sometimes gives way does nothing to change the oppression of women, because the "culture" that is thereby acknowledged and respected is often one that preserves male privilege at women's expense, that is defined by and for the interests of particular groups of men.

This dilemma is exhibited daily not only in white, middle-class feminists' interpretation (or ignorance) of the experiences of Western women of color and poor women, but also in Western feminists' reactions to various situations that women face in non-Western cultures. In this chapter, I focus on the practice of veiling. From the start, this might seem problematic, for if I am suggesting a parallel between veiling, welfare, and domestic violence, then one might assume that I believe that veiling is inherently an oppressive practice. That would be incorrect, though the suspicion is not without justification. Throughout the modern era, the West has deployed discursive representations and constructions of Islam as a barbaric source of women's inequality; and the veil is seen as the ultimate symbol, if not tool, of this inequality.[1] Fueled by media reports of the oppressive practices of the Taliban in Afghanistan, anti-American fury in Iran, and Saudi demands for restrictions on U.S. women soldiers during the Gulf War, many westerners tend to associate veiling with extreme gender oppression, even seeing the veil as the ultimate symbol of a unified, monolithic Islam.[2] This belies a great diversity in the practice, however, and ignores the fact that many Muslim women not only participate voluntarily in it, but defend it as well, indeed claiming it as a mark of agency, cultural membership, and resistance. Or rather, to the degree that such claims are acknowledged, they are viewed as false consciousness, the final effects of patriarchial colonization. Yet, as a practice, veiling differs widely among countries and regions, all of which assign it different historical and cultural meanings and adopt different styles (ranging from sheer-fabric robes, to head scarves, to dark and heavy full-length covering of the entire face and body). In various historical eras, and in different regions today, there is also a wide range of social norms concerning women's decisions to veil, running the gamut from overt coercion, in the form of state mandates and religious or cultural "police" in Afghanistan, Iran, and Algeria, to modest social pressure with an overt emphasis on women's individual choice. Additionally, many Muslim women do not veil at all, and in some countries, such as Turkey, women are actually prohibited from veiling in classrooms and other public spaces. Thus, to talk of "veiling in Islamic countries" is admittedly problematic, for the universalism such terminology seems to endorse denies these cultural variations and specificity.[3]

Why, then, should veiling be considered along with domestic violence and welfare, both of which, I have argued, restrict women's freedom? I will argue that veiling itself is not oppressive, but rather that its deployment as a cultural symbol and practice may provide (and often has done so) a form and mode by which patriarchy oppresses women in specific contexts. In this, veiling shares significant similarities with the other practices examined in this book. Welfare, for instance, is not an oppressive practice in all contexts; direct payments for labor to care for children, the sick, or the elderly do not in and of themselves challenge women's freedom. Indeed, in some nations, such as Sweden, welfare programs for mothers are quite liberating. Rather, it is the context within which welfare programs like TANF are constructed, and the forms that such programs take, that oppress poor single mothers in the United States. I have argued that this oppression stems from sexist, racist, and classist attitudes, beliefs, and knowledge claims that underwrite the construction of welfare policies. In the same vein, veiling's diversity as a practice works interactively with the power politics of patriarchy in various cultures. In some cultural contexts—indeed, such as the United States—veiling can provide a sense of identity, community, and religious faith.[4] In other contexts, such as Afghanistan under the Taliban, which forced women to wear the burqa, veiling may be less about religious identity than about power and control; as former Taliban deputy foreign minister Sher Abbas Stanakzai put it, "Our current restrictions of women are necessary in order to bring the Afghan people under control. We need these restrictions until people learn to obey the Taliban."[5] Accordingly, such examination of the specific cultural forms veiling takes can reveal shared features of gender oppression. By examining veiling as a multifaceted and complex practice located within varying and complex contexts, both specificity and commonality can be observed.

Another, perhaps even more basic, objection to my argument is that the concern with freedom that underpins my analysis displays an overt Western bias right from the start. But such a complaint obviously oversimplifies, in at least two senses.[6] First, the pervasiveness of Western colonialism and imperialism has ensured the importance of freedom and autonomy to non-Western cultures throughout the world. That Western language and conceptual vocabularies seem to dominate in international debates over human rights, nationalism and sovereignty, markets and trade—the UN Charter for Human Rights, the 1985 Nairobi Forward-Looking Strategies for the Advancement of Women, and the convention adopted by the 1995 Beijing UN Conference on Women all give a central role to women's "rights," conceptualized in individualist terms[7]—can attest to the hegemonic power of the West just as easily as it can be seen to support the Enlightenment claim for the naturalness of individual freedom. As I argued in the previous chapter, I consider feminist adoption of rights problematic unless the concept of rights is reconstructed; but international feminists, as well as women of color in the West, take issue with that position, because basic human rights that many white Western feminists take for granted are denied to women throughout the world. As Patricia Williams has argued, it is easy to talk about abandoning rights if you have been protected by them throughout your life; but for those who have been denied the protections that rights provide, being asked to give up what they have never actually had merely deepens their disempowerment. Rights are powerful tools, Williams argues, so feminists should not be too quick to give them up. Many international feminists agree, and utilize rights conceptions as powerful discursive strategies for making the point that women are human beings, that they should not be burned to death to collect their dowries, sold into sexual slavery, raped, or starved. Though such deployment of rights discourse is sometimes used to dismiss international feminists as the puppets of white westerners, it is clear that resistance to westernization and cultural "pollution" plays an important political and intellectual role in the struggles of many non-Western feminists to forge new political identities. Similarly, the concept of freedom is important to many societies in their struggle to escape the imperialist influence of the West, which suggests that the vocabulary of freedom is not alien to them but a part of their own cultural struggles. Furthermore, "the West" has not been the exclusive oppressor in history; as Martha Nussbaum points out, for instance, there is a long history of Hindu oppression of Muslims in India.[8] Nor has the West exerted the kind of unified force that would warrant labeling freedom a "Western" concern. Freedom is a fairly universal aspiration. What freedom means, however, varies in terms of cultural context, and that of course has been the central issue I have sought to confront throughout this book.

Granted the importance of freedom throughout the world, however it is defined, it is still fair to maintain that freedom is not the "obsessional core" in most Muslim societies that it is in the West. This is the second sense in which the dichotomy between East and West is an oversimplification; for much as I argued about the differences between negative and positive liberty, the key difference between East and West lies not in the degree of importance ascribed to freedom but rather in their visions of the individual, of what it means to be a person. Such visions necessarily involve the analysis of internal factors such as desire and motivation, as well as the contextual backdrops against which choices are made, desires are felt, and preferences are conceived. This focus on internal factors allows a more nuanced, complex, and sophisticated analysis of freedom. As I have argued, it is not enough for people to do what they say they want to do, for such representations of what people appear to want are often made from the perspective of privilege. Indeed, self-conceptions and self-representations of desire encode that perspective of privilege, because it has the power to define the terms in which desire is formulated. From such a perspective, oppression is often misinterpreted as free agency, and free agency is often misinterpreted as oppression, as I have already argued.

The idea that desire must always be seen as socially constructed through context requires some sort of attempt to examine and evaluate contexts, as I have suggested about domestic violence and welfare.

However, attention to cultural specificity in terms of how the "choosing subject" is constructed by differing contexts might seem to pose a considerable challenge to my project, not only because freedom may not be centrally important—or at least not important in the same way—to non-Western cultures, of which women are important members, but also because of the problematic status of the concepts of "gender" and "women," and hence of "feminism," as unqualified terms. As has been argued and documented by many, Western feminists too frequently treat women in different cultures as if they were simply variations on a basic theme defined by white, Western, middle-class experience. Yet women have been specifically and differently impacted by their locations in various classes, nationalities, ethnicities, and races. At the same time, the notion of "difference" is too often invoked by Western feminists as an excuse for failing to become involved in women's problems in other cultures. This treats non-Western women as "exotic others," which deepens their dehumanization rather than showing them respect. Thus, at the same time that many Third World and international feminists have adopted such universal concepts as human rights, they have also argued repeatedly that a genuine feminism must attend to cultural contexts, practices, and experiences.

This makes a "cross-cultural" conception of "women's" freedom ambiguous, an ambiguity that is particularly evident in regard to veiling, to which (white) Western feminism is often at least tacitly, and at times even overtly, hostile.[9] Such hostility is self-defeating, because understanding veiling as a complex practice within which women's freedom functions in correspondingly complex ways is important for feminists seeking to develop theories of concepts like "freedom" that have the potential for broad-based application. Indeed, precisely because veiling is "other" to most westerners, it may be able to reveal aspects of the West to which westerners are often blind, such as assumptions about individuality, agency, and difference, as well as Western feminists' lack of self-consciousness about our own practices, including our forms of dress. This is not to ignore the potential bias of Western feminism; but rather than argue that westerners should not talk about non-Western practices because of such potential bias, I urge a critical strategy that recognizes the need for self-criticism as well. Social constructivism can help engage such a strategy by reminding us once again of the inevitable situatedness of meaning in context, and the constructedness of desire, choice, and subjectivity. It can also help us hold onto feminism as an important element of this strategy. The argument that "feminism" is by definition a Western conception and movement denies and ignores the local and national activities of many women's groups to improve women's lives, as well as a vibrant international feminist movement. To dismiss non-Western feminists as "Westerners in disguise" simply because they are feminists is not only viciously circular but the epitome of patriarchy: to define culture, even "the East," in ways that systematically and by definitional fiat exclude the interests, concerns, and experiences of women.[10] As my discussion will show, women are important constructors of culture, and they constantly struggle to engage this construction on their own terms. How they do this can be illuminating for the question of freedom. Rather than allowing respect for "cultural difference" to silence them, feminists must recognize that respect for culture must include respect for *women's view* of culture. But such respect cannot be given unless the women concerned articulate their views. Such articulation, in turn, requires a certain degree of choice and consciousness about participation in those practices. Accordingly, I do not seek to use the category of freedom to understand veiling and to determine whether women who veil are free. Nor is my goal to define veiling as a unified practice or to show that patriarchy guarantees a reductive "sameness" running through culturally diverse practices. Rather, veiling can be used as a vehicle for developing a more complex understanding of freedom, agency, and subjectivity.

### "THE VEIL" AS DISCURSIVE AND SOCIAL SYMBOLIZATION

Despite the great cultural diversity in the practice of veiling, one thing that is fairly universal is Western reaction to it.[11] Although veiling occurs in a variety of contexts, what most westerners think about when they think of veiling are Iran and Afghanistan, which have enforced veiling with the threat, and actual execution, of physical assault on women who appear unveiled in public. From a feminist perspective, such contexts are indeed troubling. In Afghanistan, the practice seems particularly oppressive, for the revolutionary Taliban demanded that women limit their public exposure, remain sequestered in the home, and wear the burqa when in public, a heavy robe that envelopes its wearer from head to toe, completely concealing the face except for a narrow crocheted or gauze cloth across the eyes. Moreover, the Taliban enforced its dicta by physically assaulting, and sometimes even executing, women who violate them.[12]

To many westerners, the burqa seems a cumbersome and insulting outfit whose only purpose must be to restrict women's freedom of movement. And indeed, it is the cause of various health problems ranging from vision and respiratory problems to depression.[13] But the burqa is a symbol for more significant restrictions on women, such as the closing of girls' schools and prohibitions on women's wage work. Indeed, not only were women forbidden to walk abroad unless accompanied by a male relative, but the rather unpredictable attacks on women by members of the Taliban "religious police"—for infringements such as showing part of an ankle below the hem of the burqa—made women fearful of leaving their homes altogether even in the face of starvation or an acute need for medical care. Such a situation has obvious repercussions on women's agency and freedom that extend well beyond the immediacy of restriction to the home. For instance, doctors and midwives in a United Nations report indicated that after the Taliban closed the baths, which they deemed "un-Islamic," Afghan women had increased risk of gynecological infection (particularly "uterine infection after childbirth, one of four major causes of maternal mortality")[14] and skin diseases, while children were at increased risk of respiratory infection. Furthermore, women doctors were either banned from practicing or had their practices curtailed so that they could not effectively treat many illnesses women have (at the same time, male doctors were forbidden to treat women categorically).[15] Additionally, restrictions on women's work impacted harshly on the many households whose income formerly came solely from women's labor, often because husbands, fathers, or brothers were killed either in the war with the former Soviet Union or in more recent civil battles. Prohibitions on women's work has meant that the education of boys has been disrupted as well, since many women were educators, and since boys may have to work to support their mothers.[16]

Because of such associated constraints, Western feminists as well as nonfeminists often consider veiling an inherently oppressive practice. Many analogize it to domestic violence: just as staying with an abuser seems beyond comprehension, so does "choosing" the veil. Women who claim to do so are seen as brainwashed or coerced, and the veil as a key emblem of their oppression. But the Western reaction to veiling must be understood within its historical context, dating back at least to nineteenth-century British imperialists who viewed women's veiling as the ultimate symbol of Eastern backwardness. Colonial measures against veiling were asserted in the name of women's rights; but Leila Ahmed argues that this so-called feminism emerged as part of a larger nineteenth-century discourse that asserted dominance of the West over the East. In this discourse, "the veil and segregation epitomized [women's] oppression, and . . . were the fundamental reasons for the general and comprehensive backwardness of Islamic societies. Only if these practices 'intrinsic' to Islam (and therefore Islam itself) were cast off could Muslim societies begin to move forward." Western discourse thus created a dichotomy—either one embraces Islam and women's oppression, or one throws it (and the veil) off and is free—but in the process, "feminism" became part of the colonialist effort to delegitimize Islam.[17]

At the same time, however, this focus solidified the veil's symbolic force, for abandoning the veil has over the years come to be identified with westernization and imperialism. Thus, women's adoption of the veil was an important symbol in the pro-Islamist revolutionary movements of the late twentieth century in countries such as Egypt, Morocco, and Iran. Indeed, although westerners often focus on men assaulting women who do not veil, in fact the first people in contemporary movements to use the veil as a symbol of resistance were Egyptian university women.[18] In Iran in particular, the compulsory deveiling ordered by the shah was seen as an imperialist intrusion of Western custom that contributed to the fundamentalist revolution and moreover shaped the form of that revolution, for reveiling was seen as an important symbol of Iranian cultural identity.[19] Similarly, in Algeria, because women's seclusion in the home protected them from Western influence, women's veiling was seen as important to the revolutionary movement.[20] In Afghanistan, veiling was similarly seen as an important symbol of the resistance effort against the Soviet Union's occupation, and Afghan women took an active part in the resistance, as armed guerillas, among other things. Even the Revolutionary Association of Afghan Women, dedicated to promoting women's rights in Afghanistan, made resistance to Soviet occupation its primary goal.[21] And even though the Taliban's enforcement of edicts requiring women to wear the burqa were not welcomed by women in the cities, such as Kabul, one of the reasons that the Taliban came to power was because the mujahideen, who took power after the Soviets were forced out, abducted, raped, and killed three Afghan women in 1994. Indeed under the mujahideen, "abductions, forced marriages, rapes, and trafficking in little boys and girls were universally acknowledged" as widespread.[22] In such a climate, the Taliban's promises to protect women by restoring order were welcomed by many. On the one hand, then, Western attempts to "liberate" women by removing the veil simply reinscribed women's bodies as symbols of culture rather than as individual agents, replacing one form of social control with another. On the other hand, however, these attempts provided women with a method and language of resistance and agency; by adopting the veil, women could become important political actors on the stage of anti-imperialist resistance.

Does this mean that the veil, seen by westerners as a mark of oppression, is in fact a mark of agency? Not quite, for the veil's symbolic and discursive value can also be seen to entail the subjugation of women's subjectivity. This can hardly be blamed exclusively on the West; the veil is an article of clothing, and "the veil" as cultural symbol has been constructed by and through various and conflicting discourses surrounding ideals of nation, culture, personhood, and power as well as gender. Though imperialist discourses may be the easiest to identify in terms of their discursive construction of Islam's barbarism, however, Mohamad Tavakoli-Targhi argues that nineteenth-century Iranian (then Persian) observers of Western culture engaged in constructions of Western women that were just as biased. For Iranian men, "women of the West were often a displacement and a simulacrum for Iranian women. The focus and reflection on European women resulted in the production of the veil as a woman's uniform and as a marker of cultural, political, and religious difference and identity. What was perceived to be an Islamic dress for women was a product of the cultural and political encounter with the West."[23] Tavakoli-Targhi's argument is not the same as the contemporary one that Iranians were forced into a reactive stance against Western imperialism; indeed, such a reading seriously downplays men's agency and participation in shaping nationalist religious discourses and power relations. The men Tavakoli-Targhi discusses had "two conflicting images of the West. . . . One was grounded in a positive notion of freedom anchored to the memories of the French Revolution and called for the educating and unveiling of Iranian women."[24] In this view, European women were seen as "more" virtuous than Islamic women precisely because of their "freedom"; specifically, because they were educated and able to conduct reasoned discourse, they did not pose the threat of mystery that needs to be controlled.

At the same time, however, the freedom of European women was also seen as license, and therefore morally corrupt: as one late nineteenth-century Persian traveler put it, "the freedom granted to womankind in this country [England] is great, and mischief arising from this unreasonable toleration is most deplorable."[25] This second view "was grounded in a negative notion of freedom constructed on the indecency and corruption of European women and sought to protect Iranian women and the nation of Islam from the malady of the deviant gaze." In this second discourse, veiled Persian women were not only seen as morally superior but as embodying the identity and essence of the nation. The "indecency of European women" and reaction against the West may have been the starting point for the articulation of these Persian constructions, but that starting point was constructed by and through discourses, values, and perspectives that predated Western imperialism and hegemony as much as they responded to it.[26] The West had good and bad to offer, and Persian men adopted what appealed to them and shunned what did not. What did not appeal to them were practices that threatened male power to determine Iranian culture. Thus, it was the latter view—of women's freedom as morally corrupt license—that dominated in the end, for it allowed men to claim the "positive" liberty of education for themselves while denying women "negative" freedom of access. And moreover, the veil became a potent symbol—not so much a "negative" symbol of reaction against the West, but rather a "positive" reaffirmation of Eastern, Islamic morality.

Contemporary Islamic fundamentalist movements take a less ambivalent view, however, and the veil today is often seen as a symbol of resistance to the perceived "loss of cultural purity" resulting from Western power and influence. But the manner and form of such resistance has strong ties to these earlier, and more obviously gender-biased, responses. Indeed, those earlier "antagonistic articulations of European women have remained the organizing elements of twentieth century Iranian modernist and Islamicist political discourses. The Islamicization of Iran since 1979 was grounded in the rejection and condemnation of unveiled women as European dolls."[27] Beyond this construction of Western women, however, lie the possibilities of self-construction, for which the colonizer's discourse sets the terms. As Fanon suggested, efforts to resist colonization through the (re)assertion of cultural identity are always compromised by the fact that the colonizer has constructed the framework within which the oppressed must fight. Assertions of national identity are at least as much reactive as they are proactive, and efforts to "reclaim" an uncorrupted and precolonized past seek something that never actually existed. As I read Fanon, cultural movements that proclaim a return to the past never really return to the past; rather, such efforts constitute statements about the present and the future, specifically about the creation of a new society that has excised colonial influence and given the colonizer's power to the "native." Within the context of veiling, the emphasis on cultural practices constitutes an excuse and rationalization for configurations of masculine power. Unveiled women are signifiers of masculine impotence in the face of the seemingly hegemonic (but in reality porous) power of the colonizing West; by coercing women to embrace particular practices and cultural forms, such as the veil, women's bodies become the physical spaces on which men construct their illusions of power and mastery over their own lives.[28]

Such insights were particularly relevant in the autumn of 2001, following the events of September 11, for women once again emerged as a key symbol of oppression and freedom in nationalist discourses. As the United States sought international support for its military efforts in Afghanistan, the situation of Afghan women gained attention that it has sorely lacked for the past two decades. The U.S. First Lady Laura Bush addressed the media numerous times decrying the conditions of women in Afghanistan. Sensitive to the cultural symbolism of the veil (and particularly to the dangers of alienating Saudi Arabia, in which women lack many freedoms), neither she nor members of the administration overtly criticized the burqa, but rather prohibitions against education and work. Obviously, U.S. feminists must applaud our government for giving official recognition to women's plight, but whether such recognition is truly official is an open question. After all, having the First Lady, rather than a member of the cabinet or a presidential advisor, deliver such messages makes them less weighty than official policy. Indeed, as one senior administration official explained to a *New York Times* reporter, women's rights were not a priority for the Bush administration, because "We have to be careful not to look like we are imposing our values on them." The notion that "We do not try to order how women are treated in America . . . so what right does America have to tell us how to treat our women?" suggests—as was the case in the "cultural defense" that abusers have used in domestic-violence trials, which I described in chapter 4—that women are not full members of culture but only emblems of it that men can deploy. The West tacitly supports such beliefs; in a depressing echo of the nineteenth-century British imperialists Ahmed described, the Bush administration uses women's situation as a "moral cudgel" against the Taliban, to indicate the moral and cultural supremacy of the West without directly asserting it. But it may not be willing to invest the political capital needed to actually protect women's freedom.[29]

Understanding the historical context of contemporary practices and discourses suggests that the veil itself is not so much a cause of women's lack of freedom and control over their lives as it is a marker of it, and this, in turn, because wearing the veil, or shedding it, is often not optional. As Hoodfar suggests, women in Iran were just as oppressed and persecuted by the shah's mandatory deveiling as they were by the subsequent mandatory reveiling ordered by Islamic revolutionaries. And though women under the shah were not beaten up as they sometimes now are by "cultural police," they were nevertheless chased by state police for wearing veils in public, their veils were torn off them, and they were harassed. Since, for many women, not wearing the veil was akin to being naked, the ban on wearing the veil in public effectively limited women's sphere of activity to the home and made them more dependent on men, just as women's fear in contemporary Afghanistan trapped them in their homes. Indeed, in an ironic mirror image of Afghanistan, the ban on veiling in Iran severely hampered women's ability to go to the public baths, not only increasing their health risks, but also disrupting an important source of community and information for women. Additionally, women became dependent on men to sell the carpets that they made at home, which they had formerly done for themselves, thus undermining their economic as well as social autonomy and independence.[30]

Thus the shah's coercive deveiling policy cannot be seen as somehow more benign than the equally coercive reveiling instituted after the shah was deposed. What it illustrates is that the veil itself does not make women free or unfree; rather, the patriarchal use of the veil to control women sets the limits to women's agency. As Stowasser argues, Islamic customs oppressive to women arose not out of Islam per se but out of medieval customs that became intertwined with Islamic belief; and today, it is political conservatism, not Islam, that restricts women. She argues that fundamentalists view women as important and equal partners as "warriors of faith," and the veil is one important weapon that they are uniquely positioned to wield. Conservatism, by contrast, seeks women's subservience, and the veil is one of many instruments used to secure this.[31] If that is so, then it is important to acknowledge the strong role of conservatism in contemporary fundamentalist movements, for fundamentalists' assertion of the importance of the veil runs contrary to many feminist readings of the Qur'an, and the veil has been a useful historical and cultural symbol employed by patriarchy to mark and identify women's bodies and identities.[32] As such, it might seem that women's exercise of agency within the practice of veiling would be compromised; but the fact that deveiling has been seen as an equally powerful cultural symbol of patriarchical regimes problematizes such a straightforward assertion. A more interesting question might be why the veil has persisted over time as such a powerful symbol, while modes of restrictive Western dress, such as the corset, died away, and others, like the miniskirt, have resurfaced at the turn of the twenty-first century with specifically feminist twists (e.g., the power suit). It may be that since the West triggered the symbolic importance of the veil through its imperialism, it retains a certain dominance over the terms of the discourse.[33]

The issue for feminists concerned with freedom is thus how political and cultural power are used in the social and discursive construction of women's lived experience and material reality. It is less whether Western freedom is "good" or "bad" than who determines what is "good" and "bad" about the West and East. Although the West played a significant role in the cultural construction of not only the veil but political movements of resistance and identity, it did not determine such construction; the agency of, and choices made by, Islamic men were at least as influential. Thus, it is important to note that even though many Muslim women have joined the movement to veil as a sign of political protest, and Western feminists who are concerned about freedom must support them in their choice, the choice is made within a historically constructed context wherein "unveiledness and sexual liberty of women were viewed as the cause of corruption and moral degeneration of Europe."[34] Just as Western men used the veil as a symbol in their imperialist political battles so did and do Eastern Islamic men use the veil as a symbol of resistance to imperialism. Arguably, in neither case do women take part in constructing the framework within which decisions about dress take place, but rather are forced to respond in conflicting directions to frameworks constructed by men.[35]

By recognizing that the social construction of veiling is historically and culturally constituted and variable, and that it is a political as much as a religious symbol, it becomes possible to separate veiling as a practice from Islam as a set of beliefs. As several feminists have argued, the link between the veil and Islam is dubious. Claims that it is central to the Islamic faith, on this view, are complete perversions of Islam, based either in ignorance or, more cynically, patriarchal power. The Qur'an says that women should wear loose-fitting clothes that do not reveal their figures and expose only their hands, feet, and face (something the burqa does not do). The Qur'an does stress that both women and men should dress modestly (and in Afghanistan, the Taliban required men to grow beards and wear turbans; men whose beards were too short, or hair too long, were imprisoned and/or beaten).[36] But many women accommodate Qur'anic dress codes by wearing long dresses with long sleeves and head-scarves. On this view, requiring the burqa is based on an incorrect reading of the Qur'an, not just an anachronistic one. It is true that certain aspects of Islam, such as polygamy, might be difficult to reconcile with a feminist vision of freedom. But feminist scholars have noted that Islam is no more restrictively patriarchal than other religions, such as Judaism or Christianity.[37] Catholic prohibitions on abortion, as well as the surging popularity of "Promise Keepers," which urges men to forcibly assert their proper place as the leader of the family, are only two examples of the ways in which Western religions are far from egalitarian in gendered terms. And the Amish, the Mennonites, and Orthodox Jews prescribe dress codes for both men and women.

Indeed, some feminists maintain that Islam is less patriarchal than Judaism or Christianity. They point to passages in the Qur'an that declare women's right to inheritance—at half the rate of men's, admittedly, but a guaranteed entitlement, nonetheless—as well as those that urge equal respect between men and women, particularly in marriage. Nawal el Sadawi notes that "Many verses of the Qur'an refer to the fact that all people are equal before Allah, and that He created males and females so that there could be mercy and love between them." Cherifa Bouatta and Doria Cherifati-Merabtine similarly argue that "The ideas of equality, rights, women's liberation . . . . have a positive connotation when their frame of reference is Islam . . . [though] the Western women's liberation is a mystification."[38] Feminists also argue that Islam supports women's working outside the home by pointing out that the prophet Muhammad's first wife was an influential businesswoman. Furthermore, they argue that Islam encourages education for both sexes, as essential to the ability to read and interpret the Qur'an, and hence to pass on religious culture and faith. Indeed, the prophet held that those who educated two daughters had special opportunities to attain paradise. Additionally, el Sadawi also suggests that the Qur'an allows contraception, as well as abortion in the first ninety days after conception.[39] And some argue that even polygamy has its feminist aspects: it affords community among women and the sharing of housework and child care. On the other hand, some Muslim women argue that polygamy is not really supported by the Qur'an. The Qur'an instructs a man to "'Marry as many women as you wish, two or three or four. If you fear not to treat them equally, marry only one. Indeed, you will not be able to be just between your wives even if you try.'" This can readily be interpreted as a sardonic rejection of polygamy, for it is impossible to treat multiple wives "equally."[40] Such arguments are not made only by feminists, either; Lila Abu-Lughod notes an elderly Awlad 'Ali woman using this argument against her son's taking a second wife against her wishes; "It's a sin, sin, sin."[41]

Given such disagreement about the discourses of Islam and the discursive construction of gender within it, it is not surprising that there is vast disagreement on the significance, status, and meaning of veiling among Eastern feminists. Some, such as Alya Baffoun and Fatima Mernissi, see veiling as largely oppressive: "the veil can be interpreted as a symbol revealing a collective fantasy of the Muslim community; to make women disappear, to eliminate them from communal life, to relegate them to an easily controllable terrain, the home, to prevent them moving about, and to highlight their illegal position on male territory by means of a mask."[42] Mernissi argues that veiling of women is nowhere mentioned in the Qur'an, which refers to the veil only as a barrier between a married couple and the world outside, not one between men and women, a view supported by Stowasser.[43] Yet at the same time, Mernissi and others are critical of westerners', including Western feminists', readings of the veil, in which "women's liberty . . . has been viewed almost exclusively as a religious problem" instead of an economic and political one.[44] Other feminists see veiling, along with the practice of purdah, or the seclusion of women, as clear examples of resistance to westernization and the preservation of culture.[45] Valentine M. Moghadam points out that "Purdah provides the opportunity for preserving one's own identity and a certain stability in the face of external pressures," a point on which others such as Leila Ahmed agree. But Moghadam also argues that its value as a symbol of resistance has operated less for women than for men; it has served to "strengthen the men's will to resist." Her account also suggests that the heavier the veiling—the more covered women are, and the stricter and more extensive the segregation—the more oppressed they are, in a physical symbolization of the cultural and political construction of gendered (un)freedom.[46] This is a theme echoed by Marie-Aimée Hélie-Lucas, who suggests that the "need for unity" in nationalist movements means that women's needs often get submerged or ignored; "women who try to defend their rights in Muslim contexts are generally accused of importing a foreign ideology whenever they ask for more social justice." Thus, although "To be the guardians of identity and culture is an honor in the fundamentalist discourse," in actual practice, "Women are honored for as long as they keep culture and religion in the way they are told to do."[47]

Others dismiss veiling as a minor issue compared to the more pressing problems of women's education, poverty and economic dependence, violence against women, divorce and child custody, and health care for women and children.[48] Still others point out that veiling is not a practice intrinsic to Islam, but rather emerged out of other Eastern (including Semitic) cultures.[49] Some argue that the Qur'an's recommendations that hair, shoulders, and upper arms be covered, and that women should shield themselves from the sight of men to whom they are unrelated, applied only to the wives of the Prophet, who were subject to considerable public exposure, not to ordinary women.[50] Others have even questioned the gendered character of veiling; since modesty is a requirement of Muslim men as well as women, men's bodies are expected to be covered by long sleeves and trousers, as well as headgear. At the same time, veiling is not universal even among Muslim women; for instance, women do not veil in Afghanistan's neighbor Uzbekistan, despite its "powerful Islamic traditions,"[51] and as I mentioned earlier, in Turkey women are prohibited from veiling in public. Such diverse views suggest that the veil is both a marker of autonomy, individuality, and identity, and a marker of inequality and sexist oppression. This ambiguity is revealed not simply between different veiling contexts, however, but within particular cultural settings. The reason for this may be the unsettling effects of Western "penetration," or it may be an inevitable tension between individualism and cultural identity. But it may also indicate a distinctive notion of agency, one that shares certain elements of Western conceptions but introduces others quite different. The relevance of agency and freedom once again invites the image of choice, for many women themselves see veiling as a sign of devotion to Islam. Others see it as a symbol of cultural and political identity, rather than religious faith, but no less important. And indeed, it is precisely the women who choose veiling, defend it, and consider it vital to their self-identity who pose the greatest challenge to Western understandings of agency. For after all, if veiling is a mark of women's oppression—and that "if" is important to maintain—women's choosing it presents a paradox. Accordingly, I shall here focus on two specific contexts in which women talk about the veil in terms of autonomous choice. The relation of such women to the practice and discourses of veiling and Islam suggests that in contrast to Western assumptions, Muslim women in various contexts have been able to use the veil not only to establish identity and agency but to resist patriarchy as well.

## Autonomy and Freedom in Contexts of Community

This point is illustrated particularly well by two ethnographic studies of cultures in which women actively support and choose veiling. The first is Lila Abu-Lughod's study of Arab Bedouins. Abu-Lughod emphasizes that within the Awlad 'Ali Bedouin culture, individual agency is vital to women's identity. "Autonomy or freedom is the standard by which status is measured and social hierarchy determined. . . . Equality is nothing other than equality of autonomy—that is, equality of freedom from domination by or dependence on others." Echoing both negative- and positive-liberty themes, freedom is defined in terms of "the strength to stand alone and freedom from domination," and "is won through tough assertiveness, fearlessness, and pride" as well as "through self-control," regulation of the "passions."[52] Yet the concept of "honor" is also central to Bedouin identity, and although individual autonomy within tribes is important to the concept of honor, "maximization of unit autonomy"—independence *among* tribes—is also vital, as "Each tribal segment is theoretically equal to every other through opposition" (79). Thus, while the honorable man "stands alone and fears nothing" (88), honor is also measured by obedience. Tribal status and autonomy are closely tied to individual status and autonomy, and tribal autonomy and honor can be upheld only if members respect hierarchy. Thus, to be free, one must obey, but one must give that obedience freely in order to assert one's independence. The honorable individual must be strong and independent, yet also enmeshed in hierarchical family relationships, wherein the higher up one is, the more honor one has.

Women's obedience, too, must be seen as a choice; "people pity a woman who seems to obey her husband because she has no choice," due to poverty, for instance, or the lack of male kin protectors (105). Although women exhort each other to obedience, however, they also admire "willful" women. For instance, a woman who walks out on her husband declaring that she is "lonely" for her family, when actually she is angry with him for ignoring her, asserts autonomy in ways that *seem* to express deference and dependence, by invoking images of connectedness, loyalty to the family of origin, and respect for hierarchical authority, while actually challenging such values (for everyone in the tribe knows the "real" reason for the woman's actions, even though that may not be publicly expressed). Veiling and women's seclusion are seen as an expression of this independence. Women view their segregation as a source of pride and honor; it signifies that they do not need the company of men, and declares their independence (46). As a mark of modesty, the veil indicates deference but also autonomy, for it "masks" not just the body but "the 'natural' needs and passions" (115). The veil thus serves as a statement that the wearer is intent on preserving herself as separate from others, emotionally and psychologically as well as physically; it is a tangible marker of separateness and independence.

Thus, rather than a tool of oppression, veiling is an instrument of agency and freedom for these women. Abu-Lughod even notes gaps in the practice, in which women exert complete control; for instance, one woman who marries an older man decides not to veil for anyone younger than him, and then declares that in fact everyone is younger. Another woman declares she does not have to veil because she is so very virtuous (164). These discursive challenges to customary practices illustrate women's power to exert some control over the conditions of their lives by redefining those practices and categories of meaning: women reconstruct their material realities through discursive intervention in customary practice. Yet at the same time, such values are defined within patriarchal discursive parameters. Though women "share with their providers the same ideals for self-image and social reputation. . . . the situations in which they can realize these ideals, in particular those of independence and assertiveness, are circumscribed" (111). Hence, the question of why these two women's decisions are accepted, and why more women do not try to make such claims, is hazy. For such acts of resistance operate within normative parameters which women may support, intentionally or unintentionally, through their actions, but have not themselves created. This hardly proves women's oppression, of course; after all, the freedom/honor duality is a catch-22 for men too. As I argued in chapter 3, the ability to interrupt, reconfigure, and change discourse is centrally affected by power, but the paradox of social construction suggests a certain degree of remarkableness when *anyone* is *ever* able to do it.

But hierarchies of gendered power ensure that women are particularly caught. Thus, women claim to admire men who can "control all their dependents and beat their wives when the wives do stupid things" (89). And although women may be praised for their strength when they go against community norms, such rebellion is limited by patriarchal parameters. Premarital sex, for instance, results in ostracism, not admiration. As Abu-Lughod notes, the strong ideological relation between honor and modesty "serves to rationalize social inequality and the control some have over the lives of others. . . . if honor derives from virtues associated with autonomy, then there are many, most notably women, who because of their physical, social, and economic dependence are handicapped in their efforts to realize these ideals" (33). Autonomy operates within particular structures and parameters set by community, which women have participated in and helped to construct; but men have historically had the social power to set and define these cultural norms. This dynamic is a theme of Abu-Lughod's subsequent work *Writing Women's Worlds*. On the one hand, the women declare their independence from men. In the words of an old song, recited by a matriarch called Migdim with whom Abu-Lughod spends considerable time, "You who guards the female, you're fatigued." That is, "A woman can't be governed—anyone who tries to guard her will just get tired. . . . Whatever a woman wants to she can do. She's smart and she can think."[53] Yet at the same time, Migdim's sons repeatedly make their own decisions against her wishes; the eldest son "brushed her off . . . when she interfered," and he takes a third wife and transfers property despite her opposition. Among the younger men, brothers seek to control their sisters within the confines of a new conservative orthodoxy which constrains women's behavior more severely than when Migdim, or even her daughters, were girls. One of Migdim's grandsons, for instance, attempts to set fire to some shiny material purchased for his sister's dress, saying, "She wants to wear a dress that sparkles? And she's wearing bobby pins and gold fringe? She's got complete freedom!" Another of Migdim's grandsons "yells at the girls and won't let them go to get water." The women clearly disapprove of such behavior, repeatedly saying "the boys are terrible," but their disapproval seems to have no effect.[54]

The undercurrent of such attempts at control seems to concern sexuality. Migdim's song mocks men's inability to control women's sexual behavior: "One time she'll go to milk the herd and rendezvous / One time she'll get up at night to tie up the goats."[55] Sexuality discourses particularly illustrate this duality and ambiguity of women's freedom and constraint. Given that sex is seen as a dangerous area in which the self can be lost to dependence on another, both men and women who express eagerness for sex are scorned for weakness (154). But this weighs more heavily on women than men, whose sexuality is at least acknowledged, by practices such as polygamy, and allowed freer expression. Abu-Lughod cites an example of a man putting his head in his wife's lap while she is sitting with other women: unlike the man, the woman is visibly embarrassed by his expression of sexual affection, and the other women approve of her reaction. Yet she cannot refuse him, because he is her husband. This resistance/submission motif is prominent. For instance, girls traditionally cry when they learn they are to be married: "The good bride screams when the groom comes near her and tries to fight him off. She is admired for her unwillingness to talk to the groom" (154). Such resistance, however, seems to encode symbolic representations of virtue rather than expressions of desire or will, for it cannot be taken to the point of actually refusing to marry: "As a good woman she should not resist a marriage arranged by her brothers, as this would constitute defiance" (215). Thus, "the more women are able to deny their sexuality, the more honorable they are" (153). The veil and the seclusion of women are convenient and powerful ways to accomplish this denial of sexuality, for it is a way to "avoid" men's attention and to "screen" women from men, both literally and symbolically. But such denial occurs "behind the veil" as well, that is, among women, who seem to be the harshest critics of women who express sexual desire. Women encourage negative and dismissive attitudes about sex among themselves, and women who are perceived to want sex are scorned as weak.

The role of discourse and language in this process is particularly relevant, for Abu-Lughod notes that poetry is the socially accepted form through which men and women alike may express emotions and feelings. Poetry expresses emotions at the same time that it "veils" them in abstract, symbolic, and artistic forms. Despite its important place in the culture, however, such poetic expression seems rarely to affect gender relations materially. Abu-Lughod offers one particularly poignant example of a man who responded to his wife after reading a poem that Abu-Lughod had transcribed. But the significant point of the story from a feminist perspective is less that the man responded earnestly to his wife and was concerned with her desires than that normally, he would be unaware of her feelings because Bedouin poetry is oral, not written, and is not generally recited by women to men. Men can hardly be faulted for not responding to women's desires and preferences when they do not know what they are (and Abu-Lughod does offer examples of some women, particularly older women, who are fairly straightforward in expressing their desires, particularly to sons and other men lower down on the familial hierarchy).[56] But for the most part, gendered norms ensure that men are deprived of such knowledge.

Of course, the point here is not to pity Bedouin women for a repressed sexuality or false sense of agency but rather to highlight the ways in which women's agency, resistance, and freedom can be understood only by their location in a context where the control of women by men is a significant factor. As my discussion of domestic violence and welfare reveal, Bedouin women are no different from Western women in this sense. And while the emphasis I have placed on choice and self-direction may again seem to impose Western standards on a non-Western discourse, these ideals are in fact internal to this particular Bedouin discourse as well. The question, as with the other, Western practices I have discussed in chapters 4 and 5, is whether the realization of these ideals by men requires their denial to women. Though Abu-Lughod rightly asserts that "veiling is both voluntary and situational. . . . an act undertaken by women to express their virtue in encounters with particular categories of men" (159), the fact of cultural sanction in a closed community also means this choice is to some significant degree coerced, much like Foucault's claims about "freely given" sex within ancient Greek marriage. If "respectability achieved through embodiment of the code's virtues is isomorphic with self-re-

spect," then "by framing ideals as values, in moral terms, it guarantees
that individuals will desire to do what perpetuates the system, thus obviat-
ing the need for overt violence or force" (238). But this is exactly how
social control works, through the colonization of desire and will, as Foucault himself argued.[57] And as he notes, it *is* a kind of violence, because
it not only coerces individuals but redefines such coercion as freedom and
choice, thereby blinding individuals to the control they are subject to and
making them the instruments of their own oppression. Thus, the question
of women's freedom is highly ambiguous, because it always exists within
contexts not of women's making that construct women's subjectivity in
ways often at odds with understandings of agency common to both the
West and this non-Western discourse as well.

Arlene MacLeod argues, however, that such ambiguity can be used by
women to cope with restrictive contexts. In her study of women in contemporary Cairo, what she calls "accommodating protest" is an "ambiguous pattern . . . of women, who seem to both struggle in a conscious and
active way against their inequality, yet who also seem to accept, and even
support their own subordination."[58] Although proclaiming that Cairene
women "are not passive victims, and they quite actively argue their case
and seek to widen their opportunities when the chance is offered," Mac-
Leod acknowledges that women's activity is "a form of influence or manipulation within constraints which differs from the powers exercised by
the dominant groups" (41). That is, rather than having power to define
the terms of customs, like veiling, that set the parameters to individual
choice, women instead maneuver within these parameters to negotiate
their preferences, make their choices, and assert their identity.

To Western eyes, the situation in Cairo may appear extremely different
from Abu-Lughod's Bedouins, for Western dress has become a fairly common part of the cultural landscape and offers many women an apparently
wide range of choices. In fact, MacLeod reports that most women took
to the veil by choice after having worn Western fashions for much of their
lives as single adult women, and that the majority of women viewed veiling favorably (105). But at the same time, Cairene women are not faced
with simply adopting a head scarf—as the euphemism "veil" tends to
imply—but the more elaborate *higab*, which involves an entire ensemble,
including the head covering. Echoing Western notions, many of the
women she studied expressed strong sentiments of individual autonomy
and choice founded on deeply held conviction, such as one who claimed
that "putting on this dress [the higab] is an important personal decision,
and . . . it is wrong to take such a move lightly; without the proper feelings
inside, it would be wrong to veil" (109). Within such a context of choice,
however, the notion of the subject is different from the dominant Western
notion. Like Abu-Lughod, MacLeod documents among Cairene women

an understanding of individual agency that is located in community and cultural membership. This location in community is important to individual identity but does not evoke the communitarian nightmare of the selfless soul. Rather, individuals exist *within* social contexts, and the higab helps women express this "dual" location.

Community is particularly significant in the workplace, as one of the major strictures that women attempt to resist via veiling is economic. MacLeod highlights the fact that many women, particularly of the middle- and lower-middle classes, work outside the home. Although economic necessity rather than Western bourgeois ideals of career fulfillment generally motivates such employment, women nevertheless value the economic independence and "freedom of movement" (71) such work affords. Yet work puts them in an ambiguous position vis-à-vis Islam, which according to some frowns on a married woman working outside the home (though as I mentioned earlier, there is some disagreement over this claim). The higab is an important instrument in negotiating this ambiguity, because it allows women to enter the public sphere of work while at the same time making a clear statement that they adhere to the tenets of Islam. As one woman says, "it says to everyone that I am trying to be a good wife and a good mother. The *higab* is the dress of Muslim women, and it shows that I am a Muslim woman" (120).[59] The veil helps solidify community among women within the work world by presenting a visible marker of the shared cross-pressures that Islamic married working women face between economic need and traditional Islamic norms. Indeed, Stowasser argues that the economic necessity of women's work outside the home was a key factor contributing to the shift in the meaning of the term *higab* from "the home" to "a way of dress." Although it might seem somewhat paradoxical to view working out of "economic necessity" as entailing an increase in freedom, the veil, by allowing a woman to bring "the home" with her, in fact gives her freer access to the marketplace. Thus, in direct contrast to Western stereotypes that veiling expresses patriarchy, the veil can help *forestall* patriarchal expressions of women's subservience. As the visceral reminder of a woman's location in relationship—not only in kinship relations (101) but in the larger community of Islam—the veil allows women entry into the working world by protecting them from sexual harassment and visibly demanding respect from a woman's husband, men in the office, and even men on the street (133).[60] The veil is a "protest" less against the West—except in the indirect sense that being a "good woman, wife and mother" requires that one be a "good Muslim," which the women believe they cannot do in Western clothes—than against Islamic forms of patriarchy. "The *higab* voices the protest that many women dare not voice directly to their husbands, and perhaps that many cannot articulate completely even to themselves" (133). The higab can be seen as a tool of women's agency, in that it allows women to negotiate the strictures of patriarchal custom to gain what they want, to assert their independence, and to claim their own identity.

Yet is such control illusory? It is hardly the case that women control the discursive constructions of veiling any more than those of gender. For instance, the woman who emphasized the importance of having "the proper feelings inside" before making the personal choice to veil later told MacLeod privately "that she had no intention of putting on this dress and was very comfortable with her current skirts and blouses." But she "avoided making these comments to her colleagues. Instead, she confronted them within the prevailing ethos of appropriate behavior" by emphasizing that she did not "yet" have the appropriate feeling, thus leaving open the assumption that eventually, she *would* have this feeling and adopt the veil. Indeed, MacLeod notes that regardless of whether they want to veil, "few are willing to criticize the idea of veiling," and "few are willing to argue that their religion or cultural traditions are in some way wrong" (115). As was the case in Abu-Lughod's study, such responses reflect the power of the dominant patriarchal construction, as "women are not responding primarily to male pressure, but to an internalized feeling that they wish to make this accommodation to the traditional ideals of woman's identity and proper role" (140). Thus, when women claim the veil protects them from harassment, "Rather than placing the blame . . . onto men, women accommodate by altering their dress to fit the prevailing norm that men should not be tempted by women." Similarly, using the veil to allay husbands' jealousy means that "the necessity to change is placed not on men, but on women, who accommodate to the norm of women's proper behavior by adopting dress which will avoid improper comments" (107).[61] Thus, many of these women fail to bring a critical political perspective to bear on their experiences, resulting in problematic constructions of their own lived reality. As one woman says, "Today I can come and go as I please, I ask Mohammed but he almost always says of course I can go" (71). Such constructions trap women more deeply in repressive contexts by blinding them to their subordination. For instance, many women view the veil as a form of fashion, which may on the one hand undercut Western charges of oppression but on the other robs veiling of its political significance (139). Indeed, many of the women McLeod interviewed were very critical of those who took on more extreme forms of dress for political purposes, indicating not only the divisive effects of class differences among women (the fact that one woman "goes too far" in her veiling is attributed to the fact that "her family comes from the village" [111]) but how the constructions of class and gender work together to disempower women, who apparently feel threatened by those who use the veil to make overtly political statements. As one woman puts it, "Muslim women are careful about their reputation. Egypt is not like America! In America women are too free in their behavior. . . . This is not our way" (109).

## FEMINISM AND FREEDOM: CROSS-CULTURAL POSSIBILITIES

What can these different accounts of veiling tell us about Western conceptions of freedom? On the one hand, they might support the universal appeal of Enlightenment conceptions. Both MacLeod's and Abu-Lughod's accounts reveal many parallels to Western ideals: control over the self, the absence of external restraints, the importance of individuals. And most people throughout the world, including many men and women in Islamic countries, condemn the Taliban's oppressive practices. On the other hand, however, they suggest that Western conceptions are inadequate; for in contrast to Western individualism, the subject as portrayed by Abu-Lughod and McLeod is always located in contexts of kinship and community, cultural traditions, social structures, and relationships. Within such a context, the formation of desire as well as the ability to act on it becomes part of a single process rather than discrete moments. The more complex understanding this yields is much more amenable to feminist theories of freedom, which must inevitably involve analysis not just of whether the choosing subject can act on her choices but how that subject and her choices are constructed in the first place.

The emphasis on community in the foregoing discussion could be taken to suggest that westerners need to pay more attention to the positive-liberty dimensions of their own tradition; but as I have argued, most positive-liberty variants cannot accommodate the strong individualism found in the two cultures analyzed by Abu-Lughod and MacLeod. Moreover, such a conclusion would ignore what is most significant in the above analysis, namely, that women can act within parameters determined by social power structures, and indeed may be criticized for not protecting their autonomy in those terms, but do not participate in the creation of those terms, even though they may often support them. Though neither Bedouin nor Cairene society is as repressive as the Taliban, women's ability to challenge the framework is nevertheless circumscribed by patriarchy: MacLeod's office workers may be aware that gender relations are unfair, but they cannot articulate this to men even in their own homes, let alone in the political arena; and Abu-Lughod's Bedouin women would consider it a mark of dishonor, and thereby unfreedom, to challenge the hierarchy of familial agnation. As I mentioned earlier, even some Afghan women initially chose to veil as a symbol of support in the war against the former

Soviet Union but could not have anticipated how religious leaders, in entering the "vacuum left by the destruction of the civil authorities,"[62] would press their power advantage. As in Abu-Lughod's and McLeod's accounts, the Afghan situation attests to the problems women may encounter in adopting cultural and political values and discourses in contexts in which they lack cultural and political power. To say that women veil as a way to reconcile work with traditional values, or independence with honor, or to express political solidarity, may recognize women's active agency but circumvents a larger question: is it a mark of women's agency to uphold values or codes that oppress women?

Obviously, this is not simply a problem for veiling, for the same issue underlay my discussion of domestic violence and welfare. Nor is it simply a problem for women, for the ability of individual men to challenge cultural norms is often similarly hampered. But as I have already argued, a key difference is that men as a group are the primary creators and enforcers of these norms, and the norms themselves allow men more power, choice, and freedom than they do women. In the context of veiling, Muslim men, as a social group, have greater ability to challenge and change the norms, just as men do in the West: though Afghanistan and Egypt are quite diverse in their readings of the Qur'an, in both nations it is men who have the power to interpret the religious texts, and these interpretations set the conditions of women's lives. The expression of this power differential through veiling yields significant insights about the gendered character of agency and freedom. For instance, it suggests that not just the West's colonization of the East, but men's colonization of women, needs to be confronted. To take the veiled woman as symbolic of tribal or national identity or as a cultural and religious norm, as the political discourse of the veil often does, subverts the gendered dimensions of veiling. This results in a paradox: for women's ability to choose their practices is key to freedom, yet the fact that women choose to wear the veil does not of itself make wearing it a free action, or even a protest. Indeed, it could be a sign of the closed circularity of women's political disempowerment and colonization. For instance, Leila Ahmed points out that the majority of both veiled and unveiled women in Egypt favor the return of *sharia*, or religious law, without fully understanding how it would increase their subordination to men.[63] Such lack of understanding results in part from the inferior education women receive in many cultures, as well as their socialization to respect hierarchy and not become politically knowledgeable. If a "good Muslim woman" belongs in the home, then part of that construction is to be uninterested in politics and to trust in men as their political representatives. But such trust can become a trap for women, who then are systematically left out of the process of formulating the framework within which their agency can be expressed.

Thus, although the accounts I have offered of women's veiling support the claim I made in chapter 1, that choice is central to a feminist theory of freedom, the *act of choosing* is necessary but not sufficient for freedom. Women must also be able to *formulate choices*, and this requires that they have meaningful power in the construction of contexts: for instance, the development of a new religious code that would provide the moral security and certainty these women seek, without the gender repression they fear and oppose. Such a code would obviously have to derive from a different reading of the Qur'an than tends to dominate in many Muslim cultures, but it is one which many Muslim feminists have already proposed. Leila Ahmed, for instance, suggests that the reason women do not realize that the reimposition of sharia would entail gender repression is that they see Islam as favoring gender equality. Indeed, she maintains that women's "misunderstandings" are less about Islam than about politics in the patriarchal state. Similarly, Fatima Mernissi argues that patriarchy runs contrary to the tenets of Islam, and she develops a reading of the Qu'ran that is egalitarian in terms of gender.[64]

The fact that Islam is a religion, a set of beliefs based on a unitary source, the Qu'ran, might seem to limit the discursive uses that can be politically made of its text. But the history of religion and religious wars over interpretation make such claims somewhat naive. As Martha Nussbaum has argued, fundamentalists' claims that their definitions of Islamic traditions are "true" ignore the fact that cultural traditions are variable, that they change and evolve in response to changing circumstances. For instance, Jonah Blank shows that the Daudi Bohras in South Asia strictly adhere to orthodox Muslim traditions of dress (including the burqa for women, though without the face covering), prayer, and avoidance of financial interest, but eagerly embrace aspects of contemporary culture, such as technology, higher education for girls as well as boys, and careers for women. Nussbaum argues that such variability opens the door to a redefinition of "culture" that gives women a voice equal to men's, and that gives consideration of women's rights an equal place.[65] That the discourses of Islam have shifted and changed in response to political power and need is no more surprising than similar transformations in the discourses of welfare. And indeed, the connections between "East" and "West" are profound, not only in the similarities of how their discourses work to express and materialize gendered power, but in how different cultural contexts reveal things about others that are not visible from within. For instance, the need to attend to contexts within which choices are made should make Western feminists ask whether the veil is any more oppressive than Western clothing trends such as Wonder bras, makeup, miniskirts, or even blue jeans. Precisely because it challenges Western assumptions about what women "should" choose, veiling illustrates how power operates in all contexts. Women who utilize the veil to express agency may subvert the practice by turning its norms against itself, but they also reinforce its underlying power structure. In this sense, veiling may parallel domestic violence after all: not because veiling is inherently oppressive—the stereotypical Western assumption—but because of the duality and ambiguity both reveal about choice. Women negotiate the parameters of these practices to carve out space for themselves by making choices. But these choices, paradoxically, reinforce those parameters, which in turn ensure limitations on those negotiations and choices. Both domestic violence and veiling illustrate that understanding women's freedom requires understanding the material and discursive contexts within which women's choices are formed and made. But what veiling in particular reveals is the potential power of cross-cultural communication and critique in understanding context. The effort to critically evaluate women's choices must involve cross-cultural questioning that challenges the individual's construction by social norms. Women must be able to question those norms, to challenge not only practices but the contexts in which those practices are formed and take meaning. In chapter 4 I argued that intimate-partner violence demonstrated the need to shift and change contexts in order for the social construction of desire, identity, and meaning to become visible. The cross-cultural implications of Western feminists attempting to engage and understand, in all its subtle complexity, a non-Western practice such as veiling provide a useful model for seeing how contexts need to be changed, as well as offering possible alternatives for effecting such change. Envisioning these alternatives does not mean they must be adopted, any more than questioning norms necessarily entails their rejection; after all, if Muslim women moved into a Western context, they would not necessarily have greater freedom. Indeed, subjected to Western racism, they might have even *less* freedom. But the ability to question and challenge contexts is nonetheless important. By putting contexts on the table to consider their patriarchal aspects and demanding that women be able to participate in reconfiguring those contexts, feminists may be able to point out that, whatever else veiling may achieve—and what it achieves may be significant—it nevertheless supports male dominance and is at least *in part* a symbol of women's unfreedom. Indeed, as both Ahmed and Tavakoli-Targhi suggest, it even supports Western imperialism by reinscribing Western definitions and dichotomies onto Eastern practices in a reactive manner.[66] This raises serious questions about Islamic male militants' eagerness to enforce veiling in countries such as Afghanistan and Iran: if it is not as revolutionary as they claim, then why is it seen as such an important symbol? Could it be that the oppression of women is at least as important a goal as resisting the West, and that "revolution" is really about certain men's desire for power? Indeed, Shaheed argues that many of the so-called "Muslim laws" that restrict women's autonomy are not Islamic in origin at all, and that this explains the great variation in such laws from country to country.[67]

Moreover, a feminist notion of freedom requires that Western feminists be allowed to raise such challenges to non-Western practices like veiling without being automatically dismissed as imperialists, just as Eastern feminists must be able to critique Western practices that westerners may consider benign or even liberatory. It is difficult to gain a critical purchase on a context from within the context itself: one must often be "outside" it, at the same time that one is "inside" it, as Derrida noted.[68] The battered-women's shelter is a case in point. At the shelter, battered women's own stories, perceptions, and representations of their experiences interact with the perceptions and interpretations of others who are not experiencing those relationships, as well as the powers and privileges of professionals who can push for arrest, prosecution, sentencing, economic opportunities, and so forth. These different participants to the dialogue make important contributions to understanding the dominant contexts, how they need to be changed, and how to change them. Similarly, welfare advocacy requires those who can use tools such as laws, courts, legislation, and policy, but also requires attending to what welfare recipients have to say about their experiences, so that those laws and policies will accurately address the needs of caretakers and the poor. With regard to veiling, however, such back-and-forth between those "inside" and "outside" the context in question is more difficult, because the possibility for misunderstanding and misinterpretation is at its maximum. Whereas the "professionals" in IPV and welfare may be able to appreciate the nuances of their clients' experiences, in international issues the westerner is considered too much of an "outsider" to participate at all. This is where a "global" feminism can play its most radical card, however. Through cross-cultural communication that comes out of cultural specificity, but with a political goal in sight of ending sexist oppression, feminists may be able to offer insights and critiques from "outside" that are not achievable from "within." Certainly, Western feminists must be sensitive to the dangers of imperialism: as Ahmed argues, it is precisely Western imperialism that requires Islamic cultures to defend themselves so strongly against the West. This in turn makes it difficult for Islamic women to criticize their own cultures; they are caught between the rock of being ostracized as Western sympathizers, and the hard place of not having their concerns heard. In either case, they are left out of community. In this sense, Western criticism of veiling runs the danger of undermining Islamic women's attempts to affect their own cultures.[69]

Similarly, calls for cross-cultural dialogue may seem naive, given the history of such efforts, for westerners often simply say "Do it our way," and refuse to attend authentically to other cultures. Furthermore, given that Muslim women's networks have engaged similar cross-cultural exchange among specifically Muslim countries to challenge gender-repressive laws as non-Islamic, perhaps Western feminists should simply stay out of the matter.[70] But I believe it is important to have "East-West" interaction, and moreover that it can occur non-imperialistically. To begin with, Western feminists must recognize that their responsibility for promoting fruitful dialogue is greater than their Eastern counterparts', not only because the latter have already been forced to attend to the West, but also because the West has done much more damage to the East than vice versa.[71] This means that westerners must *listen*, if for no other reason than that more comprehensive understandings of our own experiences—including the way we dress and its signficance for Western women's freedom—cannot occur without such attention. Reading the works of Eastern feminists, such as Fatima Mernissi's on the ways in which patriarchy runs contrary to the tenets of Islam, or Leila Ahmed's on the populist elements of Islam that emphasize equality between men and women, or Farida Shaheed's on the important efforts toward equality that Muslim women and feminists are already making, or Homa Hoodfar's on the distressing failure of Western feminists to listen to Muslim women,[72] can help Western feminists gain a more complete and accurate understanding of women's experience without replicating the imperialist degradation of the East as "backward." Paying attention to the work of Eastern feminists can foster the recognition that women's unfreedom stems not from Islam per se but from the *use and interpretation* of Islam to feed into and support overtly political agendas and purposes, which are in turn developed by and for men and serve patriarchal interests, just as Western men have used supposedly gender-neutral value systems such as liberalism and Christianity to support Western patriarchal values and social formations.

Such insights are vital to a feminist understanding of freedom precisely because of "difference;" for "difference" may enable Western feminists to see the power which they are blind to in their own practices, but which operates no less completely. As I have argued, feminists concerned with freedom must question and challenge the social construction of women and men through institutional, cultural, and relational practices, customs, and meanings. But as I have also shown, there is a problem of infinite regress, for the third level of social construction, which concerns discourse, language, and systems of knowledge, provides us with the sense of who we are, and hence with our powers and freedoms as much as our limitations and restrictions. What this discussion of veiling and cultural difference suggests, however, is that feminist "dialogue" can address Foucault's claim that the more one resists one's context, the more one will be reinscribed in its terms of power. External or cross-cultural critique, by operating from a *different* cultural context, can provide insight into how social construction operates in *our own* context, and can suggest modes of resistance. Women's freedom may take different forms in different contexts; but to avoid the trap of cultural relativism, it is crucial that feminists from all contexts be able to make critical evaluations of different kinds, and greater and lesser degrees, of freedom and oppression, and not simply abandon critical analysis to the tyranny of indeterminate "difference." Without a critical evaluation of what is oppressive or liberating in various cultural practices and contexts, there can be no feminist account of freedom, because the terms of "cultural difference" are all too often defined by and in the interests of men who have political power. In order to break out of the vicious circularity of such constructions of difference, feminists need to make critical comparisons that attend to differences in context. Of course, such critique, precisely because it is external, is necessarily incomplete, and often incorrect, but that is why dialogue and exchange are so important. Through such a "back and forth" we may be able to operate within our cultures—which is necessary if we are to change them—with the benefit of "outside" perspectives—which are necessary to seeing what *needs* to be changed. Such a strategy can help sharpen our critical edges and facilitate our understanding, not only of "the other," but of ourselves as well. It is this strategy, as I shall argue in the following and final chapter, that holds the key to a "feminist" theory of freedom.

## Chapter Seven

# TOWARD A FEMINIST THEORY OF FREEDOM

IN CHAPTER 1, I said that a feminist approach to freedom required a political analysis of patriarchal power in particular contexts in which "freedom" is in question, and the foregoing chapters have provided this: a detailed understanding of the various factors that are involved in specific conditions of patriarchal power, and how these factors affect the social construction of women and their choices, both the material conditions—what options are available—and the psychological, emotional, epistemological, and discursive conditions that produce desire, preference, and decisions. The particular forms that patriarchal power takes in such social phenomena as domestic violence, welfare, and veiling are specific to these phenomena, but they also share certain general similarities in the ways they socially construct the contexts within which women's choices are defined. Indeed, the problems with freedom that I have discussed in these three phenomena—particularly the difficulties in identifying normative systems, like patriarchy, as barriers to freedom and the power of such systems to construct individual identity and desire—are emblematic of a broader range of unfreedoms women face. Women's oppression within existing social structures is illustrated daily by numerous restrictive phenomena, such as employment discrimination, including pay differentials, the pink-collar ghetto, the glass ceiling, and sexual harassment; stranger violence, which can keep women prisoners in their homes and in constant states of anxiety; acquaintance rape, which violates one of the few areas in which women are supposed to be able to feel safe (in the company of friends); reproductive policies ranging from restrictions on abortion and birth control to state and institutional treatment of adoptive, birth, and "surrogate" mothers; female circumcision (or female genital mutilation), abortion of female fetuses, and female infanticide, the murder of brides for dowry; the international traffic in women and girls for prostitution and sexual slavery. Any of these social phenomena could have been analyzed in the foregoing chapters, but I believe the results would have been the same: a recognition of the need to conceptualize freedom in terms of the interaction and mutual constitution of the external structures of patriarchy and the inner selves of women. A feminist approach to freedom can locate these structures in a broader context of knowledge and experience to afford a better understanding of the repressive and restrictive effects of specific social phenomena on the identities and desires of individuals who occupy various social locations within them, such as women.

In defining freedom in terms of choice, but suggesting that the formation of choice—both the material conditions in which it is made and which affect the options available, and the internal conditions of identity and self-conception that give rise to desire—I have argued that patriarchy and male domination have been instrumental in the social construction of women's choices. This recognition leads to the further suggestion that a feminist reconceptualization of liberty must begin from the basic understanding that the context in which women live constrains women's choices more than it does men's. This greater restriction produces lesser freedom procedurally, in that (most) women are less able than (most) men to formulate and act on choices, to define the choices that they would like to have, and to construct the conditions in which choices can be made. But it also produces lesser freedom for women substantively: women are less able to maximize their welfare and to pursue both things they personally see as desirable, and things that are fairly universally seen as necessary for the continued ability to make choices, such as physical safety and economic security. As Sen would put it, women's "agency freedom" and their "well-being freedom" are both compromised to a greater extent than men's.[1]

But simply understanding the complexity of women's unfreedom is not enough. I have sought not only to critique existing conceptions of freedom as masculinist but to show what a feminist vision of freedom requires as well. Obviously, I have not here engaged a feminist rendition of the two conceptions of positive and negative liberty, and I do not intend to provide that in this chapter. Such an enterprise would be self-defeating, since, as I argued in chapter 1, both models are founded on women's subordination and unfreedom. But at the same time, I maintained that each of the two models made important contributions to a feminist understanding of freedom and that project has helped guide my presentation and analysis of the three specific phenomena of intimate partner violence, welfare, and veiling. It should be clear from the foregoing chapters that I believe that negative-liberty theory's emphasis on external barriers is an important starting point for a feminist conception of freedom. External barriers to women's choices are important to recognize and remove, ranging from male violence, to workfare policies requiring women to take minimum-wage jobs even at the cost of higher education, to physical and social coercion to veil or not to veil. But at the same time, I have demonstrated that the definition of what constitutes an external barrier needs to be enlarged beyond what most negative libertarians allow. Because of social construction, understanding the productive forces of the "external" environment on the "internal" self, desire, and will is also necessary to freedom and requires us to borrow from the positive-liberty notion of internal barriers. Combining both positive- and negative-liberty elements in the idea of what constitutes a barrier means that the line between internal and external cannot be clearly drawn; rather, the two must be seen as mutually constitutive and understood together.

Similarly, I have stressed throughout this book that the negative-liberty emphasis on individual choice and self-evaluation is key to any plausibly feminist account of freedom. The history of patriarchy is a history of women's choicelessness, of choices being made for them by men rather than being able to make choices for themselves. Feminism's commitment to ending patriarchy entails a commitment to expanding choice for women. This requires the material provision of a much wider array of meaningful options and opportunities and making them genuinely available. For example, consider Susan from the opening pages of chapter 1; only if a wide range of resources existed, that provided meaningful alternatives, could we confidently say that Susan's choice to return to her husband was a free one. She must have, if she were to *leave* her partner, economic independence, including job training, education, full employment at a living wage, health coverage, and child care, in order to make *staying* a free choice. She also needs a fairly strong guarantee of physical safety, at least from her former partner, for her and her children, including protection against their abduction, as well as a rigorous criminal-justice process that takes the violence against her as a serious crime and offers her a realistic chance of conviction if she chooses prosecution. Medical treatment that recognizes the social location and significance of her injuries is also necessary, as well as social services that do not punish her for being a victim by taking away her children; psychological counseling and social services for abusive men, like her husband, to increase her sense of security from, and reduce the likelihood of, repeated violence; and social norms that not only overtly and superficially in word, but more meaningfully in deed, condem violence against women as unacceptable at all levels.

Similarly, despite her mother's insistence that Greta is responsible for her own problems, only in the face of genuine alternatives for Greta to pursue can her mother be right. It would be more plausible to maintain that she is free if Greta had well-paying and secure employment available to her, as well as employment supports such as transportation, child care, and health care; if society recognized the value of her childrearing labor by giving her better direct economic and social compensation; and if the gender division of labor that assigns women responsibility for such caring labor is abolished, so that men shared equally in its burdens. In such a context—considerably different from the patriarchal one that currently exists—Greta's mother would be justified in holding Greta responsible for her choices. Along the same lines, Charlene's choice to hide her lesbianism can be considered free only if revealing it would not result in professional penalty and social ostracism. Provision of the material conditions for choice, substantive options that are genuinely available to women, combines negative liberty's emphasis on the necessity for individuals to decide for themselves what they want with positive liberty's emphasis on the provision of enabling conditions.

Even these conditions may still not be sufficient for feminist freedom, however. Although freedom demands that individuals must be the final arbiter of their own choices, such choices, and the selves that make them, are still socially located in particular contexts that have affected and produced desire. Thus, increasing women's choices also entails engaging the social construction of desire, in order to understand the degree to which the options that women prefer and the choices that women make are themselves the products of restriction, coercion, and force. And this in turn entails understanding the social construction of discursive formations such as "the battered woman" and "the welfare mother," which in turn constitute the social meaning of "women." Understanding the social construction of desire requires the discursive reconfiguring of the concept of choice such that women are understood as beings who can make choices for themselves, "subjects" of liberty. Social construction suggests that "who I am" is central to determining "what I want"; but "who I am" is shaped by what I do, how I live, and the concrete options that are open to me, what is required of me, what is prohibited, what can be imagined as well as what is unimaginable and inarticulate. Who I am and what I want are also to a significant degree a function of discursive categories of meaning and ideological pictures of social relations that produce the material conditions within which choice is exercised. If choice is key to freedom, then what is necessary to understanding freedom is an examination not only of the conditions in which choices are made but also of the construction of choice itself: what choices are available and why, what counts as a "choice," who counts as a "chooser," how the choosing subject is created and shaped by social relations and practices. The discursive requirements of choice thus entail the recognition that the apparently negative-liberty emphasis on individual choice necessarily involves positive-liberty elements of community and social relationships, because the processes of choice making must be situated in a larger social and discursive context in order for choices to have meaning. Indeed, such contexts are needed to make choices possible, they are the logical precondition for choice. Choices must be made by individuals by and for themselves. Charlene's lover, Sally, is wrong that outing Charlene would liberate her, Charlene must decide for herself how much she wishes to share publicly about her personal life and sexuality. But because "choosing selves" are located in particular contexts of relationships, contexts in which power and production occur, the activity of choice making is itself a social process.

My emphasis on choice particularly distinguishes feminist freedom from the feminist visions of autonomy I discussed in chapter 1, and to which the feminist conception of freedom I develop here might seem to bear some similarity. In my survey of the requirements of freedom, I have not gone as far as autonomy theorists who claim that individuals must utilize reason and develop a plan of life that is rationally defensible. Autonomy theorists suggest that a person must always be able to offer coherent reasons for her choices in order for the choice to be considered autonomous. For instance, Meyers's "autonomy competence" suggests that she must be able to engage in critical analysis, weigh her options, and make a deliberate decision.[2] This process is in principle consistent with a wide range of choices, such as returning to a batterer, that would not measure up to some ideal feminist standard. But in practice the underlying message of Meyers's arguments is that self-destructive choices would most likely be eliminated if women were able to engage in critical reasoning, if they were truly "competent." Even Marilyn Friedman, whose definition of autonomy is quite similar to my conception of freedom—as "acting and living according to one's own choices, values, and identity"—requires that this choice making be conducted "within the constraints of what one regards as morally permissible."[3] By contrast, attaining freedom does not require that an individual be able to develop and follow a vision of her own life and good. Indeed, the essence of negative liberty is that she should not have to develop a sense of good at all, much less that what she does should have to meet the standards of a personally developed moral system; it only requires that she be able to do what she wants. Feminist freedom shares this negative-liberty ideal to an important extent. Hence, in the interest of freedom, the choice of a battered woman who returns or remains with an abusive partner must be respected, regardless of what anyone else—or even everyone else—thinks about that choice. As Sen notes, being able to make choices for oneself is essential to a sense of freedom, because agency is the first and most basic requirement of freedom. In this sense, feminist freedom would seem to share some of the more extreme, if not anarchic, dimensions of negative liberty. Yet at the same time a feminist conception of freedom displays a similar affinity to some of the more rigorous dimensions of positive liberty. My argument about the social construction of desire would seem to suggest that the radical self-constitution implied by an emphasis on choice is not only counterfactual but impossible. Because all choices and desires are located in context and discourse, we must inevitably face an endless regression of second-guessing over why anyone makes the choices that they do, why anyone wants what they want. Because "women's 'experience' is thoroughly constructed, historically and culturally varied, and interpreted without end,"[4] the self is not merely *embedded* in social relations but *constituted* by them. The self is only made possible by its social relations. It could not exist—logically, materially, discursively—outside of them.

The paradox of social construction thus yields a paradox of feminist freedom. Powers and freedoms are inevitably intertwined with, and even defined by, limitations and strictures. If welfare enables battered women to leave their abusers, it facilitates choice and freedom at the same time that it reinforces their submission to patriarchal scrutiny by the state. Similarly, if the veil enables women in Cairo to work for wages, it facilitates their choices and freedom even as it signals how such choices operate within larger systems of gender inequality. But we cannot therefore throw up our hands and say that there is nothing to be done because it is discourse all the way down. Feminist freedom requires a double vision: while recognizing that social construction is a phenomenon or process that happens to and is participated in by everyone through language and discourse, social practices and customs, epistemological frameworks, knowledge claims, systems of ethics and moral beliefs, feminists concerned with freedom also want to acknowledge that some groups of people systematically and structurally have more power to participate in the constructing than do others. The fact that these practices, epistemologies, systems of knowledge, and discourses set the conditions for everyone's ability to define themselves does not prevent us from seeing that it nevertheless is often more difficult for women to define themselves within a masculinist epistemology, language, and discourse, as it is for people of color in a white discourse, lesbians and homosexuals in a heterosexual discourse. This greater difficulty means that such individuals have less freedom than do members of the dominant social groups. But at the same time, I have shown that "excluded others" participate in social construction to varying degrees. The meaning that has been created by these contexts enables us to understand who we are as much as who we are not; it conceptualizes our powers as well as our restrictions. Because of this duality, it is not the case that all men are free and all women unfree. While patriarchy is about gender domination and privilege, it cannot be completely separated from other kinds of domination, such as race, class, physical ability, and so forth. In consequence, some women are better placed to support patriarchy than some men, by virtue of race, class, or other privileging factors. White women benefit from the race privilege that being white accords, just as men of color benefit from many of the privileges of gender stratification (as the cultural defense discussed in chapter 4 illustrates), and both share responsibility within the system of white patriarchy.

The greater difficulty and unfreedom that some face systematically by virtue of their social construction and context means that freedom requires the creation of new contexts. The notion of "creating new contexts" has been a theme that has threaded through the foregoing discussions. Even as social constructivism helps us understand the ways in which certain contexts constrain women, it paradoxically poses a challenge to the task of creating new ones, for our very abilities to interrogate, challenge, and resist those contexts are socially constructed as well, indeed constructed by and through the very same contexts that limit us. Saying that women's freedom is restricted by context must always already accept that women are who they are because of that context: we cannot operate from some abstract ideal of what a woman is "really" like, what her desires and preferences "truly" are, without then challenging the entire framework of social construction necessary to the critique of patriarchy in the first place. Thus, the claim that context is a barrier to women's freedom must be viewed with self-critical ambivalence. But it must nevertheless be engaged, not abandoned. Changing contexts and increasing freedom for women and other nondominant groups requires increasing their ability to participate in the processes of social construction. Once again, I describe social construction as a "process" because I consider it as ongoing, a function of relationships in language and time; and I say "participate in" because nobody has the kind of conscious control over creation of the self or others implied by the term "construction." Participation in the processes of social construction is necessary for freedom because it is as far as one can go in exerting autonomy in one's life. As Wendy Brown argues, "freedom persists as our most compelling way of marking differences between lives whose terms are *relatively* controlled by their inhabitants and those that are less so, between conditions of coercion and conditions of action, between domination by history and participation in history, between space for action and its relative absence."[5] Freedom is thus a matter of degree; though it contains some zero-sum elements, as Hobbes argues, and contains even more elements that *seem* zero-sum but are not, freedom is a term of relativity and comparison. Nobody is ever completely free any more than they are completely unfree, as those terms are used by most mainstream theorists of positive and negative liberty. However, feminists also wish to recognize that patriarchy is defined by the general dominance of men over women, across race and class. That not all men benefit as much as others from this structure, that some women do not suffer as much as others, and that some women even benefit, does not alter the fundamental discursive reality that patriarchy is premised on women's powerlessness and men's power. The paradox of social construction commits feminism to this double-edged sword.

## CHANGING CONTEXTS: THE CONTRIBUTION OF FOUCAULT

What would be required, then, for women to acquire more power to participate in the terms and processes of social construction, and thus to increase their freedom to make meaningful choices? If a feminist understanding of freedom requires the political analysis of patriarchal power in specific contexts in which freedom is at issue, and if such analysis reveals that the contexts themselves pose barriers to women's freedom, how can contexts be changed? The first and most obvious place to consider an answer to this question is discourse. Philip Pettit, for instance, defines freedom as "discursive control";[6] that is, freedom requires an individual's participation in discourse. The individual must be recognized by others as a participant to discourse, she must not be subject to undue influence or domination that compromises her ability to participate, and she also must actually participate (that is, the "capacity" to participate is not enough). When combined with his argument, discussed earlier in chapter 1, that freedom also requires nondomination, as well as with his desire to unite what he calls the "psychological" and "political" dimensions of freedom, Pettit's argument might seem similar to mine. And indeed, his understanding of freedom as nondomination and discursive control has definite feminist applications. For instance, it could help a date-rape victim establish a claim that her freedom is diminished by the rape and its sequelae, for the rape victim would seem to be left out of discourse: legal standards of evidence and social standards of sexuality are defined from a masculine point of view and prevent her from relating the event as she has experienced it. Not only the rapist—who clearly interferes with her liberty—but the judge and attorneys who do not interfere with her at all in following rules of evidence can all be seen as robbing her of discursive control, and thereby as restricting her freedom. In this sense, Pettit might seem to endorse my argument (or perhaps I could be seen as endorsing his).

But the argument I engage here is considerably different, predominantly because Pettit's definition and use of discourse are quite distinct from mine. Pettit maintains that "'discourse' . . . connotes a social exercise in which different parties take turns in exchange with one another. In this respect it has the same connotations as 'conversation'. . . . To discourse is to reason and, in particular, to reason together with others." Hence, on Pettit's account, "many practical problems are discursively resoluble; the problems are susceptible to reasoning, in particular to reasoning together, and need not be determined by the vagaries of taste or power."[7] In other words, discourse is a tool that can be used against power, rather than the key instrument of power; power is a hierarchical, top-down relationship, something specific, utilized by identifiable individuals or collectivities over others (the first two "faces" of power discussed in chapter 3). And reason is not a form of power, but the ultimate weapon against it. Pettit's understanding of discourse thus contrasts starkly to Foucault's, and to the one I employ in my own argument. For Pettit, "discourse" simply *conveys meaning*, and meaning exists independently of discourse. By contrast, I see "discourse" as a framework for the *construction and constitution of meaning*. Thus, for Pettit, discourse is more like "deliberation" than a complex of speech acts indicating a set of meanings that define, and within which we must think about, a social problem or phenomenon. In this, particularly given his conclusion that republican governmental institutions are necessary for freedom,[8] Pettit's argument is more in keeping with "deliberative democracy" theory than discourse theory.[9] Indeed, a better term for Pettit's conception of freedom would be "deliberative control."

It is surprising that Pettit does not utilize a broader understanding of discourses and acknowledge the constructive forces of language and social institutions, since a major goal of his book is to unite the psychological dimensions of freedom with the political. But his account of psychology is incomplete, for it is precisely the subtle yet pervasive kinds of power that reinforce and constitute the social construction of subjectivity that I have argued freedom theorists need to consider. The third level of social construction suggests that discourse is an important element for understanding the misrepresentation of reality and the materialization of that reality that affects women in particular ways. In this, Foucault's ideas, discussed in chapter 3, about the ambiguity of power and resistance make a useful contribution to a feminist conception of freedom. As I argued earlier, if we interpret "totalizing" not as the absolute domination and control of every aspect of an individual's life but rather as the pervasiveness of power through specific practices over the rest of existence, the connections between discourse and materiality, the macro and the micro, become politically more significant. Discursive understandings of power, resistance, production, and freedom do not simply adhere to institutions like "patriarchy" or "the family" or "the courts" in static and timeless ways but rather are produced and constituted through such institutions by means of specific events and specific individuals. Moreover, these institutions are themselves socially constructed by and through individuals and events; as Drucilla Cornell notes, "Context is not just *there*; it must be confirmed or disconfirmed, over and over again" through individual gestures that reiterate, reinforce, and reconstitute context.[10] Institutions such as prisons, hospitals, clinics, and schools have immediate effects on the construction of particular populations, and on particular aspects of an individual's identity, self-conception, and understanding of the world, but have less immediately identifiable effects on other aspects of those same individuals, as well as on entire populations that do not have direct contact with those institutions. As Foucault most famously argued, prisons have a direct effect on prisoners and criminals, but such effects work from, and in turn bring about, more general changes in social formations, institutions, relations, and practices that extend well beyond the prison: hence, as Foucault says at the very end of *Discipline and Punish*, "Is it surprising that prisons resemble factories, schools, barracks, hospitals, which all resemble prisons?"[11]

Similarly, I have argued that although welfare reform has an immediate effect on poor single mothers who depend on public assistance, it also has effects on all other women, and indeed on men as well, in its construction of gender relations and its social reinforcement of the sexual division of labor. Police policies concerning domestic violence have an immediate and direct impact on battered women, but these policies work from and reinforce gendered identity, and gendered family roles, as well as cultural associations of masculinity with violence and proprietary rights over women. Discourses of the veil and its relation to women's role in culture, religion, and the family have their most obvious effects on women in Islamic cultures and contexts, but these effects reverberate throughout the general social construction of gendered relations across culture. Each of these social phenomena produces specific tropes—the battered woman, the welfare mother, the veil, the Eastern woman—that embody, configure, and perpetuate broader, if unarticulated, constructions of gender, race, ethnicity, and class. Each construction affects many others, because the various discourses that produce them and in and through which they operate are situated in the same language. There is, in a sense, always a context for understanding and producing context; as Fish says, there is discourse "all the way down." But at the same time, by the logic of how language and discourse work, multiple discourses exist simultaneously, to ensure that there is always some room for maneuver. The "totalization" of which Foucault speaks is more like a blanket draped over all social formations, allowing some movement underneath the covers, than like concrete poured over them to lock them in place. Hence, social construction cannot get into every nook and cranny of human relations and social life to foreclose possibilities of understanding *that* we are socially constructed, of critiquing *how* we are socially constructed, and of imagining other ways of being. Discourse is thus key to understanding how patriarchal power operates politically in particular contexts to restrict individuals with particular group identities and social characteristics in specific material circumstances. But it is also vital to envisioning what is required for freedom to exist, what alternate social arrangements might enhance women's freedom.

The idea of social construction is not only relevant to understanding in what ways particular people are free or unfree, or who the subject of liberty is, or how contexts restrain and produce: it is also relevant to understanding freedom itself. In chapter 1 I argued that mainstream theorists often treat freedom as if it were a semantic rather than a normative problem and that a feminist theory of freedom sought to reclaim freedom as political, not philosophical. But it is obvious that in order to understand how the subjects of freedom are socially constructed through material and discursive contexts, the meaning of freedom must necessarily be considered. Thus, it is fairly obvious that positive and negative liberty are themselves discursive constructions. They identify different aspects of human experience and appropriate them to their own conceptual definitions. By assuming different notions of the self—as an innately separate individual, for example, as opposed to a social being in need of community—various theories of freedom create different worlds, different pictures of how social relations operate in ways that support and feed those conceptions of the self. Moreover, the particular ways that theorists describe or define humanity and human "nature" reflect the discursive contexts in which they are writing, such as the temporal, cultural, and political ideals and norms of their day. Constructions thus beget and derive from other constructions. This is not to say that the major theorists of freedom simply mirror the ideals and norms of their day, of course, for what has made many of these texts so enduring is their originality and creativity in running *against* the grain. But their "new" ideas are developed in response to those contemporary conditions (Rousseau's *Discourses*, for example, were reactions against the licentiousness of French society) and must always be understood in the context of the writer's social and discursive milieu (such as Locke's *Two Treatises*, which must be understood in the context of the Exclusion Crisis and emerging market capitalism). Acknowledgement of the social location and constitution of these theories in turn reveals that freedom itself—that is, without its positive or negative modifiers[12]—is a discursive construction. Regardless of how it is conceptualized, freedom is the most important political concept in modern and Enlightenment political theory, lying at the heart of social relations and fueling all other concepts such as rights, obligation, and justice. As the social-contract tradition particularly illustrates, entire systems of government are built and justified on a foundation of natural freedom. Yet at the same time, as I showed in my earlier discussion of these theories, this supposedly natural freedom needed to be carefully cultivated through education and appropriate political institutions. The discourse of natural freedom was in some ways the expression of genuine moral belief but in other ways stood in clear contradiction to how these theorists really imagined social life should be organized for the majority of people, notably including women.

Freedom is also a discursive construction, at a more basic level, in that how we read these theories is always affected by our own social, discursive, and political contexts. Freedom is "neither a philosophical absolute nor a tangible entity but a relational and contextual practice that takes shape in opposition to whatever is locally and ideologically conceived as unfreedom."[13] As my discussion of welfare particularly demonstrated, if dependency is unfreedom, then working constitutes freedom; if poverty is unfreedom, then a guaranteed subsistence income is freedom. The ascendancy of particular discourses is a function of power, of who has and expresses power and through which social mechanisms, but whatever conception dominates is inevitably a discursive construction; no one has the "true" discourse. The subject of liberty cannot simply be reduced to context or contextuality, however; as the foregoing chapters have shown, the beings suffering at the hands of abusers, or workfare, or cultural police, are real people, they are not creations of discourse, not abstract concepts or linguistic fabrications. That we are socially constructed does not mean that what is constructed is not real; as Cornell puts it, "Someone is only as she is exposed" through discursive constructions, "and yet there remains some*one*."[14] Although some postmodern feminists, such as Brown, Butler, and Riley, claim that focusing on discursivity does not deny the pain and suffering experienced by real humans, that often seems to be its result.[15] As I suggested in chapter 3 in considering why the first two levels of social construction were needed to complement the third level, the abstractions that are produced through a focus on language replicate the very same exclusiveness along lines of race, class, gender, and sexuality that characterize the Enlightenment liberalism that postmodernism seeks to critique and transcend. Feminism must resist such an effect, because freedom requires material conditions of choice as well as participation in social construction.

This is something that I believe Foucault realized toward the end of his life. In one of his latest interviews, "The Ethic of Care for the Self as a Practice of Freedom," Foucault explicitly rejects the vision of freedom as "liberation" and "resistance" that is generally attributed to him. Conceiving freedom as (only) resistance holds "the danger that it will refer back to the idea that there does exist a nature or a human foundation," which is something that Foucault wishes to deny. As I suggested in chapter 3, the postmodern emphasis on resistance presupposes an underlying "truth" which such resistance will reveal, a truth that reinscribes the power of what one seeks to resist. Foucault also rejects the complaint he claims is frequently made against him—"You see power everywhere, hence there is no place for liberty"—as "absolutely incomplete." Foucault maintains, in fact, that he holds the opposite view: "there cannot be relations of power unless the subjects are free. . . . if there are relations of power throughout every social field it is because there is freedom every-where." By differentiating between power and domination and viewing power as a productive force, Foucault advocates the "exercise of self upon self by which one tries . . . to transform one's self and to attain a certain mode of being" as central to the "practices of freedom."[16] Key to Fou-cault's vision is not the attainment of a "free state," as if freedom were a quality one could possess or a condition that one could attain by meeting certain preset criteria. Rather freedom is a mode of activity and thought in which people participate by engaging in practices that create the self. Again (in the seemingly endless devolution of clarifying the meaning of terms that Foucault's frequently vague use of language often demands)[17] by "creating the self" I do not take Foucault to mean the abstract individ-ual of liberal state-of-nature theory, who creates himself "from scratch," whose desires and passions and interests are "his" alone. Rather, the no-tion of "creating the self" involves the recognition that people are not merely "passive subject[s],"acted upon by social context at the first two levels of social construction (the "third face of power" articulated by Lukes). They are also "active subjects," who act upon context in daily and ongoing processes through specific actions. Such actions involve indi-viduals—in some ways intentionally, purposively, directly, consciously, in some ways not—in the creation of their selves, of who they are. As Fou-cault noted, some participate more actively than others in such construc-tion—doctors more than patients, for instance—but his insight is that the latter also have effects on their own identities and self-conceptions, as well as on those of the former. Foucault maintains, for instance, that "the mad subject is not a non-free subject," but rather "that the mentally ill constitutes himself a mad subject in relationship and in the presence of the one who declares him crazy."[18] Such constitution affects not only the identity of the self, but the identity of the doctor and her professional enterprise, and thereby the institutions within which such enterprise is carried out, and within which the patient is in turn constituted.

Many may justifiably balk at the suggestion that the mentally ill have a *choice* about how to present themselves to doctors, not to mention to the rest of the world; and indeed, it may be that an extremely elitist, and possibly sexist, perspective overshadows Foucault's entire framework, as I suggested in chapter 3. When one considers serious mental illness, such as schizophrenia and multiple personality disorder, notions of individual choice seem a false mockery of the pain the ill and their families experi-ence; and insisting that the ill choose to present themselves in particular ways (for instance, when schizophrenics stop taking their medication) drastically reduces the complexity of such illnesses, and ignores their bio-logical basis. Repeated declarations, no matter how fervent and sincere, that the body is socially constructed cannot give individuals control over the chemical reactions in their brains. But Foucault's point is actually a subtler one. He does not deny the reality of "the passive subject" produced by and through the social construction of medicine and mental illness, but he does not want us to forget about the active subject who can herself socially construct. Nor does he want to let us ignore the possibility that activity and passivity coexist and interact, that this interaction in a sense constitutes our subjectivity. As I suggested in chapter 1, a key feature of freedom, and what distinguishes freedom from autonomy, is that it involves a combination of what individuals do and what happens to them, it is about making choices within the parameters and limitations of conditions over which they have no control. Foucault's point is that if "the subject constitutes himself in an active fashion, by the practices of self, these practices are nevertheless not something that the individual invents by himself. They are patterns that he finds in his culture and which are proposed, suggested and imposed on him by his culture, his society and his social group."[19] For instance, "hysteria" may have been one of the few ways in which women were able to respond to cultural strictures, even if the mode of response did not result in the best quality of life for them. Similarly, a woman who goes limp during a beating to minimize her injury may appear complicitous in the battering but actually may have chosen the best of the poor options available to her, just as a young, black, single woman who intentionally gets pregnant and goes on welfare may seem to be her own worst enemy but may in fact be rebelling against racism and poverty, or a woman who adopts the veil may seem to be mindlessly adhering to patriarchal religious customs but in fact is resisting patriarchal strictures on women's paid employment. Choices that individuals make are not necessarily well thought out, objectively rational, or even fully self-conscious, but to deny the role and power that individuals have to make choices and that these choices help to constitute the self is equally mistaken.

Care of the self thus coheres with the picture of freedom developed in the foregoing chapters: that we have desires, regardless of where they come from, that we can evaluate those desires, regardless of by what criteria, and that we make choices, regardless of why we choose what we do. By this I do not mean that the "where, what and why" are not vital; they have been a central focus of my discussion of patriarchal power. And indeed, Foucault's concern with social construction, I have suggested, is fundamentally about such questions. But because those questions can be answered at best only partially and tentatively, at a certain level people must act *as if* they know the answers. Because we are individuals within the world, situated within particular historically constituted sets of relationships, we always must be the ones to act for ourselves, as negative-liberty theory asserts. We may be subjected to pressures and obstacles that seem overwhelming, but that does not mean that our existence is determined for us, that we do not exist as beings who can affect and influence those social formations and practices. Hence, a battered woman may have to make choices within severely constrained parameters, but she does make choices and must do so every day in order to survive. As I read Foucault, however, what is relevant to understanding her freedom is not simply the fact that she makes choices but rather the degree to which she can participate in creating the options from which she must choose. As positive-liberty theory recognizes, individual choices cannot always be taken at face value; individuals and their choices must always be understood in the social contexts that shape and guide desires and options. Participation in affecting those contexts is key to the distinction between "power" and "domination," and between freedom and unfreedom.

Or more specifically, it is key to the distinction among varying *degrees* of freedom and unfreedom. For being able to participate in such processes does not guarantee that you will get what you want; indeed, it assumes that "what you want" is not set and determined but may shift in and through the processes of constructing the options that are available and the parameters for choosing among them. But what is relevant to freedom is the participation. As Les Thiele puts it in his Nietzschean reading of Foucault, "Humanity is involved in the struggle of becoming, of creating itself." That is, freedom lies in the struggle, not necessarily in the outcome; it lies in the notion "not that one *is* something but that one may *become* many things." So the goal of freedom is the "perpetuation and ameloriation of the conditions that make struggle itself possible," which "must include the conditions that influence [individuals'] means of understanding and identifying themselves."[20] Thiele believes this shows that Foucault eschews both negative and positive liberty, but on my reading Foucault embraces both negative freedom, in advocating resistance and liberation—to which, I agree, Foucault's theory cannot be reduced but which nevertheless play an important part in it—and positive freedom, in advocating "care for the self," which, significantly, Foucault says "implies also a relationship to the other . . . in order to really care for self, one must listen to the teachings of a master. One needs a guide, a counselor, a friend—someone who will tell you the truth."[21]

It may seem rather jarring to hear Foucault talk about "the truth," considering that he is commonly believed to reject the possibility of truth.[22] But here, I believe, he means not timeless universals, nor absolutes, but rather critical observation; the struggle against the quicksand of social construction to claim (some measure of) control over (some portion of) the self, which cannot be done without someone to help pull you out. And although Foucault does not state this directly, I believe that my previous chapters indicate that this struggle and the insights of "truth" require not only relationship with others who share similar experiences, similar discourses and materializations, but others who are embedded in different discourses and material relations as well. Lucie White's account of her representation of an African American woman on welfare demonstrates how Foucault's formulation complements feminist insights about power, relationship, truth, and freedom. Her client "Mrs. G." was sent an over-payment by the state welfare office. When she tried to pay it back, she was assured that it was not an error, but after she cashed the check and spent the money she was charged with fraud. White plotted out a line of testimony for the client to take that would persuade those in judgment; she wanted Mrs. G. to emphasize that she spent the money on "necessity items" like sanitary napkins and not reveal that a portion of the money was spent on "Sunday shoes" for her daughter, because White believed that these would be considered luxury items and result in a judgment against her client. Mrs. G. needed White to represent her in this fraud hearing, and although she expressed some reluctance to stretch the truth as White wished her to do, she appeared to acquiesce. But during the hearing she changed her testimony and yet still won the case. By testifying about the Sunday shoes, Mrs. G. resisted the stereotype of the poor, help-less, downtrodden black woman, a trope that White wanted to exploit in order to win the case. Admitting proudly that she purchased the shoes for her daughter to wear to church, Mrs. G. revealed to White the "truth" about her life and her humanity, that life on welfare is difficult and restric-tive, but that her humanity nevertheless persists in the act of making choices and taking control of those choices. By being forced to respond to Mrs. G.'s unexpected testimony, White developed a different under-standing of the complicated relationships between welfare recipients and case workers, as well as strategies for resisting state bureaucracy. She be-lieves this experience has given her a better—a "truer"—perspective from which to consider her legal strategies of resistance against the welfare state and to free poor women from its restrictions. Thus, though the "counselor" might at first seem to be White, since she is the professional who must lead Mrs. G. through the legal system, in the end it is Mrs. G. who guides White to greater understanding about herself and others.[23]

A similar understanding of relationship and its importance to freedom is illustrated by the Milan Women's Bookstore Collective's *Sexual Differ-ence*, in which they develop a theory of "female freedom." In an echo of Foucault's call for "a guide, a counselor, a friend," the collective argues that relationships of "entrustment" are key to women's freedom. Free-dom entails a "symbolic debt. . . . to other women—to the one who brought her into the world, to those who have loved her, those who have taught her something, those who have spent their energies to make the world more comfortable for her." The debt that women owe each other pertains to the centrality of social, political, cultural, and gendered discursive contexts to freedom, to restraint, and to women's participation in social construction. As an individual I always exist and operate in a social structure which I help to support by my actions. This structure provides meaning to all I do and say: "language is part of the fabric of social relations." But under patriarchy, "these are not favorably disposed to women's experience." Hence, individual women cannot achieve freedom as such. Because all meaning requires context, and because contexts are created through social interaction and not individual will, the conventional understandings of freedom require a dependence on existing patriarchal contexts, which are premised on women's oppression. If it is unavoidable to rely on and thereby reinforce and support context in order to live and act, the issue thus becomes *which* social structure I wish to promote: the existing patriarchal one, by invoking and supporting existing meanings, or a new feminist one that challenges and changes meaning? As the Milan authors put it, there is always a "debt" to be paid; the trick is not to pay it to the "wrong creditor." That is, we always unavoidably utilize and thereby reinforce some context through our actions, and all contexts have substantive meaning that reflects and reproduces power relations. The key is to be aware of the context one supports and to make a conscious choice between contexts, for "if the social translation of the human value of being a woman is not done by women, it will be done by men according to their criteria." Hence, "We are not free with regard to payment of the symbolic debt," they say, "yet its payment is liberating for us."[24]

Patricia Hill Collins similarly argues that relationships of guidance and counsel among African American women provide the basis for freedom; by creating a different context, they allow affirmation of identity and resistance of white patriarchal social constructions of black womanhood. As what she calls "outsiders within," African American women both adopt and internalize the discourse of white patriarchy because their lives are structured by its ideology. Yet because they are outsiders within that culture—not accepted as members—they also can contest the truth claims of this ideology. Black women can see the contradictions between the ideology and the reality of their experience, Collins argues, because the contradictions affect them in immediate and concrete ways. Relationships among black women in which they can critique the dominant ideology and its dissonance with lived reality can produce what Collins calls "safe spaces," arenas in which women produce freedom through resistance to the dominant discourse's construction of them and affirmation of alternative and self-defined self-understandings. Freedom for Collins does not consist merely in the absence of external restraints, the legal, social, and physical restrictions of racism, ranging from slavery and apartheid to corporate tokenism and glass ceilings, but also involves "consciousness as a sphere of freedom." That is, freedom involves internal factors of identity and self-conception which can provide "the conceptual tools to resist oppression."[25] In a clear echo of Foucault's vision of care for the self,[26] Collins posits an interdependent relationship between the ability to change existing contexts and the ability to reshape and redefine the self. Since black women are socially constructed by white patriarchy not as individuals but as a faceless group to be feared and scorned, each individual black woman must address the social construction of black femaleness in order to confront the social construction of herself as an individual. Freedom thus involves responsibility to other African Americans, and particularly African American women, for it is only through such collective rethinking of contexts that each individual's self can be reconstituted and freedom can occur.

The interaction between relationship and freedom has clearly underwritten my analysis of IPV, welfare, and veiling. Relationships among women have played an important role in changing the discursive and material contexts in which women are oppressed by various forms of patriarchal power. Such new contexts are crucial not only to new theoretical formulations of abstract concepts like freedom but to the political realization of these concepts through social practices, policies, and laws. Violence, poverty, and oppression are concrete daily experiences in many women's lives; ending these social ills requires questioning their acceptability and challenging their normalization. The new contexts needed to make this questioning and challenging possible will be importantly shaped by and for women. As I discussed in chapter 4, battered-women's shelters provide new contexts in which a woman can come to understand her experiences and her selfhood in new and different ways that can help her end the violence, whether by leaving the batterer or by more effectively identifying and accessing the tools at her disposal. Similarly, the relationships women form together in seclusion from men provide spaces to express feelings, beliefs, and ideas they are constrained from expressing to, or in the company of, men. Muslim women's networks are key to their abilities to change cultural practices that are restrictive and harmful to them, without rejecting their faith or culture. Welfare rights organizations like the NWRO or the Kensington Welfare Rights Union, as well as informal women's networks through which child care arrangements are often set up, contribute to women's ability to survive poverty and take control of defining their identity away from powerful, predominantly male politicians.[27] Though entirely different in their origin, foundation, structure, and particular function, purdah, battered-women's shelters, and welfare rights organizations have served similar functions of providing "safe spaces" for women to define who they are and how they envision their lives.

Of course, the notion of relationship or solidarity among women has become quite passé in light of the sometimes acrimonious debates over difference, racism, classism, and heterosexism within a dominantly white, middle-class feminism. The voluminous feminist literature critiquing the "essentialism" that is presupposed of any effort to define "women," much less to locate "women" as a source of political power, suggests that positing women's relationships as necessary to women's freedom is a political and theoretical dead end. This is where the term "feminist," denoting a commitment to end sexist oppression, could be helpful, for a notion of *feminist* community avoids the problem of defining "woman," thereby embracing a wide diversity of "women," with a variety of self-definitions and commitments. Feminist community also includes space for men who are concerned to achieve women's equality and freedom. But even this strategy for defining community is obviously limited by the fact that many women, including many battered women, many welfare mothers, and particularly many Islamic women, do not consider themselves feminist, and indeed consider feminism as antithetical to their conceptions of themselves as women. The infinite regress of qualifiers, exceptions, and rejections that the notion of "community" entails within feminism poses yet another quandary to feminism in dealing with the paradox of social construction, because the issue of where new and liberating contexts are supposed to come from, what they are supposed to build on, seems to elude a straightforward answer. It suggests that the paradox of social construction may in fact be irresolvable, and that feminist freedom, if not women's freedom, is an illusion.

## THE POLITICS OF FREEDOM

I believe this conundrum that feminists face has to do with an inadequate understanding of politics. I have argued that feminist freedom requires a *political* analysis of patriarchal power in specific contexts in which freedom is in question, and such an analysis will necessarily turn on what is meant by politics. The truism that politics is about power is not particularly informative without any further articulation of what constitutes "power," and thereby begs the question rather than answers it. The obvious reason is that the subject of politics, like the subject of liberty, is so firmly set as male—perhaps even the archetypal bourgeois white male—that the particularity of its identity is easily forgotten. As I demonstrated in chapter 2, when freedom emerged as an important political concept in the Enlightenment, the two subjects of liberty and politics merged. All of the theorists I discussed constructed the citizen as specifically male and constructed freedom as the core value of human nature which government was to protect and promote, in both the negative-liberty sense of protecting the individual from injury and his property from encroachment by others and the positive-liberty sense of creating citizens through public practices of participation and private practices of education that trained individuals to exercise reason and thereby recognize their true and best interests. If the subject of politics, like the subject of liberty, is a specific formation of Western culture in liberal bourgeois democracies (of various forms), then certain questions do not need to be asked, because their answers are previously established. Some of these questions, in circular fashion, center on the meaning of politics. Feminists have long critiqued the traditional liberal vision of politics as the clash of interests. As feminists such as Carole Pateman, Nancy Hartsock, and myself have argued—and as I have noted at various points throughout this book—ever since the emergence of social-contract theory in the seventeenth century, liberal, interest-based politics have been animated by a propertied-white-male conception of citizenship that not only excludes white women, the poor, and men and women of color but depends on such exclusion.[28] A supposedly newer model of politics, which has gained some ascendancy within the Left in recent decades, including the feminist Left, centers on "identity," but is similarly inadequate for reconfiguring freedom. It holds no more potential than interest politics for changing oppressive contexts, only for modifying specific conditions within existing contexts—contexts that are in part founded on the oppression of these identity groups and which will therefore never grant full recognition to their members. Brown argues that because identity politics is constituted by a reaction against liberal interest-based politics, it has little chance of changing the status quo. Rather, it can only "naturalize and thus entrench the powers of which those identities are the effects."[29] She claims that as long as identity is based on "injury," the injury cannot be let go without the loss of identity; thus, groups like feminists hold onto their injuries by exaggerating and oversimplifying the power of patriarchy and fail to envision new ways to change it.

I believe that Brown is unfair to feminism, for the experiences I have articulated in the previous chapters attest to the pervasive effects of patriarchy as a cultural construct that assigns greater value to men than to women, provides more options to men, and supports men's pursuit of choice more than women's. Hence, identity provides an important ingredient for changing women's unfreedom. But I do agree that identity is a poor foundation for politics because the women I have discussed in the previous chapters all have distinctive relationships to the discursive categories of gender. I suggest that the way to address these paradoxes is to recognize that politics is neither about interests nor identities. Politics is about issues: the concrete identification of oppressive power in specific contexts. Issues are temporal and specific, discursive and social constructions in the most literal sense: they come into existence as a result of expressly felt need and desire, but they must be identified and named in order to exist. Like identity, issues arise out of experiences that socially and historically constitute the meaning of who I am and what I want. Like interests, however, issues are not given or fixed but rather change in response to variable experience and material need. Hence, sometimes an issue's importance is affected by who one is, such as when women who had never experienced sexual harassment were nevertheless outraged to see Anita Hill dismissed by male members of the Senate Judiciary Committee as hysterical and sexually frustrated. Sometimes issues become important to people because of what is happening to them, as when a feminist academic's research is rejected for publication because it is seen as "biased" by virtue of its feminist perspective. Sometimes issues become significant because of what is happening to others with whom we have various kinds of connections, such as when a white professor's African American student is racially harassed; sometimes by what is happening to others with whom we have no ostensible connection at all, such as when a Quebecois businessman supports aid to peasant victims of an earthquake in Colombia. The notion of "issues" captures the idea that what I believe is important, what I think needs to be done, is not necessarily a function of interest or identity (support for earthquake victims) and yet may be in part stimulated by both (support for Hill). It recognizes that my identity is neither uniform nor all-encompassing of what is important to me, and that what benefits me directly cannot adequately account for my concern for other living beings and shared social life. It recognizes the possibility of—dare I say it?—universal humanity, even as it recognizes the divisions and differences between and among humans, that groupings can be organic and manufactured, that who we are and what is important to us are socially constructed.

A feminist vision of politics thus involves the basic struggle among people of differing experiences, views, judgments, and preferences to persuade others, or be persuaded by others, to agree with their judgments or give them what they want. If we are to avoid the second-guessing characteristic of positive-liberty theory, then feminists such as Brown are correct to maintain that politics must replace the repeated efforts that feminists make toward stating the "truth" about women's experiences by postulating reductive and universalistic identities. But at the same time, she and other feminists of the poststructuralist persuasion view politics as a somewhat random, if not utopian, "cacophony of unequal voices clamoring for position";[30] people are so "different" from one another that they have little foundation for agreement except perhaps random chance, and there is thus no basis for deciding their competing claims. By contrast, I suggest that politics is subject to the very same discursive constructions as are the individuals engaging in politics. Those constructions involve the social ascription of certain kinds of individuals into categorical groupings that affect experience. As I have shown throughout this book, regardless of differences among individuals who are categorized as "women" in any given social context, that categorization produces particular sets of experiences and social meanings that are beyond any individual's control. Accordingly, just as we must ask about the foundation of desire, and acknowlege that women may appear to want certain things because patriarchy has constructed them to, so must we ask about political advocacy, for the effects of oppression do not magically disappear when we enter the voting booth or march in a parade against the World Bank. "Empowerment" is limited by the prior context of subjugation to which it responds. People hold all sorts of political beliefs for a variety of reasons, many of which would seem to run contrary to the supposed interests of the people holding them; and those political beliefs are shared by large numbers of people who see themselves as connected by experience and identity. Such tension cannot be dismissed either on grounds of abstract individualism, as when we assume that a battered woman who defends her abuser must not mind being beaten up, or on grounds of false consciousness, as when we assume that women who veil have simply identified with patriarchy. Rather, debate and dialogue must engage the process of challenging and questioning various political claims and beliefs. I believe that this is what Foucault meant by counselors and guides who tell us the truth, who challenge us to dig more deeply into the meaning of who we are, what we want, and how we are constituted and produced by power.

As the foregoing chapters have suggested, politics comes out of experience, which shapes our evaluations of both what is important and how political goals should be achieved. Thus, for instance, the experiences of battered women reveal that physical security and preserving relationship are both of utmost importance. The fact that domestic violence seems to create a tension between these two goals suggests that it is not only the dominant patriarchal discourse of domestic violence (in which men are entitled to hit women, women cause men to be violent, and women are not genuine individuals entitled to legal protection) that produces contexts that restrict the freedom of battered women; feminist discourses that seek to explain and end IPV may do so as well. Rather than calling relationships and safety mutually exclusive, feminists should be asking how these two goals can be reconciled. In this, the experiences of women in relationships where violence has stopped may be a good starting point for reconstructing the discursive understanding of domestic violence and determining what resources are needed to stop it. But such experiences are not an ending point, because the paradox of social construction means that women's perceptions and understandings of their own experiences of violence and oppression have constructed them in ways that force certain kinds of desires into prominence and coercively repress others. Hence the need within the battered-women's movement for interaction and dialogue between battered women and advocates, professionals, volunteers, people who sit "outside" an individual woman's experience and can provide a different perspective on her perceptions, as well as other battered women (including some advocates, volunteers, and professionals), people whose experiential framework provides a basis for understanding through similarity. Similarly, in chapter 6 I advocated cross-cultural dialogue between Eastern and Western feminists to enhance understanding not only of other experiences and cultures but of one's own; one must be inside one's culture and yet at the same time outside it in order to gain a clearer understanding of practices of oppression and freedom. Hence, Western women who challenge Islamic women's endorsement of the veil as a protection against patriarchy must in turn be challenged about the social significance of their own modes of dress and how they reflect patriarchal values and the social construction of gender. In chapter 5 I suggested that women on welfare needed to participate more actively in the construction of welfare policy. This was not to say that they should determine it by themselves, for if the conditions of welfare have produced the very subjectivities that undermine women's ability to effect genuine change, then the existing power dynamics may simply be repeated. But women on welfare should be included in the process of policy creation; they should be contributing authors and not merely subordinated, solitary objects, for the experience of being on welfare provides insights that cannot be attained by privileged lawmakers, as PRWORA demonstrated, and as Lucie White attested.

"Experience," like "relationships among women," is a contested concept in feminist theory, of course. Feminist poststructuralists in particular eschew experience as "feminism's epistemologically positivist moment."[31] This view depends on a confusion of the three levels of social construction, however. To say that experience provides a foundation for feminist theory does not entail an essentialist reading of gender, but it does assume that what is constructed is real, and that for it to have an active and conscious effect on the construction of future identities and practices, we have to understand what it is. As I hope is clear by now, the fact that women's experience is socially constructed does not mean it evaporates as discursive fiction, that feminists cannot make political judgments about it, or that it cannot serve as the foundation for critical insights into the workings of power and future alternatives. As Amartya Sen argues, a vital element of women's freedom is the presence of their voices within political discourse; and what those voices express is largely informed by their experiences. As I have shown, important insights emerge when we explore the particularity and detail of women's experiences, when we look at those experiences from the perspectives of those having them. Such insights do not tell the entire story, of course, but must be engaged, challenged, questioned, and interpreted within discourse. What women think they need from social relations, institutions, practices, customs, laws, and public policy to establish and maintain their freedom—to develop their capabilities, to exert control over their lives by participating in the processes that construct the material conditions in which they live and the discursive parameters of who they are—is a necessary starting point for theoretical consideration of the practical requirements of freedom.

That is why I define politics in terms of issues rather than identities or interests, because such a definition recognizes people's shared concerns without making assumptions about who they are or how they live their lives, as identity politics does, and without reducing politics to self-interested rational action, as interest group politics does. It allows for a wider diversity of values and goals, as well as of reasons for commitment to those values and goals. Casting politics in terms of issues also accommodates the different orientations toward feminism that many women have: even if some women refuse to identify with feminism, or reject feminist values as contrary to their interests, they are nevertheless concerned with particular aspects of women's well-being and agency. Because their experiences lead them to consideration of particular material conditions that restrict women, they can coalesce around issues such as funding for battered-women's shelters, or mandatory arrest policies, or workfare, or health care, or differing interpretations of the Qur'an, without having such politics reduced to essentialized identities or individualist interests that fail to recognize the systematic structure of the problems these issues represent. Communities based on issues are more solid and enduring than interest groups, but they are less totalizing and essentializing than identity groups.[32]

## CHANGING CONTEXTS: THE ROLE OF EQUALITY

Equality is also essential to such a political process, and indeed, equality, along with discourse and politics, is a third tool for feminist freedom. The demand for women's greater participation in social construction is fundamentally a call for equalization of power. Such equalization is key to Foucault's claim that freedom requires struggle, and it is key to the ability to differentiate among contexts as producing greater or lesser degrees of freedom for various groups of people, such as women. Hence, the foregoing chapters have all ended on the theme of equal participation in social structures and processes: coordinated community policies that provide victims of IPV with resources to access a variety of public and private choices, and battered-women's shelters where women participate side by side with staff to engage in constructions of new understandings of self and choice (chapter 4); welfare policies defined, created, and exercised with the participation of women on welfare and providing the full array of resources needed to produce economic and social equality for single mothers and other poor women and men (chapter 5); women's networks where Eastern and Western women exchange perspectives, views, cultural critiques and ideological challenges in a way that avoids Western imperialism, and develop definitions of "culture" in ways that include women's voices, experiences, and perspectives (chapter 6).

Equality is obviously central to the idea of freedom that emerges from the Enlightenment: negative-liberty theorists like Locke, in declaring all men to be free in the state of nature, asserted that formal equality, of right and of liberty, was central to the social contract. Positive-liberty theorists like Rousseau declared that equality of a more substantive kind was central, viz., equal power among community members seeking liberty through self-rule. In setting the conditions for the civil state, Kant ascribed considerable importance to "*equality . . . as a subject*" along with "*independence . . . as a citizen.*"[33] And virtually all liberty theorists—even Mill, though perhaps less blatantly—have denied this equality to women. Moreover, both positive- and negative-liberty theorists have always had great difficulties incorporating sexual difference into their notions of equality. Some would suggest that difference is at the heart of negative liberty's conceptualization of equality as strictly formal and procedural; it is recognition of difference that motivates the definition of freedom as the absence of external impediments and the theorization of freedom as space within which individuals can act as they wish. Yet negative-liberty theory incorporates its own conception of sameness; indeed, the universalism of discourses of liberal rights and formal equality *denies* the reality of concrete differences among people, and is fundamentally biased along lines of race, class, and gender. For women, equality is generally defined as "the same as white men," a definition which ignores that women experience a multiplicity of differences from men and from each other. Taking (white) men as the standard for equality catches women in a double bind: either they are treated exactly the same as men, thus denying their specific needs—as when women are denied pregnancy leave—or else they are treated as completely different from men and in need of special protection.[34] Such a conception of equality, however, merely means that everyone is "equally abstracted from the social powers constituting our existence, equally decontextualized from the unequal conditions of our lives."[35] As Rousseau argued, formal equality's guise of neutrality helps solidify preexisting inequalities of power, denies differences in situation, resources, and needs, and thus perpetuates real, substantive inequality. Yet even his model of economic and political equality among men was founded on women's difference from men, a difference that translated into inequality. Positive liberty's second-guessing presupposes a notion of equality that requires a profound sameness of the will, such as Rousseau's general will or Hegel's *Geist*. This sameness of will is premised on and produced by women's exclusion from political participation and their subordination to men. It is perhaps this history—as well as the history of the feminist movement, in which women of color have suffered inequalities and accompanying erasure of experience in the name of "sisterhood"—that makes claims to difference and heterogeneity so important to contemporary feminism and a feminist conception of freedom and equality.

The conception of equality necessary to a feminist vision of freedom must pay attention to the concrete specificities of difference in particular times, cultures, and social formations: in Foucaultian terms, an "archeology," if not a "genealogy," of difference. Conceiving equality through difference requires considering the material conditions of women's lives in various cultures and classes, the labor that they do, the conditions of power in which they do it; seeing what actually is rather than extrapolating grand theories of human nature from narrow culture- and time-specific samples. Obviously, such seeing is never objective, as it occurs through interpretive discursive processes. But a commitment to equality demands that these processes include the perceptions and understandings of participants as well as observers and formulates its picture out of a diversity of voices and experiences. As my discussions of veiling, welfare, and domestic violence have shown, it is only by understanding specific, concrete experiences of particular women in specific contexts that a more complete descriptive picture of them can be achieved, and the commonalities of gender oppression can be identified and theorized accurately. But such pictures cannot approach adequacy, much less accuracy, without including the perspectives of those having the experiences. Understanding differences between groups as well as within groups (including our own) can produce a more complete descriptive picture of those differences. Such completeness is necessary to any plausible conception of difference, equality, or freedom. The history of modern political theory illustrates the ease and power of falsely universal claims made under the guise of equality. Only by gaining more complete pictures can we develop and achieve a genuine equality that addresses the lived experiences of different people.

Amartya Sen engages in such specific and detailed analysis to argue that equality is key to women's freedom. Sen's "capability approach" focuses on "a person's freedom to achieve well-being," and this requires "real alternatives," not merely formal ones. What makes alternatives real is often economic resources; he argues that dire poverty is the primary barrier for most people throughout the world in achieving well-being and pursuing the goals they would like to pursue. But this is partly because poverty is tied to an array of broader and more abstract inequalities. Hence, he argues that when westerners talk of "development," we must consider not merely "growth of GNP" in developing nations, but a much more expansive array of "social and economic arrangements . . . as well as political and civil rights."[36] By considering development as an issue of freedom, wealth is transformed into an indicator of other kinds of goods that people need if they are to nurture and exercise their capabilities. If everyone must be equally free, as liberalism has long asserted, then everyone must have relatively equal access to economic resources, if not equal resources themselves. Economic equality produces a substantive freedom as much as a formal freedom; equality of outcome as much as of process, equality of the goods which rights are supposed to protect as much as of the rights themselves.[37] Freedom is constituted by opportunities, as negative-liberty theory asserts, but these must be *real opportunities . . . to accomplish what we value*."[38]

Sen's distinction between "well-being freedom" and "agency freedom" is useful for feminism, for it highlights the tensions between making our own choices and making the right choices, which have persisted in freedom theory from the early modern era to today. Locke's notion of tacit consent, which ensured that the uneducated majority would be bound to state authority, and Rousseau's concept of the general will, which determined what people not only should want but really do want, even if they do not know it, were both ways to protect people's well-being freedom from a misguided use of their agency freedom. Similarly, many feminists believe that battered women who choose to remain with their abusive partners because they feel responsible or at fault abdicate their well-being through acts of agency; these feminists therefore support mandatory arrest policies or insist that these women go into psychotherapy.[39] But such a position is problematic for feminism, as I have already shown. As Sen notes, a concern with well-being inevitably involves treating people as "patients" rather than agents, as objects of state action whose fate depends on evaluations by others. Certainly, well-being might involve claims of the self about what she perceives as her own best interest, but the problem of adaptive preferences, the effects of oppression on desire and self-perception, compromise the reliability of such self-evaluations. Because of these effects, well-being cannot be collapsed into agency, Sen suggests: "the active agency of women cannot, in any serious way, ignore the urgency of rectifying many inequalities that blight the well-being of women and subject them to unequal treatment." (So just because a battered woman chooses to stay with an abusive partner does not mean she is free, in Sen's view.) Well-being assessments must rely on some sort of "objective" criteria, Sen suggests, such as empirical evidence on mortality rates, education, literacy, and so forth. But at the same time, Sen maintains that agency freedom is still centrally important: "any practical attempt at enhancing the well-being of women cannot but draw on the agency of women themselves in bringing about such change." Accordingly, he argues that we must attend to agency and well-being simultaneously, because they mutually constitute one another:

> The relative respect and regard for women's well-being is strongly influenced by such variables as women's ability to earn an independent income, to find employment outside the home, to have ownership rights and to have literacy and be educated participants in decisions within and outside the family. Indeed, even the survival disadvantage of women compared with men in developing countries seems to go down sharply—and may even get eliminated— as progress is made in these agency aspects.[40]

This is an insight that feminists such as Catherine MacKinnon seem to ignore. Basing her legislative attempts to outlaw pornography on the equal-protection clause of the Fourteenth Amendment, Mackinnon's use of equality sacrifices agency freedom in the interest of well-being freedom. For she maintains that the conditions of patriarchy completely forestall women's agency; women are socially constructed to choose precisely what patriarchy wants them to choose. Women's desires are completely determined by patriarchy, their preferences have completely adapted to their oppression.[41] Hence, freedom and equality for MacKinnon require not abstract rights to choose or consent but substantive legal intervention to protect women from exploitation by restricting activities that she asserts are harmful to women and engaged in primarily by men, such as pornography. In maintaining that the cultural expression of female subordination in pornography robs women of the ability to make choices that reflect their true interests, she logically commits feminism to a state that forces women to be free by outlawing those freedom-robbing practices. Indeed, one could even argue that she is not really concerned with freedom at all, for she views freedom as a myth that men use to exploit and dominate women. But in Sen's view, feminists like MacKinnon who seem to care more about well-being than agency end up actually undermining women's well-being. For making choices for oneself, acting in the world, participating in community and political life as active agents are all important to women's well-being, both materially—because such power reduces their exploitation by men—and psychologically—because acting in the world makes one feel more competent and gives one a sense of positive control over one's life.

But such power also increases women's well-being discursively, for it enhances women's ability to participate in the social construction of their identities and the social meanings of gender. Sen would not put it in these terms, for he discusses women's agency and participation in much more basic and literal terms of "the political, economic, and social participation and leadership of women." But such participation is essentially linked to the constitution of discourses and the processes of social construction. Though the most obvious and immediate outcome of equalizing women's political and economic power and social membership is a material change in women's well-being, as well as their ability to develop and express their agency by making choices, such material changes inevitably affect the social construction of "women." Women's participation in the labor economy not only enhances individual women's independence from specific men, but in the process elevates women's status as a group, changing social attitudes about women's role in the family and particularly their place in family decision making, as well as girls' understandings of their life chances and possible futures. Sen does not recognize these discursive dynamics, for he is much more concerned with the second level of social construction, and possibly the first, than he is with the third. But his concern with material reality results in an apparent retreat from his insights about the interdependence of well-being and agency. Hence, in contrast to Mill, who believed that it was enough for women's equality that they have the opportunity to work outside the home (because it produced an exit option which would balance men's power over them), and that being a wife and mother was legitimately seen as a "career," Sen asserts that it is not enough that women have the *opportunity* to pursue education or engage in paid employment; they must actually be educated and earn money. The associations he draws between literacy, earning power, and fertility, for instance, are not between fertility and the availability of *options* to learn how to read and engage in paid employment, regardless of whether women pursue those options; rather they are between fertility, being able to read, and actually earning money.[42] Such a position could be seen as taking agency away from women, like the battered-women's advocate who supports mandatory arrest and prosecution policies. Sen seems to resolve this by assuming that providing women with the means to express agency will automatically result in their expression of agency; and indeed, it is hard to imagine a legitimate argument supporting illiteracy as a "choice," because it is so fundamental to the ability to express agency in the contemporary world. But at the same time, Sen's assumption not only undercuts somewhat his argument about adaptive preferences but also collapses agency into well-being. In the context of overwhelming poverty and oppression, Sen is suggesting, differences among people tend to flatten out; "difference" may be a luxury that only those who do not have to worry about daily survival can indulge in. But as a result, the individual Sen works with is decidedly the liberal individual—perhaps not one who emerges from a state of nature, but one who is fairly identical to most others.

Drucilla Cornell, by contrast, who also develops a feminist vision of freedom that gives a central place to equality, emphasizes the necessity of including difference "at the heart of freedom." Cornell argues that equality produces the freedom to imagine myself as a "sexuate being" (which she defines as the "sexed body of our human being when engaged with a framework by which we orient ourselves") without the oppressive interference of rules, norms, and values that not only limit how I can see myself but dictate how I should see myself as well.[43] Cornell might seem to agree with my argument that context creates barriers to women's freedom through the social construction of desire, because if the "framework by which we orient ourselves" is always already patriarchical, then the only way that women can gain autonomy and freedom for our "sexuate being" is through what Cornell calls "the imaginary domain." "The freedom to struggle to become a person" requires "the space for the renewal of the imagination and the concomitant re-imagining of who one is and who one seeks to become."[44] Patriarchy provides blockages to such imaginings, especially regarding women's "sexuate being," for its power over women depends on constructing women's sexuality in very specific ways that guarantee masculine control over it. Yet precisely because women's self-conceptions are constructed by and through oppressive social relations of institutionalized gendering, "imagining" is the only way for women to be able to achieve freedom.

Although I support Cornell's effort to develop a feminist theory of freedom through material experiences such as adoption, however, her specific focus on *sexual* difference is limiting and problematic. In the first place, as she presents it, sexual difference is highly individualistic; what equality produces is the ability to imagine *myself*, as if simply thinking my way around oppressive practices is all that stands between me and an infinite number of possible futures and self-identities. Such a picture denies the ways in which such imagining is always and of necessity socially constructed by particular contexts, social relations, institutions, and practices. Where would alternative visions of myself come from? Cornell seems to believe that a kind of naturalist sexuality is the answer. Although she acknowledges, along with feminists like Judith Butler, that the "sexed body is symbolically constructed,"[45] Cornell also "distinguish[es] sexual difference from femininity, as the imposed social constructs that define our gender identity as women within patriarchy." For "without the affirmation of feminine sexual difference, we will consciously perpetuate the gender hierarchy under which the feminine is *necessarily* devalued."[46]

Her placement of sex "at the heart of freedom,"[47] and particularly individuals' ability to "imagine" their "sexual imago,"[48] for themselves, puts too much weight on a rather romanticized conception of sex, however. In the first place, it denies the social constructedness that she claims to recognize; for even the imagination, and the possibilities that humans have for imagining, are always already socially constructed by and through context and language. Like MacKinnon, Cornell tends to view social construction as "oppressive socialization"; if patriarchy would simply stop constructing women, women would be "free" to imagine their sexualities for themselves.[49] In the second place, like Wendy Brown, Cornell exaggerates difference; sexuality is *so* different for each woman in Cornell's view that it cannot be critically and categorically analyzed, only recounted in the most abstract terms. For instance, Cornell defends prostitution as a way for women to express their sexuate being because a prostitute she interviews says that her work has helped her recover from the trauma of childhood sexual abuse.[50] But Cornell never critically engages the social conditions, such as the structure of patriarchal power in the family through which such child abuse takes place, that forced this women to make such a choice, any more than she explores the economic conditions that much more frequently lead women into prostitution because it is the best-paying employment they can find. The failure to locate individual experience within broader contexts of social construction cannot bring about the "radical" political change she claims to seek.

The importance of such change to feminist freedom is why I maintain that what equality produces is not an individualist freedom of abstract imagining, but rather material participation in the social structures and contexts that construct us—as women, poor, white, black, middle-class, Western, heterosexual, Islamic, and so forth. If such categories are discursively unavoidable, then rejecting them accomplishes nothing politically; indeed, by rejecting them and declaring that the self's essential core, the imagination, is independent of such discursive limitations, Cornell actually reinforces their social power. By contrast, what I argue for is women's self-conscious and self-critical engagement with discourse so as to redefine terms like "freedom" in ways that reflect lived reality and desire, as well as possible alternative future realities and desires. Although individuals perform such engagement, they do so in recognition of their location in contexts and of the need for others to share in their endeavor. Thus, my equivalent of Cornell's individualistic "imaginary domain" is a social process in which people acting together—though not always in agreement—work to change contexts so as to produce new meanings and possibilities. Greater participation in the processes of social construction allows greater freedom not for *self*-imagining per se but for *group* imagining *within which* individuals can partially define and construct themselves.

Without the discursive categories defining the larger context, the individual has no vocabulary with which to imagine the self.

A second problem with Cornell's argument is that *sexual* freedom is not the primary concern of the women I have discussed in the previous chapters, much less the women that Sen is talking about. Women on welfare are not worried so much about their sexuality as about feeding their children and paying the utility bills. Battered women may have been sexually assaulted as well, but IPV victims are less concerned about their sexuality than about their physical and psychological safety and economic and emotional security. Women who veil are not necessarily concerned with the oppressive or liberating effects it might have on their sexuality, but rather with issues of religious and national identity, as well as (in the case of the Cairene workers) economic security. Obviously, as I noted earlier, sexuality is not irrelevant to these experiences; "man in the house" rules, marital rape and sexual assault, sexual jokes and feelings expressed among women in purdah are all relevant aspects of women's experiences. But sexuality is not the primary issue of freedom. For instance, sex is not the *reason* that men abuse their female intimate partners; rather, it is a *tool* that men use to reinforce their social, political, and legal power. Women on welfare are clearly "punished" for being single mothers, and hence at some level for engaging in sex; and significant aspects of welfare reform explicitly target reproductive sexuality through family caps and bridefare. But women who care for adopted or foster children suffer the same economic restrictions as "biological" mothers, and work requirements and time limits are much more motivated by racism than by a concern with sexuality. The Bedouin women whom Abu-Lughod interviewed may be disturbed when their husbands do not sleep with them in equal measure with co-wives, but their concern is clearly about social standing and power rather than sexuality. Thus, although sex is relevant to women's experiences, it is only a part of a large constellation of issues "at the heart of freedom," and indeed it is not the issue which most women would identify as their major concern. Cornell's focus on sex as the *primary* concern of freedom may thus misrepresent what is important to women themselves.

Despite the shortcomings of Cornell's focus on sexuality, however, her attention to difference "at the heart of freedom" is nonetheless on the right track. Difference is indeed logically key to the agency freedom that Sen wishes to promote, even if he does not acknowledge it. For without difference, why would agency be necessary? As the theorists discussed in chapter 2 tacitly assume, if everyone needs to make the right (and hence the same) choices in order to be free, then others can make such choices for them, and thus force them to be free. My discussions of welfare, domestic violence, and veiling have shown the importance of difference to a feminist understanding of both agency and well-being. Attention to difference forestalls the problematic assumption of what battered women, or Islamic women, or welfare mothers "really" want, because their desires will be affected and shaped by their particular situations. Understanding the social construction of desire requires analyzing the broad social forces at work in shaping discourses and defining categories (such as "battered women" and "welfare mothers"). But it also requires attention to the specific needs, identities, and desires of individual women as they have been produced (for instance, when love leads a woman to stay with an abusive mate, or when Bedouin women feel inhibited from sharing feelings with their husbands).

The most important contribution that equality makes to women's freedom is the role it can play in distinguishing between and evaluating contexts: both subjectively, by ensuring that women play a role equal to men's in constructing discursive meanings and their material expression, and objectively, by setting forth principles for the evaluation of contexts. Specifically, equality can help determine whether a particular context constrains any group of people less or more than it does any other. For instance, if a society repeatedly, systematically, constrains women more than men, blacks more than whites, lesbians more than heterosexuals, then there is a theoretical presumption in favor of the conclusion that the society—or the rules, norms, institutions, practices, and values in question in a particular context where freedom is at issue—presents a barrier to the more constrained group. If it does not, and all are equally limited in similar ways by a particular context, then there is a theoretical presumption in favor of the conclusion that it does not constrain per se, but only defines the choices, as poor as those choices may be, for all of us. I state it in terms of a "presumption" because cases can always be made to the contrary, but the presumption places the burden of proof on those who defend unequal limitations on choice. For example, gravity limits us all; it is not the case that some are freer to fly than others, and the burden of proof is on those who seek to challenge this claim. On the other hand, racial economic policy in the United States may result in the majority of airplane riders being white, while the majority of bus riders are black; here, inequality is an indication that some are constrained in their liberty by social-structural forces, and the burden of proof is on those who wish to deny this. Such constraints are not necessarily obvious; they may be indirect and hidden. Laws concerning leave for pregnancy and childrearing appear to limit us all equally, by referring to "pregnant persons" and "parents," but in fact single out a particular group—namely, women—because of social custom as well as biology. Certainly, the capacity or incapacity to become pregnant should not be considered a restraint, or even a "disability," yet the larger social context of sexual discrimination results in social policy that inhibits women's ability to formulate and make choices about pregnancy. The barrier to freedom is thus not women's pregnant bodies but, rather, patriarchal social attitudes and customs pertaining to pregnancy and women.

Such attention to patterns and the systematic quality of differential treatment and outcome can help settle some of the controversies I identified earlier over the definition of a barrier. For instance, it would no longer matter whether poverty is seen as an unavoidable and morally neutral outcome of capital or the result of evil exploitation of the poor by the wealthy; in either case, since poverty is necessary to the reproduction of wealth, what would matter is how poverty systematically prevents certain groups of people from achieving certain things while other groups, who benefit from the wealth, are permitted or enabled to achieve those same things. Thus, if it were demonstrated that African Americans were disproportionately unable to afford home ownership, the presumption would be that African Americans are restricted economically compared to whites, and the task of freedom would be to identify how such restriction operates and how to remedy it. Similarly, the question of whether patriarchy is a barrier to women's freedom is less important than the fact that the majority of welfare recipients are women, and that welfare as a public assistance program provides much lower benefits, and involves more conditions and requirements than, say, Social Security or unemployment insurance, of which men are the majority of recipients. Such inequality suggests a presumption in favor of the notion that women are restricted in their freedom more than men. This presumption would then require analysis of a variety of further questions about relative equality—why women, rather than men, raise most children, why women have a harder time finding well-paid employment, why child care is so difficult to obtain— that are not in themselves economic, but nevertheless provide answers to questions of economic disparity and hence to considerations of women's freedom.[51] The role of equality in discriminating between contexts involves in this case consideration of the social construction of gender and the gendered division of labor.

But even more importantly, making equality the criterion for evaluating contexts means that the crucial distinction for freedom is not between inner and outer restraint—which social constructivism shows us is a false dichotomy—but rather between equal and unequal restraint, between the process of restraint and its outcome, between the form of restraint and its content. It shifts our focus from the procedures for treating people the same under the law to the outcomes of those procedures—an equality of result rather than of process. Feminism does not require that we simply reject procedure, of course, only that we not isolate it from its product. When equality of procedure produces inequality of outcome, the procedure has to be questioned as to whether it is truly "impartial," or only superficially—and misleadingly—so. Outcome, substance, and particularity become not so much ends in themselves as warning beacons to direct our theoretical and political attention to the possibility of power imbalances. Feminism should thus reject the opposition of procedure and substance found in many feminist critiques, and yet draw on the insight inherent in such critiques—that procedures can appear to be neutral while perpetrating gross inequities—to help create a notion of equality that attends to differences in context and situation and is sensitive to substantive needs and outcome.

This conception of equality thus attends to differences between individuals and between larger social groups, but at the same time, focusing on difference in the context of equality reduces the substantive importance of difference. Recognizing that difference is a social construction—not only are women and men socially constructed to embody certain characteristics and not others, but the discursive meaning of those characteristics assigns them disparate social value—the relevant point becomes not whether women are, for instance, more nurturant or less aggressive than men—whether they are "different"—but rather whether such differences result in systematically unequal treatment and dominance. Difference does not provide an excuse to deny freedom to particular individuals or groups, as has often been the case for women. Rather, difference is a signal light indicating times when equality and freedom may be particularly at issue; it marks out occasions when misunderstanding and conflict may arise and indicates the possibility for appropriate state protection, not to repress differences but to ensure that differences are respected and accommodated equally. Examples would be self-defense laws that recognize and accommodate women's often lesser physical strength; welfare policy that recognizes and seeks to alter women's primary social responsibility for children; international aid policy that gives women's voices equal weight in defining the "culture" to which such aid responds.[52]

## CONSTRUCTING FEMINIST FREEDOM

This view of equality in turn involves the recognition that the state is central to politics. Feminism invented the phrase "the personal is the political," and politics exists in many social relations that most of us paradoxically seek to keep private. I hardly want the state to intervene if my husband shirks his share of the housework, even though I see the division of household labor as an important example of gender politics; that is a battle I would prefer to wage for myself. But the state needs to be conceptualized as a resource that can be brought into some private-political contexts; for instance, if I want the state to prevent my husband from beating me up. The state is a meaningful and useful resource that women need to be able to access if they are to increase their participation in the processes of social construction, for the state is an important instrument in such construction. Hence, feminism should be less hostile to state intervention per se than some feminists advocate, particularly those who recognize the importance of discourse to freedom. Both Cornell and Brown, for instance, are skeptical of, if not hostile to, feminist reliance on the state as "protector." Cornell, for instance, argues against censorship of pornography and the outlawing of prostitution because such supposedly feminist efforts merely replicate obviously sexist uses of the state, such as regulation of abortion. Similarly, noting that "the state has acquired a historically unparalleled prominence—political and economic, social and cultural—in millions of women's lives," Brown chides feminists for failing to "consider the state as a vehicle of domination or to reflect on 'protection' as a technique of domination." Because "the state is an insignia of the extent to which politics between men are always already the politics of exchanging, violating, protecting, and regulating women," using the state for feminist liberatory purposes is, in her view, a self-contradiction. Not only does "women's deepening involvement with the state entail exchanging dependence upon individual men for regulation by contemporary institutionalized processes of male domination." Worse, the terms of neutrality, universalism, and abstraction in which the state is conceptualized hide its power and dupe women into thinking they are empowered when instead they are further subordinated, thus reiterating rather than resisting—much less reworking—patriarchal constructions of women.[53]

Certainly my discussion of welfare reform in chapter 6 has shown that Brown's fears are not unfounded. Women on welfare, whether they are ashamed of it and struggle to meet the work requirements of welfare reform (despite hardships of inadequate child care and transportation), or have consciously sought out welfare as a means to secure independence from abusive husbands, or have decided that welfare is a way to attack and get back at the racism and classism of the liberal state and economy, are all subjected in similar ways to the scrutiny, regulation, and disciplinary power of the state. And it is a state that, despite its ideological discourse, clearly does not have an interest in women's freedom, either in the negative-liberty sense of genuine independence or in the positive-liberty sense of autonomous control over their own lives. I have argued that in attempting to develop a "woman-friendly" public welfare policy, feminists have often become caught up in the framework dictated by the Right and have replicated the very power structures they desire to destabilize. The point of that argument, however, was not to eschew the state but rather to reconfigure it. I believe that Brown, like Cornell, overstates the case against the state and against feminism. It is not state intervention per se, but rather the *form* of such intervention, reflecting the interests of (certain groups of) men, that generally hurts women. Compared to feminist welfare policies, the ideal of the state as noninterventionist is even less likely to "transform the masculinism of bureaucracy" than to "reiterate it."[54] For the notion that a noninterventionist state is even possible, and that it can allow women to define themselves and achieve liberation from the social construction of gender, is uncomfortably reminiscent of the negative-liberty liberal ideals that Brown clearly opposes, sustainable only from the perspective of privilege. From the perspective of powerlessness, by contrast, the state often intervenes most intrusively and egregiously precisely when it claims to be doing the contrary, such as when, under the rubric of privacy, its failure to arrest and prosecute domestic abusers results in the restriction of women's freedom. In this sense, then, the position that the state should simply not involve itself in matters of domestic violence, abortion, sexual harrassment, pornography, or economic support of single parents makes problematic assumptions about the state, and indeed about the ability to escape the state. As Ulrike Liebert maintains, the social developments necessary to achieve gender inequality "can hardly be expected to be the result of the 'free play of market forces.' Rather, they require state regulations and legal frameworks."[55]

This does not mean that feminists should be sanguine about state power. Feminists, Brown most notably among them, have been instrumental in revealing the ways in which state power is used against women's freedom. But rather than abandoning the state as a potential feminist tool, such feminist insights attest to the need to rethink what the state should be in a feminist vision and how feminists want to relate to it. As Brown herself suggests in passing,[56] feminists seeking a better world that allows women greater freedom need to articulate both a feminist vision of democracy (which I take to be the starting point for an egalitarian state) and a feminist *public policy*—which by definition comes from and is expressed through a state—that would reflect what women in specific contexts and situations need and want to enhance both their well-being and their agency. By acknowledging difference, a "woman-friendly" feminist state would be in a better-informed position to intervene—and to refrain from intervention—in ways that respond to contextualized need, rather than in ways that systematically benefit some at others' expense. Indeed, such an approach could actually reduce such intervention by equalizing power among citizens, strengthening those who are currently less powerful. At the least, such an approach is not likely to increase intervention; rather, such intervention—in the protections and penalties it assigns to men and women—will be distributed more equitably.

Feminist fear of the state is based on the very same liberal fears of positive liberty that Berlin expressed: a fear of second-guessing, of being told what is in our best interest, of being forced to be free. But such fears once again miss an important insight about social construction and about freedom. As I indicated earlier in this chapter, a feminist theory of freedom demands that the individual self must make her own choices. Yet that self, its status and content, is continually in doubt and requires context and relationship with others in order to provide and sustain its meaning. Understanding this paradox requires a subtle distinction. Specifically, granting that second-guessing must be rejected by a feminist theory of freedom because it is antithetical to women's agency and self-determination does not mean that the interrogation of desire—which is what often *leads to* second-guessing—should itself be avoided. On the contrary, it is vitally important to freedom that critical questioning about desire, about who we are and what we want, be constantly engaged. The issue is where we draw the line in the process of asking questions and coming up with answers. Feminist freedom says that others can, and indeed should, ask me questions. But only I can come up with the answers, nobody else can answer those questions for me. Autonomy theorists, for instance, as well as positive-liberty theorists like Rousseau, tend to provide external standards for what answers are legitimately autonomous—or in the case of "procedural" autonomists like Meyers and Dworkin, what standards the answers must meet.[57] Freedom, however, cannot really involve itself with the answers. Indeed, it does not even require that you come up with any reasoned answers at all; you can say, "I don't really know, I just want to do it" and still be considered free, even if your decision fails the autonomy test. However, freedom does require that we ask questions, that we continue a critical engagement with the foundation and meaning of desire and choice. If I disapprove of your answers, as a shelter worker might when a battered woman decides to return to her abuser, I cannot force or require you to act as I wish. I can persist in asking more questions, however. Indeed, in a sense I have an obligation to continue asking, for being exposed to the questioning—being "subjected" to it, if you will—is necessary to freedom, or at least to being as sure as possible that the conditions for personal choice have been maximized, if not attained. As Foucault said, we require "counselors" to "tell us the truth," by which I believe he means—since most of his writings reject the notion of universal "truth"—asking pointed and hard questions that challenge the answers we have come up with. The point of this constant questioning is to engage the process of social construction, to entangle oneself in the messy paradox of desires that are constituted and produced through social formations.

Note that in my formulation here, freedom requires *others* to ask questions, not the self. Whereas autonomy theorists require that I go through certain procedures and perform certain tasks in order to achieve autonomy, thereby demonstrating a satisfactory level of intellectual self-awareness and even rationality, such requirements are reminiscent of the paradox of positive liberty's forcing you to be free. Indeed, precisely because of social construction, I am often not the best person to interrogate my own situation. Precisely because others occupy a position outside my particular context, they can pose questions that challenge the assumptions and givenness that experience has produced in my self. At the same time, however, because I am the one who has the experience, I must be the filter and arbiter of such questions, challenges, and information, even to the point of deciding to reject them; and I must be the one to come up with the answers, no matter how imperfect, or imperfectly formulated, they might be.

This might seem like a fairly radical negative-libertarian position; I am the final arbiter of what choices I will make: those choices do not have to measure up to external standards of reason but need only reflect desire; and whatever desires I happen to have must, in the end, be accepted as legitimate. Such a view would seem to contradict most of the foregoing argument that desire is a social construction and must be critically engaged; it might seem to agree with the negative libertarian who shrugs his shoulders when a battered woman stays with her abuser, inferring that abuse must be what she wants. But there is in fact no contradiction; I am simply differentiating between requiring an individual to engage her own desires and requiring that her social context provide the necessary resources to permit, and even encourage, such engagement. Only if others are engaged with her, asking her questions about her choices, and making sure that she has a reasonable range of realistic options that are genuinely available, can we call her decision free. Indeed, the notion that others have an *obligation* to question her, and the importance of dialogic critical questioning to freedom, require relationship or community very much in the positive-liberty vein. Though freedom must be expressed by individuals, its conditions are made possible by community. This obligation is not only moral but logical: freedom, by definition, requires a social context out of which desire emerges and in which desire and freedom obtain meaning. Indeed, as both Collins and the Milan Collective argued, community as an instrument of change is dictated by the logic of social construction: if patriarchal contexts restrain women, new contexts cannot evolve without the establishment of a different "world," a different material and intellectual framework, a different discourse. At the same time, however, contexts cannot materialize out of thin air, but only out of other contexts that already exist.

I do think that feminist freedom requires that women's decisions be respected, regardless of what they choose; feminists must support, in principle if not politically, women's choices to oppose abortion, stay with abusers, not report rape or sexual harassment, or become full-time mothers and housewives. Feminism needs to be open to a much broader diversity of views than it has generally allowed. But such respect is motivated at least as much by recognition of oppression—as in the case of the battered woman who returns to her abuser because she has nowhere else to go or fears for the safety of her family—as respect for freedom—as in the case of pro-life women who believe that abortion is murder.[58] Moreover, such respect may consistently be limited by the parameters of feminist politics. For instance, a pro-life argument that many abortions result from economic hardship and social stigma inflicted by a sexist society, so that to talk of "women's choice" is hypocritical at best, is worlds apart from the more common pro-life argument for a "right to life" for the "unborn." While this latter position could arguably be legitimated through appeal to liberal ideals, by couching its claims in terms of "rights" for the fetus, it cannot be reconciled with feminist ones any more than the argument that abortion is wrong because women are destined by scripture to reproduce: in both arguments, fetuses take unilateral precedence over women. The importance of feminist parameters lies in the recognition that not just anything can count as "feminist"; to invoke Wittgenstein's phrase, there is a "family resemblance" among political and normative ideals that can legitimately be called feminist.[59] This is not to say that a Christian fundamentalist woman must be forcibly freed from her reasons for opposing abortion; rather, it is to say that in order for this woman to sustain a belief that she is free, she must put up with continual feminist challenges to her reasons. Even so, expanding what can be labeled a "feminist" position enhances freedom, not only enlarging the feminist tent to allow for a greater diversity of voices but also fostering such diversity. For the feminist attention to relationship requires a context that allows and even encourages a broader diversity of views: not simply a context that will tolerate views that are developed independently, but rather one that will provide the means for the development of such views by constructing subjectivities that are able to think and see in different directions. The central importance of social relationships to the context within which individual identities are constructed means that freedom cannot simply be a more robust version of letting others alone but must logically involve the recognition that those others come to be who they are through the social contexts in which they exist. Understanding the subject of liberty is key to understanding the meaning and practice of liberty, for it is only through such understanding that the particularities of human experience can be incorporated into theory, and political theory can produce new and better meanings.

# NOTES

1. Tamar Lewin, "Hurdles Increase for Many Women Seeking Abortions," *New York Times*, March 15, 1992, 1, 18. "Meg" is the fictional name I have given her to facilitate later reference in the text.

2. Evan S. Connell, *Mrs. Bridge* (San Francisco: North Point Press, 1959).

3. Throughout this book I will discuss specific women's "stories," and a note should be made on those that are not obviously drawn from other research. These stories are not the result of systematic interviews in the tradition of qualitative empirical political science. But neither are they fiction, in the hallowed philosopher's tradition of creating hypothetical examples to illustrate philosophical points. Some stories come from individuals I have met and talked with; some, from individuals whom colleagues have met or interviewed. Still others are composites: they combine the markedly similar and overlapping experiences of several such individuals. Precisely because these stories are not based on systematic interviews, I do not offer any of them as systematic "proof" of women's experiences, or of their oppression or freedom; but at the same time, I think it is important to acknowledge that the stories I relate are "real," that they are not the fantasies of angry feminists, out to blame men for all the evils of the world, but rather represent the experiences of real, live women.

4. This would be independent of our stance on abortion; for instance, a "pro-life" advocate *could* argue that by not having an abortion, the woman is "freer," in that she will be realizing her true nature, and he or she could also argue that abortion interferes with the fetus's freedom as well. But most pro-life arguments instead seem to hold that women *should not* be free to abort, that such freedom is immoral.

5. I will use the terms "freedom" and "liberty" interchangeably throughout the book, as do most contemporary theorists; but see Hanna Fenichel Pitkin, "Are Freedom and Liberty Twins?" *Political Theory* 16, no. 4 (1988): 523–52.

6. See Richard Flathman, *The Philosophy and Politics of Freedom* (Chicago: University of Chicago Press, 1987) for an excellent survey of the range of definitions of freedom.

7. Isaiah Berlin, "Two Concepts of Liberty" in *Four Essays on Liberty* (New York: Oxford University Press, 1971), 118–72.

8. Ibid., 123.

9. Ibid.

10. See Charles Taylor, "What's Wrong with Negative Liberty?" in *The Idea of Freedom: Essays in Honor of Isaiah Berlin*, ed. Alan Ryan (New York: Oxford University Press, 1979).

11. Ibid., 176.

12. Berlin 1971, 125.

13. John Rawls, *A Theory of Justice* (Cambridge: Harvard University Press, 1971), 204.

14. Ibid., 121–22.

15. Taylor 1979, 177.

16. Berlin 1971, xlii.

17. Isaiah Berlin, " 'From Hope and Fear Set Free,' " in *Concepts and Categories: Philosophical Essays* (New York: Viking Press, 1979), 190.

18. Ibid., 191. See also Hillel Steiner, "How Free?: Computing Personal Liberty," in *Of Liberty*, ed. A. Phillips Griffiths (New York: Cambridge University Press, 1983), 73; and Ian Carter, "The Measurement of Pure Negative Liberty," *Political Studies* 40 (1992): 38–50.

19. Berlin 1979, 193. Richard J. Arneson makes a similar observation in "Freedom and Desire," *Canadian Journal of Philosophy* 15, no. 3 (1985): 426, 444–45.

20. Berlin 1979, 193.

21. Stanley I. Benn, *A Theory of Freedom* (New York: Cambridge University Press, 1988), esp. 132. S. I. Benn and W. L. Weinstein, "Being Free to Act and Being a Free Man," in *Concepts in Social and Political Philosophy*, ed. Richard E. Flathman (New York: MacMillan, 1973): freedom means "to be able to choose among available courses . . . deciding between alternative courses lies at the heart of freedom" (312). Joel Feinberg, "The Interest in Liberty on the Scales," in *Rights, Justice, and the Bounds of Liberty: Essays in Social Philosophy* (Princeton: Princeton University Press, 1980): "interest in liberty *as such* . . . is an interest in having as many *open options* as possible" (35). Christine Swanton, *Freedom: A Coherence Theory* (Indianapolis: Hackett Publishing Company, 1992): "freedom cannot be identified with mere want satisfaction" (48).

22. See Flathman (1987) on "autarchy" (216–20), first- and second-order desire (45–51), and the critique of "open options" (27–31, 224–27); also Robert Nozick, *Anarchy, State, and Utopia* (New York: Basic Books, 1974) (on his famous principle "From each as they choose, to each as they are chosen" [160]); and William A. Parent, "Some Recent Work on the Concept of Liberty," *American Philosophical Quarterly* no. 3 (1974): 156–57.

23. Berlin 1971, 124.

24. Taylor 1979; see also Charles Taylor, "Atomism," in *Powers, Possessions, and Freedom*, ed. Alkis Kontos (Toronto: University of Toronto Press, 1979a).

25. Taylor 1979, 184.

26. Ibid., 177.

27. Berlin 1971, 133–34.

28. Taylor 1979, 185.

29. Marilyn A. Friedman, "Autonomy and the Split Level Self," *Southern Journal of Philosophy* 23, no. 1 (1986): 19–35, makes this point as well.

30. See, for instance, Michel Foucault, *Language, Countermemory, and Practice* (Ithaca: Cornell University Press, 1977), as well as *The Foucault Reader*, ed. Paul Rabinow (New York: Pantheon, 1984), esp. 381–82; Jacques Derrida, *Positions* (Chicago: University of Chicago Press, 1972).

31. Michel Foucault, *The History of Sexuality* vol. 1, *An Introduction* (New York: Vintage Books, 1990a); Jacques Derrida, *Margins of Philosophy*, trans.

Alan Bass (Chicago: University of Chicago Press, 1982); Jean Francois Lyotard, *The Postmodern Condition: A Report on Knowledge* (Minneapolis: University of Minnesota Press, 1979).

32. Diana Coole, "Constructing and Deconstructing Liberty," *Political Studies* 41 (1993): 83–95.

33. Jon Elster, *Sour Grapes* (New York: Cambridge University Press, 1983). See also Amartya Sen, *Inequality Reexamined* (Cambridge: Harvard University Press, 1992).

34. Paul Benson, "Autonomy and Oppressive Socialization," *Social Theory and Practice* 17, no. 13 (1991): 385–408; Diana T. Meyers, "Personal Autonomy and the Paradox of Feminine Socialization," *Journal of Philosophy* 84, no. 11 (1987): 619–28.

35. Amartya Sen, "Well-Being, Agency, and Freedom: The Dewey Lectures 1984," *Journal of Philosophy* 82, no. 4 (1985), esp. 191.

36. Amartya Sen, *Development as Freedom* (New York: Alfred A. Knopf, 1999), 104–5.

37. Kathy Ferguson, *The Man Question: Visions of Subjectivity in Feminist Theory* (Berkeley: University of California Press, 1993), 129. See also Wendy Brown, *States of Injury: Power and Freedom in Late Modernity* (Princeton: Princeton University Press, 1995), 145, for a similar contrast between socialization and social construction.

38. Gerald MacCallum, "Negative and Positive Freedom," in *Concepts in Social and Political Philosophy*, ed. Richard Flathman (New York: Macmillan, 1973), 301. See also Orlando Patterson, *Freedom: Freedom in the Making of Western Culture* (New York: Basic Books, 1991), 296.

39. MacCallum 1973, 298.

40. Ibid., 301, 303.

41. John Gray, "On Positive and Negative Liberty," *Political Studies*, 28, no. 4 (1980): 510–13.

42. Benn 1988; Carter 1992; Coole 1993; Flathman 1987; Gray 1980; Quentin Skinner, "The Idea of Negative Liberty: Philosophical and Historical Perspectives," in *Philosophy in History*, ed. Richard Rorty, J. B. Schneewind, and Quentin Skinner (Cambridge: Cambridge University Press, 1986); Hillel Steiner, "Individual Liberty," *Proceedings of the Aristotelian Society* 75 (1974–75): 33–50; Robin West, "Taking Freedom Seriously," *Harvard Law Review* 104, no. 1 (1990): 43–106.

43. MacCallum 1973, Patterson 1991.

44. Philip Pettit, *A Theory of Freedom: From the Psychology to the Politics of Agency* (New York: Oxford University Press, 2001).

45. Flathman 1987, 17.

46. Ibid., 324.

47. Berlin 1971, xxxix.

48. "Physical restraints imposed (by man or natural forces) on or around a person which prevent him from moving except within a limited space . . . moral coercion employed so effectively and/or unexpectedly that it serves as a sufficient causal condition of the victim's not acting in a specified way, or . . . institutional arrangements which make it impossible to undertake certain kinds of activities."

William A. Parent, "Freedom as the Non-restriction of Options," *Mind* 83 (1974): 166.

49. Ibid., 156.

50. Carter 1992.

51. Kristjan Kristjansson, "What Is Wrong with Positive Liberty?" *Social Theory and Practice* 18, no. 3 (1992).

52. David Miller, "Constraints on Freedom," *Ethics* 94 (1983): 66–86.

53. Ibid., 67.

54. Kristjansson 1992, 293.

55. Miller 1983, 81.

56. See, for instance, Benn and Weinstein 1973, 315.

57. Miller 1983, 74.

58. S. I. Benn and W. L. Weinstein, "Freedom as the Non-Restriction of Options: A Rejoinder," *Mind* 83 (1974): 437.

59. Benn and Weinstein 1973, 314.

60. Benn 1988, 138, 133.

61. John Gray, *Liberalisms: Essays in Political Philosophy* (New York: Routledge, 1989), 176, and ch. 3.

62. G. A. Cohen, "Freedom and Money: In Grateful Memory of Isaiah Berlin," 12. This paper was presented in several different academic venues during 2000 and 2001. It will be cited subsequently as Cohen 2001. Full text is available online at http://www.utdt.edu/departamentos/derecho/publicaciones/rtj1/pdf/finalfreedom.PDF.

63. Ibid., 13, 14. See also G.A. Cohen, "Capitalism, Freedom, and the Proletariat," in *The Idea of Freedom: Essays in Honor of Isaiah Berlin*, ed. Alan Ryan (Oxford: Oxford University Press, 1979), esp. 11–15; and *Self-Ownership, Freedom, and Equality* (Cambridge: Cambridge University Press).

64. Cohen 2001, 5, emphasis added.

65. Ibid., 13.

66. Sen 1999, 20, 8, 15; ch. 4 more generally on poverty as a barrier to freedom; ch. 6 on the relationship between economic and political freedom. See also Sen 1992.

67. Sen 1999, 194, 96–98.

68. Amartya Sen, "Capability and Well-Being," in *The Quality of Life*, ed. Martha Nussbaum and Amartya Sen (Oxford: Clarendon Press, 1993), 35.

69. Sen 1999, ch. 8.

70. Benn 1988, 143.

71. Katie Roiphe, *The Morning After: Sex, Fear, and Feminism* (Boston: Little, Brown, 1993); Christina Hoff Sommers, *Who Stole Feminism? How Women Have Betrayed Women* (New York: Simon and Schuster, 1994), ch. 10.

72. See Susan J. Brison, "Surviving Sexual Violence: A Philosophical Perspective," *Journal of Social Philosophy* 24, no. 1: 5–22.

73. For those who do not recall (or who may be too young to have lived through this infamous event), the "Central Park jogger" was a twenty-eight-year-old white female Wall Street executive who was severely beaten, raped, and left for dead by a group of eight to twelve fourteen-and fifteen-year-old boys in New

York City's Central Park on April 19, 1989. Details of the criminal case against one of the accused attackers, *The People &C., Respondent, v. Yusef Salaam, Appellant* 83 N.Y. 2d 51, 629 N.E. 2d 371, 607 N.Y.S. 2d 899 (1993), can be accessed online at http://www.law.cornell.edu/ny/ctap/081_0051.htm. See also Patricia J. Williams, *The Alchemy of Race and Rights: Diary of a Law Professor* (Cambridge: Harvard University Press, 1991) for a discussion of the racial implications of the attention garnered by the attack, which, according to her, was due to the fact that the victim was white and upper-middle-class, while the attackers were young black and Hispanic men. Indeed, many racial activists at the time argued that the attack was a case of "wilding," an activity in which groups of young black and Hispanic men looked specifically for whites to victimize with brutal violence. Because "wilding" made the attack an issue of racial inequality more than sexual violence, a number of black and Hispanic newspapers, most notably the *Amsterdam News* out of Harlem, repeatedly reported the woman's name (even though the mainstream press has always declared that the identity of the woman has never been revealed). I have wrestled with the question of whether such revelation makes her identity public knowledge, and hence burdens me with the responsibility to report it here, but I leave it to readers who wish to know the victim's name to perform the research on their own.

74. Camille Paglia, *Sexual Personae: Art and Decadence from Nefertiti to Emily Dickinson* (New Haven: Yale University Press, 1990).

75. Benn 1988, 142.

76. See Andrea Parrot, *Acquaintance Rape and Sexual Assault Prevention Training Manual* (Ithaca: Cornell University College of Human Ecology, 1990); and Emilie Buchwald, Pamela Fletcher, and Martha Roth, eds., *Transforming a Rape Culture* (Minneapolis: Milkweed Editions, 1993).

77. Pettit 2001, 78.

78. Ibid., 137, emphasis added.

79. See, for instance, Vivienne Walt, "Afghanistan: Inside the Burqa," *USA Today*, January 9, 2002, 1A; Andrew Higgins, "The Fabric of Change: The Bottom Drops out of the Burqa Market in Afghanistan," *Newsday*, December 26, 2001, B3; Amy Waldman, "Behind the Burka: Women Subtly Fought Taliban," *New York Times*, November 19, 2001.

80. A similar problem undermines his critique of freedom as "nonlimitation." As mentioned earlier, Pettit's objection to freedom as "nonlimitation" is that limits that exist naturally, or at least through nobody's fault, are morally distinct from limits that are the result of intentional and purposive action. But the examples he offers of "limitations" include "handicap and illness, lack of education and information, insecurity and poverty," all of which I have suggested are, to at least a significant degree, socially constructed (Pettit 2001, 131). Equating "poverty" with "illness," for instance, denigrates the social causes, structures, and frameworks of poverty; it accepts poverty as a fact of nature, much like catching the flu, rather than a social force involved in the construction of subjectivity. Even worse, Pettit fails to account for the ways in which disability and illness may themselves be products of interference or even domination, such as when the failure to produce cures for particular illnesses or disabilities results from policy deci-

sions that, say, fund military expenditures or corporate tax cuts at the expense of medical research.

81. Brison 1993.

82. Sarah B. Pomeroy, *Goddesses, Whores, Wives, and Slaves: Women in Classical Antiquity* (New York: Schocken Books, 1975); Susan Estrich, *Real Rape* (Cambridge: Harvard University Press, 1987).

83. bell hooks, *Feminist Theory: From Margin to Center* (Boston: South End Press, 1984).

84. Nancy J. Hirschmann, *Rethinking Obligation: A Feminist Method for Political Theory* (Ithaca: Cornell University Press, 1992), 60.

85. John Stuart Mill, "The Subjection of Women," in *On Liberty and Other Essays*, ed. John Gray (New York: Oxford University Press, 1991), 522–23. See also Christine Di Stefano's chapter on Mill in her *Configurations of Masculinity* (Ithaca: Cornell University Press, 1991).

86. Jean-Jacques Rousseau, *Emile*, ed. Allan Bloom (New York: Basic Books, 1979), esp. book 5; G.W.F. Hegel, *The Phenomenology of Spirit*, ed. A.V. Miller (New York: Oxford University Press, 1977), esp. 274–78; Immanuel Kant, *Observations on the Feeling of the Beautiful and Sublime*, trans. John Goldthwait (Berkeley: University of California Press, 1960).

87. Thanks to Joan Tronto for this phrasing.

88. Cass R. Sunstein, "Preferences and Politics," *Philosophy and Public Affairs* 20, no. 1 (1991): 11.

89. See Catriona MacKenzie and Natalie Stoljar, "Introduction: Autonomy Refigured," in *Relational Autonomy: Feminist Perspectives on Autonomy, Agency and the Social Self* ed. Catriona MacKenzie and Natalie Stoljar (New York: Oxford University Press, 2000), and Brown, 1995, 156–57, for critiques of this negative-liberty version of liberal autonomy.

90. Emily R. Gill, *Becoming Free: Autonomy and Diversity in the Liberal Polity* (Lawrence: University Press of Kansas, 2001), 17.

91. John Christman, introduction to *The Inner Citadel: Essays on Individual Autonomy*, ed. John Chrisman (New York: Oxford University Press, 1989), 3; Joseph Raz, *The Morality of Freedom* (Oxford: Clarendon Press, 1986).

92. See, for instance, the essays in *Autonomy and Community: Readings in Contemporary Kantian Social Philosophy*, ed. Jane Kneller and Sidney Axinn (Albany: State University of New York Press, 1998); and MacKenzie and Stoljar, 2000.

93. Wright Neely, "Freedom and Desire," *Philosophical Review* 83 (1974): 32–54; see also Christman, introduction to Christman 1989, 13.

94. Robert Young, *Personal Autonomy: Beyond Positive and Negative Liberty* (New York: St. Martin's Press, 1986), 5; Jennifer Nedelsky, "Reconceiving Autonomy: Sources, Thoughts, and Possibilities," *Yale Journal of Law and Feminism* 1, no. 1 (1989): 8.

95. Flathman 1987; also Christman, introduction to Christman 1989, 13.

96. MacCallum 1973, 301.

97. Diana T. Meyers, *Self, Society, and Personal Choice* (New York: Columbia University Press, 1989); Christman, introduction to Christman 1989, 10.

98. Gerald Dworkin, "The Concept of Autonomy," in Christman 1989, 60. See also Gill 2001, 18.

99. MacKenzie and Stoljar, introduction to MacKenzie and Stoljar 2000.

100. In order, these quotes are taken from: Marilyn Friedman, "Autonomy, Social Disruption, and Women," in Mackenzie and Stoljar 2000, 37; Nedelsky 1989, 24; Gerald Dworkin, *The Theory and Practice of Autonomy* (New York: Cambridge University Press, 1988), 20; Raz 1986, 204; Young 1986, 42; Christman, introduction to Christman 1989, 10; Meyers 1989, 96; Gill 2001, 29.

101. Meyers, 1987, 619; Robert Young, "Autonomy and the Inner Self," in Christman 1989, 83; Gill 2001.

102. Meyers 1989, 51; Meyers 1987, 619. Paul Benson makes a similar argument that Meyers's definition of autonomy in terms of "autonomy competence . . . has much in common with the traditional acounts of freedom." Paul Benson, "Feminist Second Thoughts about Free Agency," *Hypatia*, 5, no. 3 (1990): 63. However, he himself deploys notions of rationality in his own conception of "critical competence"; see Benson 1991, 398–99.

103. Dworkin 1988, 20.

104. Susan Brison, "Outliving Oneself: Trauma, Memory, and Personal Identity," in *Feminists Rethink the Self*, ed. Diana T. Meyers (Boulder: Westview Press, 1997).

105. Meyers 1987, 626.

## Chapter Two

1. John Locke, *Two Treatises of Civil Government*, ed. Peter Laslett (Cambridge: Cambridge University Press, 1960; rpt. New York: New American Library, 1963), 347. Hereafter cited as *First Treatise* or *Second Treatise*, followed by page number.

2. But see Kirstie M. McClure, *Judging Rights: Lockean Politics and the Limits of Consent* (Ithaca: Cornell University Press, 1996), which argues, somewhat differently, that natural law provided absolute limits on human freedom, since it demarcated the boundaries within which individuals could make choices and pursue their interests. Rights constituted the realm of freedom and individual "convenience," whereas law defined the realm of virtue and duty.

3. John Locke, *An Essay Concerning Human Understanding*, ed. Peter N. Nidditch (Oxford: Clarendon Press, 1975), 278.

4. John Locke, *Questions Concerning the Law of Nature*, ed. Robert Horowitz, Jenny Strauss Clay, and Diskin Clay (Ithaca: Cornell University Press, 1990), 173–75, 109, 111. Hereafter cited in the text as *Questions*, followed by page number.

5. John Locke, *Of the Conduct of the Understanding*, ed. Thomas Folwer (New York: Lenox Hill-Burt Franklin, 1971), 9, 12. Hereafter cited in the text as *Conduct*, followed by page number.

6. C. B. Macpherson, *The Political Theory of Possessive Individualism: Hobbes to Locke* (New York: Oxford University Press, 1962).

7. John Locke, *An Essay on the Poor Law*, in Locke, *Political Essays*, ed. Mark Goldie (New York: Cambridge University Press, 1994).

8. Jacobus tenBroeck, "California's Dual System of Family Law: Its Origin, Development, and Present Status," *Stanford Law Review* 16 (1994): 1249.

9. John Locke, *Some Thoughts Concerning Education* in *The Educational Writings of John Locke*, ed. James L. Axtell (New York: Cambridge University Press, 1968), 129. Hereafter cited as *Thoughts* followed by page number.

10. Uday Mehta, *The Anxiety of Freedom: Imagination and Individuality in Locke's Political Thought* (Ithaca: Cornell University Press, 1992), 132.

11. Locke, "Epistle Dedicatory," in *Thoughts*, 32.

12. Rogers Smith, *Liberalism in American Constitutional Law* (Cambridge: Harvard University Press, 1985); Lorenne Clark, "Who Owns the Apples in the Garden of Eden?" *Canadian Journal of Philosophy* 7, no. 4 (1977).

13. Locke, *The Reasonableness of Christianity*, ed. I. T. Ramsay (Stanford: Stanford University Press, 1958), 76. At the end of *A Discourse of Miracles*, he takes another swipe at the intellectual capacities of "poor bricklayers," though not, this time, at women (86).

14. Whether Locke believes women can hold property is, like the issue of their rationality, somewhat contested; I maintain that, at best, in the chapter "Of Conquest" in the *Second Treatise*, Locke recognizes the potential of *femme sole* status, a special dispensation from a court that allows a woman to take control of property when she has no male relative to act on her behalf. But even this is less a property right for women than an example of men's duties to women and children: that is, in a situation of conquest, one cannot seize property that the wife and children of the vanquished need to live on. See Nancy J. Hirschmann, *Rethinking Obligation: A Feminist Method for Political Theory* (Ithaca: Cornell University Press, 1992), 53–54. Similarly, Clark 1977 argues that Locke is not articulating rights that women have, but rather rights that states do not have. Locke seeks "to ensure that no . . . victor in conquest or usurpation could alienate the male's property from his legitimate heirs . . . regardless even of the father's transgressions" (713).

15. Locke's differentiation between "perfect" and "imperfect members" of the social contract was founded on the distinction between express and tacit consent, but these categories of civil membership also entailed a series of further differences between them in terms of rights and duties. See Locke, *Second Treatise*, esp. 393–94, as well as John Dunn, "Consent in the Political Theory of John Locke," in Dunn, *Political Obligation in Its Historical Context* (Cambridge: Cambridge University Press, 1980), and Hirschmann 1992, 54–56.

16. Isaiah Berlin, "Two Concepts of Liberty," in *Four Essays on Liberty* (New York: Oxford University Press, 1971), 125.

17. Jean-Jacques Rousseau, *The Origin of Inequality*, in *The Social Contract and Discourses*, ed. G.D.H. Cole (London: J. M. Dent, 1973), 55. Hereafter cited as *Origin*, followed by page number.

18. Jean-Jacques Rousseau, *The Social Contract*, in Rousseau, 177. Hereafter cited as *Social Contract*, followed by page number.

19. Hirschmann 1992, 61–70.

20. Jean-Jacques Rousseau, *Principles of Political Economy*, in Rousseau 1973, 135.

21. Jean-Jacques Rousseau, *Emile; or, On Education*, trans. Allan Bloom (New York: Basic Books, 1979), 40. Hereafter cited as *Emile*, followed by page number.

22. For various feminist criticisms and analyses of Rousseau, see Zillah Eisenstein, *The Radical Future of Liberal Feminism* (New York: Longmans, 1981); Jean Bethke Elshtain, *Public Man, Private Woman* (Princeton: Princeton University Press, 1981); Lynda Lange, "Rousseau and Modern Feminism" in *Feminist Interpretations and Political Theory*, ed. Mary Lyndon Shanley and Carole Pateman (University Park: Pennsylvania State University Press, 1991); Carole Pateman, *The Sexual Contract* (Stanford: Stanford University Press, 1988); Linda Zerilli, *Signifying Woman* (Ithaca: Cornell University Press, 1994); Elizabeth Wingrove, *Rousseau's Republican Romance* (New York, Routledge, 2000).

23. Rousseau, *Emile*, 405.

24. Rousseau insists that "every woman must . . . produce nearly four children; for nearly half of the children who are born die before they can have others, and the two remaining ones are needed to represent the father and the mother." *Emile*, 362.

25. Richard L. Velkley, *Freedom and the End of Reason: On the Moral Foundation of Kant's Critical Philosophy* (Chicago: University of Chicago Press, 1989).

26. Hans Reiss, introduction to Immanuel Kant, *Political Writings*, 2d ed., ed. Hans Reiss (New York: Cambridge University Press, 1991), 39.

27. Immanuel Kant, *Groundwork of the Metaphysics of Morals*, trans. H. J. Patton (New York: Harper and Row, 1964), 49. Subsequent citations will be made as *Groundwork*, followed by page number. As I have already indicated, however, some attribute "negative liberty" to Bentham.

28. Allen Wood, "Kant's Compatibilism," in *Self and Nature in Kant's Philosophy*, ed. Allen Wood (Ithaca: Cornell University Press, 1984), 49.

29. See also Henry Allison, *Kant's Theory of Freedom* (Cambridge: Cambridge University Press, 1990), 38.

30. Immanuel Kant, *The Metaphysics of Morals*, trans. Mary Gregor (Cambridge: Cambridge University Press, 1991), 126. Subsequent citations will be made as *Metaphysics*, followed by page number.

31. Immanuel Kant, *Education*, trans. Annette Churton (Ann Arbor: University of Michigan Press, 1960). Subsequent citations will be made in the text as *Education*, followed by page number.

32. Immanuel Kant, *Anthropology From a Pragmatic Point of View*, trans. Mary J. Gregor (The Hague: Martinus Nijhoff, 1974), 167. Subsequent citations will be made as *Anthropology*, followed by page number.

33. Because of this, Kant says that sex is *only* permissible in marriage; to have sex outside of marriage is to abandon your humanity (*Metaphysics* 97).

34. Immanuel Kant, *Observations on the Feeling of the Beautiful and Sublime*, trans. John Goldthwait (Berkeley: University of California Press, 1960), 78. Subsequent citations will be made as *Observations*.

35. In a more prosaic argument, Kant notes that indigenous Canadian women "deliberate upon the most important regulations of the nation, even upon the question of war and peace. They thereupon send their deputies to the men's coun-

cil and generally it is their voice that determines the decision. But they purchase this privilege dearly enough. They are burdened with all the domestic concerns, and furthermore share all the hardships of the men" (*Observations* 114). Though such disadvantages are purely phenomenal and thus not relevant to freedom, here again Kant indicates that women have the capacity for reason, but it is not in their interest to use it, an argument all the more surprising because of Kant's repeated arguments that non-European *men* are incapable of reason.

36. Nancy Tuana, *Women and the History of Philosophy* (New York: Paragon House, 1992), 69, 65.

37. Immanuel Kant, "On the Proverb: 'That May be True in Theory, but It Is of No Practical Use,'" in *Perpetual Peace and Other Essays*, trans. Ted Humphrey (Indianapolis: Hackett Publishing Co., 1983), 72.

38. John Stuart Mill, *The Subjection of Women* in Mill, *On Liberty and Other Essays* (New York: Oxford University Press, 1992), 493, 532. All references to the four essays discussed in this section—*On Liberty, Utilitarianism, On Representative Government*, and *The Subjection of Women*—are to this volume and will hereafter be cited as *Liberty, Utilitarianism, Representative Government*, and *Subjection*, respectively.

39. Berlin 1971.

40. David Hume, *A Treatise of Human Nature*, ed. L. A. Selby-Bigge (New York: Oxford University Press), book 3; Nancy J. Hirschmann, "Sympathy, Empathy, and Obligation: A Feminist Rereading," in *Rereading the Canon: Feminist Interpretations of Hume*, ed. Anne Jaap Jacobson (University Park: Pennsylvania State University Press, 2000); John Rawls, "Two Concepts of Rules," *Philosophical Review* 64 (1955): 3–21.

41. Mill learned Greek, Latin, and mathematics by a very young age. He also had a nervous breakdown at sixteen, but this apparently did not shake his faith in extraordinary education; rather, he believed that his father had left out an essential aspect of education, namely, sentiment. See John Stuart Mill, *The Autobiography*, in *John Stuart Mill on Education*, ed. Francis W. Garforth (New York: Teachers College Press, Columbia University, 1971).

42. Ibid., 65.

43. Ibid., 41; Stefan Collini, introduction to *The Collected Works of J. S. Mill*, Vol. 21, *Essays on Equality, Law and Education*, ed. John M. Robson (Toronto: University of Toronto Press, 1984), xlix.

44. John Stuart Mill, "Inaugural Address Delivered to the University of St. Andrews," in Mill 1984, 217.

45. Ibid., 256.

46. F. W. Garforth, *John Stuart Mill's Theory of Education* (New York: Harper and Row, 1979), 106, 132, 121, 143.

47. Mill, "Inaugural," 217, 250, 244.

48. Richard E. Flathman, *The Philosophy and Politics of Freedom* (Chicago: University of Chicago Press, 1987).

49. Thomas Hobbes, *Leviathan*, ed. C. B. Macpherson (New York: Penguin, 1985), 332, 192, 229, 388.

50. Ibid., 377, 380, 381.

51. Ibid., 254, 253, 185, 156, 383. See also Hirschmann 1992, 42–44.

52. Hobbes 1985, 261.

53. Karl Marx, "The German Ideology," in *The Marx-Engels Reader*, 2d ed., ed. Robert C. Tucker (New York: W. W. Norton, 1978), 197.

54. See Nancy C. M. Hartsock, *Money, Sex and Power: Toward a Feminist Historical Materialism* (Boston: Northeastern University Press, 1984).

CHAPTER THREE

1. See Richard Ashcraft, *Revolutionary Politics and Locke's Two Treatises* (Princeton: Princeton University Press, 1986); Isaac Kramnick, *Revolutionary Politics and Bourgeois Radicalism* (Ithaca: Cornell University Press, 1990); C. B. Macpherson, *The Political Theory of Possessive Individualism: Hobbes to Locke* (New York: Oxford University Press, 1964).

2. Stanley I. Benn, *A Theory of Freedom* (New York: Cambridge University Press, 1988), 168.

3. William Connolly, *The Terms of Political Discourse* (Princeton: Princeton University Press, 1993), 148, 163.

4. Ibid., 169.

5. Kathy Ferguson, *The Man Question: Visions of Subjectivity in Feminist Theory* (Berkeley: University of California Press, 1993), 129. See also Wendy Brown, *States of Injury: Power and Freedom in Late Modernity* (Princeton: Princeton University Press, 1995), esp. 145.

6. Judith Lorber, *Paradoxes of Gender* (New Haven: Yale University Press, 1994), 1, 35, and ch. 10, "Guarding the Gates: The Micropolitics of Gender."

7. Paul Benson, "Autonomy and Oppressive Socialization," *Social Theory and Practice* 17, no. 3 (1991): 386–88.

8. Ibid., 399. This would particularly be the case for Heather Whitestone, Miss America for 1995, who, as a deaf person, was the first physically disabled Miss America.

9. Ibid., 389, emphasis added.

10. Mary Astell, *A Serious Proposal to the Ladies, for the Advancement of Their True and Greatest Interest*, ed. Patricia Springborg (Brookfield, Vt.: Pickering and Chatto, 1997); Mary Wollstonecraft, *A Vindication of the Rights of Woman*, ed. Miriam Brody (New York: Penguin Books, 1992).

11. John I. Kitsuse and Malcolm Spector, "Toward a Sociology of Social Problems," *Social Problems* 20 (1973): 407–19. See also the essays in *Constructivist Controversies: Issues in Social Problems Theory*, ed. Gale Miller and James A. Holstein (New York: Aldine de Gruyter, 1993); Michel Foucault, *Discipline and Punish: The Birth of the Prison*, trans. Alan Sheridan (New York: Random House, 1977); Michel Foucault, *The History of Sexuality*, vol. 1, *An Introduction* (New York: Vintage Press, 1990a).

12. Gayatri Chakravorty Spivak, *In Other Worlds: Essays in Cultural Politics* (New York: Routledge, 1988), 77–78.

13. Judith Butler, *Gender Trouble* (New York: Routledge, 1990), 143–44.

14. Ludwig Wittgenstein, *Philosophical Investigations*, trans. G.E.M. Anscombe (New York: Macmillan, 1968).

15. Stanley Fish, *Is There a Text In this Class?* (Baltimore: Johns Hopkins University Press, 1980), 356.

16. Indeed, this has been the most commonly asked question when I have presented this work publicly, which is why I feel compelled to address it here. Particular thanks to the New York Society for Women in Philosophy's challenges to my inclusion of language in social construction, which helped me to clarify the "levels" imagery.

17. Peter Bachrach and Morton S. Baratz, "Two Faces of Power," *American Political Science Review* 56 (1962): 947–52. Bachrach and Baratz were, of course, responding to Robert Dahl's "The Concept of Power," *Behavioral Science* 2 (1957): 201–15.

18. Steven Lukes, *Power: A Radical View* (New York: Macmillan, 1974).

19. Peter Digeser, "The Fourth Face of Power," *Journal of Politics* 54, no. 4 (1992): 979–80.

20. It could also be argued that it includes identifiable agency as well, though that would require an "expanded" notion of agency that applied not only to particular individuals but to classes or groups of individuals, such as "capitalists" or "men."

21. Michel Foucault, "Two Lectures," in *Power/Knowledge: Selected Interviews and Other Writings, 1972–1977*, ed. Colin Gordon (New York: Pantheon Books, 1980), 93. See also Foucault, "Power and Strategies" and "The Eye of Power" in the same volume.

22. See Foucault 1990a.

23. Foucault, "Two Lectures," in Foucault 1980, 98.

24. Nancy Fraser, *Unruly Practices: Power, Discourse, and Gender in Contemporary Social Theory* (Minneapolis: University of Minnesota Press, 1989), 25.

25. Foucault, "Power and Strategies," in Foucault 1980.

26. Digeser 1992, 981.

27. Diana Coole, "Constructing and Deconstructing Liberty," *Political Studies* 41 (1993): 86.

28. Fraser 1989, 25.

29. Nancy J. Hirschmann, *Rethinking Obligation: A Feminist Method for Political Theory* (Ithaca: Cornell University Press, 1992).

30. Brown 1995, 167.

31. Drucilla Cornell, *Transformations: Recollective Imagination and Sexual Difference* (New York: Routledge, 1993), 1.

32. Judith Butler, *Bodies That Matter: On the Discursive Limits of "Sex"* (New York: Routledge, 1993), ix.

33. See "Afterword: Democracy, Difference, and Reconstruction," in Hirschmann (1992), for an overview of these debates.

34. Denise Riley, "A Short History of Some Preoccupations," and Judith Butler, "Contingent Foundations," both in *Feminists Theorize the Political*, ed. Judith Butler and Joan W. Scott (New York: Routledge, 1992).

35. Rosemary Hennessy, *Materialist Feminism and the Politics of Discourse* (New York: Routledge, 1993), 34; see also Alice Jardine, *Gynesis* (Cambridge: Harvard University Press, 1985) and Susan Hekman, *Women and Knowledge* (Boston: Northeastern University Press, 1990).

36. The fact that some men are treated like this—for instance, gay men, and perhaps particularly gay men of color—does not invalidate this specificity, since such men are treated as they are because of their so-called femininity, perceived as all the more dangerous because exhibited by a male body. On the issue of gay men's "passing," however, and the systematic advantages this gives them over women within the context of "heteropatriarchy," see Jacquelyn N. Zita, "Male Lesbians and the Postmodern Body," in *Hypatia: A Journal of Feminist Philosophy* 7, no. 4 (1992): 106–27.

37. Butler 1993, esp. the concluding chapter.

38. Jean Grimshaw, "Autonomy and Identity in Feminist Thinking," in *Feminist Perspectives in Philosophy*, ed. Morwenna Griffiths and Margaret Whitford (Bloomington: Indiana University Press, 1988).

39. Cornell 1993, 21.

40. Connolly 1993, 151.

41. See Nancy J. Hirschmann, "Feminist Standpoint as Postmodern Strategy," *Women and Politics* 18, no. 4 (1997).

42. Foucault 1990a, 31.

43. Linda Alcoff makes a similar point in "Dangerous Pleasures: Foucault and the Politics of Pedophilia," *Feminist Interpretations of Michel Foucault*, ed. Susan Hekman (University Park: Pennsylvania State University Press, 1996): 99–136.

44. Foucault 1980, particularly "Two Lectures."

45. This is a notion with which he also concludes volume 1; see Foucault 1990a, esp. 150–59.

46. Michel Foucault, *The History of Sexuality*, vol. 2, *The Use of Pleasure* (New York: Vintage Books, 1990b), 22.

47. Ibid., 169.

48. Ibid., 163.

49. Adriana Cavarero, "Toward a Theory of Sexual Difference," in *Diotima* (Milan: La Tartaruga, 1987), quoted in Teresa de Lauretis, "The Essence of the Triangle or, Taking the Risk of Essentialism Seriously: Feminist Theory in Italy, the U.S., and Britain," *Differences* 1, no. 2 (1989): 16.

50. Sharon Marcus, "Fighting Bodies, Fighting Words: A Theory and Politics of Rape Prevention," in *Feminists Theorize the Political*, ed. Judith Butler and Joan W. Scott (New York: Routledge, 1992), 391, 387.

51. Ibid. However, despite this focus on language, she seems to reject a feminist focus on legal reform, because it is premised on accepting patriarchy as inevitable and monolithic; it "implies that rape can only be feared or legally repaired, not fought" (Ibid., 388). But as feminist legal scholars would argue, efforts to prevent a victim's sexual history from being admitted into evidence and to remove the requirement that she show bruises to demonstrate nonconsent, have been important steps toward undermining key aspects of the "rape script."

52. Ibid., 389.

53. Catherine MacKinnon, *Feminism Unmodified: Discourses on Life and Law* (Cambridge: Harvard University Press, 1987), and *Only Words* (Cambridge: Harvard University Press, 1993).

54. "Not a Moral Issue," in MacKinnon 1987.

55. Michel Foucault, *Language, Countermemory, Practice: Selected Essays and Interviews*, ed. Donals F. Bouchard (Ithaca: Cornell University Press, 1977), 231–33. John McGowan also points out that "MacKinnon's description of patriarchy's omnipresence" is similar to both "Derrida's revelation of Western metaphysics' grounding distinctions in every text" and "Jameson's arguments for the encroachment of late capitalism everywhere," though I think he makes the obverse of my point: whereas I am here suggesting that MacKinnon is more discursively oriented than she admits, McGowan is suggesting that postmodernism has a more "top-down" view of power domination than many are willing to acknowledge. John McGowan, *Postmodernism and Its Critics* (Ithaca: Cornell University Press, 1991), 24.

56. Indeed, it is argued that social constructivism really came into its own through work on sexuality, particularly in the area of gay studies (see Edward Stein, *Forms of Desire: Sexual Orientation and the Social Construction Controversy*, [New York: Garland Publishers, 1982]). But I find that the dichotomous categories postulated in much of this literature—between social construction and "the real," between nominalism and essentialism—set up a "straw man" version of social constructivism (see, e.g., James Weinrich, "The Reality of Social Construction," in Stein [1982]).

57. Butler 1990, 30.

58. Ibid., 93–106, 28; Foucault 1990a, as well as "Two Lectures," "Body\Power," and "Truth and Power," in Foucault 1980.

59. Butler 1993, 223.

60. Brown 1995, 166–67.

61. Michel Foucault, *The Birth of the Clinic: An Archeology of Medical Perception* (New York: Vintage, 1994).

62. Jacques Derrida, *Margins of Philosophy*, trans. Alan Bass (Chicago: University of Chicago Press, 1982), 135.

63. Simone de Beauvoir, *The Second Sex*, trans. H. M. Parshley (New York: Vintage Books, 1968), 587–89, 604–5. On knowledge of the "subaltern," see Spivak 1988.

CHAPTER FOUR

1. In *Emile et Sophie; ou, Les Solitaires*, Rousseau's unfinished sequel to *Emile*, Sophie becomes pregnant with another man's child. She reveals this fact to Emile when he attempts to force himself on her; but Emile ceases his efforts when he realizes that her repeated refusals have not been the "wise refusals" which "give value to that which is granted," which Jean-Jacques recommended to the couple on their wedding night (Jean-Jacques Rousseau, *Emile: or, On Education*, trans. Allan Bloom [New York: Basic Books, 1979], 479), but rather genuine aversion. Desolated by her betrayal, Emile then abandons Sophie, and she dies. As perversely as Rousseau's writings invert gendered power, as I discussed in chapter 2, particularly when he denies the logical possibility of rape (*Emile* 358–59; see also my discussion in ch. 2), there is still a significant difference which feminists need to acknowledge between Emile's behavior and the perpetration of physical and sexual violence in the form of hitting, punching, and completed rape. Jean-Jacques

Rousseau, *Emile et Sophie; ou, Les Solitaires*, preface by Michel Feher (Paris: Rivage Poch/Petite Bibliothèque, 1994); see also Elizabeth Wingrove, *Rousseau's Republican Romance* (Princeton: Princeton University Press, 2000), 88–90.

2. Suzanne K. Steinmetz, "The Battered Husband Syndrome," *Victimology: An International Journal* 2, nos. 3/4 (1978): 499–509; Suzanne K. Steinmetz and Joseph S. Lucca, "Husband Battering," in *Handbook of Family Violence*, ed. Vincent B. Van Hasselt (New York: Plenum Press, 1988).

3. Elizabeth Pleck, Joseph H. Pleck, Marlyn Grossman, and Pauline B. Bart, "The Battered Data Syndrome," *Victimology: An International Journal* 2, nos. 3/4 (1977): 680. They pointed out that even if one conceded all of Steinmetz's claims—which were based on speculative and even absurd "evidence" of husband battering, such as comic strips—her data still showed wife abuse to be six times more frequent than husband abuse (681). They also showed Steinmetz's speculations about why battered husbands do not leave to be unfounded; the belief that battered husbands would be impoverished by alimony and child-support payments if they left flew in the face of statistics on disturbingly low rates of payment by divorced men, and showing that divorced men's standard of living rises while women's uniformly decreases (682). See also Trudy Mills, "Victimization and Self-Esteem: On Equating Husband Abuse and Wife Abuse," *Victimology: An International Journal* 9, no. 2 (1984): 254–61, which points out that woman battering lowers women's self esteem but that women's violence against husbands does not affect men's self esteem.

4. Pleck et al. (1977), 682–83. See also Arthur Z. Cantos, Peter H. Neidig, and K. Daniel O'Leary, "Inquiries of Women and Men in a Treatment Program for Domestic Violence," *Journal of Family Violence* 9, no. 2 (1994): 113–24; and Daniel G. Saunders, "Wife Abuse, Husband Abuse, or Mutual Combat? A Feminist Perspective on the Empirical Findings," in *Feminist Perspectives on Wife Abuse*, ed. Michelle Bograd and Kerstie Yllo (Newbury Park, Calif.: Sage Publications, 1988).

5. Rudy J. Aguilar and Narina Nunez Nightingale, "The Impact of Specific Battering Experiences on the Self-Esteem of Abused Women," *Journal of Family Violence* 9, no. 1 (1994): 35–45.

6. Murray A. Straus, Richard J. Gelles, and Suzanne K. Steinmetz, *Behind Closed Doors: Violence in American Families* (New York: Doubleday, 1981); Richard J. Gelles, *The Violent Home: A Study of Physical Aggression between Husbands and Wives* (Beverly Hills, Calif.: Sage Publications, 1974).

7. Patricia Tjaden and Nancy Thoennes, *Full Report of the Prevalence, Incidence, and Consequences of Violence against Women: Findings from the National Violence Against Women Survey*, report prepared for the U.S. Department of Justice (Washington, D.C., 2000), 29.

8. Tjaden and Thoennes 2000a, 27.

9. Straus, Gelles, and Steinmetz 1981.

10. Linda Gordon, *Heroes of Their Own Lives: The Politics and History of Family Violence* (New York: Viking, 1988); John Stuart Mill, *The Subjection of Women*, in *On Liberty and Other Essays* (New York: Oxford University Press, 1992).

11. Tjaden and Thoennes, 2000a; Ronet Bachman, "A Comparison of Annual Incidence Rates and Contextual Characteristics of Intimate-Perpetrated Violence against Women from the National Crime Victimization Survey (NCVS) and the National Violence against Women Survey (NVAWS)," *Violence Against Women* 6, no. 8 (2000): 839–67; Martin D. Schwartz, "Methodological Issues in the Use of Survey Data for Measuring and Characterizing Violence against Women," *Violence Against Women* 6, no. 8 (2000): 815–38.

12. Carol Hagemann-White, "European Research on the Prevalence of Violence against Women," *Violence Against Women* 7, no. 7 (2001): 732–33.

13. See, for example, American Psychological Association, *Violence and the Family* (Washington, D.C.: American Psychological Association, 1996); Panos Institute, *The Intimate Enemy: Gender Violence and Reproductive Health*, Panos Briefing no. 27 (London: Panos Institute, 1998), 1–20. U.S. Senator Paul Wellstone (D-Minn.), who has introduced legislation requiring employers to provide emergency leave for domestic-violence victims, has put the figure at one woman every thirteen seconds (http://www.senate.gov/~wellstone/dvstats.htm). Take Back the Night puts it at one woman every nine seconds (http://www.metdesigns.com/takeback/stats.html).

14. Renzetti maintains that lesbians are battered at the same rate as heterosexual women. Claire M. Renzetti, *Violent Betrayal: Partner Abuse in Lesbian Relationships* (Newbury Park, Calif.: Sage Publications, 1992). See also Kerry Lobel, ed., *Naming the Violence: Speaking Out about Lesbian Battering* (Seattle: Seal Press, 1986); David Island and Patrick Letellier, *Men Who Beat the Men Who Love Them: Battered Gay Men and Domestic Violence* (New York: Haworth Press, 1991). The National Lesbian Health Care Survey found that lesbians experienced even higher rates of abuse than heterosexual women (J. Bradford, C. Ryan, and E. D. Rothblum, "National Lesbian Health Care Survey: Implications for Mental Health Care," *Journal of Consulting and Clinical Psychology* 62 (1994): 228–42. But such figures often include lesbians' experiences of child abuse and incest, and not just intimate-partner violence. Moreover, Tjaden and Thoennes found that the majority of lesbians abused by partners were abused in prior relationships by *male* partners; 11 percent of lesbians were battered by female partners. Patricia Tjaden and Nancy Thoennes, *Extent, Nature, and Consequences of Intimate Partner Violence: Findings from the National Violence Against Women Survey*, report prepared for the U.S. Department of Justice (Washington D.C.: 2000b), 30.

15. Jay G. Silverman, "Dating Violence against Adolescent Girls and Associated Substance Use, Unhealthy Weight Control, Sexual Risk Behavior, Pregnancy, and Suicidality," *Journal of the American Medical Association*, 286 (August 1, 2001): 421–26; Barrie Levy and Patricia Giggins, *What Parents Need to Know about Dating Violence* (Toronto: Groups West Canada, 1995); Stacy L. Burstin, "Legal Responses to Teen Dating Violence," *Family Law Quarterly* no. 2 (1995): 331–56 (though she includes perpetrators as well as victims when numbering teens who experience intimate violence); Bernard Schissel, "Boys against Girls: The Structural and Interpersonal Dimensions of Violent Patriarchal Culture in the Lives of Young Men," *Violence Against Women* 6, no. 9 (2000): 965–66; Francine LaVoie, Line Robitaille, and Martine Hebert, "Teen Dating Relation-

ships and Aggression: An Exploratory Study," *Violence Against Women* 6, no. 1 (2000): 6–36.

16. Lawrence A. Greenfield, Michael R. Rand, Diane Craven, Patsy A. Klaus, Craig A. Perkins, Cheryl Ringel, Greg Warchol, Cathy Matson, and James Alan Fox, *Violence by Intimates: Analysis of Data on Crimes by Current or Former Spouses, Boyfriends, and Girlfriends, 1976–1996*, report prepared for the U.S. Department of Justice, Office of Justice Programs (Washington, D.C., 1998), v, 13, 43, 9, 42.

17. Federal Bureau of Investigation, *Crime in the United States 1998: Uniform Crime Reports* (Washington, D.C., 1998), 281.

18. Federal Bureau of Investigation, *The Structure of Family Violence: An Analysis of Selected Incidents* (Washington, D.C., 1995).

19. FBI 1998, 278.

20. Ruth E. Fleury, Cris M. Sullivan, Deborah I. Beybee, "When Ending the Relationship Does Not End the Violence: Women's Experiences of Violence by Former Partners," *Violence Against Women* 6, no. 12 (2000): 1364; Martha R. Mahoney, "Legal Images of Battered Women: Redefining the Issue of Separation," *Michigan Law Review* 90, no. 1 (1991): 1–94, 3; Madelaine Adelman, "No Way Out: Divorce-Related Domestic Violence in Israel," *Violence Against Women* 6, no. 11 (2000): 1223–1252.

21. Greenfield et al. 1998, v.

22. Ibid. Again, if the remaining 25 percent of victims are males, even allowing that a substantial portion of these incidents reflects women's efforts at self–defense, violence against men may be a serious problem.

23. Callie Marie Rennison and Sarah Welchans, *Intimate Partner Violence: Bureau of Justice Statistics Special Report* (Washington, D.C., 2000), 1–3. Though they cite the same decline in intimate-partner murders (from 3,000 in 1976), they also note that just over half of those had female victims. Thus, the actual number of females murdered by intimates declined only slightly, from just over 1,500 to just under 1,400.

24. Tjaden and Thoennes 2000a, iv.

25. Callie Marie Rennison, *Crime Victimization 2000: Changes 1999–2000 with Trends 1993–2000*, report prepared for the U.S. Department of Justice (Washington, D.C., 2001), 8.

26. L. Heise, M. Ellsberg, and M. Gottemoeller, "Ending Violence against Women," *Population Reports*, series L., n. 11 (Baltimore: Johns Hopkins School of Public Health, Population Information Program, 1999).

27. Ibid.

28. Hageman-White 2001, 734–38.

29. Adelman 2000, 1232.

30. Ola W. Barnett and Alyce D. LaViolette, *It Could Happen to Anyone: Why Battered Women Stay* (Newbury Park, Calif.: Sage Publications, 1993), xxi. Though I follow them in including pets under "property" violence, I believe there is a much more serious effect produced by killing or hurting a pet—a living creature capable of experiencing pain and fear—than, say, a lamp, no matter how "treasured" the lamp may be. Particularly significant is the emotional support that pets can provide battered women. See Clifton P. Flynn, "Woman's Best Friend: Pet

Abuse and the Role of Companion Animals in the Lives of Battered Women," *Violence Against Women* 6, no. 2 (2000), 162–77.

31. Roberta L. Valente, "Addressing Domestic Violence: The Role of the Family Law Practitioner," *Family Law Quarterly* 29, no. 2 (1995): 187–96, 188.

32. See, for instance, Burstin 1995, 335; Schissel 2000; Larry Tifft, *The Battering of Women* (Boulder: Westview Press, 1993), 18–22; and Edward W. Gondolf, "How Batterer Program Participants Avoid Reassault," *Violence Against Women* 6, no. 11 (2000): 1218–19, et passim, on the preponderance of "interruption" and the infrequency of "respect" as strategies used by batterers to prevent abusive incidents.

33. Jeffrey L. Edleson, Zvi Eisikovits, and Edna Guttman, "Men Who Batter Women: A Critical Review of the Evidence," *Journal of Family Issues* 6, no. 2 (1985): 229–47, 243.

34. Barnett and LaViolette 1993, 17.

35. Rennison and Welchans 2000, 4; Greenfield et al. 1998, 14, 43, Rennison 2001, 7.

36. Richard M. Tolman and Daniel Rosen, "Domestic Violence in the Lives of Women Receiving Welfare," *Violence Against Women* 7, no. 2 (2001): 146–47; Laura Lein, Susan E. Jacquet, Carol M. Lewis, Patricia R. Cole, and Bernice B. Williams, "With the Best of Intentions: Family Violence Option and Abused Women's Needs," *Violence Against Women* 7, no. 2 (2001): 194; Melanie Shepherd and Ellen Pence, "The Effect of Battering on the Employment Status of Women," *Affilia: A Journal of Women and Social Work* 3, no. 2 (1988), 55–61, 58.

37. Stephen French Gilson, Elizabeth DePoy, and Elizabeth Cramer, "Linking the Assessment of Self-Reported Functional Capacity with Abuse Experiences of Women with Disabilities," *Violence Against Women* 7, no. 2 (2001). See Pagelow (1992), 104, on how abused women's struggle for child custody is also affected negatively by physical handicaps, even when their disabilities were caused by the abuse.

38. Linda C. Lambert and Juanita M. Firestone, "Economic Context and Multiple Abuse Techniques," *Violence Against Women* 6, no. 1 (2000): 49–67.

39. Susan Moller Okin, *Justice, Gender and the Family* (New York: Basic Books, 1989), ch. 7; Joan Zorza, "Recognizing and Protecting the Privacy and Confidentiality Needs of Battered Women," *Family Law Quarterly* 29, no. 2 (1995): 273–311, 276.

40. Indeed, the reality of domestic violence transferred to the workplace and the cost to productivity has prompted corporations like Liz Claiborne and Mary Kay Cosmetics to develop organizations such as the Corporate Alliance to End Partner Violence (http://www.caepv.org), and intervention programs to assist battered women. See also Schafer 2001, H1.

41. Zorza 1995, 276. See also Anne Menard, "Domestic Violence and Housing," *Violence Against Women* 7, no. 6 (2001): 707–20; Jody Raphael, "Public Housing and Domestic Violence," *Violence Against Women* 7, no. 6 (2001): 699–706.

42. Fleury, Sullivan, and Beybee 2000; Mahoney 1991; Kurz 1996; Adelman 2000; Jean Giles-Simms, *Wife Battering: A Systems Theory Approach* (New York: Guildford Press, 1983), 62. But also see Tjaden and Thoennes 2000b, 37.

43. Mahoney 1991, 6; Walker 1989, 46–47, also suggests that women who leave are more likely to be killed.

44. Tjaden and Thoennes 2000b, 37, emphasis added.

45. C. W. Harlow, *Female Victims of Violent Crimes*, report prepared for the U.S. Department of Justice, NCJ-126826 (Washington, D.C., 1991).

46. L. Bensley, S. MacDonald, J. Van Eenwyk, K. Wynkoop Simmons, and D. Ruggles, "Prevalence of Intimate Partner Violence and Injuries: Washington, 1998," *Journal of the American Medical Association* 284, no. 5 (2000), 559–60.

47. Tifft 1993; Ellen Pence, "Some Thoughts on Philosophy," in *Coordinating Community Responses to Domestic Violence*, ed. Ellen Pence and M. F. Shepard (Thousand Oaks, Calif.: Sage Publications, 1999); Rebecca E. and Russell P. Dobash, "Violent Men and Violent Contexts," in *Rethinking Violence Against Women*, ed. Russell and Rebecca Dobash (Thousand Oaks, Calif.: Sage Publications, 1999).

48. Lenore Walker, *Terrifying Love: Why Battered Women Kill and How Society Responds* (New York: Harper and Row, 1989), 51–52; Richard Gelles, *Family Violence* (Newbury Park, Calif.: Sage Publications, 1987). See Schissel 2000, 968–69, on the links between "unpremeditated and nondisciplinary" violence (i.e., not corporal punishment) and boys' tendency to be abusive in dating relationships.

49. Liz Kelly, "How Women Define Their Experiences of Violence," in *Feminist Perspectives on Wife Abuse*, ed. Ellen Bograd and Kersti Yllo (Newbury Park, Calif.: Sage Publications, 1988), 114–32; Gail E. Wyatt, Julie Axelrod, Dorothy Chin, Jennifer Vargas Carmona, and Tamra Burns Loeb, "Examining Patterns of Vulnerability to Domestic Violence among African American Women," *Violence Against Women* 6, no. 5 (2000): 495–514.

50. Alison Towns and Peter Adams, "'If I Really Loved Him, He Would Be Okay': Women's Accounts of Male Partner Violence," *Violence Against Women* 6, no. 6 (2000): 573.

51. Ibid.; Judith Lorber, *Paradoxes of Gender* (New Haven: Yale University Press, 1994), 71.

52. Barnett and LaViolette 1993, 17, 78, 20; Renzetti 1992.

53. Kathleen J. Ferraro, "Hard Love: Letting Go of an Abusive Husband," *Frontiers: Journal of Women Studies* 4, no. 2 (1979): 16–18; Kathleen B. Jones, *Living between Danger and Love: The Limits of Choice* (New Brunswick, N.J.: Rutgers University Press, 2000); Wendy K. Taylor, Lois Magnussen, and Mary Jane Amundson, "The Lived Experience of Battered Women," *Violence Against Women* 7, no. 5 (2001): 581.

54. Richard Gelles and Claire Pedrick Cornell, *Intimate Violence in Families* (Newbury Park, Calif.: Sage Publications, 1990); Pagelow 1981.

55. Lorber 1994, 72; see also Taylor, Magnussen and Amundson 2001 on women's use of the police not to separate from the abuser but simply to interrupt a violent event.

56. Walker 1989, 37.

57. Mahoney 1991, 14–19.

58. Michele Cascardi and K. Daniel O'Leary, "Depressive Symptomatology, Self-Esteem, and Self-Blame in Battered Women," *Journal of Family Violence* 7 (1992): 249–59; Mary Ann Dutton, *Empowering and Healing the Battered*

*Woman: A Model for Assessment and Intervention* (New York: Springer, 1992); Lenore Walker, *The Battered Woman Syndrome* (New York: Springer, 1984).

59. Greenfield et al. 1998, 20.

60. Kathleen J. Ferraro, "Cops, Courts, and Battered Women," in *Violence against Women: The Bloody Footprints*, ed. Pauline Bart and Eileen Moran (Newbury Park, Calif.: Sage Publications, 1993), 166, and "Policing Woman Battering," *Social Problems* 36, no. 1 (1989): 61–74; Edem Avakame and James J. Fyfe, "Differential Police Treatment of Male-on-Female Spousal Violence: Additional Evidence on the Leniency Thesis," *Violence Against Women* 7, no. 1 (2001):22–45; Cheryl Hanna, "No Right to Choose: Mandated Victim Participation in Domestic Violence Prosecutions," *Harvard Law Review* 109 (1996); 1857; Raphael 2000, 699; Tifft 1993, 8.

61. Greenfield et al. 1998, 20.

62. Ferraro 1993, 166; Hanna 1996, 1858.

63. Alisa Smith, "It's My Decision, Isn't It? A Research Note on Battered Women's Perceptions of Mandatory Intervention Laws," *Violence Against Women* 6, no. 12 (2000): 1384.

64. Eve Buzawa, Gerald Hotaling, and Andrew Klein, "The Response to Domestic Violence in a Model Court: Some Initial Findings and Implications," *Behavioral Sciences and the Law* 16 (1998): 185–206.

65. Ferraro 1989, 64. For instance, police interpreted the statute to apply to married couples only, not cohabiting couples (65–66) and "community property" laws to mean that a man could not be arrested for damaging his wife's property (68–69). Though the point of the new law was to mandate arrest for misdemeanor violence, police still required "a level of evidence high enough for felony arrests" to establish probable cause (66). They made sexist assumptions about aggression: "a man physically assaulting a woman who was screaming and yelling at him could be construed as mutual combat," so that no arrest was made because the officers could not determine who was at fault (70). Police asserted that although a woman might want to press charges because she "was angry that night, she would cool down the next day and forget about charges" (69), and that domestic violence was unimportant and trivial in comparison to crimes like robbery (71), despite the pervasive belief that domestic violence calls put the police at greatest risk for injury. Finally, they perceived violence as "normal" for people of color, who as a whole were viewed as "deviant" (67–68).

66. Susan E. Bernstein, "Living under Seige: Do Stalking Laws Protect Domestic Violence Victims?" *Cardozo Law Review* 15 (1993): 525–67; Wayne E. Bradburn, "Stalking Statutes: An Ineffective Legal Remedy for Rectifying Perceived Problems with Today's Injunction System," *Ohio Northern University Law Review* 19 (1992): 271–88; Tjaden and Thoennes 2000a; Judith McFarlane, Pam Willson, Dorothy Lemmey, Ann Malecha, "Women Filing Assault Charges on an Intimate Partner: Criminal Justice Outcome and Future Violence Experienced," *Violence Against Women* 6, no. 4 (2000): 396–408.

67. Ferraro 1993, 170–73; J. David Hirschel, Ira W. Hutchison, III, and Charles W. Dean, "The Failure of Arrest to Deter Spouse Abuse," *Journal of Research in Crime and Delinquency* 29, no. 1 (1992): 7–33, 8.

68. Hanna 1996.

69. Carolyn Copps Hartley, "'He Said, She Said': The Defense Attack of Credibility in Domestic Violence Family Trials," *Violence Against Women* 7, no. 5 (2001): 510–44.

70. James Ptacek, *Battered Women in the Courtroom: The Power of Judicial Responses* (Boston: Northeastern University Press, 1999); Mahoney 1991; Zorza 1995, 282–83; "Victim's Protection Plea Ignored," *Philadelphia Inquirer*, February 15, 1996, A6; "New York Judge Refuses to Move Criticized Colleague," *Philadelphia Inquirer*, February 22, 1996, A10; "Judge Expresses Sympathy for Freed Man's Victim," *Philadelphia Inquirer*, February 29, 1996, A9.

71. Family Violence Project of the National Council of Juvenile and Family Court Judges, "Family Violence in Child Custody Statutes: An Analysis of State Codes and Legal Practice," *Family Law Quarterly* 29, no. 2 (1995): 197–227, 201. "Friendly parent" (not "parent friendly") laws award custody to the parent who is more likely to permit and encourage frequent contact with the child: the parent who is more "friendly" to the other is awarded custody.

72. Marjorie D. Fields, "The Impact of Spouse Abuse in Children and Its Relevance in Custody and Visitation Decisions in New York State," *Cornell Journal of Law and Public Policy* 3 (1994): 236–37; Rochelle F. Hanson, Benjamin E. Saunders, and Janet Kistner, "The Relations between Dimensions of Interparental Conflict and Adjustment in College-Age Offspring," *Journal of Interpersonal Violence* 7, no. 4 (1992): 435–53; Howard A. Davidson, "Child Abuse and Domestic Violence: Legal Connections and Controversies," *Family Law Quarterly* 29, no. 2 (1995): 357–73, esp. 358–59.

73. Family Violence Project (1995), 197–227, 204.

74. Fleury et al. 2000, 1376. The assumption that women use child custody vindictively also underlies the "friendly parent" laws discussed earlier.

75. Hanna 1996.

76. Greenfield et all 1998, 19.

77. Angela Brown, *When Battered Women Kill* (New York: Macmillan, 1987), 171–75. Ferraro (1993), 169, points out this down-side of mandatory-arrest policies, namely, that they result in more arrests of women who have tried to defend themselves.

78. Elizabeth Rapaport, "The Death Penalty and the Domestic Discount," in Fineman and Mykitiuk 1994, 238, 228.

79. James Ptacek, "Why Do Men Batter Their Wives?" in *Feminist Perspectives on Wife Abuse*, ed. Ellen Bograd and Kersti Yllo (Newbury Park, Calif.: Sage Publications, 1988), 152–55. See also Adam Jukes, *Why Men Hate Women* (London: Free Association Books, 1993), xxiii, 8.

80. Bensley et al. 2000, 559.

81. L. Kevin Hamberger, Bruce Ambuel, Anne Marbella, and Jennifer Donze, "Physician Interaction with Battered Women: The Women's Perspective," *Archives of Family Medicine* 7 (November/December 1998): 575–82; E. Stark, A. Flitcraft, W. Frazier, "Medicine and Patriarchal Violence: The Social Construction of a 'Private Event,'" *Intern Journal Health Service* 9 (1979): 461–93; Demie Kurz and Evan Stark, "Not-So-Benign Neglect: The Medical Response to Battering," in Bograd and Yllo 1988.

82. Smith 2000, 1395.

83. Zorza 1995, 285.

84. Barnett and LaViolette 1993, 34, 31–36, Evelyne C. White, *Chain, Chain, Change: For Black Women in Abusive Relationships*, second edition (Seattle: Seal Press, 1994), 71–72.

85. Greenfield et al. 1998, 13; Tjadan and Thoennes found that racial minorities experienced more IPV than whites, with the highest rates among American Indians and Alaska Natives (2000b, 25). The FBI's Uniform Crime Reports, however, indicate that whites experience more family violence than minorities (FBI 1998, 281–83.)

86. Callie Rennison, *Violent Victimization and Race 1998 with Trends 1993–98*, report prepared for the U.S. Department of Justice (Washington, D.C., 2001), 8. See also Edward W. Gondolf, Ellen Fisher, and J. Richard McFerron, "Racial Differences among Shelter Residents: A Comparison of Anglo, Black, and Hispanic Battered Women," and Lettie L. Lockhart, "Spousal Violence: A Cross-Racial Perspective," both in *Black Family Violence: Current Research and Theory*, ed. Robert L. Hampton (Lexington, Mass.: Lexington Books, D. C. Heath and Company, 1991).

87. Greenfield et al. 1998, 19; White 1994, 22–23, 25.

88. Kimberle Crenshaw, "Mapping the Margins: Intersectionality, Identity Politics, and Violence Against Women of Color," *Stanford Law Review* 43 (1991): 1241–99; White 1994, 41.

89. Nilda Rimonte, "A Question of Culture: Cultural Approval of Violence against Women in the Pacific-Asian Community and the Cultural Defense," *Stanford Law Review* 43 (1991): 1311–26.

90. Leslye E. Orloff, Deeana Jang, and Catherine F. Klein, "With No Place to Turn: Improving Legal Advocacy for Battered Immigrant Women," *Family Law Quarterly* 29, no. 2 (1995): 313–29, 313, 326–27; Crenshaw 1991, 1247–49.

91. Rosemary Ofeibea Ofei-Aboaguy, "Altering the Strands of the Fabric: A Preliminary Look at Domestic Violence in Ghana," *Signs: Journal of Women in Culture and Society* 19 no. 2 (1994): 924–38. See also Tibamanya Mwene Mushanga, "Wife Victimization in East and Central Africa," *Victimology: An International Journal* 2, no. 3/4, (1978): 479–85, and Orloff, Jang, and Klein 1995, 316.

92. For instance, a Chinese man who killed his wife by bashing her head with a hammer because she had an affair cited a cultural ritual where a man whose honor is so violated customarily threatens to kill his wife, but neighbors prevent the killing. The lack of such a community in the United States resulted in his carrying out his threats. Several such cases resulted in an increase in domestic violence within Asian communities in New York, and women reported that their batterers explicitly cited the case when confronting their victims as evidence that the judicial system allowed them to kill their wives. Melissa Spatz, "A 'Lesser' Crime: A Comparative Study of Legal Defenses for Men Who Kill Their Wives," *Columbia Journal of Law and Social Problems* 22 (1991): 597–638, 620. Alice J. Gallin, "The Cultural Defense: Undermining the Policies against Domestic Violence," *Boston College Law Review* 35 (1994): 723–45, esp. 728, 730, 735.

93. Asma Jahangir, *Civil and Political Rights, Including Questions of Disappearances and Summary Executions* (New York: United Nations Commission on Human Rights, 2000). See also Arin 2001 and Araji 2001.

94. United Nations Population Fund, *The State of the World Population*, ch. 3, "Ending Violence against Women and Girls," (New York: United Nations, 2000). See also Canan Arin, "Femicide in the Name of Honor in Turkey," *Violence Against Women* 7, no. 7, (2001): 821–25.

95. Sherene Razack, "What Is to Be Gained by Looking White People in the Eye? Culture, Race, and Gender in Cases of Sexual Violence," *Signs: Journal of Women in Culture and Society* 19, no. 2 (1994): 894–923, 918.

96. Ibid., 902.

97. Ibid., 913.

98. Uma Narayan, *Dislocating Cultures: Identities, Traditions, and Third-World Feminism* (New York: Routledge, 1997), ch. 3.

99. James W. Zion and Elsie B. Zion, "Hozho' Sokee'—Stay Together Nicely: Domestic Violence under Navajo Common Law," *Arizona State Law Journal* 25 (1993): 407–26.

100. Ibid., 422, quoting Charlotte Johnson Frisbie, "Traditional Navajo Women: Ethnographic and Life History Portrayals," *American Indian Quarterly* 6, nos. 1/2 (1982): 20.

101. Zion and Zion 1993, 417.

102. Crenshaw 1991, 1262–63.

103. Sarah Lucia Hoagland, *Lesbian Ethics: Toward New Values* (Palo Alto, Calif.: Institute of Lesbian Studies, 1989); see also the essays in *An Intimacy of Equals: Lesbian Feminist Ethics*, ed. Lilian Mohin (New York: Harrington Park Press, 1996).

104. Renzetti 1992, 90, 123, 100, 102, 93–96.

105. Some women report that fighting back reduces domestic violence, but most report it makes the violence worse, and that going limp is the most effective way to reduce injury. See Brown 1987; R. Emerson Dobash, Russell Dobash, Cathy Cavanagh and Monica Wilson, "Wife Beating: The Victims Speak," *Victimology: An International Journal* 2, nos. 3/4 (1978): 608–22.

106. Barnett and LaViolette 1993, 8.

107. Kersti Yllo and Murray A. Straus, "Patriarchy and Violence against Wives: The Impact of Structural and Normative Factors," *Journal of International and Comparative Social Welfare* 1 (1984): 1–13.

108. Michael D. Smith, "Patriarchal Ideology and Wife Beating: A Test of a Feminist Hypothesis," *Violence and Victims* 5, no. 4 (1990): 257–73, 268. Moreover, his finding of a secondary and equally direct connection between levels of education, employment, and income with such patriarchal values supported Bowker's theory of a "'patriarchal subculture' of wife beaters composed mainly of low-SES males who socialize their peers into the ideology of male dominance and the importance of keeping wives 'in line,' by force if necessary." See Lee H. Bowker, *Beating Wife Beating* (Lexington, Mass.: D. C. Heath and Co., 1983), and "The Effects of National Development on the Position of Married Women in the Third World: The Case of Wife-Beating," *International Journal of Comparative and Applied Criminal Justice* 9 (1985): 1–13.

109. Charles P. Ewing and Moss Aubrey, "Battered Women and Public Opinion: Some Realities about Myths," *Journal of Family Violence* 2 (1987): 257–64.

110. Karen M. Genteman, "Wife Beating: Attitudes of a Non-Clinical Population," *Victimology: An International Journal*, 9, no. 1 (1984): 109–19, 109, 111.

111. Ayaga Agula Bawah, "Women's Fears and Men's Anxieties: The Impact of Family Planning on Gender Relations in Northern Ghana," *Studies in Family Planning* 30, no. 1 (1999): 54–66.

112. United Nations Population Fund, 2000.

113. Donileen Loseke, *The Battered Woman and Shelters: The Social Construction of Domestic Violence* (Albany: State University of New York Press, 1992), 43.

114. Ibid., 153.

115. Ibid., 54, 39.

116. Walker 1989, 37 et passim; Jane C. Murphy, "Lawyering for Social Change: The Power of the Narrative in Domestic Violence Law Reform," *Hofstra Law Review* 21, no. 4 (1993): 1243–93; Mary Ann Dutton, "Understanding Women's Responses to Domestic Violence: A Redefinition of Battered Woman Syndrome," *Hofstra Law Review* 21, no. 4 (1993): 1191–1245.

117. Towns and Adams 2000.

118. Walker 1984. Barnett and LaViolette note that this self-blame decreases "over time as they realize that nothing they do makes a difference." Barnett and LaViolette 1993, 81 (see also Cascardi and O'Leary 1992). This may in part motivate women to kill their abusers, as fear mingles with rage.

119. Albert Memmi, *The Colonizer and the Colonized*, trans. Howard Greenfeld (Boston: Beacon Press, 1967).

120. Mildred Daley Pagelow, *Women=Battering: Victims and their Experiences* (Beverly Hills, Calif.: Sage Publications, 1981), 105, emphasis added; Tifft 1993, 82, emphasis added.

121. Gelles 1987, 140.

122. Barnett and LaViolette 1993, 13, 9, 13. See also Schissel 2000.

123. Towns and Adams 2000.

124. Barnett and LaViolette 1993, xxvi, 1.

125. Straus, Gelles, and Steinmetz (1981), Pagelow, Pleck, et al. 1978, Davidson 1995, Donald Dutton, *The Batterer: A Psychological Profile* (New York: Basic Books, 1995); Diana Doumas, Gayla Margolin, and Richard S. John, "The Intergenerational Transmission of Aggression across Three Generations," *Journal of Family Violence* 9, no. 2 (1994): 157–75.

126. Donald Dutton 1995, 141, 71.

127. Ibid., 84.

128. Philip Pettit, *A Theory of Freedom: From the Psychology to the Politics of Agency* (New York: Oxford University Press, 2001), 89, 120. I discuss Pettit's views on the relation between discourse and freedom in chapter 7 below.

129. Gondolf 2000; Ptacek 1988.

130. Sharon Marcus, "Fighting Bodies, Fighting Words: A Theory and Politics of Rape Prevention," in *Feminists Theorize the Political*, ed. Judith Butler and Joan W. Scott (New York: Routledge, 1992).

131. Martha R. Mahoney, "Victimization or Oppression? Women's Lives, Violence, and Agency," in *The Public Nature of Private Violence*, ed. Martha Albertson Fineman and Roxanne Mykitiuk (New York: Routledge, 1994), 62.

132. The most common legal defenses for a battered woman who kills her abuser are temporary insanity and battered-woman syndrome, viz., the argument that because the battered woman has become incapable of perceiving exit options, she inappropriately kills the abuser (for instance, when he is sleeping) rather than escaping. Angela Brown, Lenore Walker, and others, however, have argued that such killings should be described as self-defense. For instance, Brown discusses several similar case studies in which a man severely beats his partner and then lies down to go to sleep (often under the influence of alcohol or drugs), warning that he is going to kill her when he gets up. Given the violence of the recent attack, as well as a history of being tracked down when she has escaped before, the woman may believe such threats pose an "imminent" danger and see killing him while he is asleep as the only way to survive. Additionally, given that inequalities of strength reduce her chances of defending herself once the attack begins, a woman may resort to killing her abuser when she is most likely to succeed, often when the abuser is asleep (Brown 1987, 171–75). See also Elizabeth Schneider, "Equal Rights to Trial for Women: Sex Bias in the Law of Self Defense," *Harvard Civil Rights–Civil Liberties Law Review* 15 (1980): 623–47; and Walker 1989.

133. Mahoney 1994, 65

134. Homosexual battering could present a similar challenge, since a woman is not the victim. But many feminist critiques of patriarchy easily accommodate men's domination of other men; see Smith 1990 on "social patriarchy" versus "familial patriarchy," and Carole Pateman, *The Sexual Contract* (Palo Alto, Calif.: Stanford University Press, 1988) on "father patriarchy" versus "husband patriarchy." Lesbian battering thus provides a stronger potential challenge to the feminist claim, since there would seem to be no "patriarch" to begin with.

135. Renzetti 1992, 103, 34.

136. Jan Horsfall, *The Presence of the Past: Male Violence in the Family* (North Sydney, Australia: Allen and Unwin, 1991), 16.

137. National Institute of Justice, "At a Glance: The Impact of Arrest on Domestic Violence: Results from Five Policy Experiments," *National Institute of Justice Journal*, October 1999, 27.

138. Ibid., 27–28, emphasis added.

139. Greenfield et al. 1998, 19.

140. Mahoney 1991, 30.

141. Dutton 1992. See also Barnett and La Violette 1993, 124.

142. L. M. Tutty, B. A. Bidgood, and M. A. Rothery, "Support Groups for Battered Women—Research on Their Efficacy," *Journal of Family Violence* 8 no. 4 (1993): 325–43.

143. Judy Woods Cox and Cal D. Stoltenberg, "Evaluation of a Treatment Program for Battered Wives," *Journal of Family Violence* 6 (1991): 395–413.

144. Margrit Brückner, "Reflections on the Reproduction and Transformation of Gender Differences among Women in the Shelter Movement in Germany," *Violence Against Women* 7, no. 7 (2001): 770, 773. See also Sarah Haffner, "Wife Abuse in West Germany," *Victimology: An International Journal* 2, nos. 3/4 (1978): 472–76.

145. Tifft 1993, 134. See Maryann Syers and Jeffrey L. Edleson, "The Combined Effects of Coordinated Criminal Justice Intervention in Woman Abuse," *Journal of Interpersonal Violence* 7, no. 4 (1990): 490–502.

146. Smith 2000, 1386.
147. Mahoney (1991), 55.

CHAPTER FIVE

1. Demi Kurz, "Women, Welfare, and Domestic Violence," in *Whose Welfare?* ed. Gwendolyn Mink (Ithaca: Cornell University Press, 1999); Mary Ann Allard, Randy Albelda, Mary Ellen Colten, and Carol Cosenze, *In Harm's Way? Domestic Violence, AFDC Receipt, and Welfare Reform in Massachusetts* (Boston: McCormack Institute, University of Massachusetts-Boston, February 1997); Laura Lein, Susan E. Jacquet, Carol M. Lewis, Patricia R. Cole and Bernice B. Williams, "With the Best of Intentions: Family Violence Option and Abused Women's Needs," *Violence Against Women* 7, no. 2 (2001): 194; Anne Menard, "Domestic Violence and Housing," *Violence Against Women* 7 no. 6 (2001): 708; Richard M. Tolman and Daniel Rosen, "Domestic Violence in the Lives of Women Receiving Welfare," *Violence Against Women* 7, no. 2 (2001): 142.

2. As Mimi Abramovitz notes, ADC was "designed to release [mothers] . . . from the wage-earning role" so they could care for their children and "make them citizens capable of contributing to society." Mimi Abramovitz, *Regulating the Lives of Women: Social Welfare Policy from Colonial Times to the Present* (Boston: South End Press 1988), 315. See also Frances Fox Piven, "Women and the State: Ideology, Power, and Welfare," in *For Crying Out Loud: Women's Poverty in the United States*, ed. Diane Dujon and Ann Withorn (Boston: South End Press, 1996); and Julia S. O'Connor, Ann Shola Orloff, and Sheila Shaver, *States, Markets, Families: Gender, Liberalism and Social Policy in Australia, Canada, Great Britain and the United States* (Cambridge: Cambridge University Press, 1999), e.g., 148.

3. This is arguably truer in the United States and "liberal" welfare regimes than in the social democratic or even conservative-corporatist welfare regimes of northern Europe, which tend to provide more generous benefits to mothers and others. See Evelyne Huber and John Stephens, "Welfare State and Production Regimes in the Era of Retrenchment," Occasional Paper no. 1, Institute for Advanced Study, School of Social Science February 1999, which can be accessed at http://www2.admin.ias.edu/ss/home/papers.html.

4. Kathy Ferguson, *The Feminist Case against Bureaucracy* (Philadelphia: Temple University Press, 1984); Wendy Brown, *States of Injury: Power and Freedom in Late Modernity* (Princeton: Princeton University Press, 1995), 192.

5. Ann Shola Orloff, "Ending the Entitlements of Poor Single Mothers: Changing Social Policies, Women's Employment and Caregiving in the Contemporary United States," in *Women and Welfare: Theory and Practice in the United States and Europe*, ed. Nancy J. Hirschmann and Ulrike Liebert (New Brunswick, N.J.: Rutgers University Press, 2001).

6. Drucilla Cornell, *At the Heart of Freedom: Feminism, Sex, and Equality* (Princeton: Princeton University Press, 1999).

7. Catherine R. Albiston and Laura Beth Nielsen, "Welfare Queens and Other Fairy Tales: Welfare Reform and Unconstitutional Reproductive Controls," *Howard Law Journal* 38, no. 3 (1995): 473–519; Nell Irvin Painter, "Hill, Thomas, and the Use of Racial Stereotype," in *Race-ing Justice, En-gendering Power: Es-*

*says on Anita Hill, Clarence Thomas, and the Construction of Social Reality,* ed. Toni Morrison (New York: Pantheon Books, 1992), 201–2.

8. Elizabeth Bussiere, *(Dis)Entitling the Poor: The Warren Court, Welfare Rights, and the American Political Tradition* (State College: Pennsylvania State University Press, 1997), 167; Karen Seccombe, *So You Think I Drive a Cadillac? Welfare Recipients' Perspectives on the System and Its Reform* (Boston: Allyn and Bacon, 1999), 11; U.S. Department of Health and Human Services, "Clinton Administration Makes Awards to Change the Culture of Welfare," press release, November 6, 1995.

9. See, for instance Martha Fineman, "Images of Mothers in Poverty Discourses," *Duke Law Journal* 102, no. 2 (1991): 274–95; and Lucy A. Williams, "The Ideology of Division: Behavior Modification Welfare Reform Proposals," *Yale Law Journal* 102, no. 3 (1992): 719–46.

10. The U.S. Department of Health and Human Services reports that although people of color constituted two-thirds of families on TANF, whites are still the largest single group, slightly larger than African Americans. Cole 2001, 227. See also Gwendolyn Mink, *Welfare's End* (Ithaca: Cornell University Press, 1998), 120; Laura Flanders, with Janine Jackson and Dan Shadoam, "Media Lies: Media, Public Opinion, and Welfare," in Dujon and Withorn 1996, 34; Seccombe 1999, 15.

11. Roberta M. Spalter-Roth and Heidi I. Hartman, "AFDC Recipients as Care-Givers and Workers: A Feminist Approach to Income Security Policy for American Women," *Social Politics: International Studies in Gender, State, and Society* 1 (1994): 190–210; LaDonna Ann Pavetti, "Dynamics of Welfare and Work: Exploring the Process by Which Women Work Their Way off Welfare," U.S. Deptartment of Health and Human Services, May 1992; Heidi Hartmann and Hsaio-Ye Yi, "The Rhetoric and Reality of Welfare Reform," in Hirschmann and Liebert, 2001.

12. Albiston and Nielsen 1995; Nancy Fraser and Linda Gordon, "A Genealogy of Dependency: Tracing a Keyword of the U.S. Welfare State," *Signs: A Journal of Women and Culture in Society* 19, no. 2 (1994): 309–36; Martha Albertson Fineman, "Dependencies," in Hirschmann and Liebert 2001.

13. House Committee on Ways and Means, Subcommittee on Human Resources, *Hearing on Welfare and Marriage Issues,* May 22, 2001; Statement of David Popenoe. Available online at http://waysandmeans.house.gov/humres/107cong/5–22–01/5–22pope.htm.

14. Douglas J. Besharov and Peter Germanis, "Welfare Reform—Four Years Later," *Public Interest,* no. 140 (Summer 2000); Marcia K. Meyers, "How Welfare Offices Undermine Welfare Reform," *American Prospect* 11, no. 15 (2000).

15. See Bussiere 1997, Gwendolyn Mink, *The Wages of Motherhood: Inequality in the Welfare State, 1917–1942* (Ithaca: Cornell University Press, 1995); Wendy Sarvasy, "Beyond the Difference versus Equality Policy Debate: Postsuffrage Feminism, Citizenship, and the Quest for a Feminist Welfare State," *Signs: A Journal of Women and Culture in Society* 17, no. 2, (1992).

16. John Rawls, *A Theory of Justice* (Cambridge: Harvard University Press, 1971); Nancy J. Hirschmann, *Rethinking Obligation: A Feminist Method for Political Theory* (Ithaca: Cornell University Press, 1992), ch. 2.

17. Cole 2001; Lein et al. 2001; Levin 2001.

18. See the essays in Hirschmann and Liebert 2001.

19. See Sarah Lyall, "Blair Scolds British 'Workless Class' in Outline of Welfare Plan," *New York Times*, June 3, 1997, A3; Warren Hoge, "First Test for Britain's Camelot: Welfare Reform," *New York Times*, January 4, 1998, 1; and Joyce Mushaben, "Challenging the Maternalist Presumption: The Gender Politics of Welfare Reform in Germany and the United States," in Hirschmann and Liebert 2001.

20. William Kelso, *Poverty and the Underclass: Changing Perceptions of the Poor in America* (New York: New York University Press, 1994).

21. Brown 1995, 18.

22. Although in Illinois pursuing education is considered equivalent to working for purposes of continuing to receive welfare, this is the exception, not the rule. In Pennsylvania, for instance, "General and vocational education, English-as-a-second language or job skills training" (but not college or graduate education) can be used to meet the work requirement for a maximum of twelve months; after that period, recipients may pursue education in addition to working, but such pursuits do not "count" as work that permits continuation of benefits (Pennsylvania Department of Public Welfare, *Temporary Assistance for Needy Families: State Plan*, 1999, which can be accessed at http://www.dpw.state.pa.us/oim/pdf/TANFstateplan.pdf). For various accounts of welfare's resistance to recipients' pursuit of education, see Diane Dujon, "Out of The Frying Pan: Reflections of a Former Welfare Recipient," in Dujon and Withorn, 1996; James M. O'Neill, "New Rules Alter Course of Students on Welfare," *Philadelphia Inquirer*, April 25, 1999, B1; and Rena Singer, "Welfare Cutoffs Need Adjustments, Committee Told," *Philadelphia Inquirer*, Feburary 17, 1999, B1.

23. Mink 1998, 66.

24. CLASSP 2001; Lein et al. 2001; however, they argue that two-thirds of battered women on welfare do not in fact utilize the Family Violence Option, because other barriers such as inadequate child care, housing, transportation and pay, were more significant in blocking their efforts at employment.

25. Pennsylvania Deptartment of Public Welfare, "1999–2000 Budget Highlights" (Harrisburg, Pa.: February 2, 1999); Monica Yant, "Imagining Her Life, No Longer on Welfare," *Philadelphia Inquirer*, February 16, 1999, A1, A8.

26. Hartmann and Yi 2001; Roth and Hartmann 1994.

27. Linda Gordon, *Pitied but Not Entitled: Single Mothers and the History of Welfare* (New York: Free Press, 1994); Mink 1995.

28. Lucy White, "No Exit: Rethinking 'Welfare Dependency' from a Different Ground," *Georgetown Law Journal* 81 (1993): 1961–2002, 1971.

29. Ibid., 1997.

30. Ibid., 1976.

31. Kathryn Edin, "Surviving the Welfare System: How AFDC Recipients Make Ends Meet in Chicago," *Social Problems* 38, no. 4, (1991): 462–74. See also White 1993.

32. Lisa Dodson, *Don't Call Us Out of Name: The Untold Lives of Women and Girls in Poor America* (Boston: Beacon Press, 1998); Lisa Dodson, "At the

Kitchen Table: Poor Women Making Public Policy," in Hirschmann and Liebert 2001.

33. See, for instance, Dodson 1998, esp. 126–28; Edin 1991; Marta Elliott, "Impact of Work, Family, and Welfare Receipt on Women's Self-Esteem in Young Adulthood," *Social Psychology Quarterly* 59, no. 1 (1996): 80–95; Robin Rogers-Dillon, "The Dynamics of Welfare Stigma," *Qualitative Sociology* 18, no. 4 (1995): 439–56; Laura Walker, "If We Could, We Would Be Someplace Else," in Dujon and Withorn 1996.

34. Flanders et al. 1996; Jason DeParle, "Despising Welfare, Pitying Its Young," *New York Times*, December 18, 1994, B1; Seccombe 1999.

35. Edin 1991, 469–70.

36. Dodson 2001.

37. Though Bussiere and Mink detail women's contribution to sexist, racist, and classist discourses surrounding welfare, Susan J. Carroll and Kathleen Casey argue that Republican and Democratic women were largely responsible for alleviating some of the harshest aspects of PRWORA. "Welfare Reform in the 104th Congress: Institutional Position and the Role of Women," in Hirschmann and Liebert 2001.

38. Seccombe 1999.

39. Gloria T. Hull, Patricia Bell Scott, and Barbara Smith, eds., *All the Women are White, All the Blacks are Men, but Some of Us are Brave: Black Women's Studies* (Old Westbury, N.Y.: Feminist Press, 1982).

40. Lisa Catanzarite and Vilma Ortiz, "Racial/ Ethnic Differences in the Impact of Work and Family on Women's Poverty," *Research in Politics and Society* 5 (1995): 132–33. See also House Committee on Ways and Means, Subcommittee on Human Resources, *Hearing on Welfare and Marriage Issues*, May 22, 2001, Statement of Kathryn Edin, for female welfare recipients' reluctance to marry because they see men as unfaithful, untrustworthy, and exploitive. Edin points out, however, a thematic undercurrent expressed by the women she interviewed, namely, the inability of poor men, and particularly men of color, to obtain steady employment. Her statement is available online at http://waysandmeans.house.gov/humres/107cong/5-22-01/5-22edin.htm. See also Kathryn Edin and Laura Lein, *Making Ends Meet: How Single Mothers Survive Welfare and Low-wage Work* (New York: Russell Sage Foundation, 1997).

41. Thanks to Liz Bussiere for some stimulating email exchanges on this topic.

42. Fineman 2001; Eva Feder Kittay, "From Welfare to a Public Ethic of Care," in Hirschmann and Liebert 2001.

43. Sarvasy 1992, 346.

44. Bussiere 1997; Fraser and Gordon 1992; Mink 1998.

45. For a discussion of Hobbes's well-known argument about the compatibility of force, necessity, and free choice, see Hirschmann 1992, 35–39; and Carol Pateman, *The Problem of Political Obligation: A Critique of Liberal Theory* (Berkeley: University of California Press, 1985), ch. 2.

46. Ronald Dworkin, *Taking Rights Seriously* (Cambridge: Harvard University Press, 1977).

47. Brown 1995, 158.

48. Hirschmann 1992, Carole Pateman, *The Sexual Contract* (Palo Alto, Calif.: Stanford University Press, 1988).

49. Bussiere 1997, ch. 7, discussing *Shapiro v. Thompson*, 394 U.S. 618 (1969).

50. See *Saenz v. Roe*, 119 S. Ct. 1518 (1999); *Maldonado v. Houstoun*, no. 97–1893 (3d Cir. September 9, 1998), Clearinghouse no. 52168.

51. Carol Gilligan, *In A Different Voice: Psychological Theory and Women's Development* (Cambridge: Harvard University Press, 1982).

52. Including, some might argue, myself. In Hirschmann 1992, I use the work of Gilligan and others to develop an argument that social-contract theory is "structurally sexist," and that feminist values of caring and connection derived from such psychological research pointed toward a redefinition of the concept of "obligation." In the process, I critiqued standard rights discourse as similarly masculinist. Some will undoubtedly read this chapter as a retraction, but that would be to misinterpret both my earlier book and the present one. My critique of "rights" in *Rethinking Obligation* was a critique of the classic liberal vision but did not preclude the feminist rethinking of rights that I am engaged in here. Both here and in *Rethinking Obligation*, I argue that women's historical experiences of care need to *inform*—not to *replace*—public discourses and political theories, and that their doing so should lead the way to reconfigurations of central liberal conceptions, such as obligation and rights. Just as obligation, which is seen in liberalism as a product of individualistic choice, had to be rethought through notions of connection, relationship, and positive responsibility, so do rights, which are seen in liberalism as similarly individualistic and importantly related to choice and consent, need to be rethought in terms of care, connection, and positive responsibility. See Nancy J. Hirschmann, "Difference as an Occasion for Rights: A Feminist Rethinking of Rights, Liberalism, and Difference" in *Critical Review of International Social and Political Philosophy* 2, no. 1 (1999): 27–55, for a fuller explication of my views on how such a reconfigured conception of rights should be developed.

53. Pateman 1988; Hirschmann 1999.

54. Brown 1995, 158

55. Ibid., 18.

56. Joan Tronto, "Who Cares? Public and Private Caring and the Rethinking of Citizenship," in Hirschmann and Liebert 2001.

57. Mink 1995; Bussiere 1997.

58. Kittay 2001.

59. O'Connor, Orloff, and Shaver 1999, 148, 144.

60. Orloff 2001. Indeed, even in Sweden, which is often cited as *the* model of a woman-friendly welfare state, and which allows fifteen months of caretaker leave for either parent, such benefits are market driven: one has the "right," not to be compensated for care work per se, but to a job in the market economy, a right that in turn entails not being penalized for the work interruptions that having and caring for a baby brings about. Furthermore, benefits are linked to wages; specifically, benefits total 80 percent of the caretaker's working wage, with much

lower amounts going to caretakers not in the labor force. Thanks to John Stephens for pointing this out.

61. Judith Butler, *Bodies That Matter: On the Discursive Limits of "Sex"* (New York: Routledge, 1993). Of course, as I discussed in chapter 4, Butler would not appreciate the use to which I have put her words, for she would reject the notion that "reconstituting the system" is even possible.

## CHAPTER SIX

1. As Roxanne Euben notes, "the Muslim woman covered head to foot in the Iranian *chador*" is "the most common visual image of Islamic fundamentalism," though the Afghan woman in the burqa has probably already replaced that image. Roxanne L. Euben, *Enemy in the Mirror: Islamic Fundamentalism and the Limits of Modern Rationalism* (Princeton: Princeton University Press, 1999), xiv.

2. See, for instance, "Islam's Many Faces," *Economist*, May 31, 1997, 16; Barbara Freyer Stowasser, *Women in the Qur'an, Traditions, and Interpretation* (New York: Oxford University Press, 1994), 127–28; Deniz Kandiyoti, "Women and Islam: What are the Missing Terms?" *Dossier* 5/6 (1988–89).

3. Farida Shaheed distinguishes between the adjectives "Islamic" and "Muslim," holding that the former refers to "that which is ordained" and the latter to "the assimilation of Islam into prevailing structures, systems, and practices." Farida Shaheed, "Controlled or Autonomous: Identity and the Experience of the Network, Women Living under Muslim Laws," *Signs: Journal of Women in Culture and Society* 19, no. 4 (1994): 998. Her distinction between religion and the *interpretation and use of* religion to express something else, such as culture or political resistance, is a theme I pursue here; but since many of the scholars to whom I refer in this chapter do not follow Shaheed's terminology, I use the adjectives "Islamic" and "Muslim" interchangeably.

4. See for instance Laurie Goodstein, "Muslims Nurture Sense of Self on Campus," *New York Times*, November 3, 2001; Um Yaqoob, "Lifting the Veil," *Women's International Net Magazine* 46, part A (September 2001).

5. Jan Goodwin and Jessica Neuwirth, "The Rifle and the Veil," *New York Times*, October 19, 2001.

6. See, for instance, Amartya Sen, "Human Rights and Asian Values," *New Republic* 217, nos. 2–3 (1997): 35–40.

7. See Stanlie James, "U.N. Treatment of Multiple Oppressions: A Black Feminist Perspective," *Journal of African Policy Studies* vol. 1, no. 1 (1995): 53–69. See also Arati Rao, "The Politics of Gender and Culture in International Human Rights Discourse"; Maria Suarez Toro, "Popularizing Women's Human Rights at the Local Level: A Grassroots Methodology for Setting the International Agenda"; Sima Wali, "Human Rights for Refugee and Displaced Women"; and Nadia H. Youssef, "Women's Access to Productive Resources: The Need for Legal Instruments to Protect Women's Rights"; all in *Women's Rights, Human Rights*, ed. Julie Peters and Andrea Wolper (New York: Routledge, 1995).

8. Martha C. Nussbaum, *Women and Human Development: The Capabilities Approach* (New York: Cambridge University Press, 2000), 178.

9. See particularly Homa Hoodfar, "The Veil in Their Minds and on Our Heads: The Persistence of Colonial Images of Muslim Women," *Review of Feminist Research* 22, nos. 3/4 (1993): 5–18.

10. Margot Badran, "Gender Activism: Feminists and Islamists in Egypt," in *Identity Politics and Women: Cultural Reassertions and Feminisms in International Perspective*, ed. Valentine M. Moghadam (Boulder: Westview Press, 1994a), 208; Marie-Aimée Hélie-Lucas, "The Preferential Symbol of Islamic Identity: Women in Muslim Personal Laws," in ibid., 399; Uma Narayan, *Dislocating Cultures: Identities, Traditions, and Third World Feminism* (New York: Routledge, 1997).

11. Hoodfar 1993, 5.

12. Amy Waldman, "Behind the Burka: Women Subtly Fought Taliban," *New York Times*, November 19, 2001a. For an account of violence against women in Iran for improper dress, see Akram Mirhosseini, "After the Revolution: Violations of Women's Human Rights in Iran," in *Women's Rights, Human Rights*, ed. Julie Peters and Andrea Wolper (New York: Routledge, 1995).

13. Deborah Ellis, *Women of the Afghan War* (Westport, Conn.: Praeger Publishers, 2000), 62.

14. Quoted in "Kabul's Women Face Tough Winter," United Press International, November 27, 1996.

15. Jackie Rowley, "The Invisible Sex," *Times*, London, October 12, 1996; Goodwin and Neuwirth 2001; Waldman 2001a. Also see Afghan Women's Network list-serve mailing, October 17, 1996, Save the Children Organization. But Amy Waldman reports that the written penal code promulgated by the Taliban's leader, Mullah Muhammad Omar, which the Ministry for the Promotion of Virtue and Prevention of Vice was supposed to enforce, actually permitted male doctors to treat women in a medical emergency, as long as they "only look at the part that the patient needs looked at; nowhere else can be touched or seen." The only restriction on female doctors is to wear "old clothes, and no ornamentation." Obviously, the enforcement of this written code exceeded its mandate. Amy Waldman, "No TV, No Chess, No Kites: Taliban Penal Code, from A to Z," *New York Times*, November 22, 2001b. See also Nancy Hatch Dupree, "Afghan Women under the Taliban," in *Fundamentalism Reborn? Afghanistan and the Taliban*, ed. William Maley (New York: New York University Press, 1998), 156. The translation she offers of the rules regarding dress for female doctors is "simple clothes," rather than "old."

16. Suzanne Goldberg, "Women Wait to Lift Veil of Silence," *Guardian* (London), December 27, 1996, 12; Sarah Horner, "Women of Kabul Hide Behind Veil of Fear," *Independent* (London), September 30, 1996, 11; Waldman 2001a; Ellis 2000, 62.

17. Leila Ahmed, *Women and Gender in Islam* (New Haven: Yale University Press, 1992), 152.

18. Ibid., 220. Also, Shahin Gerami, "The Role, Place, and Power of Middle-Class Women in the Islamic Republic," in Moghadam 1994a, 332.

19. Hoodfar 1993, 10.

20. Leila Ahmed, "Feminism and Feminist Movements in the Middle East, a Preliminary Exploration: Turkey, Egypt, Algeria, People's Democratic Republic

of Yemen," in *Women and Islam*, ed. Azizah al-Hibri (New York: Pergamon Press, 1982), 164.

21. Ellis 2000, 8–9, 217.

22. Dupree 1998, 145, 147.

23. Mohamad Tavakoli-Targhi, "Women of the West Imagined: The *Farangi* Other and the Emergence of the Woman Question in Iran," in Moghadam 1994a, 98.

24. Ibid., 99. It should be noted that Tavakoli-Targhi's "positive" and "negative" conceptions of freedom do not draw on Berlin's, the ones that I have deployed in this book. Although the latter conceptions do have a loose relationship to hers, she uses the terms "positive" and "negative" normatively, that is, as equivalent to "good" and "bad."

25. Ibid., 104, 102, 105.

26. Ibid., 99, 114.

27. Ibid., 99.

28. See Frantz Fanon, "On National Culture," in Fanon, *The Wretched of the Earth*, trans. Constance Farrington (New York: Grove Press, 1963); and Frantz Fanon, "Algeria Unveiled," in Fanon, *A Dying Colonialism*, trans. Haakon Chevalier (New York: Grove Press, 1965). Though Fanon is criticized by feminists for his views on veiling as part of the Algerian nationalist movement, I agree with Madhu Dubey that Fanon's arguments actually cohere with feminist ideals. See Madhu Dubey, "The 'True Lie' of the Nation: Fanon and Feminism," in *Differences* 10, no. 2 (1998):1–29. For criticisms of Fanon, see Diana Fuss, *Identification Papers* (New York: Routledge, 1995) and Anne McClintock, *Imperial Leather: Race, Gender, and Sexuality in the Colonial Conquest* (New York: Routledge, 1995).

29. Alessandra Stanley, " U.S. Tempers Its Voice on Women's Status to Avoid Alienating Muslim Allies," *New York Times*, October 27, 2001; Goodwin and Neuwirth 2001; Waldman 2001; Ahmed 1992.

30. Hoodfar 1993, 10.

31. Stowasser 1994, 38, 6, 21.

32. Euben 2000.

33. Ahmed 1992.

34. Ibid., 110.

35. Shaheed 1994, 1003.

36. Dexter Filkins, "In Fallen Taliban City, a Busy, Busy Barber," *New York Times*, November 13, 2001.

37. Shaheed 1994, 998.

38. Nawal el Sadawi, "Woman and Islam," in al-Hibri 1982, 199; Cherifa Bouatta and Doria Cherifati-Merabtine, "The Social Representation of Women in Algeria's Islamist Movement," in Moghadam 1994a, 194. Also see Fatima Mernissi, *Beyond the Veil: Male-Female Dynamics in a Modern Muslim Society* (Bloomington: Indiana University Press, 1987), xvi.

39. El Sadawi 1982.

40. Ibid., 198.

41. Lila Abu-Lughod, *Writing Women's Worlds: Bedouin Stories* (Berkeley: University of California Press, 1993), 74.

42. Fatima Mernissi, "Virginity and Patriarchy," in al-Hibri 1982, 189. See also Alya Baffoun, "Women and Social Change in the Muslim Arab World," in al-Hibri 1982.

43. Fatima Mernissi, *The Veil and the Male Elite*, trans. Mary J. Lakeland (Reading, Mass.: Addison-Wesley, 1991); Stowasser 1994, 90–94.

44. Mernissi 1987, vii.

45. See particularly Ahmed 1982, 164, and Badran 1994, esp. 203.

46. Valentine M. Moghadam, "Reform, Revolution, and Reaction: The Trajectory of the 'Woman Question' in Afganistan," in *Gender and National Identity: Women and Politics in Muslim Societies*, ed. Valentine M. Moghadam (Atlantic Highlands, N.J.: Zed Books, 1994b), 82.

47. Hélie-Lucas 1994, 399, 394. See also Badran 1994, 208; Gerami 1994, 336.

48. Ahmed 1992, 166; Shaheed 1994, 997–98.

49. Hélie-Lucas 1994, 395; Azizah al-Hibri, "A Study of Islamic Herstory: Or How Did We Ever Get into This Mess?" in al-Hibri 1982, 216.

50. Arlene Elowe MacLeod, "Hegemonic Relations and Gender Resistance: The New Veiling as Accommodating Protest in Cairo," *Signs* 17, no. 3 (1992): 539. See also Nesta Ramazani, "The Veil—Piety or Protest?" *Journal of South Asian and Middle Eastern Studies*, 7, no. 2 (1983): 20–36.

51. Marcia Kunstel and Joseph Albright, "Focus on the Wealth of New Nations," *Atlanta Constitution*, June 15, 1997, 8A. In Albania as well, where headscarves are the only "veiling" engaged in, many Muslim women do not cover their heads. This could testify to the effects of communism in decomposing Islam in these countries; see Sima Wali, "Repatriation and the Reconstruction of Afghanistan: The Role of Women," *Migration World* 22, no. 4 (1994): 26–28.

52. Lila Abu-Lughod, *Veiled Sentiments: Honor and Poetry in a Bedouin Society* (Berkeley: University of California Press, 1986), 79, 87. Subsequent references will be made in the text.

53. Abu-Lughod 1993, 78.

54. Ibid., 74, 77.

55. Ibid., 78; goats appear to have a lascivious connotation.

56. Particularly in Abu-Lughod 1993.

57. Michel Foucault, *The History of Sexuality*, vol. 1, *An Introduction* (New York: Vintage Books, 1990).

58. Arlene Elowe MacLeod, *Accommodating Protest: Working Women, the New Veiling, and Change in Cairo* (New York: Columbia University Press, 1991), xiv. Subsequent references will be made in the text.

59. Stowasser 1994, 129

60. It is not clear whether the veil really does protect women from street harassment, or whether this is simply a rationalization. For instance, when a man told MacLeod that a woman "walking alone" on the street was inviting sex, she mentioned that his sisters often walked alone coming home from work. He immediately replied, "That is completely different!" (84). But there is no linking of this "difference" to the veil; the man was not clearly referring to *unveiled* women walking alone, nor did he except his sisters from the charge of "inviting sex" simply because they are *veiled*. Rates of sexual assault vary whether veiling is

practiced or not, and low statistical findings of sexual assault could result from sexist standards of reporting and prosecution rather than from a low incidence of assault. For instance, in Iran a charge of rape requires verification from three male witnesses.

61. MacLeod also asserts that "Veiling allows women into the workplace by, in essence, removing the reminders of gender" (107), but unless she means sex— that is, by hiding women's sexuality—then she would seem to contradict herself, since the veil is a distinct *mark* of gender, and indeed, would seem to reinscribe gender difference. If she means "sex," then I agree with her, because it is through desexualization that the veil facilitates women's movement in the public realm. However, as feminists like Butler might assert, whether such desexualization is compatible with freedom is another open question.

62. Rowley 1996, 11.

63. Ahmed 1992, 226–28.

64. Ibid.; Mernissi 1991; also Shaheed 1994.

65. Jonah Blank, *Mullahs on the Mainframe: Islam and Modernity among the Daudi Bohras* (Chicago: University of Chicago Press, 2001); Nussbaum 2000, 45–48.

66. Ahmed 1992; Tavakoli-Targhi 1994.

67. Shaheed 1994, 1004–5.

68. Jacques Derrida, *Margins of Philosophy*, trans. Alan Bass (Chicago: University of Chicago Press, 1982), 135, discussed in chapter 3 above, pp. 99–100.

69. Ahmed 1992, 162.

70. Shaheed 1994, 1005–18.

71. See Maria Lugones and Elizabeth V. Spelman, "Have We Got a Theory for You! Feminist Theory, Cultural Imperialism, and the Demand for the Women's Voice," in *Women's Studies International Forum* 6, no. 6 (1983): 573–81. I realize that the events of September 11, 2001, make such statements more difficult to accept, but the history of imperialism is longstanding, and the dominance of the West in contemporary globalization cannot be ignored.

72. Mernissi 1991; Ahmed 1992; Shaheed 1994; Hoodfar 1993, 13–14.

CHAPTER SEVEN

1. Amartya Sen, *Development as Freedom* (New York: Alfred A. Knopf, 1999).

2. Diana T. Meyers, *Self, Society, and Personal Choice* (New York: Columbia University Press, 1989).

3. Marilyn Friedman, "Autonomy, Social Description and Women," in *Relational Autonomy: Feminist Perspectives on Autonomy, Agency and the Social Self*, ed. Catriona MacKenzie and Natalie Stoljar (New York: Oxford University Press, 2000), 37.

4. Wendy Brown, *States of Injury: Power and Freedom in Late Modernity* (Princeton: Princeton University Press, 1995), 41.

5. Ibid., 5.

6. Philip Pettit, *A Theory of Freedom: From the Psychology to the Politics of Agency* (New York: Oxford University Press, 2001), 5.

7. Ibid., 67.

8. Idid., esp. chapter 7.

9. See, for instance, Amy Gutmann and Dennis Thompson, *Democracy and Disagreement* (Cambridge, Mass.: Belknap Press, 1996); *Deliberative Politics: Essays on Democracy and Disagreement*, ed. Stephen Macedo (New York: Oxford University Press, 1999).

10. Drucilla Cornell, *Transformations: Recollective Imagination and Sexual Difference* (New York: Routledge, 1993), 16.

11. Michel Foucault, *Discipline and Punish: The Birth of the Prison*, trans. Alan Sheridan (New York: Pantheon, 1977), 227–28.

12. Rawls's distinction between concepts and conceptions is relevant here: positive and negative liberty are, despite Berlin's famous article, two particular conceptions of freedom; freedom *simpliciter* (if that is not oxymoronic) is the concept. John Rawls, *A Theory of Justice* (Cambridge: Harvard University Press, 1974).

13. Brown 1995, 6.

14. Cornell 1993, 21.

15. Brown 1995, Judith Butler, *Bodies That Matter: On the Discursive Limits of "Sex"* (New York: Routledge, 1993); Denise Riley, "A Short History of Some Preoccupations," in *Feminists Theorize the Political*, ed. Judith Butler and Joan W. Scott (New York: Routledge, 1992).

16. Michel Foucault, "The Ethic of Care for the Self as a Practice of Freedom: An Interview with Michel Foucault on January 20, 1984," conducted by Raùl Fornet-Betancourt, Helmut Becker, and Alfredo Gomez-Müller, trans. J. D. Gauthier, *Philosophy and Social Criticism* 12, nos. 2–3 (1987): 124, 123, 114.

17. Such imprecision is admittedly partly due to the problems of discourse I articulated in chapter 3: the contradictory logic of having to create new meanings through existing terms, concepts, and intellectual frameworks that are opposed to the new meanings one is trying to develop and communicate. But it is also partly due to Foucault's own vague phrasing, and partly to the sometimes absurd deification of Foucault that has resulted in such a preponderance of his "writings" taking the form of interviews with intellectuals who seem afraid to ask the basic question: What do you mean by that? Foucault's answers thus remain uninterrogated, unchallenged, and unanalyzed within the context of the interview. How ironic that the scholar most responsible for "discursivity" in the academy should have had so few peers able to engage in genuine discourse with him. See Tom Dumm's *Michel Foucault and the Politics of Freedom* (Thousand Oaks, Calif.: Sage Publications, 1996), for similar ambivalence about the state of Foucault scholarship, as well as an interpretation of Foucault's views on freedom that complements my own.

18. Foucault 1987, 122.

19. Ibid., 122

20. Leslie Paul Thiele, "The Agony of Politics: The Nietzschean Roots of Foucault's Thought," *American Political Science Review* 84, no. 3 (1990): 918–19.

21. Foucault 1987, 118.

22. See, for instance, Michel Foucault, "Two Lectures," in Foucault, *Power/Knowledge: Selected Interviews and Other Writings, 1972–1977*, ed. Colin Gordon (New York: Pantheon Books, 1980).

23. Lucie White, "Subordination, Rhetorical Survival Skills, and Sunday Shoes: Notes on the Hearing of Mrs. G.," *Buffalo Law Review* 1 (1990).

24. The Milan Women's Bookstore Collective, *Sexual Difference: A Theory of Social-Symbolic Practice*, trans. Patricia Cicogna and Teresa de Lauretis (Bloomington: Indiana University Press, 1990), 129, 28, 129, 147, 138. I discuss their arguments more fully in Nancy J. Hirschmann, "Revisioning Freedom: Relationship, Equality, and the Politics of Entrustment," in *Revisioning the Political: Feminist Reconstructions of Traditional Concepts in Western Political Theory*, ed. Nancy J. Hirschmann and Christine Di Stefano (Boulder: Westview Press, 1995).

25. Patricia Hill Collins, *Black Feminist Thought* (Boston: Unwyn Hyman, 1990), 96, 99–103.

26. Ibid., 227–28.

27. Lisa Dodson, "At the Kitchen Table: Poor Women Making Public Policy," in *Women and Welfare: Theory and Practice in the United States and Europe*, ed. Nancy J. Hirschmann and Ulrike Liebert (New Brunswick, N.J.: Rutgers University Press, 2001).

28. See, for instance, Nancy Hartsock, *Money, Sex, and Power: Toward a Feminist Historical Materialism* (Boston: Northeastern University Press, 1984); Nancy J. Hirschmann, *Rethinking Obligation: A Feminist Method for Political Theory* (Ithaca: Cornell University Press, 1992); Carole Pateman, *The Sexual Contract* (Palo Alto, Calif.: Stanford University Press, 1988).

29. Brown 1995, 120.

30. Ibid., 43

31. Brown 1995, 41. Brown also unfairly misrepresents feminist standpoint theory by collapsing it into "consciousness raising." In Hirschmann 1992, I established that feminist standpoint theory clearly cannot be reduced to "narrative" or "consciousness raising," that the "achieved character" involves political struggle as well as theoretical analysis. Saying that a standpoint is epistemological does not necessarily entail a notion of "Truth," because multiple feminist standpoints should emerge out of the various material experiences of differently situated women. Part of those differences, as I have shown here, include discourse, but they cannot be reduced to discourse without denying the materialization that discourse produces. See also Nancy J. Hirschmann, "Feminist Standpoint as Postmodern Strategy," in *Women and Politics* 18, no. 4 (1996): 73–92, for the ways in which standpoint theory actually accomplishes much of what Brown and other feminist postmodernists seek from feminism. For another important feminist postmodernist account of the theoretical significance of experience, see Joan W. Scott, "Experience," in *Feminists Theorize the Political*, ed. Judith Butler and Joan W. Scott (New York: Routledge, 1992).

32. This vision thus complements and expands on the arguments I make for "caucus democracy" in Hirschmann 1992, chapter 6.

33. Immanuel Kant, *On the Proverb: "That May Be True in Theory, but It Is of No Practical Use,"* in Kant, *Perpetual Peace and Other Essays*, trans. Ted Humphrey (Indianapolis: Hackett Publishing Co., 1983), 72.

34. Joan Scott, "Deconstructing Equality-Versus-Difference: Or, The Uses of Poststructuralist Theory for Feminism," *Feminist Studies* 14, no. 1 (1988): 33–50.

35. Brown 1995, 110.

36. Sen 1999, 3.

37. Amartya Sen, *Inequality Reexamined* (Cambridge: Harvard University Press, 1992), 49.

38. Ibid., 31.

39. Margrit Brückner, "Reflections on the Reproduction and Transformation of Gender Differences among Women in the Shelter Movement in Germany," *Violence Against Women* 7, no. 7 (2001).

40. Sen 1999, 190–91.

41. Catherine MacKinnon, *Feminism Unmodified: Discourses on Life and Law* (Cambridge: Harvard University Press, 1987), esp. ch. 3 and 13.

42. Sen 1999, 198.

43. Drucilla Cornell, *At the Heart of Freedom: Feminism, Sex, and Equality* (Princeton: Princeton University Press, 1998), 7.

44. Drucilla Cornell, *The Imaginary Domain: Abortion, Pornography, and Sexual Harassment* (New York: Routledge, 1995), 5.

45. Cornell 1998, 7.

46. Drucilla Cornell, *Transformations: Recollective Imagination and Sexual Difference* (New York: Routledge, 1993), 5; Judith Butler, *Gender Trouble* (New-York: Routledge, 1990).

47. A concept which, it should be noted, she never explicitly defines in this book but rather assumes; she begins *At the Heart of Freedom* with the question "Where does women's freedom begin? It should begin with the demand that we free ourselves from the use of gender comparison as the ideal of equality," a circular argument that assumes a liberal, individualist, negative-liberty conception of freedom. Her statement that "a person's freedom to pursue her own happiness in her own way is critical for any person's ability to share in life's glories" (18) is as revealing for the classically liberal—downright Millian—concept of freedom she deploys as for the fact that she never even sees the need to acknowledge that she *is* implicitly deploying the liberal definition of freedom, that there are many other possible ways to conceptualize freedom, and that her tacit choice of this definition is itself a political choice, not just a philosophical one.

48. Cornell 1998, 36.

49. "I believe that feminists are right to argue that many women have so deeply internalized their own degradation that they have lost the ability to imagine themselves as equal" (Cornell 1998, 169).

50. Cornell 1998, 54–57.

51. See also Sen's theory of relative and absolute deprivation in Sen 1999, 70–74, 89–92.

52. See, for instance, the essays in *Patriarchy and Development: Women's Positions at the End of the Twentieth Century,* ed. Valentine M. Moghadam (Oxford: Clarendon Press, 1996).

53. Cornell 1998, chap. 2; Brown 1995, 168, 15, 188, 173.

54. Brown 1995, 173.

55. Ulrike Liebert, "Degendering Care and Engendering Freedom: Social Welfare in the European Union," in Hirschmann and Liebert 2001.

56. Brown 1995, 169.

57. Meyers 1989; Gerald Dworkin, *The Theory and Practice of Autonomy* (New York: Cambridge University Press, 1988).

58. Kay Castonguay, "Pro-Life Feminism," in *Feminist Philosophies*, 2d ed., Janet A. Kourany, James P. Sterba, and Rosemarie Tong (Upper Saddle River, N.J.: Prentice-Hall, 1999).

59. Ludwig Wittgenstein, *Philosophical Investigations*, trans. G.E.M. Anscombe (New York: Macmillan, 1968).

# NAME INDEX

*Since no bibliography has been provided for this book, the name index below refers readers to the location of full bibliographic information, indicated by boldface type. In the case of sources with more than two authors, the lead author alone is cited.*

# SUBJECT INDEX